D1479009

HUNTER S. THOMPSON

HUNTER S. THOMPSON

Fear, Loathing, and the Birth of Gonzo

Kevin T. McEneaney

ROWMAN & LITTLEFIELD
Lanham • Boulder • New York • London

Published by Rowman & Littlefield
A wholly owned subsidiary of The Rowman & Littlefield Publishing Group,
Inc.
4501 Forbes Boulevard, Suite 200, Lanham, Maryland 20706
www.rowman.com

Unit A, Whitacre Mews, 26-34 Stannary Street, London SE11 4AB

British Library Cataloguing in Publication Information Available

Library of Congress Cataloging-in-Publication Data

Names: McEneaney, Kevin T., author.
Title: Hunter S. Thompson : fear, loathing, and the birth of Gonzo / Kevin T. McEneaney.
Description: Lanham, Maryland : Rowman & Littlefield, 2016. | Includes bibliographical refer-
    ences and index.
Identifiers: Identifiers: LCCN 2015044459 (print) | LCCN 2015045691 (ebook) | ISBN
    9781442266209 (hardback : alk. paper) | ISBN 9781442266216 (electronic)
Subjects: LCSH: Thompson, Hunter S.—Criticism and interpretation. | Thompson, Hunter S.—
    Influence. | Thompson, Hunter S. Fear and loathing in Las Vegas. | American literature—20th
    century—History and criticism. | Reportage literature, American—History and criticism.
Classification: LCC PS3570.H62 Z75 2016 (print) | LCC PS3570.H62 (ebook) | DDC 813/.54—
    dc23

∞ ™ The paper used in this publication meets the minimum requirements of
American National Standard for Information Sciences Permanence of Paper
for Printed Library Materials, ANSI/NISO Z39.48-1992.

Printed in the United States of America

To historian Douglas Brinkley,
who dubbed me Mr. Angles

And perspective it is the best painter's art.
—William Shakespeare, Sonnet 24

CONTENTS

PREFACE

To you only do I tell the enigma that I saw—the vision of the lone-somest one.—Friederich Nietzsche

This book provides a study of literary themes in the work of Hunter S. Thompson. Thompson is known primarily as a political writer and social commentator. As a populist writer, he was also a serious intellectual with deep literary roots. Investigation of those roots reveal Thompson's unique manner of absorbing and transforming varied influences. Many of those influences became a starburst of activity in the creation of *Fear and Loathing in Las Vegas*, a book that since its 1971 publication has sold at least 60,000 to 70,000 copies a year, a novel that has continued to appeal to each new generation of readers. Half of this study will be devoted to that book because I hope to deepen the subtlety of its appreciation among general readers, and even the academic commu-nity, which has been somewhat reluctant to embrace's Thompson's vi-brant and raucous humor.

Thompson's work offers a parallel to Francois Rabelais, the creator of the Renaissance movement, who sought to revitalize Christianity through humor and political satire. Thompson sought to revitalize the spirit of America's Founding Fathers through a backwoods pessimistic humor that centered upon failure and disappointment rather than the braggadocio boast of achievement. Like Rabelais, Thompson perceived humor as a revitalizing force in life. And as with Rabelais, below the candied surface of humor resided the nut of wisdom. Thompson's prin-cipal theme was the American Dream of freedom and its vital spirit, which he saw as on the decline in the populace at large and in our national and local laws. His view was that of an outsider looking into the glittery shop window of luxury but with an empty pocket, belly full of hunger, and tongue wittily wagging. Thompson was America's greatest literary and political humorist of the second half of the twentieth century.

Humor's central characteristic remains courage to confront the unpredictable. A nation's psychological health may be measured by its ability to laugh at itself. If there comes a time when a person or nation loses its sense of humor, then that nation (or person) is in considerable trouble. I hope that the example of Thompson's laughter, and its robust intellectual health, may serve as inspiration for future lovers of this country in times of stress and turmoil.

Much of the book discusses how Thompson employed literary templates: he twisted or warped them in unusual ways to create original commentary. The deeper layer of how these bent literary templates functioned would not be available to the average reader; it has also led to the peculiar situation of a major writer not being taken too seriously by the literary establishment because of his complex sense of humor. In this process I have relied on his letters, as well as literary allusions, in an attempt to see what is written from the author's point of view. The book's title uses the word enigma, indicating something difficult to explain. While there usually isn't anything funny in explaining jokes, much of Thompson's work cries out for exegesis. A comedian requires a plausible aura of mystery to protect the legerdemain of the work and administer variations on it. I hope I have explained the enigmatic difficulties of Thompson's work without damaging it, leaving his legacy as an example of resonant literature that should influence other writers.

ACKNOWLEDGMENTS

I wish in particular to thank historian Douglas Brinkley's extraordinary wisdom, empathetic understanding, and dedication during his Hunter S. Thompson seminar at the Norman Mailer Writer's Colony at Provincetown. His fierce intellectual depth stimulated me to finish this work much quicker than it would have otherwise proceeded. At Norman Mailer's house, cheerful Jessica Zlotnicki and witty Guy Wolf created an invisible and seemingly effortless aura of hospitality and efficiency. The presence of Norman's benevolent ghost lurking amid bookshelves must have transmitted to me some of his inspiration and industry. I thank seminar participants, possessed during the séance, whose lively observations, offhand remarks, and stimulating ideas may have contributed to my thinking. Those august personnel consisted of journalists Michael Keane, James Kirchick, Mathew Mercier, Dan O'Sullivan, and Bill Shea; fiction writers Jo Lennan and Liz Moore.

My gratitude extends to several people who read in part or whole my rough draft and offered helpful comments: Ed McNicoll in the early and rougher going, Gerald Williams as chapters neared completion yet were not complete; the Reverend Douglas Grandgeorge and Martha Moffett for special comments; Liz McNicoll and Veronica Towers for cogently perusing other parts of the manuscript. Above all, the inspiration of Douglas Brinkley looms. Any shortcomings sit squarely on my shoulder, like a terrified cat sinking its claws into sunburned skin. For my Renaissance education, I thank A. Bartlett Giamatti, James Mirollo, and Joseph Mazzeo, the latter two of Columbia University.

Slowly
Uncloud the borealis of your eye
And show your iceberg secrets, your midnight prizes
To the green-eyed world and to me.

—George Barker, "Turn on Your Side and Bear the Day to Me"

I

LOUISVILLE SLUGGER

From Delinquent to Celebrity

Until I myself read and then met Hunter, I would have thought it impossible for anyone whose brains were so saturated with mind-benders to make sense on a telephone, let alone write so well.—Kurt Vonnegut

The machinery of the gods stood ready. The black Freak Power[1] memorial thrust 150 feet upward to the starry heavens, culminating in a large, double-thumbed red fist that bloomed as the cannon's muzzle. Preparations were made for lighting the long fuse. The weather cooperated as 150 invited guests assembled for the singular commemoration at the edge of the deceased's land. Juan Thompson drove his father's Great Red Shark convertible to the base of the extraordinary monument. Huge spotlights focused on the monument cast up overhead three "gonzo fist" shadow images of the cannon's muzzle onto slow-drifting, low-ceilinged clouds.[2] Music for the event was provided by the Nitty Gritty Dirt Band and a Tibetan gong-and-drum band.[3] The Memorial Blast-Off was about to begin.

Hunter S. Thompson had died a few months earlier amid the heavy snows of winter after having published fifteen books. Actor Johnny Depp, a close friend of Thompson, had financed the extravagant monument at an estimated cost of $2.5 million, transporting the enormous structure from California over the Rocky Mountains with great difficulty. Thompson had conceived of the monument cannon back in 1977, when he had explained his idea to an undertaker in West Hollywood, specifying the placing of his ashes within a fire bomb on the palm of the fist-muzzle.[4]

Among invited guests: journalists Ed Bradley (Thompson's Woody Creek neighbor), Michael Isikoff, Carl Bernstein, and Charlie Rose, on whose program Hunter genially appeared three times; Senator John Kerry and former Senator Gary Hart; actors John Cusack, Benicio Del Toro, Bill Murray, Jack Nicholson, and Sean Penn; movie producers Laila Nabulsi and Bob Rafeslon; novelists Jim Harrison, William Kennedy, and Kurt Vonnegut; publisher Jann Wenner of *Rolling Stone*; artists Tom Benton and Ralph Steadman, who designed the magnificent structure; and former presidential candidate George McGovern, who expressed regret for not having chosen Hunter S. Thompson as his vice-presidential running mate. Lyle Lovett, to whom Thompson bequeathed his gun collection, performed "If I Had a Boat." Then Johnny Depp and David Amram joined Lovett in Amram's "Theme and Variations on My Old Kentucky Home." Anita Thompson read the whole of "Kubla Khan," a populist, visionary poem that offers a stinging indictment of racist upper-class poetry. On the surface that Coleridge poem appears to be about opium, yet below the surface lurks the message that Ethiopian folk song remains superior to English parlor-room poetry, which prized class and French neoclassical theories of formal construction over authentic poetic sentiment.

Most of the celebrity crowd who mingled in the cool mountain air at Owl Farm knew Thompson as the beloved author of a novel some deemed to be the "Great American Novel": *Fear and Loathing in Las Vegas* (1971). Author and painter, political columnist and father, hillbilly humorist and outrageous satirist, Thompson left behind a hoard of unpublished manuscripts in the basement of his Woody Creek compound with an enormous archive of journalistic tape recordings. His widow, Anita Bejmuk Thompson, and historian Douglas Brinkley, literary executor, would supervise Thompson's legacy. Some manuscripts have been recently published, yet more await publication.

Sheriff Bob Braudis cautioned the crowd not to shed any tears because Hunter had told him that after his death, his friends should assemble and recollect him with "the tinkling of ice in glasses."[5] For the cosmic launch, Bob Dylan's "Mr. Tambourine Man" and Norman Greenbaum's "Spirit in the Sky" accompanied the booming cannon shot. Borne aloft into the stratosphere on August 20, 2005, to explode amid spectacular fireworks, were the ashes of an author who enjoyed an extravagant funeral ritual, the most extravagant one perhaps being Qin Shi Huang, the first emperor of China, was buried along with over 8,000 terra-cotta soldiers, 130 chariots, and about 800 horses.

The man whose cold ashes were shot skyward[6] was born in Louisville, Kentucky, on July 18, 1937, the eldest of the three sons of Virginia Ray Davison Thompson and Jack Robert Thompson, an insurance salesman, who had a son from a previous marriage. From the age of six, Thompson grew up in the middle-class Cherokee Triangle neighborhood of Louisville, designed by Frederick Law Olmstead. Thompson learned the friendly art of persuasion by knocking on doors to collect past-due bills the milkman could not collect.[7]

When Thompson was nine, the FBI knocked at his front door, informing his parents that Hunter was the prime suspect in the overturning of a mailbox, by means of a pulley and ropes, into the path of a bus. His friends had squealed on him, said the FBI agents, who threatened Hunter with five years in prison. His mother wept, yet Hunter doubted his friends had "squealed" on him. Not wanting to be the first to confess, he defied the two dark-suited agents: "What witnesses?" he insisted repeatedly. His father was annoyed by the intrusion into his house and encouraged Hunter to stand firm. Having accomplished nothing, the FBI agents departed, never to return: "I learned a powerful lesson. Never believe the first thing an FBI agent tells you about anything."[8] That lesson of standing up to authority imprinted on the young boy an emboldened self-confidence.

Hunter's mother introduced him to Mark Twain and Jack London, and he began to live out those authors' books with pranks, fistfights, and even war games with BB guns, using animals or other kids as practice targets. He developed a dark sense of humor that other kids feared.[9] As a youngster, Hunter accidentally met the sportswriter Grantland Rice playing golf in Cherokee Park. Rice gave him the freedom to sit at the press table and television booth, and permitted him to mingle with players and fetch loose balls during Southeastern Conference tournament basketball games.[10]

When Hunter was fourteen, his elderly father died of myasthenia gravis, an immune muscle disease usually connected with a thymus disorder. Hunter became the "man of the family," mentoring younger brothers Davison and James, taking a job at a local bank. His mother worked as a newspaper secretary, then local public librarian, struggling to raise her sons to be proper middle-class successes. With no father at home to restrain him and with only his grandmother to look after him, Hunter became the traditional juvenile delinquent, drinking beer and cruising the neighborhood in his mother's car, projecting his mischievous charm on everyone he met, leaving tire tracks on rich people's manicured lawns. And yet he traveled with a dog-eared copy of Plato's *Republic*,[11] which denounces Homer and Athenian civic virtue. Although he toted this academic "bible" of aristocracy, the wealthy parents of his peers never accepted him. Six feet tall, he walked with a limp, one leg shorter than the other from birth.

His school literary essays featured a startlingly forceful style and, despite an occasional descent into obscenity, at sixteen Thompson found himself recommended to the Athenaeum Literary Association, whose members contributed essays to its annual publication. His Athenaeum friend gave Hunter the nickname "Dr. Hunto."[12] Thompson's heroic theme was: "Who is the happier man, he who has braved the storm of life and lived, or he who has stayed securely on shore and merely existed?"[13] An existentialist by temperament, Thompson was more interested in action than theory; at the age of twenty-six, he labeled Jean-Paul Sartre "an eloquent windbag."[14] Here Hunter appears to be thinking of *Being and Nothingness* (1943) rather than Sartre's novels or plays. Thompson took Sartre's political observations seriously, especially concerning how liberal neocolonialism was destined to fail.[15]

At seventeen Thompson and two friends were arrested for robbing a couple of eight dollars in a local park. Thompson himself did not take the money, but because of his previous record of four arrests for underage drinking and vandalism, as well as his self-styled reputation as "Louisville's answer to Billy the Kid,"[16] he was up on a bogus rape charge (later dropped), but unlike the blue bloods who walked, he received sixty days in jail, plus suspension from school, which prevented him from graduating. Released after thirty days, he befriended the robbed couple.[17] Hunter was a rebel, yet someone with honest contradictions who wanted to do the right thing. He was thrown out of the Athenaeum Literary Association because of the arrest.

Thompson joined the Air Force at eighteen after scraping a new truck by doing sixty in an alley, not expecting another vehicle to be parked there.[18] He wanted to fly, but was shunted into electronics at Scott Air Force base in southern Illinois, where his only consolation was his interest in tape recorders.[19] Hunter was reassigned to Eglin Air Force Base in the Florida panhandle—later noting that Cold War preparations "for doom and dress rehearsals for death were key to the ethos of Eglin."[20] Thompson deceitfully but persuasively described himself as editor of his high school newspaper. He then went to the base library and glanced through a few books on journalism until the library closed. He was able to fill a sudden vacancy due to an editor being jailed for public urination—that's how he became sports editor of a column he called "The Spectator" for the base newspaper *Command Courier*.[21]

While he wrote acceptable articles, Thompson's satiric jibes at officers required censorship. Mingling on furlough weekends with the upper-crust café society in the city of Fort Walton, Thompson reveled in his role as spontaneous gossip spigot. Violating military regulations, he wrote for a professional wrestler newsletter under pseudonyms and also wrote sports articles for a local civilian paper, the *Playground News*.[22] For one issue of the base paper, he broke into the office late at night and remade the front page, exposing his superiors for giving an improper discharge to a star football player in order to improve his career prospects.[23] The brass mulled over the embarrassing publicity; Thompson received an honorable discharge (Airman First Class) in 1958, two years before his enlistment period ended,[24] departing the Air Force with a portfolio of articles to prove he was indeed a journalist.

At the *Middletown Daily Record* in upstate New York, Thompson worked as a small-city reporter, speeding around the countryside in his Jaguar with an attractive black girlfriend. The wife of a prominent local resident would often visit his cabin for intimate satisfaction.[25] He was fired after two months for "a vicious fight with an advertiser."[26] This pattern of disruptive employment was repeated at a number of newspapers. Working as a copy boy for *Time* magazine in New York City,[27] where he attended the School of General Studies at Columbia University, Thompson appropriated armloads of office supplies to type Fitzgerald's *The Great Gatsby* as well as some of Faulkner's stories—an unusual method for learning prose rhythm. He was fired for his unpardonable, insulting wit at a Christmas party.

Thompson began a relationship with a blonde Goucher College graduate, Sandra Conklin, in early 1959, while he worked on his apprentice novel, *Prince Jellyfish*. Wearing Bermuda shorts, he drifted west, happily hitchhiking 3,200 miles.[28] He explored San Francisco and Big Sur while subsisting on temporary odd jobs supplemented with freelancing. In the fall Thompson briefly trudged to South America as a freelance correspondent for the *New York Herald Tribune*.

Pursuing a sportswriting job, Thompson landed in Puerto Rico a few days after New Year's Day, 1960. There he met and befriended another aspiring writer, William Kennedy. Girlfriend Sandy arrived to join Thompson and his high school friend Paul Semonin, who were sharing a tiny concrete beach house with an expansive ocean view on Luquillo Beach. When the sports magazine *Sportivo* folded, and Thompson's male-modeling jobs dried up, the three returned to New York City, where on August 1, Thompson won $50 as a contestant on Johnny Carson's game show, *Who Do You Trust?* Sandy worked as airline stewardess. That autumn Semonin resumed his studies at Columbia, while Thompson redrafted his novel and explored Manhattan. When Kennedy's apprentice novel, *The Angels and the Sparrows*,[29] was rejected, Thompson commiserated with him because Grove Press had just rejected *Prince Jellyfish*.[30]

After a year of the trio living together, Semonin in the spring found a drive-away Ford Fairlane destined for Seattle. He and Hunter thoroughly enjoyed their Kerouac-like road trip. Thompson admired Kerouac for his autobiographical approach to writing.[31] Hunter and Paul then hitched south to San Francisco, where they delved into the Beat scene. Once Hunter secured a job as property caretaker at a nudist spa in Big Sur, about six miles from where Henry Miller, whom he wanted to meet but never did, lived,[32] Sandy quit her job and flew to San Francisco, where she found work as a secretary.[33] On July 2, 1961, Thompson's hero, Ernest Hemingway, committed suicide. At the time, Thompson's good friend Gene McGarr was visiting him; he says Thompson was devastated by the news. Thompson was fired in August for an unfortunate incident surrounding his rebuking a paraplegic bather (probably for engaging in public sex). This led to a retaliation attack organized by outraged bathers.[34] Hunter was ambushed on the shrubbery path to the baths and badly beaten by several men. Venting anger, Thompson repeatedly emptied his shotgun out of his cabin windows without opening them.

Hunter went home to visit his mother and concoct his own high-octane basement brew as he wrote journalistic pitches, while Sandy left for New York City to find an apartment. Thompson visited Sandy on East 81st Street for a few months before pushing off in April as a South American stringer for the *National Observer*, which wanted human-interest portraits on several countries.[35] Injecting an autobiographical perspective, Hunter provided engaging sociological articles on Columbia, Peru, Ecuador, Bolivia, Uruguay, and Brazil, while enduring several bouts of debilitating dysentery. He was based in Rio de Janeiro with Bob Bone, a friend from Puerto Rico who worked at a financial magazine. Thompson wrote to Semonin: "All the Brazilians I have met have been zanies, to use your (and Mencken's) term."[36] Hunter nearly spent time in jail for recreational rat shooting with his pistol at a garbage dump.[37] Hearing a distorted drag in his voice and concerned about his health, Sandy flew down to join him.

On their return to the States, Thompson married Sandra Dawn Conklin at an Indiana "marriage parlor" not too distant from Louisville, on May 20, 1963. Hunter had acquired a severe mumble, probably the result of a minor stroke triggered by malaria. Later in life, to help allay the possibility of a stroke and counter the effects of alcohol and drug use, Thompson consumed several grapefruits every day.

The *National Observer* paid expenses for authorized articles by the roving on-the-road reporter as the honeymoon couple toured the country.[38] The assassination of John Fitzgerald Kennedy in November traumatized Thompson. The two settled into the Haight-Ashbury district of San Francisco, where Sandy worked as a hotel maid[39] before Juan Fitzgerald Thompson was born on March 23, 1964.

Thompson was miffed when the paper turned down a pitch on Mario Savio and the Free Speech Movement, subsequently limiting submissions to book reviews. Hunter, who had spent much of his life satirizing people, was fired from the *National Observer* for writing a complimentary book review of Tom Wolfe's first book, *The Kandy-Kolored Tangerine-Flake Streamline Baby* (1965). Carey McWilliams at *The Nation* magazine then rescued him with an assignment that eventually became *Hell's Angels: A Strange and Terrible Saga* (1967), which established Thompson as a leading writer of the New Journalism movement. Thompson had a follow-up contract for a book in which to vent venom at the president, but *The Johnson File* went up in smoke when President Lyndon B. Johnson announced he would not seek another term.

Hunter and Sandy had spent a couple of months visiting Semonin in Aspen during their honeymoon. When the family left San Francisco in late fall of 1966, headed for New York City, they drove through Aspen to revive pleasant memories. They discovered a cheap rental in Woody Creek, a few miles from the city. Instead of proceeding to New York, they nestled in Woody Creek and eventually were able to buy 110 acres.[40] Once established at Owl Farm, Thompson (like Flannery O'Connor and South American Catholic bishops) raised peacocks; he became an active local environmentalist.

During the summer of 1967, at an Aspen bar, Thompson was introduced to Oscar Zeta Acosta by Hunter's friend Michael Solheim. Oscar and Hunter became close friends. Acosta, as a character and political activist, eventually became an inspiration for some of Thompson's best work, and the exchange of letters between them conjures remarkable frankness and earthy humor. Acosta's description of how they became friends appears in chapter 15 of his *The Autobiography of a Brown Buffalo* (1972), wherein Thompson is depicted as Karl King,[41] a nod to Thompson's unwavering support of Martin Luther King Jr., whom they both admired. In tribute to Acosta following his mysterious death-disappearance in the summer of 1974, Hunter and John Kaye produced a film script. The movie based on this film script, *Where the Buffalo Roam* (1980), starred Bill Murray (whose extraordinary performance boosted his movie career) as Thompson and Peter Boyle as Lazlo (Acosta).

Thompson had covered the 1964 Republican New Hampshire primary for *Pageant* magazine. While hardly a fan of Richard M. Nixon, Hunter recognized that Nixon, whom he doggedly followed everywhere, possessed a keen political mind and was an excellent campaigner, adapting well to unforeseen situations. At the end of the campaign, Nixon speechwriter Ray Price needed a reporter to talk football, and football *only*, with Nixon during an hour's limo ride to the Manchester airport in sub-zero weather. Thompson was the only reporter on hand with the requisite sports background, so he sat next to Nixon talking football. Once he discovered that Hunter had known Grantland Rice, Nixon professed that he would have preferred to be a sportswriter like Rice to being a politician. Thompson thought Nixon the archetypal con

man, yet he was astonished at Nixon's detailed knowledge of football—
Nixon knew which colleges many pro players attended, their college
school songs, and the statistics for many players. [42] While Thompson
loathed Nixon from the day he entered Congress, it was this up-close
interview that fueled Thompson's contemptuous comedy when he
wrote about Nixon in numerous pieces, culminating in his notorious
1994 *Rolling Stone* obituary, "He Was a Crook," later retitled as "Chapter 666: The Death of Richard Nixon." [43] One biographer declared:
"Richard Nixon was Hunter's muse. Hunter's most memorable work
was inspired by Nixon's venality." [44] Covering the Democratic primary
in New Hampshire, Thompson wrote to his mother: "McCarthy is the
only human being in the race, so he's naturally doomed. But he's fun to
travel with. Nixon is a nightmare of bullshit, intrigue and suspicion." [45]

Random House supplied Thompson with press credentials to cover
the 1968 Democratic National Convention in Chicago. There he was
thoroughly drubbed by cops during Mayor Richard Daley's police riot,
one of sixty-five press members who would be beaten and/or arrested
that last week of August. [46] This event transformed him into a hardened
radical, yet he never filed his coverage of the event. Thompson later
declared to another journalist, "I went to the Democratic convention as
a journalist and returned a raving beast." [47] Thompson's "Chicago '68"
has never been published, [48] possibly because the account remains too
personal.

Thompson couldn't crack mainstream magazines, but the times were
changing and new venues opened. He wrote for *Scanlan's Monthly*,
which was the first magazine to call for President Nixon's impeachment;
in retaliation, Nixon ordered the Internal Revenue Service to harass the
magazine, which led to its folding. [49] One Thompson article never published in 1969 was "The Gun Lobby," a piece for *Esquire* magazine on
the National Rifle Association, of which he had been a member since
1962. [50] Commissioned at three thousand words, the article took on a
life of its own, and by the time it was finished, it ran to about eighty
thousand words. *Esquire* had given a fifty-page excerpt conditional ac-
ceptance, but ultimately turned it down. [51] Hunter couldn't sell the
book. [52] The historian Douglas Brinkley judges it among Hunter's best
work. [53] Another great disappointment that year, even more wrenching,
was the birth of Hunter and Sandy's daughter Sarah, who died shortly
after delivery. The hospital said they would dispose of the body. Hor-

rified, Hunter and his coroner friend Billy Noonan (from his Louisville childhood) broke into the morgue and stole Sarah's body. They buried her at Owl Farm.[54]

In 1970, shaving his head, Thompson ran unsuccessfully for sheriff of Aspen on the Freak Power ticket. He didn't really want to be sheriff, but he attempted to draw publicity to himself as a wacky exception to the Freak Power Party ticket, whose real agenda was to elect Ned Vare as county commissioner and Billy Noonan as coroner. During the campaign, Hunter received death threats, including one delivered personally from the Hells Angels.[55] Thompson's imaginative campaign—the brazen rhetoric, satire, and publicity artwork—provided a conceptual ideology and approach that influenced several generations of writers, musicians, and artists.[56] The Aspen Wall Posters created for the campaign were so incendiary the local Aspen printer refused to continue the series and a Boulder printer had to be enrolled.[57] When notified of his narrow loss, Hunter posed satirically for pictures, wearing a woman's long blonde wig. Thompson's account of his campaign and an analysis of it appeared in *Rolling Stone* as "Freak Power in the Rockies."[58]

When *Scanlan's* magazine folded in January of 1971, Jann Wenner hired Thompson as a staff writer for *Rolling Stone* magazine. The following year Wenner asked Thompson to set up and head a national headquarters office for the magazine in Washington, but when the office was moved to Manhattan, Thompson found the corporate atmosphere stultifying and left to pursue freelance writing.

For years Hunter had been laboring on a sociological opus, a book about the "Death of the American Dream" as it related to exploitation of the Horatio Alger syndrome and the Vietnam War. The book was under contract to Random House. Thompson despairingly wrote that the project he had labored at for years "was the most monstrous waste of time I've ever got bogged down in."[59] In 1971 themes from that uncompleted manuscript emerged in his series of articles for *Rolling Stone* that became the New Journalism novel that transformed him into a celebrity: *Fear and Loathing in Las Vegas*. Essentially an anti-war novel, it synthesized a multitude of cultural and literary strands.

In another series of articles Thompson covered the 1972 elections for *Rolling Stone*, which (when re-edited) became *Fear and Loathing on the Campaign Trail* (1973), the first subjective depiction of political campaigns and personalities. Hunter encouraged Timothy Crouse, who was covering George McGovern, to spill gossip and anecdotes about reporters covering the election, which became *The Boys on the Bus* (1973). Although he was assigned to cover Edmund Muskie, Thompson favored the historian Dr. McGovern; Thompson's surreal speculation that Muskie *might* be taking ibogaine, a drug derived from the root of the iboga plant and used to terminate heroin or cocaine addiction, helped to end Muskie's bid for the presidency.[60]

"Fear and Loathing at the Super Bowl" appeared in the February 15, 1973, issue of *Rolling Stone*. Regarded by sports fans as an iconic landmark in journalism, it exposed the hypocrisy and corruption of team owners, and drug use by both players and reporters (whom he labeled as gullible "hired geeks"). Thompson compared Oakland Raiders owner Al Davis to Sonny Barger of the Hells Angels, and concluded: "Any society that will put Barger in jail and make Al Davis a respectable millionaire at the same time is not a society to be trifled with."[61] Thompson compares Davis to Grantland Rice's hero Vince Lombardi, concluding they are hardly in the same league.

Summoned by *Rolling Stone* to cover the Watergate scandal, Thompson, with his first full-time job in years, spent a year in Washington with Sandy and their talking black mynah bird Edward, who chanted "What's goin' on?" Hunter provided intense, eloquent coverage of Watergate. In July of 1974, when it was clear that Nixon would resign, Jann Wenner demanded Thompson write an article entitled "The Quitter." Quitting was antithetical to Nixon's personality—instead, Nixon acted like a tough football coach determined to score one more field goal in a losing blowout. Asked to spin something he did not believe in at the behest of his friend Wenner, Thompson was faced with a dilemma: How could a participant journalist become involved in his enemy's resignation, except to make silly boasts that would be ridiculed? He sat before his typewriter for days on this absurd assignment, never moving beyond the given typed headline. *Rolling Stone* was compelled to slap together a retrospective collage of Thompson's previous articles on Nixon. That was the first time that the iron man who was a reliable typing machine—known to attack the typewriter for sixteen-hour stretches or even several days—faltered on a major assignment, but there was to be a series of such incidents in the future. Two months later his epic denunciation "Fear and Loathing in Limbo: The Scum Also Rises" appeared in *Rolling Stone*.[62]

In April 1973 *Playboy* sent Thompson down to Key West to cover the Cozumel fishing tournament. The assignment, "Old Gonzo and the Sea," was to be a parody of Hemingway and deep-sea fishing. Michael Solheim accompanied him as sidekick "Yail Bloor" ("Bloor" being one of Thompson's favorite pseudonyms when he performed prank telephone calls at parties when he was younger).[63] "The Great Shark Hunt," a lengthy antic essay of mischievous shenanigans in the Florida Keys, appeared in the December 1974 issue of *Playboy*.

In late March 1975, a month before its April 28 collapse, Thompson departed for Saigon to cover the city's fall for *Rolling Stone*. His friend Loren Jenkins was the *Newsweek* bureau chief in Saigon. From Hong Kong Thompson smuggled $40,000 into Saigon for *Newsweek*, so that Jenkins could meet the magazine's last payroll and evacuation expenses.[64] Meanwhile, Jann Wenner, reacting in anger to a ranting letter from Hunter, took him off retainer, which had the effect of canceling his life insurance policy in the war zone. Relations with *Rolling Stone* magazine naturally grew frosty; his only publication at the time was an open cable about the canceled insurance.

Several short pieces written during April, including Thompson's impossible letter requesting an interview with North Vietnamese Colonel Giang, wherein Hunter declares: "I'm not an especially good typist, but I am one of the best writers currently using the English language as both a musical instrument and a political weapon."[65] These pieces were later gathered in *Songs of the Doomed* (1990). Thompson decided it would be "better" to cover the fall from Laos, but had no story to file. Jenkins fled on one of the last helicopters out of Saigon, and Hunter later jovially joined him in Bali for rest and recuperation, bringing Sandy (who had been staying in Hong Kong) plus a large jar of powdered mescaline.[66]

With strains developing in Hunter's marriage when his wife discovered infidelities,[67] Thompson spent much time on the college lecture circuit; he was the favorite Halloween costume of college sophomores.[68] Meanwhile, singer Jimmy Buffett bought a house in Aspen. Thompson and Buffett became friends through Aspen novelist and lyricist Tom Corcoran, who sometimes worked as a seasonal bartender in Key West at Captain Tony's (where Hemingway had preferred to drink). Buffett, who had not yet married, gave Thompson keys to his bachelor flat in Key West to use when Buffett was on tour.[69] Thompson partied with other writers, accompanied by the many groupies attracted by Buffett's growing fame. From a literary point of view, this was not a productive period in Thompson's life. In 1977 he met Jim Belushi's assistant, Laila Nabulsi, backstage in 1977 before a *Saturday Night Live* skit. They quickly became lovers, and Laila eventually came to live with Thompson as his assistant for several years. Sandy and Juan moved out in August 1978. Sandy, who had considerable secretarial skills and had been Hunter's emotional and technical support as typist, editor, and research assistant, now worked at the Aspen Bookstore. Thompson hired and fired several lawyers, owed arrears to the Internal Revenue Service, and was seriously behind in his mortgage.[70]

Thompson's discussion of possible suicide in the introduction to his anthology, *The Great Shark Hunt* (1979), strikes the note of a burnt-out writer, yet it may also have expressed the frustration of a man going through a bitter divorce. After the divorce, his working habits became erratic. Thompson was able to retain his house and straighten out his financial problems, yet he became a gadding philanderer with a series of interesting temporary girlfriends and numerous incomplete projects. Being both a celebrity and local activist brought Thompson a carnival of daily distractions, and his propensity for humorous mischief entangled him in frequent legal conundrums, for which he needed both his resourceful imagination and the lightning aid of a sharp lawyer.

While Thompson enjoyed the economic perks of being a celebrity, he did not take kindly to people who treated him with awed regard. He usually treated such people with contempt, sometimes humiliating them.[71] Thompson was also annoyed by Gary Trudeau's popular *Doonesbury* cartoon character, "Uncle Duke," based upon Thompson's *Fear and Loathing in Las Vegas*. The depiction of Duke at the *Rolling Stone* magazine office swatting at bats with a ruler particularly infuriated him, as did the realization that Trudeau's satiric depiction of Duke was one element that had helped catapult Trudeau to a readership of over 60 million.

In Washington, DC, where Hunter was easily recognizable, people on the street sometimes jeered at him as being the incarnation of a dimwitted cartoon character.[72] After Trudeau won the Pulitzer Prize in 1975 and appeared on the cover of *Time* magazine, Wenner hired him to cover the 1976 presidential election, which Thompson then declined to do. To Thompson it did not seem fair that Trudeau could base part of his meteoric career on mocking his masterpiece. Years later, Conan O'Brien permitted Thompson to machine-gun cardboard cut-outs of the cartoonist on his television show.[73]

With Loren Jenkins, Hunter covered the American invasion and subjection of Grenada in the fall of 1983, rejoicing in the success of the quick American intervention. He clowned around with other reporters, yet his account of their silly capers did not appear until twenty years later in *The Kingdom of Fear* (2003).

Except for *The Curse of Lono* (1983), Thompson produced no more long fictional narratives. There had been a series of proposed novels: *Guts Ball* (a depiction of physically sadistic games by Nixon's inner circle aboard a DC-10), *The Silk Road* (about drug smuggling in the Florida Keys), *The Night Manager* (about the pornography industry, in the manner of Gay Talese's *Thy Neighbor's Wife*), and *Polo Is My Life* (a satire on the upper class and exposé on the assassination of John Fitzgerald Kennedy). Yet most of these works never received much more than cursory drafts; some scraps were eventually gathered to bulk out books. Thompson concentrated on his weekly musings for the *San Francisco Examiner* and then ESPN news, political and sports columns that tossed pertinent "irrelevancies" into the mix. His brilliantly funny observations on American life were gathered in several anthologies.

Hunter's short pieces varied from the hilarious to the outraged to the bemusingly frivolous. On big occasions he still rose to publish marvelous articles, such as his coverage of the 1983 Roxanne Pulitzer scandal for *Rolling Stone*, in which he revived his Horatio Alger and American Dream themes, or his *Examiner* column the day after 9/11, in which he prophesied an unending, global Christian jihad. He was ubiquitous, if not exactly sober, on the college speaking circuit in the 1980s and early 1990s, generously giving numerous entertaining interviews (sometimes in a satiric mood) to varied publications. When he spoke, he required a small sum of single dollar bills to be handed to him in a brown paper bag before he spoke—similar to the poet Dylan Thomas's demand that periodical publishers pay him for poems by surreptitiously passing him cash under the table at a pub (as well as picking up his current bar tab or, in the case of Cyril Connolly, the tab for the past six months). Like the singer and songwriter Dr. John, Hunter signed himself in at hotels under pseudonyms to avoid being harassed by fans, one of his favorites being Benjamin Franklin.

The Rum Diary, Thompson's gritty, melancholy novel about journalists, appeared in 1998 to acclaim nearly forty years after it had been written. That same year the film version of *Fear and Loathing in Las Vegas*, produced by Laila Nabulsi, was released. Fellow Kentuckian Johnny Depp produced and starred in the film treatment of *The Rum Diary* (2011). Several documentaries about Thompson have been made, the most significant and successful being Wayne Ewing's *Breakfast with Hunter* (2003) and, especially, Alex Gibney's *Gonzo: The Life and Work of Dr. Hunter S. Thompson* (2008).

In his personal life, like James Thurber, Hunter was clumsy during unguarded moments (but well coordinated when playing sports or swimming), yet they both turned awkwardness to comic advantage. Actress Margot Kidder said: "He was so munglingly ineffectual as a human that I adored him. I just thought anyone who was this bumbling was wonderful."[74]It was Thompson who accidentally knocked over a television camera during Nixon's impeachment hearings. Riotous anecdotes about Hunter's confusion and daily pranks appear to be endless.

When Thompson covered the 1991 William Kennedy Smith rape trial in Palm Beach for *Rolling Stone* (although he did not file a story), he stayed near Palm Beach as the guest of Larry Haley, a *National Enquirer* reporter. One day he had to fly to New York City for an appearance on the *Tonight Show*. Back in Palm Beach that evening, he settled in front of Haley's television set to watch his four minutes. When Thompson saw that his segment had been cut to one minute, he hauled out his gun and shot out the television set. Haley (an ex-marine) left the room, returned a minute later with an AK-47 and put it against Hunter's head, saying, "Give me $600 for that TV now." Thompson forked it over.[75]

Thompson first met Anita Bejmuk in 1997 when she volunteered to work on the second volume of his correspondence. She moved in with him in 1999, and they married in 2003. Shortly afterward, his health began to decline. He underwent hip replacement surgery, and then back surgery when his spinal column became inflamed. Hunter redamaged his hip and broke his left leg, both tibia and fibula, for the second time on a trip to Hawaii in December 2004 while making a bowl of dried noodle soup[76] and then broke his right ankle at home reaching for ice cubes.[77] He was confined to a wheelchair and was in continual pain, but doctors could do nothing but write him ineffective prescriptions.

He knew that the inflammation in his spinal cord was rising up to his brain. On February 20, 2005, Thompson took his own life with a single pistol shot from a .44 through the mouth,[78] as described in the conclusion to his satiric story, "Death of a Poet."[79] According to the coroner death was instantaneous.[80]

Thompson did not live to see the results of his last legal crusade. As a celebrity, Hunter regularly received enormous bags of fan mail. Deborah Fuller, Thompson's faithful and extraordinarily competent secretary and handler for over twenty years, sorted through this mail, reading selected letters to him.[81] His attention was caught by a letter of appreciation from a young woman, Lisl Auman, serving life without possibility of parole. The result was a public campaign to free her from an unjust sentence. Hunter announced the campaign to his friends at the Super Bowl halftime and publicly in his February 5, 2001, column, "Hey Rube," under the headline "Lynching in Denver." "The Most Dangerous Sport of All," published on May 14, described a courthouse-steps rally for the twenty-year-old girl, who was given that life sentence for being handcuffed in the back of a police car while cops chased her skinhead boyfriend, chase concluding in a fatal shootout that killed both a cop and her boyfriend.

The "Hey, Rube!" circus shout was coded slang for carnies to come help a fellow worker being attacked by outsiders. Thompson's column and his book by that name was a call for others to help out the nation by trying to free it from injustices perpetrated from within. Thompson was not in a position to be sheriff or governor, but he could shout outrage and produce laughs like no one else. Lisl Auman, after serving eight years in jail, walked out of prison on April 26, 2005, several months after Thompson's death. Wearing an ankle bracelet, she continues under probation for twelve years, yet for the past several years has lived as a productive member of society.[82] This modest legal victory in the matter of felony law represents a triumph of "profane" law over "sacred" law in the sensibility of Rousseau, who delineated the difference between rational law and unthinking customs,[83] also the theme of Russell Banks's *Lost Memory of Skin*, which features an innocent with an ankle bracelet.[84]

Although there have been many anecdotal memoirs and several critical biographies of Thompson, as yet none are definitive. The life of this tall-teller of wild fables[85] was filled with contradiction and absurd ironies. He became a global celebrity through mocking the Horatio Alger motif, although he himself embodied the Horatio Alger story of the hardworking boy who did not graduate from high school, succeeding far beyond the wildest dreams of his family and ambitious peers who attended Ivy League colleges.

In a letter to his visual collaborator Ralph Steadman, Thompson explained that Steadman was not getting paid for his artwork but for smashing windows: "And that is an art in itself. The trick is getting paid for it."[86] As a practiced contrarian humorist, Hunter loved to cause chaos, upsetting preconceived notions, whether of eating, walking, or playing—an iconoclast who would leave everyone laughing.

Thompson employed the honorific title Doctor, his friends often calling him "Doc." He had bought a Doctor of Divinity certificate from the Universal Life Church in the late Sixties. He frequently called himself a Doctor of Journalism or Dr. Gonzo. Late in life some of his friends began calling him Doctor of Strangeness because of his uncanny ability to re-imagine himself and his varied interests in unusual ways, from inventing the sport of shotgun golf to odd perspectives of social critique.

While he did not live up to his potential of becoming America's greatest novelist, Thompson left one enduring literary masterpiece and two very good novels, along with two acclaimed (and much imitated) landmarks of journalism, a dozen glittering jewels of journalistic essay, and a posthumous legacy of fascinating letters. Thompson's invention of gonzo sensibility has gone viral in American culture, while popular sales of his books continue their climb, mainly because most amused readers want to read everything he wrote, even if it be a memo expressing momentary exasperation. Thompson was America's most incisive and savvy political commentator since H. L. Mencken and, according to journalist and novelist Tom Wolfe, "Hunter was the only twentieth-century equivalent of Mark Twain."[87]

2

PLAY IT AGAIN, HUNTER

The Rum Diary

One afternoon, Wenck, feeling the front desk was choking him on space, grabbed his typewriter and heaved it across Fulton Street into St. Paul's Chapel cemetery.—Grantland Rice

In Thompson's fledgling first attempt at fiction, *Prince Jellyfish*, Thompson says his narrator, Welburn Kemp, attended college at Washington and Lee[1] (where his friend Tom Wolfe excelled), and Kemp brags about the respect value of falsely claiming to having attended university at Yale (where Tom Wolfe received his prestigious doctorate). While the disjointed sample chapters of *Prince Jellyfish* that appeared in *Songs of the Doomed* have little literary merit, *The Rum Diary: A Novel*[2] (1998) remains exciting. For both novels the main character's name, Welburn Kemp, was a tribute amalgam of two high school friends: Welburn Brown, who died in a sports car accident, and Kenny Kemp, brain damaged from another car accident.[3] *The Rum Diary*'s concerns run parallel to those of Thompson's friend, William Kennedy, whose first novel, *The Ink Truck* (1969), limns the journalistic world of deadlines, organized labor, and societal conflict during a newspaper strike in an Albany, New York, of his imagination.[4]

Kennedy's *The Ink Truck* floats on the skein of surreal and buffoonish blarney—that is to say, on the wit of language more than plot, although odd characters remain well drawn. Thompson's novel, written in the American Realist tradition, walks through the streets of a particular time and sociology while advancing character study amid a love triangle. In the end both novels focus on the theme of exploited journalists betrayed by both employers and colleagues.[5] Like Nathaniel West's *Day of the Locust* (1939), which depicts low-paid (at that time) screenwriters who provide memorable grotesques, both Thompson and Kennedy (influenced by the tinge of surrealism in West) dramatize poorly paid journalists.

Thompson's approach in *The Rum Diary* presents a study of American expatriates abroad, much as Hemingway had done with *The Sun Also Rises* (1926) and Dennis Murphy with *The Sergeant* (1958). Murphy's accomplished novel, vivid in intensity of feeling, good with character and evocative atmosphere, yet too narrowly a two-character novel, sported excited blurbs from John Steinbeck, Mark Schorer, and Wallace Stegner. Thompson played touch football and drank with Murphy when he was in Big Sur. Murphy doubted Sandy's assertions that Hunter would one day be a great writer. When he broke into Hunter's cabin, he was astonished to find a draft of *The Rum Diary* as well as a copy of *The Sergeant*, with copious underlining and massive annotations. Murphy exclaimed: "Hunter had studied my book like a Bible, and I didn't even know he had a copy."[6]

Kennedy and Murphy later read a running draft of *The Rum Diary* during the summer of 1963 and proffered advice to Thompson, both advising a sharpening of plotline and further delineation of minor characters.[7] By that fall, another rewrite centered on what Thompson called "The Rage,"[8] which indicates extended development of Yeamon, whose angry edge somewhat resembles Fitzgerald's Tom Buchanan, as a character. The sergeant in Murphy's novel brims with a ferocious rage from his suppressed homosexual impulses; Thompson morphs Murphy's portrayal of homosexual rage directed against mediocrity—Thompson's counterpart, Yeamon (Yeah-man, in the sense of someone possessing integrity and life-affirming force, perhaps even a distillation of Nietzsche's phrase "Yea and Amen" from *The Birth of Tragedy*), explodes with rage at being betrayed by employer and girlfriend.

Kennedy had been the managing editor of the *San Juan Star* from the fall of 1959 through early 1962. Kennedy's narrator Bailey[9] becomes increasingly hysterical and unhinged during a writer's strike, thus entering the portal of absurd humor. Thompson had applied to Kennedy for a job with a rather crazed letter and had been rejected, yet later

Kennedy met Thompson when Hunter became a sportswriter down in Puerto Rico where he spent eight months.[10] In 1964 Thompson wrote of the *Star* that "On any given night the city editor was just as likely to pick up the phone and get a routine story as he was to hear that half his staff had been locked up for creating a riot."[11] This applied as well to the bowling magazine *Sportivo*, which often paid Thompson in bounced checks for accounts of legendary left-handed local bowling tournaments.[12]

In his subsequent work Thompson often extracted riotously absurd humor from the most bleakly mundane situations—after all, he had been initiated into the high-voltage rhythms of bowling and the mind-blowing explosions of lightning pins on a near-daily schedule. The bowling comedy *Kingpin* (1996), with Woody Harrelson, Bill Murray, and Randy Quaid, adopts elements of Thompson's trademark humor: Harrelson and Murray compete for a woman, much like Kemp and Yeamon from Thompson's novel. At the film's climax, Harrelson bowls left-handed in a tournament, his right having been amputated as a result of an attempt to hustle gangsters. Thompson's gonzo brand of humor has percolated into American culture at large.

William Kennedy's preface to *The Proud Highway* observes that Thompson's journalism often operates as fiction,[13] and I think it fair to say that Thompson's self-consciously labeled fiction supplies somewhat exaggerated and dramatized autobiography. *The Rum Diary* reads like what the Japanese call the "I novel," a novel grounded in first-person exploit and perceptual embroidery.[14] Thompson's model for his procedure must have been Kerouac's *On the Road* (1957), the most conspicuous and successful first-person fictional narration outside of memoirs. *The Rum Diary* declares its autobiographical slant and requires the subtitle, *A Novel.* Jimmy Buffett's flattering blurb labels the book "a brilliant tribal study." The tribe? Wandering journalists lost in the backwoods of a sleazy profession.

Kennedy's *The Ink Truck* centers on journalists and a union strike; unlike Ken Kesey's point of view in *Sometimes a Great Notion* (1964), Kennedy supports unions. Thompson, a compulsive satirist, remains ambivalent—supporting the concept of better pay and working conditions, but averse to mass assembly bordering on hysteric psychosis, more interested in observing violence (like George Orwell) as an amused spectator rather than a participant. For Thompson, the strike functions as chaotic and futile background atmosphere, his foreground being the carousing self-indulgence of drunken journalists along with the incompetence and corruption of editorial direction, accompanied by the comedy of cultural clash that underscores paranoid misunderstandings between Puerto Rican and Yankee culture.

The well-written prologue of *The Rum Diary* dramatizes the 1958 plot as the "senseless odyssey" of young ambitious journalists eager to force their idealism on a world that may opportunistically provide them with their "impending doom." The tag "senseless" offers supercilious self-parody; the novel provides comedy, but also insidious realities to be taken seriously. Doom for journalists is perhaps even more real now than it was back in that grubby heyday when the cost of living was in fact cheaper. This band of confederate journalists believes investigative journalism can create a better world, or at least a critical interpretation of society and what is happening to it. While the novel remains somewhat diminished by the blatant narcissism and wishful hedonism of its apprentice narrator, and especially the seasoned reporters in early background chapters, subsequent chapters sparkle with wit and narrative drive as we see Kemp shed much of his adolescent narcissism for greater sociological understanding. Kemp slowly uncovers the menacing manipulators behind the Oz-like curtain of propaganda and its relationship to politics.

The novel opens with the narrator downing drinks with friends in the White Horse Tavern at Hudson and 11th Street, the favorite hangout of Dylan Thomas and Jack Kerouac during the early Fifties; the Clancy Brothers, Joel Oppenheimer, James Baldwin, Seymour Krim, Norman Mailer, and Hunter S. Thompson in the late Fifties when he worked as a copyboy for *Time* magazine; as well as an assortment of oddball bohemians from varied professions over the years. During the winter of 1958 Thompson was residing on Manhattan's Upper West Side, collecting parking tickets, and "this morning doing controlled skids around Sheridan Square in the Village"[15] in the freshly fallen snow, feeling he'd rather remain in Manhattan and die like the bohemian poet, essayist, and novelist Maxwell Bodenheim, who with his wife was brutally axe-murdered by a crazed drifter dishwasher whom they had sheltered. His motto at the time was "To hell with the rent. . . . I'll drink instead."[16]

Without a steady girlfriend, Hunter experienced the city as a huge tomb. By the end of January he had moved to 113th Street, closer to Columbia University where he took classes, but by April he had relocated to Greenwich Village at Perry Street near the White Horse Tavern. His windowless bachelor-pad walls were painted a macabre black[17] as he began to pen his apprentice novel, *Prince Jellyfish*.

Kemp barely makes the plane flight, one of Thompson's obsessively recurring incidents both in journalism and fiction. As a journalist on the go in South America when he wrote for the *National Observer* in the early Sixties, this situation appears to have been a commonplace anxiety for Thompson. Ahead of Kemp in the check-in line stands a girl with whom Kemp becomes instantly fascinated. The scene resembles the momentary fascination recorded by Tom Swanson, the main character of Murphy's *The Sergeant*, when Swanson, from the passing window of a car, spots a solitary girl standing on a Paris sidewalk. Swanson registers overwhelming electric sexual attraction, but actually goes on to meet the girl he's in love with at a café. Kemp falls in love at first sight with the in-line blonde, whom he pegs as a tourist out for fun. Self-consciously clumsy, he makes a fool of himself over her on the plane. Kemp's awkward beginning contrasts with the smooth confidence of Swanson when he is confronted by his girlfriend's brother who displays his role as his sister's protector, lightly grilling the handsome foreign soldier.

In the plane there's a comic scene with Kemp attempting to save a window seat for the blonde, but a fat man belligerently grabs it. Frustrated, Kemp awkwardly blocks the fat man from leaving his seat as he awaits the passing of the blonde. A stewardess calls Kemp a sadist for his behavior toward the fat man. The comedy of the fat man was another Hunter obsession. During his copyboy stint at *Time* magazine, Hunter had boasted in a letter that at an office party he had loudly told the publisher and his friends that the business manager was a "FAT LECHER,"[18] even saying this to the manager's face.

Thompson inverts the aspect of Murphy's serious novel where the sergeant is a homosexual sadist. The heterosexual Kemp finds himself being unjustly labeled as a sadist; this scene is traditional slapstick. While subtle opposing parallels run between both novels, Thompson's novel operates as a refutation of Murphy's novel, which also deals with

dislocated Americans abroad amid a culture that neither fully compre-
hends.

After landing, Kemp muses that he's wandering in a den of hustlers
as he overhears conversations about beach property development, thus
introducing one of the novel's principal themes. His characteristic humor surfaces, as if he were intimately talking to the reader in a Greenwich Village bar: "Their voices set my teeth on edge. I have no valid
complaint against hustlers, no rational bitch, but the act of selling is
repulsive to me. I harbor a secret urge to whack a salesman in the face,
crack his teeth and put red bumps around his eyes."[19]

The scenery of waterfront hotels and standardized suburban housing
becomes symbolic of automated conformity rather than mere background, as it would in most novels. Kemp enters the newspaper office
and introduces himself around as many of the novel's characters appear.

The position of Kemp's boss, Lotterman, the managing editor, remains awkward. As a former communist, he's under pressure to prove
he's a reformed capitalist with a visceral hatred of communism. At this
point the U.S. State Department was advertising Puerto Rico as a show-
case for how American capitalism could operate in all of South America.
This meant that America was investing in Puerto Rico, something that
most Puerto Ricans naturally approved of, since that would better their
lives. As a foreigner and former communist, Lotterman was not perceived as trustworthy by the populace.

The category of "The Fear" first appears in *The Rum Diary* as the
fear of being trapped in the small-town womb of one's childhood as it
applies both to continental Americans and Puerto Rican islanders
yearning to flee and explore the expansive life of the continent and its
brashly urban cities.[20] This fear "warps" the narrator Kemp, who wants
to flee the claustrophobia of family and background, just like Puerto
Ricans who want to emigrate. "The Fear" stems from entrapment (described as being caught in a sack), confinement to backwater mediocrity, the agony and guilt of knowing one has not explored the larger
world, the fear of not attempting a potentially liberating odyssey with its
real threat of doom. That latter aspect was the fear and apprehension
expressed in the gospel of Mark in recounting the Achilles-like doom
that awaited Jesus.

Although journalists and Puerto Ricans alike share this same fear, it
produces a mutual paranoia mirrored and mired in cultural distrust.

"The Fear" stalks everyone as the unconscious thread that warps the weft of life on the island, yet also remains the prospect of pointless odysseys doomed to disaster and failure. Kemp titles his five-part feature story on emigration as "Rubber Sacks, The Fear." Lotterman ratchets his exasperation to hysteria, accusing Kemp of hysteria. Lotterman favors the Horatio Alger myth as the motive for emigration, but not the fear of small-town life, yet he ironically admits that fear of small town life brought him to Puerto Rico from Tallahassee.

Kemp feels disgustingly petty when he realizes he's stuck on the same rock as the Puerto Ricans who dream of landing in New York, but he refuses to bowdlerize his truth-telling observations, so the article ends up spiked (canceled). This article provides an example of the kind of writing Thompson aspired to before arriving in Puerto Rico—his ambition to attack the "The Dry Rot of the American Press," a theme essay Thompson had promised in a letter to William Kennedy, yet instead mailed to him in the form of a one-act drama.[21]

The narrator remains ambivalent about his own project, half-ambitious work afflicted with hedonistic daydreams, much like Jake Barnes in *The Sun Also Rises*. But unlike the perfunctory glimpses of Barnes as a journalist, we see Kemp hard at work. His daydreams tempt him to flee Puerto Rico to any point on the globe at the slightest temptation or momentary reverie. He curses "the warped impulse that brought him to this dull and steaming rock"[22] and resumes drinking after a drunken night that led to jail after he, Yeamon, and Sala wanted to run a tab at a restaurant where they were not regulars, a genuine autobiographical episode of the time Hunter and a friend walked out on a check. In the novel Sanderson magically appears at midnight to bail them out, but in real life it was William Kennedy.[23] The in-joke transforms the ruggedly heterosexual Kennedy into a certain type of character with upper-echelon newspaper connections that Kennedy never had. Thompson's trademark was always to present his fictions as based upon autobiographical reality, yet those fictions were so twisted and transformed by Thompson's compulsive sense of humor that their very appearance as a connection to his life sometimes sails by as tenuously as a puff of smoke, a mumble to the initiated inner circle.

The cursing scene becomes a symbolic display of a change wrought in Kemp where, like Rick in *Casablanca* after he feels burned by Elsa, he will temporarily think harder about his interests rather than those of others, but as in the movie, this will be only a short phase of reactive behavior. In a 1971 letter Thompson describes the novel as a "flawed masterpiece," displaying his habitual self-denigration when it comes to assessing his own achievement, while affirming the vitality of the plot. He alludes to a theme in the novel that is more explicitly obsessive in *Fear and Loathing in Las Vegas*: "The San Juan drink/drug/madness underground, as a backdrop to the American Dream destroying one of its main worshippers."[24] Although Kemp simmers with anger, his eyes are opened, as in many coming-of-age novels. He will remain alert to the madness seething below the surface of life on the island, behaving no longer as a tourist but as an engaged reporter.

The thought of even renting a room or car looms as a confining commitment to Kemp. While he displays some comprehension of the demeaning frustrations Puerto Ricans dwell in, after his beating by the police, he reverts in anger to a traditional colonial mentality that Thompson satirizes: "Puerto Rican jails were for Puerto Ricans—not Americans who wore paisley ties and button-down shirts."[25] In *The Sun Also Rises* Hemingway had boldly treated the problem of anti-Semitism, while Thompson dramatizes anti-Puerto Rican sensibility among Yankees.

Kemp is so immersed in doldrums, he recollects the hobby of clock-watching in high school, but the self-pitying aspect of Kemp that often attempts to take center stage, though honest, does little to endear the cynically bewildered solipsistic character to the reader. Although the convention remains autobiographical, Kemp clearly does not have Thompson's expansive personality, which is left to Yeamon.

After Kemp's arrest for resisting arrest, and a bout of monstrous paranoia, Thompson manages to conjure some sympathy for the lonely wastrel Kemp in his roach-infested hovel, yet the blatantly imitative and supercilious Walter Mitty fantasy-meditation on revenge firearms re-creates an alienated pathetic delirium. This underground disorientation presents a mere hiccup as Kemp pulls himself together, garnering opportunities to advance his budding career as an upcoming journalist, which happens primarily as his boss sees Kemp as least responsible for the scandal.

Yeamon, from a small rural town in Kentucky, confides in Kemp about his troubled relationship with Chenault, expressing disillusionment with his profession as a journalist, evaluating most at the paper as mere drunks. He muses about traveling to Europe; he sees himself as a rebel, wondering where his reward for being a rebel lies. Kemp, in friendly fashion, gently mocks him for such narcissistic optimism. Thompson has split himself in two, leaving his more practical side to Kemp, his physical stature and idealism to temperamental Yeamon.

When Kemp sees the group mug shot of the drunken colonial trio of *News* journalists splattered on the front page of the rival Spanish-language *El Diario*, he grows understandably depressed and begins "to get the fear."[26] The seedy and apparently deranged Moberg, a wonderfully sinister minor character in the novel, advises Kemp to carry a gun for self-protection against the striking union of bellicose Puerto Rican printers while the paper's manager Lotterman employs scab printers. When Kemp had first arrived at the newspaper's offices, his first glimpse of the outfit was the tall Yeamon fighting with the strikers. Lotterman, thoroughly scared, fires the intransigent Yeamon after Yeamon makes threatening wringing gestures with his huge hands to throttle him.

Yeamon's attractive blonde girlfriend, Chenault, a Smith College graduate and wealthy Connecticut rebel (her name being a compound of Ché, the intimate form of an Argentinean greeting, and the Renault auto) at whom Kemp had clumsily gawked on his flight down to Puerto Rico, sponges off Yeamon as his live-in girlfriend. After the abrasive and ornery Yeamon is fired without pay, Kemp visits the couple at their cheap beach-side love shack beyond paved roads—in real life a concrete shack without running water that Thompson shared with painter Paul Semonin.[27] Kemp remains sexually attracted to party-girl Chenault, who loves to sunbathe nude; it's clear Yeamon has become exasperated with Chenault's compulsive exhibitionism.

Yeamon has a freelance article to do on the upcoming St. Thomas carnival. He persuades Kemp to meet them at the carnival. Yeamon hints that his relationship with Zelda-like Chenault has run its course, and that the carnival might be an opportunity for him to pass Chenault off to Kemp, but Yeamon's real agenda is that he suspects he needs another hand to keep Chenault in check.

Kemp must juggle a freelance assignment on the carnival's first day, which he has acquired from the senior editor, Sanderson, who has his own downtown office atop one of the city's tallest buildings. Sanderson had worked the bailout and the court system deferment of the impending railroad trial of the drunken trio. Others on the staff are nasty and prejudiced toward Sanderson because he's gay, but Kemp treats him like a regular human being, so Sanderson offers Kemp the plum job of doing a stringer article for the *New York Times* and its companion piece, a brochure about the prospects for a booming resort development on Vieques, an island just off Puerto Rico that the American military used for ordinance practice for planes, artillery, and tanks.[28] The expectation remains that Kemp will collude with fixer Sanderson in writing the perfect fantasy tourism article, then puff Vieques in a commissioned brochure for small-time middle-class investors being fleeced by the Miami mob. The money to be made in journalism oozes as a form of sleazy promotional prostitution in the wake of Conrad Hilton's wizard developments: "Conrad had come in like Jesus and all the fish had followed."[29]

With the prospect of increased income, Kemp locates a room rental and plunks down money for a used car. Although the site of the proposed development at Vieques presents a gorgeous beach, it's crystal clear that vacationers wouldn't want to mix with stewed military personnel binge-drinking on weekend leave or listen to the constant round of concatenating explosions—the whole project being completely absurd. The management of the newspaper revolves around Miami mob interests gouging the tourist trade.

Kemp would like to be a rebel against the establishment phonies, but he also harbors daydreams of fast cars and fast girls. The tension in his character consists of his dilemma—will he become another commercial sellout ad man, or will he find a way to rebel and avoid the doom of inglorious servility? The Faustian temptation to sell his soul explicitly appears to him when Kemp eyes a forty-foot racing sloop with a teakwood deck: Kemp thinks he might be willing to sell his soul for that trim yacht. In an unusual time-warp retrospective rumination that sounds like it came from a later draft, the narrator ruefully confesses that in his youth he might have jumped at the opportunity to sell his soul.[30]

Kemp hitches a boat ride to St. Thomas, the scene of a carnival that is a drunken parody of an authentic carnival. He hooks up with Yeamon and Chenault; they engage in heavy drinking with the mashing dance lines chugging and churning about the island. The parody of the sloppy, drunken dancing can be seen as a reverse tribute (Thompson once more turning things upside down, like insults for compliments) to Dana Kennedy, the onetime professional Puerto Rican dancer whom William Kennedy married. Thompson's novel is dedicated to her. They remained good friends and Thompson often sent her some of his stage persona props when he was finished with them: his googly eyeglasses, his blonde wig, red scarf, lipstick, trick plastic hammer, and, incredibly, the hospital X-ray of his smashed pelvis (autographed). She archives these items under her bed.[31] These comic gifts echo a friendly relationship between H. L. Mencken and the actress Anita Loos, whereby she would send Mencken a comic gift each year, like a Christmas stocking with a small New Testament jammed into its toe for the atheist.[32] Loos's sketch of Mencken's empty-headed women friends eventually became, with Mencken's encouragement, the best seller *Gentlemen Prefer Blondes* (1925) and later a successful movie.[33]

Meanwhile, the island riot continues—Yeamon and Kemp participate in the farcical looting of a liquor store after the windows have been smashed by rioters. At a debased late-night private party Chenault finds herself transported into a dancing trance and removes all her clothes. This scene surpasses the suggestive dancing between the bullfighter and Lady Brett at a hotel. When Yeamon and Kemp object, they are soundly beaten and tossed from the party.[34] They bring the police back the next morning to no avail: Chenault had vanished.

The carnival parallels the seven-day fiesta in Hemingway's *The Sun Also Rises* where Jake, Bill, Robert, and Mike, along with Lady Brett, enjoy round-the-clock chaos and nearly daily bullfights. Brett has an affair with Robert, then with the star nineteen-year-old bullfighter. Both carnivals feature tourists slumming in a foreign culture, yet Thompson's fiesta provides more exciting drama. For Hemingway, the bullfight enacts a primitive erotic allegory that incites sex, while in Thompson the African mode of dancing into a trance state leads to group activity: the robbing of the liquor store in which Yeamon and Kemp participate, and the orgy from which they futilely attempt to extract Chenault. For Hemingway's Jake, Lady Brett's affair with Robert is damaging, but the affair with the bullfighter is terminally traumatic, just like Chenault's behavior at the party.

When ex-boxer and ex-lover Robert beats up the bullfighter in the hotel bedroom, he terminates his relationship with Brett. For Yeamon, Chenault's public orgy furnishes the last straw to her persistent promis-

cuity. Carnival, once a vibrant medium of black protest, has been reduced to a parody of itself, ironically enslaving Chenault who sees herself as the new liberated woman. Hemingway's Bill utters a sardonic
postmortem: the fiesta was a "wonderful nightmare."[35] For Yeamon, it's
a humiliating nightmare. While Robert subdued the bullfighter, outnumbered Yeamon and Kemp receive their lumps. Thompson indulges
his habit of warping literary templates, providing parallels with a twist,
often a reversal modality—the template functions to be overwritten in
Dionysian reversal. The European fiesta functions as a spirited denial of
English Puritanism, while the New World carnival, shorn of its history,
acts as exploitative consumption.

The surreal bathhouse orgy at the end of Kennedy's *The Ink Truck*
leaves the reader with uncertainty—not quite sure about events, witnessed through the mist of nightmare, the bleak epilogue of failure
supplying the hangover. Kennedy's parallel revolves around disgust: the
orgy has no real consequence other than being an irresponsible distraction, which he satirizes as ugly through his distorting surreal lens, while
in Hemingway the fiesta leads to Jake becoming disgusted with Lady
Brett after she secretly departs on a train with the bullfighter. In stark
contrast, Thompson has Kemp appropriate a more active role in claiming Chenault by confronting Yeamon.

A hungover Kemp responsibly returns for Monday work. On Tuesday morning Chenault wakes him by tapping like a mouse at his door.
On the one hand, Kemp now despises Chenault for the gang rape abuse
she subjected herself to, but on the other hand, he can't resist his fatal
attraction to her, and he succumbs to making love in the shower. When
Kemp finally gets the girl he so lusts after, the reader can finally feel
sorry for him. We learn Chenault can't ever achieve orgasm and that
propels her promiscuity—hence her search for the right earth-man who
might magically provide it, an interpretation that today might appear as
a superficial sexist cliché. This drama of her sexuality parallels the compulsive promiscuity of Lady Brett in *The Sun Also Rises*, but also functions as a sexual wound paralleling Jake Barnes's impotence, a medieval
theme connected in Gottfried von Eschenbach's *Parzival* to the Holy
Grail where the king's life, imperiled by a groin war wound, finds daily
preservation with communion from the Grail.

Jake and Lady Brett, who were in love with each other, couldn't
consummate their love sexually in Hemingway's novel because Jake had

lost his male member while retaining his testicles. Hemingway told A. E. Hotchner that the wound was physical, not psychological. [36] But Chenault has a psychological wound—a comic theme of unholy quest for the true and ultimate orgasm—in contrast to Lady Brett's insatiable wanton orgasms; Hemingway at one point compares Lady Brett to Homer's Circe. [37] Just as Lady Brett matures somewhat and demythologizes the phallic bullfighter, Chenault discovers a more maternal attraction to Kemp over Yeamon's more brutal masculinity. [38]

That afternoon Kemp hears the newspaper will fold. On Wednesday morning Kemp humbly retrieves Chenault's clothing and luggage from a bitter, angry Yeamon. On Friday Lotterman tells the staff the paper will close: there will be no immediate severance pay, their past week will be paid next week. The journalists know they won't be paid next week—there's a near riot. Kemp returns home to discover Chenault reading *Heart of Darkness* (ironic, since she has just emerged from a sexual heart of darkness). Kemp informs Chenault that everything's over between them because he won't be able to pay next month's rent. He urges her to return to New York; they make love once more. The reference to Conrad (Joseph, not Hilton) provides the meta-text key for the structure of Thompson's novel, alerting the reader to the iceberg element in the plot. It appears that gangsters actually own the newspaper and have been using the paper as an advertising front for the development schemes whereby they intend to fleece investors.

Miami is the equivalent of Conrad's Belgian capitol building, the "whited sepulcher." Lotterman incarnates the Kurtz-like figure, whose corruption vectors the vortex of colonial mayhem. Lotterman appears to have run the newspaper as if he were running a street-numbers lottery. There has been no sane method or rationale behind the existence of the newspaper. If Lotterman "had a million dollars and all the freedom in the world he'd still put out a worthless newspaper because he wasn't smart enough to put out a good one." [39] Chenault, the drifter, has provided some comic relief in the same way the Russian clown and his colorful shirt functions in Conrad's novel. [40] Like Conrad, Thompson even calls attention to the motif of Chenault's shirt. The horror consists of a thousand media punks, "pompous little farts, waving the banner [of freedom, truth, and honor] with one hand and reaching under the table with the other." [41] Chenault and Kemp make sensuous love for the last time before she departs.

After a sumptuous hotel breakfast with Chenault, Kemp departs for Al's, where the journalists collect to pool angry stories. Kemp drives to a beach club to compose witty diary entries about the failed newspaper. For inspiration he reads the preface to Conrad's *Nigger of the Narcissus*, a rather famous manifesto proclaiming literary impressionism. Kemp abandons all hope of being anything but a failure when he compares himself to Conrad's monumental literary achievement. This presents a frank admission that, in terms of stylistic achievement, Thompson knew he wasn't reaching what his ambition desired in *The Rum Diary*. Yet this passage is itself a virtual reproduction of a passage from Fitzgerald's introduction to the 1934 Modern Library reprint of *The Great Gatsby*:

> I had just re-read Conrad's preface to *The Nigger*, and I had recently been kidded half haywire by critics who felt that my material was such as to preclude all dealing with mature persons in a mature world. But, my God! It was my material, and it was all I had to deal with. [42]

Thompson offers another warped template—what on the surface appears to be a confession of failure merely supplies irony if the reader recalls Fitzgerald's own defiant apology. Thompson omits Fitzgerald's last sentence, but the educated reader would pick up on the allusion to Fitzgerald's preface. The doubling motif (of the two prefaces) is a hallmark signature of Thompson's tricky postmodern use of allusions, although an intriguing argument has been made that the novel teeters on the cusp between the modern and the postmodern. [43]

Kemp returns to his room to discover Chenault's departure note expressing the romantic hope of a future Manhattan rendezvous. This explicitly warps the ending of *Casablanca*. In a characteristic twist, the novel's conclusion differs from *Casablanca*'s ending, which remains unusual by Hollywood standards: Rick (Bogart) doesn't get Elsa (Ingrid Bergman). Patriotic causes trump personal love engagements in time of war, but in peacetime Chenault flies off solo with the possibility or promise of romantic reunion. And unlike the Bogart figure, Kemp will not stay behind. In his impressionistic novel, *Big Sur* (1962), Jack Kerouac drew a parallel between his hallucinatory drunken hangover with Humphrey Bogart in *The Treasure of the Sierra Madre* (1948) when

Bogart, who has just killed his partner, stares insanely into the campfire.[44] But Thompson does not indulge in Kerouac's self-pity.

Reporting to work on Monday, Kemp hears of the newspaper's bankruptcy. In the evening Kemp attends a social given by the Rum League and the San Juan Chamber of Commerce. Lotterman and other journalists mill about the party. Moberg, Sala, and the sportswriter Donovan (who has a hidden butcher knife) boldly threaten to kill Lotterman. Yeamon appears menacing in his black nylon gloves, although he's thoroughly distracted by a beautiful young girl. Moberg aggressively demands from Lotterman his back pay. Lotterman cruelly bashes him to the ground. As Moberg rises, Lotterman bops him again, then chases him when Moberg struggles up. Yeamon springs to Moberg's rescue, staggering Lotterman with a solid punch, smashing him to the ground in a spurt of blood. A mysterious bodyguard, dressed all in black, jumps in the air like some fabled cartoon ninja, knocking down Yeamon, Sala, Moberg, and Donovan. Amid the subsequent riot and confusion, Yeamon, Donovan, and Kemp flee.

After worriedly driving about aimlessly, Kemp chances an appearance at Al's where Sala tells him Moberg has been arrested for the murder of Lotterman who died of a heart attack. While this can happen, it remains a rare occurrence.[45] Donovan and Yeamon are also wanted by the police as accessories to the crime. Earlier in the novel Sala had complained to Lotterman that the incensed union strikers will eventually kill someone from the paper. The irascible Lotterman had replied, "Nobody's going to be killed."[46] Lotterman's sudden death glimmers off-page in karmic irony, yet it's not quite as dramatic as the on-page delirious death of Kurtz in Conrad's novel.

Kemp returns to his tiny digs, finding Yeamon in his shower, a doubling of the motif of finding Chenault in his shower. Panicking in sudden flight, Yeamon had bashed his motorcycle headlight and can't drive to the airport in the dark. Kemp decides to drive Yeamon to the airport, thereby becoming guilty of assisting a fugitive. On the way to the airport a sudden torrential squall, aptly described, delays their arrival and they arrive in time to see the last plane take off down the runway with Donovan's profile decorating a window seat. Kemp now becomes an outlaw harboring a fugitive, and has achieved the status and danger of an existential hero.

In *The Sun Also Rises* violence furnishes an ambiance: a bullfighter
is killed in the ring and a man is killed during the running of the bulls.
The tourists deride these deaths as death for sport to test a reaction,
and to their surprise the local tavern owners glumly agree. Both deaths,
in the background, remain accidental. Lotterman's death remains center stage, yet Thompson introduces an element of the accidental—
Lotterman dies from a heart attack, from the shock of being hit rather
than being battered, stabbed, or shot.

Yeamon had no intention of killing Lotterman—he merely wanted
to rescue the persecuted Moberg. While this event traduces the prescriptions of Aristotelian tragedy—that the doer must knowingly be
responsible for one's fate—it works effectively and convincingly for the
newspaper milieu in which there's nearly always a truer story hidden
behind the explanation available to the public, yet the reporter may not
have the full proof needed or political muscle to publish the real story.
The death of Lotterman also dramatizes the false, presumed aloofness
of the management class, who are immune from the vengeance of the
street. To the average Puerto Rican, Yeamon appears as a rebel hero for
vanquishing the man suspected of being a communist at heart. But for
Yeamon such iconic status looms as pathetically ironic—he will no longer be able to make a living in the profession.

Kemp drives Yeamon forty miles to the obscure St. Thomas ferry
dock. Yeamon will limp off to South America with the shirt on his back
and a hundred dollars in his pocket. On the way back to his apartment,
Kemp halts to pick up *El Diario*. Yeamon's wanted mug graces the front
page. Kemp motors on to Al's to see Sala. Depressed, disillusioned, and
resigned, they converse, but fall to silent meditation after much rum
while the piano player tinkles "Laura," the song Gene Tierney made
famous in the 1944 movie of that name, depicting a fleeting and dream-
like Angelica double from Ariosto's *Orlando Furioso*. Then the imaginary music of a thousand hungry clocks ticking in the Caribbean night
records the wan poetic boredom of exhaustion in the concluding sentence. The ticking clock motif presents a parody of the cliché in the
thriller genre, while it recalls the boredom experienced by every young
student in the confined classroom who has outgrown the level of education offered.

Kemp will begin a new perilous quest for job security, riches, and
women on another corrupt rock in the trenches of sleazy propaganda

driven by the whimsical wallets of the wealthy. In real life, it was feature travel writer Thompson,[47] facing the prospect of a year in jail for resisting arrest after his police beating, who fled, nestling in a small sailboat to other ports.[48] Thompson had boarded a sloop bound for Lisbon, but the ship's head-stay (the support for the main mast) broke, and they hauled into Bermuda for repair. The repair was taking so long that Thompson grew impatient and flew to New York City,[49] but the nerve-wracking ordeal of the sea voyage provided the setting for his short story, "Burial at Sea,"[50] which describes a well-to-do husband losing his wife during a sea vacation to the grubby skipper of a small yacht named "Sebastian."

Thompson has evoked the atmosphere of the film *Casablanca* (1942) in the novel's prologue and epilogue, explicitly citing the film in the middle of the novel when Kemp hops to Vieques: "It was the kind of town that made you feel like Humphrey Bogart: you came in on a little bumpy plane."[51] The epilogue references Homer: this has been a ten-year odyssey on the part of Kemp, who has wandered the Southern Hemisphere in search of a stable journalistic living. While interesting events have happened, no journalistic home, no Ithaca, has been found. Kemp will return to the island of Manhattan, his longed-for Ithaca where he will love his Penelope, Chenault.

If there are other upstart suitors, he will fight both them and the whole edifice of journalistic corruption. From the crucible of Puerto Rico, Kemp emerges as an outlaw journalist ready to take on the whole corrupt profession. But his Homeric war with the establishment will erupt in comedy: his weapons will consist of biting comic barbs he has been privately honing in his letters over the past decade. Like Pietro Aretino, Francois Rabelais, or Edgar Allan Poe, he will assert a raw honesty, sociological critique, and savage dignity that will distinguish him as a journalist's journalist, clothed in the jesting court mantle of Mark Twain, America's own down-home Homer.

Compared to the Conradian allegory of imperial horror, the holocaust theme of Conrad's Belgian colony in Africa, or its revivified metaphor in the script of Francis Ford Coppola's 1979 *Apocalypse Now* epic about American soldiers in Vietnam,[52] Kemp's aspirations may appear as grandiose affection, yet the book may be deeply appreciated as a young journalist's heroic vow to be the new Odysseus who will return to his former island home, Manhattan, to slay the false suitors who corrupt journalism. The grumbling camaraderie of jousting journalists that Thompson depicts remains closer to the ethos of desperate beachcombers than socially concerned intellectuals who wallow in self-righteous cynicism. Management as fraudulent phonies strikes a contemporary and enduring critical note within the business of journalism, where advertising prescribes the formulaic script behind closed office doors, promoting clichés that appeal to seven-year-olds. These journalists scratch their living on the edge with constant fear of unemployment, especially if they abrade their shoe leather and produce unwanted real journalism. Loathing remains the deadline rush work required to staunch "The Fear"; loathing becomes incarnated in the typewriter that the writer must pound every day to ensure that he can survive his destined doom. Thompson was also known to have indulged in occasionally shooting up his typewriter with a .454 Magnum pistol.[53]

The nostalgic film daydreams of *Casablanca* that flit through the novel must be interpreted in the light of Thompson's warping technique. The black-and-white past has given way to a new world of color cinema in which the villains are not as easily defeated as in past movies. The film world upholds illusions—at the end of the novel, corrupt management still holds sway over the young journalists.

As a major category of philosophical, religious, or literary significance, there is nothing knew about fear. Stendhal employed the concept of fear and trembling in *On Love* (1822), Soren Kierkegaard subsequently used fear as a philosophical and religious category[54] for grounding absurdity in *Fear and Trembling* (1843), and the American Puritan divine Jonathan Edwards employed fear and trembling somewhat humorlessly in his vivid sermons.[55] Nor is its use peculiar to the Protestant tradition—Dante Alighieri made eloquent and comic use of it in his *Inferno*, and Francis Thompson converted fear into a haunting guilt in his narrative poem, "The Hound of Heaven." In these works the category of fear is less dangerous than the arrogance of pride, and fear becomes transformative redemption, as in Gertrud von Le Fort's epistolary novella, *Song of the Scaffold* (1932).

Whether Thompson himself was aware of such precedents remains problematic,[56] yet, as so often in the history of writing, things which appear new often have forgotten precedents. While Albert Camus was the reigning journalist-novelist-philosopher in the West during the Fifties, his influence—other than the vague continuum of absurdity—does not mark Thompson's novel. Thompson never displayed much interest in philosophy, although in *Hell's Angels* he cites Kierkegaard: "The daily press is the evil principle of the modern world, and time will only serve to disclose this fact with greater and greater clearness."[57] Thompson always remained well aware of the press's capacity for distortion and myth-building, a central theme of *Hell's Angels*.

The work of the Argentinean Roberto Arlt may be seen as a general predecessor. Arlt made his living as a journalist and employed semi-autobiographical narrative in his fiction, working impulsively on the edge of destruction. He conjured fevered projective fictions to embroider his narratives and, like the hero of his 1926 coming-of-age novel *El juguete rabioso (Mad Toy)*,[58] Thompson's Kemp wants desperately to be somebody, but finds neither self-redemption nor the possibility of a decently sane society. In Arlt's fiction the hero usually mingles with half-mad alienated characters amid a surreal and sinister landscape.

As in Arlt's *The Seven Madmen* (1929), there are seven desperate characters: loudmouthed Segarra, headstrong Yeamon, pessimistic Sala, menacing Moberg, whacko Donovan, bemused Kemp, and the homosexual rebel Sanderson. The names identify a motley international crew of professional wanderers. While Thompson's characters are nearly half-crazed, they never quite achieve the phantasmagoric surrealism Arlt provides, although Moberg and Yeamon nearly do; Thompson's atmosphere of hysteria and manipulative paranoia in his plot bear a significant resemblance to Arlt's fictional technique, but in terms of style, the plainer American realism Thompson that employs runs closer to the sense of implacable *doom* evoked by Curzio Malaparte's journalistic account of World War II in *Kaputt* (1943), which offers both eyewitness authenticity, as well as imaginative re-creation of events so horrifying, especially in the scenes of Nazi activity in Romania, that the book remains at times difficult to read.

Thompson's novel limns a world of struggling bohemian outcasts amid their pathetic and absurd, largely self-inflicted, dead-end melodramas. While it satirizes the rat race of competitive male egos and their clashing demonic impulses, it romanticizes male bonding over the warping powers of drink (which often ironically turns them into blockheads), as well as a lost paradise where beautiful and willing women-rebels fulfill men's temporary sexual needs without any need for domestic commitment like the compulsive Baudelaire-like fantasies of Arlt's

Ernesto Erdosain in *The Seven Madmen*.[59] Like Ernesto, Kemp day-dreams of living in an American movie, yet for both Arlt and Thompson such daydreams linger as romantic temptations that are not real; as in Arlt, characters "are tremendously unhappy, but no diagnosis or possible remedy for their sorrow is ever specified."[60] Amid alienation and poverty, Arlt's characters face a corrupt society with mysterious Romantic conspiracies doomed to fail, although Thompson more astutely locates conspiracy in the upper echelons of corporate power. The attempt to rebel also remains disfigured by personal romance, lust, and the desperate behavioral excesses that alienation produces. For both Arlt and Thompson the result resembles Camus's Sisyphean rebel doomed to failure, yet both Arlt and Thompson add the comic ingredient of eccentric histrionics and fevered longing that readers find so captivating. As in *The Seven Madmen*, which appears, along with *The Sun Also Rises* (and to a lesser degree *The Sergeant*), to be the inspirational template for *The Rum Diary*, a reader is encouraged to assemble a version of reality from various character problems and delusions amid the phantasmagoria of social distortions imposed by the iron fist of society.

Thompson's novel, set in 1958 (the year Arlt's novel was republished and re-appreciated, with enthusiastic reviews) casts a gritty glance back to a time when colonial journalism was run like a civilian military propaganda operation, temporarily employing globe-hopping outlaw wetbacks, since they were the only available pens to be exploited on the colonial frontier where bankers and gangsters colluded, speculating beyond the reach of the law. The only way these nonconformist journalists could conceive of escaping the tightrope they walked amid the conformity of a formula job was to become independent writer-contractors through feature journalism, or achieve the near-impossible dream of commercial literary success. Thompson half-managed the former and aspired to the latter more successfully in subsequent brilliant journalism cunningly disguised as fiction, as Kennedy perceptively noted.

Despite the novel's dated limitations about the sociology of Puerto Rico, the plot offers a lively read, yet the cosmetic and nostalgic film-script sugar-coating romantically depletes *The Rum Diary* of the doomed alienated grittiness one finds in an autobiographical masterpiece like Dazai Osamu's *No Longer Human* (1948, trans. 1958). Thompson, like his character Kemp, lusts after monetary success more than the obscure achievement of art that one finds in a hermit writer like the Argentine Macedonio Fernández. As Thompson forcefully articulated in a 1978 interview (finally managing to shock his jaded interviewer), his only motivation was writing for money: "What else is there?"[61] Such remains the traditional position of the professional writer, noted by Boswell when he cited Samuel Johnson's frank observation that "No man but a blockhead ever wrote, except for money."[62] *The Rum Diary* records the young Thompson's aspiration to lounge in the parlor of legendary immortals, drinking rum with his flip-flops on, yet three decades later (1988) Thompson humorously complained, "I spent half my life trying to get away from journalism, but I am still mired in it—a low trade and a habit worse than heroin, a strange seedy world full of misfits and drunkard and failures."[63] Thompson's gift remains his ability to create popular entertaining comedy from his own failures—as well as his country's failures—while he combines his branded gonzo humor with trenchant moral critiques. Much of that humor leaked into the 2011 Johnny Depp film version of the novel, yet a movie traditionally runs as a crude cover of a novel.

Conrad's *The Heart of Darkness* also appears as a meta-text theme in the writings of Thompson's longtime friend, Tom Wolfe. Both *The Bonfire of the Vanities* and *I Am Charlotte Simmons* feature explicit references to Conrad, just as Wolfe's satiric critique of *Time* magazine's Henry Luce in *The Right Stuff* later parallels Thompson's attack in *Hell's Angels*.[64] The roots of satiric New Journalism in both Thompson and Wolfe can be traced to Curzio Malaparte's neo-Proustian masterpiece, *Kaputt* (1944), where the debasement of habitual lying, posturing, and boasting permits some people to survive the tsunami of death during the madness of World War II. Malaparte was the first modernist to introduce the on-scene journalist who provides a first-person mix of satiric exaggeration and reportorial observation (although Mark Twain accomplished that in his 1869 *Innocents Abroad*), blending interior personal fiction with conversational settings.[65] Wolfe transferred Malaparte's elegant salon settings with old European royalty, relocating Malaparte's technique to the obviously less-cultured Upper East Side of Manhattan in his 1970 "Radical Chic" essay about Leonard Bernstein and the Black Panthers, while Thompson followed the ironic interior strain of madness in Malaparte, developing a hallucinatory satire the following year with *Fear and Loathing in Las Vegas*. While both

Thompson and Wolfe were indebted to Norman Mailer's breakthrough journalism of *Advertisements for Myself* (1959), which initiated political satire from Mailer's self-consciously bumptious ego, the satire of Thompson and Wolfe had darker embellishing roots in Malaparte's more complex novelistic journalism, with its backdrop tableaux of literary meta-texts and mocking exaggeration.[66]

Because *The Rum Diary* provides a close-up of a singular profession, it lacks the broad questing appeal of New Englander Jack Kerouac's hipster novels, *On the Road* and *The Dharma Bums*; etched in the minimal realism of Hemingway's early spare style, *The Rum Diary* contains an element of the zany, desperate, loony qualities one discovers in the fevered fantasies of Arlt's South American tribulations or the surreal flights in William Kennedy's novels.

The version of the novel that we now have was discovered in Thompson's basement by friend and historian Douglas Brinkley, who retreated to a country cabin with cartons of pages that Curtis Robinson photocopied to edit the manuscript—thrice the size of the current novel. Episodes concerning pirates were cut.[67] Perhaps the film version of the novel will stimulate the publication of a longer unedited version, as was done with the recent "scroll" republication of Kerouac's *On the Road*. The novel would have been published in the late Sixties after the success of *Hell's Angels*, but due to a dispute about its editing, Thompson had the manuscript stolen. Mary Sue Rucci at Simon and Schuster and Douglas Brinkley were able to edit it to Hunter's satisfaction.[68]

The film made from *The Rum Diary* injects gonzo comedy into the gritty novel. Like any movie, this version includes scenes not in the novel, and some scenes in the novel are dropped. Near the end of the film, the futile theme of putting out a journalist's exposé edition of the paper arrives via Kennedy's *The Ink Truck*. And that works well, yet it would have been better if Sala had lost the last cockfight. The final scene of the movie attempts to tag onto the tragic-comic a purely comic ending that doesn't work. The villain Sanderson, played by Aaron Eckhart, virtually steals the film from the hero Kemp (Johnny Depp). The novel contains a showdown between the heroes and the villain. While any good novel or film needs such a climax, the film punks out—diminishing the hero, literally turning the hero into a criminal when he casually steals Sanderson's boat. This remains ironic because of the novel's interior monologue episode that Kemp experiences by the docks, when he endures his Faustian temptation that he might sell his soul for a yacht.

The film could have attained a climatic catharsis by adhering more closely to the novel. At the concluding party Kemp and Sanderson would have argued. Sanderson could have lost his temper and hit Kemp, and Kemp could have decked Sanderson, sending him to the hospital. The next morning Sala shows Kemp his picture on the front page of the newspaper, reading him excerpts. Sala happily discovers that charges against him have been dropped, but there's a manhunt on for Kemp, charged with attempted murder. Sala tells Kemp he lost the war and must flee. Kemp tells Sala that he has everything backward—that he has merely lost a battle, not a war, wars being composed of a series of battles. The war between corrupt corporations and the exploited populace presents an endless war; Kemp means to win a few battles in this war. Sala drives Kemp (with the mere hundred dollars Chenault left) to the ferry in a storm, but they miss the ferry. Kemp spends the next night on the beach, taking the ferry in the morning with vagabond chin stubble. Then the text epilogue about battles Kemp has won.

The reason why the film presents the sloop ending is that Hollywood prefers a happy ending; box office analysts frown on tragic endings. American exceptionalism means that heroes always triumph, that Horatio Alger always gets the sailboat and sails off. Hollywood money managers turned *The Rum Diary* into a John Wayne film. The fact that these Alger-like figures employ corporations as covers to steal wealth was the point Thompson was making in the novel; the film's ending deprives the general populace of catharsis and endorses a point of view the book denounces. I don't see in Thompson's writing any advocacy of blatant criminality (drug use is universally human, not criminal) or any advocacy of revolutionary violence, although Kerouac in *On the Road* depicts the stealing of cars as casual underclass heroism outside of any sociopolitical context.

Stealing the boat runs counter to faith in journalism: that if the lies and hypocrisy of the wealthy are exposed, democracy still has a chance, even if it means one is betting against the odds. Stealing the yacht subtly defends the corporate point of view: Thompson was a criminal, not a serious journalist. While not above pilfering hotel accessories or lifting petty items as pranks, Thompson would have been more likely to pen a positive review of Lawrence Lessig's *Republic Lost* (2011) than to steal the svelte sloop of Roger Ailes or Rupert Murdoch (although it is true that Thompson once entertained the idea of using a stolen car rental incident in his short story "Polo Is My Life").[69] As Thompson later wrote, "I have worked with the criminally insane all my life. These are my people, but I usually try to keep them at arm's length."[70] Despite Thompson's avowed pessimism, he remained a Jeffersonian, not a disciple of Vladimir Lenin or Jean Genet. Thompson later recollected:

> When I was 20 years old I harangued the editors of the *Louisville Courier-Journal* to send me to Cuba so I could join Fidel Castro in the Sierra Maestra mountains and send back dispatches about the triumph of the revolution. I was a Believer—not a Marxist or a Communist or some kind of agrarian Stalinist dilettante—but I was also a working journalist, and editors were not eager to pay my expenses to go to Cuba to fight with Castro in the mountains.[71]

Jefferson placed his faith in the press rather than the government's ability to remain honest or sane.

Thompson's novel has benefited from a revived currency because news outfits are currently engaged in Darwinian downsizing while reporters discover themselves under pressure to report expected corporate truisms rather than perform investigative journalism. Just as Mark Twain's satiric *The Gilded Age* (1873) humorously depicted post-boom Civil War amid lobbyist corruption—and still endures as relevant social critique—so will *The Rum Diary* abide as an entertaining critique of entrenched conspiratorial corruption in journalism.

As an Anglo-Caribbean novel, *The Rum Diary* lacks the resonating cultural ironies Russell Banks developed in *The Book of Jamaica* (1980) and *Rule of the Bone* (1995), but its submerged iceberg theme of opportunistic corruption rises to the murderous conspiratorial levels Banks profiled in *Affliction* (1989).[72] While Hemingway's *The Sun Also Rises* profiles the party mentality of upper-class American expatriates, Thompson portrays the after-hours partying of working-class journalists who sweat from one deadline to the next; they party in working-class fashion for relief from frustration, not out of boredom like Hemingway's elite drifters. While Hemingway offers satire in depicting the empty partying of the elite as a way of life, Thompson defends the practice among journalists as an important venue for the exchange of insider information and freelance job opportunities, confining his satire to the deranged excesses of drunken behavior. And as time tramps by, has anything really changed, despite the digital revolution, in the habits of journalists or those tycoons who cynically exploit them?

The Rum Diary memorably etches a sociological portrait of manipulated young professionals from obscure places, restlessly wanting to explore whatever moral illusions they think the American Dream may offer them, even if that dream aligns an assortment of rebellious and provocative Western "outlaws" with a handful of loose beach sand and a rain bucket to collect the treasured drops of drinking water that may occasionally fall from the distant and laughing empyrean heavens.

3

ODDBALL JOURNALISM, UNDERCLASS CULTURE

Hell's Angels

Hunter, why are you writing about these losers?—Dr. Bob Geiger

At *The Nation* magazine Carey McWilliams who, like his mentor Mencken, reveled in discovering young writers, spotted an article about trendy topless joints in San Francisco in the November 2, 1964, issue of the *National Observer*. McWilliams commissioned a twenty-nine-year-old starving writer in the Haight-Ashbury district to write a short piece on the Hells Angels motorcycle gang, which started out as "just another down-and-out assignment."[1] At that time Hunter was momentarily disgusted with journalism, concentrating on his novel, hunting for odd jobs, lining up on Mission Street with derelicts for temporary jobs at 5 a.m., but not being picked from the lineup.[2] Offered $100 by McWilliams for the article, which amounted to exactly one month's rent, Thompson buoyantly wrote to Charles Kuralt, who was paying his rent,[3] on March 26, 1965, that he was doing the piece just for kicks:

> Before I let them into the house last night I explained to them that I didn't go much for fist-fighting, but preferred to settle my beefs with a double-barreled 12-gauge shotgun. They seemed to grasp the concept and we got along fine; Sandy's hysteria abated, I was a gallon of wine and a case of beer poorer, but in the end I think I got the makings of about five fine stories.[4]

Sandy Thompson said the cyclists were polite and considerate of their baby Juan when in their house, yet when Hunter went drinking beer with them in bars, which was usually about two or three days a week in the summer of 1965,[5] he usually left when they began taking Seconal because then "they would be *monsters*."[6]

The piece, "Losers and Outsiders," addressed a rape charge (later dropped) and was directed at the Hells Angels, appeared in *The Nation* on May 17, 1965.[7] Its publication by a little-known writer, who had been a stringer for varied outfits writing about South America for the past five years, along with its sensational coverage by various press publications, elevated Thompson into the elite company of the limply labeled "New Journalism"—including journalists like Norman Mailer, Thomas Wolfe, Jimmy Breslin, and George Plimpton, who had transformed sports journalism into a participatory affair. Plimpton had pitched against the National League, chronicled in his modestly titled *Out of My League* (1961), and on assignment from *Sports Illustrated* had boxed several rounds with super-stylists Archie Moore and Sugar Ray Robinson. Mailer attempted to project what the middle class thought about the zeitgeist of politics; Wolfe's freelancing profiled popular yet peculiar oddities like the invention of the demolition derby, as well as a contemporary backwoods distiller; Breslin conjured the daily angst of shouts in the street.

These journalists were cutting-edge writers who thought journalists shouldn't sit at their desks reading official wires, but like George Orwell in *A Homage to Catalonia* (1938), troop out into the field where the real action exploded in random insanity. Orwell, inspired by the wanderlust slumming of Jack London, had penned a gritty and bleak underclass landmark in *Down and Out in Paris and London* (1933). Even Ralph "Sonny" Barger, the Oakland president of the Hells Angels, liked the article (although he said a few facts were exaggerated). The piece gave Thompson entrée into the Hells Angels gang for the price of two kegs of beer.[8] About Hunter's book, Barger, whom Thompson depicted as three inches taller than he was, later said: "It was junk. The worst part is that it became a law enforcement guide on the club. . . . Plus, Hunter never delivered on the beer kegs."[9] Barger was annoyed at what he claimed were Thompson's exaggerations on gang initiation practices, especially the dung-and-oil clothes-dipping claim.[10] Yet after a serious beating, would anyone reward thugs with beer kegs?

Living amid the squalor of Haight-Ashbury with a wife and baby, Hunter foresaw the future gestalt of popular American culture. He replied to his sympathetic landlord Dr. Bob Geiger's query about these losers: "No, these guys [the Hells Angels] are really showing us where society is going."[11] With his first assignment on American underclass culture, Thompson foresaw that the demographics of American society would produce an explosive growth of underclass street culture, something that Beat writers like Jack Kerouac, Bob Kaufman, and Gregory Corso were exploring individually. But Thompson prophetically envisioned the strident sociological split in American culture between high and low culture:

> It may be that America is developing a whole new category of essentially social criminals . . . persons who threaten the police and the traditional social structure even when they are breaking the law . . . because they view The Law with contempt and the police with distrust, and this abiding resentment can explode without warning at the slightest provocation.[12]

The eye-catching stylistic ellipses and attitude, reminiscent of Celine's signature style and trademark cynicism, captures an attitude that a few years later went viral on some college campuses as frustration over the Vietnam genocide mounted among students.

Journalism could also become investigative sociology or even whimsical anthropology, as Tom Wolfe famously announced in his iconic over-the-top introduction to *The Kandy-Kolored Tangerine-Flake Streamlined Baby* (1965), published as light summer reading, but soon to become a shelf-life classic of curious offbeat journalism. In that collection Wolfe had profiled the inventor of the demolition derby, a white-lightning distiller, and a custom car maker, among other feature stories—offbeat articles that today flourish under the banner of oddball journalism. Thompson loved the book, wrote a review of it for the *National Observer*, for which he had written book reviews in the past, but the review was spiked by an editor who did not like Wolfe. Thompson sent on his unpublished review to Wolfe and a friendly correspondence ensued.

Thompson realized there was something troubling and emblematic about the confused anger of American subculture that involved F. Scott Fitzgerald's disgruntled disillusionment with the so-called American

Dream. Thompson would ride that dangerous road into the underclass heart of darkness to prefigure the coming culture wars between high and low. In a generic manner, sinister adumbrations of this cultural split had been chronicled previously by Henry Miller in his depressing but illuminating cross-country tour of the American people and landscape, *The Air-Conditioned Nightmare* (1945).

The motorcycle article, with its disciplined and bemused tone of a reporter who appeared to know the business from the inside out, impressed many editors. Thompson quickly received offers to write for *Playboy, Cavalier, Esquire,* and *Saturday Evening Post,*[13] as well as seven book offers, but only one offer was specific about money: Angus Cameron at Knopf, who was familiar with Thompson's work and admired it, encouraged Bernard Shir-Cliff at Ballantine to sign Thompson. Shir-Cliff proposed sending immediately $1,500, which in those days was a considerable sum for a struggling writer.[14] Sara Blackburn, wife of the poet Paul Blackburn, at Random House temporarily became Thompson's "fringe" book editor. In his May 7, 1965, reply, Thompson notes that, aside from his poverty, he perhaps could do an outline for a book on "Hard-Rock Diggers, Carny Hustlers, *Braceros* [migrant workers], Hells Angels, Aspen Philosophers, free-lance foreign correspondents, ski-bums, and Kentucky Mountain disc jockeys,"[15] lamenting the latter would cost a great deal in expenses because of the travel involved, but that at the moment he was concentrating on his novel *The Rum Diary.* Thompson had previously published an impressionistic travelogue article on Kentucky bluegrass music for the *Chicago Tribune,* February 18, 1962.[16]

When Thompson landed the paperback Ballantine contract for a book on motorcycle gangs at the end of June, he was finally able to pay his rent and get his guns and camera out of hock,[17] but he also boasted that he used the money to buy a motorcycle, a BSA 650 Lightning that didn't much impress the Angels, who were into Harleys with showboating extras.[18] Barger later expressed rueful regret that the gang's image was wedded to the Harley-Davidson brand (the brand *required* by all members) after some British and Japanese bikes offered riders more exciting options, but part of the gang's identity resided in a made-in-America patriotic sensibility.[19]

While the advance kept Thompson afloat, in a letter to his editor Jim Silberman at Random House, where the book had been upgraded to a first-printing hardback, Thompson observed that during the writing of the book, "nobody came to see me because they were afraid I'd ask for a loan."[20] It wasn't until the book was purportedly finished after a booze-and-pill madcap writing session of the book's second half in four days, including a one-hundred-hour stint of straight writing.[21] Many writers have recorded boasting exaggerations of fantastic output, from Liam O'Flaherty to Harry Martinson (author of the 1956 masterpiece *Aniara*) to Jack Kerouac,[22] who may have provided the model here—announcements of such manic activity usually attract useful publicity copy. Thompson met his March 1, 1965, deadline, so that he could collect the second half of the advance and pay his rent.

In his book on the Hells Angels, Thompson had focused on the cult aspect of edgy subgroups that in some bizarre fashion acclaimed the American Dream while unconsciously illustrating its doomed failure. To cue the reader, Thompson fronted his book with an eloquent epigraph from literature's most famous underclass cult figure—Francois Villon, sardonic lyrical genius and outlaw poet, whose outlandish habit of going to bed at the first streak of dawn Hunter would soon emulate throughout his life.

Douglas Brinkley observantly notes that what makes *Hell's Angels* a classic is "Thompson's way of capturing the rococo political and cultural theater that defined the San Francisco Bay Area in the psychedelic sixties,"[23] and while that atmosphere and its attendant ingenuous tactics in the widening cultural divide between the peace movement and the developing police state is memorably limned, I think what also makes the book a classic remains it's exposé of shoddy mainstream journalism and how journalism finds itself manipulated by the machinations of what the hippies would call the gratuitous paranoia of the conspiratorial police state. By promoting fear and angst between the middle class and the working class over the hyped issue of drugs and sex, a cultural divide could be opened, and that divide could be exploited to ridicule egalitarian policies developed during the Great Depression. With the middle class fearful of losing their children to sexual excess and drug abuse, the culture of the working class could be vilified, and elites would be free to amass wealth with less scrutiny by the general public. It was as if, among politicians and those serving them, the infamous exploitation flick *Reefer Madness* (1936) had gone viral in the established media while the journalistic establishment hyped it up because sensationalism sold papers, a lesson that Thompson was later to exploit as he successfully turned journalism on its head.

The genius of Thompson's critique of the newspapers and police reports that he repeatedly cites in his book consists of exposing the gross banality and feckless incompetency of both the media and police, thus marking him as a true disciple of George Orwell: "Facts are lies when they're added up, and the only kind of journalism I can pay much attention to is something like *Down and Out in Paris and London.*"[24] In fact, the systematic harassment of citizens goes back to police treatment of the Hells Angel's once their media boom started—the tactic of randomly seizing peace protesters on the streets and jailing them, if they had so much as an outstanding traffic ticket, had its origins in harassing the Angels.[25] Thompson charts mainstream journalism's complicit nexus with the police state, the early wooing media interlude before their symbiotic and demonic marriage in the religion of patriotic sensationalism.

That social critique becomes deflated amid Thompson's rambling autobiographical humor, bloated with amusing exaggeration,[26] yet tinged with a curious blend of cynical audacity and outraged naïveté, not unlike the bemused narrator of Mark Twain's early successful travelogue, the best seller of his life, *The Innocents Abroad* (1869), wherein Twain skewers the panoramic pretentions of history and religion with the backdrop of a global grand tour. For Thompson, rumor and the news media replace the oppressive and fuddy-duddy role of history in daily life that astonished Twain; San Francisco becomes a microcosmic college frat house at war with a staid and out-of-touch administration.

Amid exaggerated chaos and bemused good-humored rage, both Twain and Thompson itemize extended anecdotes with such clarity of detail that a reader surrenders a lifetime of sober skepticism, accepting the finely etched cartoon for a sociological portrait that one might contemplate framing to hang on the bathroom wall or the mildewed basement bar. Thompson even subtly evokes a tall story of Twain's when telling a brief anecdote about a gas-filling attendant near the Sierra town of Angels Camp, the remote site of Twain's short story, "The Celebrated Jumping Frog of Calaveras County."

While Twain glories in the intricate and fanciful pseudo-history of legendary Roman Catholic relics, Hunter excavates the tantalizing legend-making ability of Hollywood to manufacture a substitute reality, including the name Hells Angels from a 1930 Jean Harlow flick of that title featuring gonzo pilots in the First World War.[27] Thompson's treatment of the Marlon Brando and Lee Marvin movie, *The Wild One* (1954), snugly resembles Twain's preferred technique of thorough demythologization. Thompson mainly depicts American behavior as reflexive Pavlov-like conditioning derived from Hollywood movies—"assault victims" of Hells Angels are most often themselves "victims of the John Wayne complex,"[28] those who swing at the first perceived insult. Thompson convinces the reader that as a reporter, he is living the quintessential adolescent fantasy—living in a movie: "I had a feeling that at any moment a director would appear, waving cards saying 'Cut' or 'Action.'"[29]

In contrast, the seriously disorganized and menacing Hells Angels were out to have some random fun if they couldn't pay their rent, or perhaps they had a friend who was able to buy them a drink or three, and yet they, too, had their own heightened pride, and while they wanted to benefit monetarily from any media publicity, they were distrustful of being exploited by media (which most commonly did exactly that). Thompson was begrudgingly accepted after he published his famous essay on bike riding, yet still resented as the intellectual opportunist bound to get more out of the cooperative interchange than they were. Thompson hung out with the gang, taking biking runs with them, but never dressing like them, maintaining his professional status as a transplanted East Coast reporter.[30] But like Orwell in *Homage to Catalonia*, he was out in the field, engaged in whatever anarchy would erupt. While at this point in his life, Thompson remained skeptical about lottery pill popping—he bonded with gang members over numerous drinks in bars.

The unpredictable behavior of the Angels contrasts with the programmed movie behavior of Americans burdened with Hollywood tropes reeling through their unconscious minds. Thompson dubs the Angels accomplished street artists: "The concept of the 'motorcycle outlaw' was as uniquely American as jazz."[31] Yet such high artistry of scorning foresight before getting involved translates into "No compromise. If a man gets wise, mash his face. If a woman snubs you, rape her."[32] Obviously, improvisation might be dangerous terrain in the proximity of a gang member.

Much of the success of the book resides, of course, in its wickedly absurd humor. When the Hells Angels rocket from obscurity to fame, desiring quantity above accuracy or fairness, and developing "a prima-donna complex,"[33] the gamut of bribery, extortion, barker promoters, faux rip-off T-shirts, desperate ad men, obscure con men, and bilked newspapers with spiked photo essays proffer a reeling carnival atmos-phere where even poets and mystics seek to worship at the foot of the momentary, whorish fame bestowed upon the Angels. This was the lurid, freak-show mirror view of the American Dream as an illusionary white puff of sideshow smoke with the bumbling and corrupt news industry as the insider freak show, its mirrors garishly distorting reality week by week. Thompson's personality simultaneously splits as the cyn-ical insider and set-upon outlaw outsider, concluding with a raucous grin like Lewis Carroll's Cheshire Cat, with a Kentucky bourbon mum-ble. Yet when a journalist nails a responsible article, the reader recoils in near shock, while Thompson promptly tips his hat to the reporter.

The elongated digression on the fictional Linkhorn family from Nel-son Algren's *A Walk on the Wild Side* (1956), which presents the con-temporary Hells Angels as *nouveau* hillbillies displaced in an urban setting, firmly links Thompson's work to the tradition of working-class realism. Thompson had originally wanted to employ an extended quota-tion of six paragraphs on the Linkhorns. Algren was not amused, not inclined to cooperate, and circumspectly advised that "It's always a good idea for a writer to do the best he can with what he has."[34] Unable to acquire the longer quotation to hammer in his point that "a Linkhorn on a Harley is a new kind of animal,"[35] Thompson left it to Random House to sort out the legal limit of his wish, but added a critical foot-note that cites William Faulkner's story "Barn Burning," which "pro-vides the dimension of humanity that Algren's description lacks."[36]

Algren had suspected either a satiric use of his material or mere filler by a writer who wanted to capitalize on his reputation, while Thompson wanted to use Algren's fiction as if his fiction were a docu-mentary artifact. The passage also makes the obvious boast that while Algren and Faulkner wrote fiction about this class of people, Thompson pens documentary realism while living in the midst of it, allocating his own fantasies to bracketing sidebars, although one sometimes wonders how much fictive enhancement capered the wording of incisive and memorable real-life anecdotes. Algren's suspicion of an over-going, a going beyond his work, appears in hindsight to be well founded, although Algren remained polite and genial in their correspondence. With less on the Linkhorns at his disposal, Thompson effectively made his point while being less labored. Thompson subsequently wrote to Norman Mailer, complaining, "I quoted Algren on white trash and got myself in a hell of an argument with him and his agent. He threatened to sue me. I thought I was paying the man a compliment, but he came at me like Nixon."[37] Thompson could never resist a comic exaggeration.

While this rambling aside on the mythical Linkhorns functions as sociological background,[38] literary maneuvering, and homage to Algren, its speculative genealogical argument percolates with such specious fantasy that the passage indulges in the hippie genre of down-home goof rap in a marijuana haze. It also functions as a medicinal antacid tablet before the consumption of a backwoods gallon of crude white lightning, dramatically delaying the promised action of a Hells Angels all-night orgy.

Thompson makes clear through a variety of citations that outlaw motorcyclists remain antagonistic toward the press, yet Thompson presents himself as the outlaw's hero with a successful beer trip in his car during the day and the more exciting nighttime trip where his press credentials (phony, he says) play a role. During the dark firelit night of gargantuan beer swilling, he's able to provide more anecdotal profiles of various motorcycle outlaws, which have the effect of a sumptuous coffee-table sketchbook, the sketches so memorable and concisely honed, as one finds in the war journalism of Curzio Malaparte. Thompson remains the enemy journalist spy, tolerated despite his dubious status as a journalist, an actor and recorder whose rebellious tendency leads him to identify more with the habits of downtrodden motorcycle outlaws than the rigid police attempting to control and supervise them, just as Curzio Malaparte sympathized with Nazi resisters in his masterpiece *Kaputt* (1944) where his deft portraits of Nazi officials and collaborators glow with malice, menace, and brutal banality. While Malaparte dealt with outright fascism in the wide European theater, Thompson traces the incipient development of fascism in the San Francisco area as well as in the national press.

Despite the litany of sensational anecdotes about rape and the destruction of property by outlaws, his sympathy remains clearly with the devil, as he explains how the police and court system routinely abuse underclass motorcyclists. The systematic abuse becomes emblematic of the growing tendency toward a monolithic police state, where the implicit freedom of all citizens are jeopardized on the Fourth of July—an iconic irony further buttressed by the fact that the holiday celebration occurs in the remote wilderness owned by the government. The overarching irony consists of the fact that irrational fear in both the general populace and the police will ultimately undermine the freedom that Americans so proudly profess to cherish. The outlaws remain admirable because they retain their dignity, living without fear, like the traditional heroes of Western epics.

Like Milton's Satan, the uneducated outlaws understand that the profound nature of liberty borders on anarchy, that liberty itself breathes the fresh air of impromptu risk, something of which William Blake remained acutely aware. Part of that edge was provocation play with police. Sonny Barger observed: "Getting into trouble with the law forces you to think on your feet. It's a game. They use their crazy rules and end-around strategies to put you away, and you use your wits to find a way out."[39] Yet such living on the edge in quest of laughs, reputation, and euphoria had its downside. Thompson grimly noted the "sense of despair is one of the most pervasive realities of a Hells Angels existence."[40]

As with many medieval epic heroes, we know that the motorcycle knights face ultimate doom, that their reckless worship of independent pride and nonconformity will not survive the coming decades. That they are corralled and imprisoned in a state park illustrates the final closing of the Western frontier—the park has been turned into an ad hoc containment camp, ringed by threatening law officers. If the untamed wilderness can be converted into an overnight prison, what can't be? Despite the emblematic nature of Thompson's subversive critique, there's an honesty concerning the menace of sexuality in the Edenic wilderness—just as in Genesis, the forbidden fruit of sexuality remains problematic, with alcohol and its casual appropriation (as well as pills) providing the role of tempter among bikers. The sexual drive retains its dark and uncontrollable potential, for both men and women, as the promiscuous anecdotes of biker mamas ardently proclaim. Thompson's American Genesis echoes the biblical labyrinthine profusion in the Garden of Eden, with its constant meditation on how the press divinely "clothes" the fun-loving American wilderness.

Thompson makes it clear that girls were along for the ride and commanded little respect. This was the legacy of Sonny Barger's leadership:

> When I became president of the Oakland chapter, women were no longer welcome as members of the club. I felt we didn't need girls in our club. The Hells Angels is an elite men's club. Maybe we're sexist, male chauvinists, whatever, but since we don't take any money from the government, they can't take us to court and force us to change our bylaws and start accepting women . . . none will ever be voted in as members. [41]

Thompson provides information about the status classification of women: "old ladies," wives or steady girlfriends attached to a specific biker; "strange chicks" who are temporary drifters out for a thrill and judged fair game for mating brawls; and "mamas," groupies who've traveled with the gang and have usually been with more than one biker at the same time. The mamas occupy the lowest rung. Thompson recounts an anecdote about a mama who was once auctioned off in a dive bar for twelve cents, and the story of a biker who ran out of gas in Baker, unable locate a gas station attendant who would have a go at her for a gallon of gas. [42] For biker ladies who require Emily Post behavior guidance on the taboo of shaking hands with gloves on or how to take good care of your ole man and his patch, *The Biker Babe's Bible: A Guide to Being a Good Ole Lady* by "Throttle" (Holly French) has been available since 2005 for your oil-blackened backpack.

What on the surface appears to be a wayward exercise in oddball journalism, with a roll call of sensational anecdotes shunted in as conversational slides like Turgenev-style capsule biographies, begins to resonate as a defining parable about the American Dream of paradise lost in the quest for unlimited freedom, and the inevitable totalitarian inclinations of any government apparatus faced with that prospect. The real enemy consists of neither the motorcycle outlaws nor the police, but the pervasiveness of fear in the general populace as epitomized by the six young drunken citizens who attack the solo biker, Dirty Ed. [43] And in this instance we have an example of hope: the police observe what Thomas Paine would call common sense; they overreact on behalf of neither side, and everyone saves face. The young men find themselves arrested and sent home; the restrained bikers violate their own version of the Three Musketeer code by not beating the offensive young drunks. The reader sees the privileged irony with which these drunken miscreants are treated—if it were a reverse tale of several bikers beating up a citizen for sport, we know what the outcome would have been like and how this would have been reported by the press—and the incident functions as an emblematic anecdote of how common sense and mercy can avoid apocalyptic confrontations.

After a lurid and lusty digression on the subject of rape among the Hells Angels to whet a reader's appetite, the conclusion to the second part of the book, "The Hoodlum Circus and the Statutory Rape of Bass Lake," serves up a comic red herring. Over the course of the holiday weekend, nothing really happens outside the consumption of nearly endless six-packs of beer, except the arrival of some hydroplanes, and the awkward sight of some bikers bathing in their clothes with women splashing around in panties and T-shirts: "It looked like the annual picnic for the graveyard shift at the Never Swear copper mine in Butte, Montana."[44] Despite the dramatic buildup and the sensational promise of the section's title, we've just witnessed nothing more than a traditional Fourth of July celebration one might find in the neck of any woods or down the end of a dead-end street in any small town or city, the sole exception being the presence of both competent and incompetent reporters trying to manufacture copy for their headline-addled rag.[45]

That anarchic Fourth of July celebration appears seedy, in contrast to Orwell's intoxicating description in *Homage to Catalonia* of the joyous crowds in Barcelona: the colorful banners waving in the streets, the revolutionary songs of solidarity erupting with heartfelt hope, and the varied communal efforts to secure armed freedom with inventive, practical initiative. The American Fourth of July illustrates not only a lack of optimism, but individuality and narcissism incapable of community.

After a hymn to the expertise of the Angels individually sequencing the roar of their engines to kick-start like godly thunderbolts while entertaining and entrancing the crowd, we are treated to a second-string comic parody by non-Angel outlaws:

> Buck, a massive Joker, crashed into a police car before he got out of first gear and was taken straight to jail. Frip from Oakland went flying off the road and hit a tree, breaking his ankle and blocking traffic on the narrow lakeside road.[46]

Barking police dogs follow, and the keystone cops seize a piteously screaming photographer instead of the Angel they were after; they slam the photographer's skull against a dirt cliff until eloquent silence reigns. While the handcuffed photographer speeds away in a paddy wagon, we sit with worry waiting for the ambulance to arrive for poor Frip. The photographer, predictably, spends three long nights in jail and must pay a heavy fine for obstructing justice, thus illustrating the fickle perils of motorcycle journalism for second-rate journalists. The morning newspapers trumpet holiday riot stories—in the Midwest and at Lake George, where over two hundred were arrested: "It seemed like the only people who hadn't erupted on the Fourth of July were the Hells Angels."[47] The peculiar emergency order restraining the Hells Angels at Bass Lake is dismissed at the request of the attorney general who concocted the mysterious unconstitutional document. The couple of hundred cops were happy to have collected overtime; we get a relevant footnote—four weeks later, the infamous Watts riot erupted. Like the cops, we've been had by this prank, and had our laugh, but the fear of social disruption, anarchy, and police repression remains the ultimate reality in our not-so-Edenic society.

The comic second section of the book serves as a foil for the more serious third section, "The Dope Cabala and a Wall of Fire," whose subject is a more and tragic meditation on irrational violence in American life. Thompson exposes three press stories about the Hells Angels to be sheer fiction, one of them being a spurious story about a cabal of Angels smuggling marijuana from Mexico; two other spurious stories are ridiculed, one about a knife stabbing in New York City and one about a riot in Laconia, New Hampshire. There appears to be a fashionable viral sociological trend afoot to blame the Hells Angels for anything imaginable, but blaming them for a planned police riot in New Hampshire to grab national attention presents the most perverted and sinister scenario. The wall-of-fire motif derives from a quotation by the mayor of Laconia, who explained that the phantom Hells Angels at the so-called riot disappeared "behind a wall of fire."[48] Thompson's attack on senseless tabloid journalism offers a picture of American newspapers encouraging Americans to believe that other Americans remain inherently and habitually violent, and thus in need of ever-increasing police intervention in a lurching march toward a police state encouraged by such characters as the mayor of Laconia.

While Thompson serves up wicked satire on the fashionable reputation of the Angels in the Bay area among academics, he warms to Ken Kesey, boasting of his role in linking affable Kesey with the Angels. At Kesey's famous party the day after drug charges against him were dropped, when Hells Angels mingle with Merry Pranksters, Thompson and his family hang out with Allen Ginsberg. They amuse themselves with interviewing the police at the cordon ringing the party, the price of such good copy being a ticket for a cracked car taillight. Thompson, no longer an outlaw, revels in his momentary role of bohemian socialite chameleon in-the-know, connecting motley social strands of society with LSD experiments, which were legal at the time.

The lengthy insert of Allen Ginsberg's laborious "poem," actually a speech to students about a free-speech march against the draft and the Vietnam War, first printed in the *Berkley Barb*, presents rhetorical encouragement with emphatic line breaks as if it is free-verse poetry—is a self-righteous political rant about freedom offering sane psychological advice, which today might appear tame because of hindsight, and yet students still are sometimes harassed by tear-gas wielding riot police for no obvious reason.[49] Nine months later Thompson comically groused that "bedrock madman" Ginsberg, who had kindly assisted Thompson with the recording of the Merry Prankster–Hells Angels party,[50] was now "copping out with tolerance poems and the same sort of swill that normally comes from the Vatican."[51]

In the long digression on LSD use, Thompson derides the Timothy Leary approach about controlled settings and personal guides, approves Kesey's approach in making these experiments available to the general public, and offers sundry comic anecdotes on how LSD has had beneficial effects on mellowing the Hells Angels, yet he hammers his press theme on how the Angels were corrupted by media attention, taking note of intricate ironies with regard to racial tensions among cyclists. After a general consideration of alienation and anomie in American culture, Thompson offers a masterly summation on the difference between a "loser" and an "outsider" that make the Hells Angels attractive to the public:

> The streets of every city are thronged with men who would pay all the money they could get their hands on to be transformed—even for a day—into hairy, hard-fisted brutes who walk over cops, extort free drinks from terrified bartenders and thunder out of town on big

motorcycles after raping the banker's daughter. Even people who think the Angels should all be put to sleep find it easy to identify with them. They command a fascination, however reluctant, that borders on psychic masturbation.[52]

Like the witty Will Rogers, the Thompson oracle speaks as the country's backwoods psychiatrist and accomplished outlaw journalist.

The concluding chapter features the ritual funeral of Mother Miles, with all Angels attending in tribute and displaying disgust at the hired Cotton Mather–style sermon. An Angel Thompson doesn't know appears in a black leather jacket with "Loner" in white italics scrawled on his back. Then Thompson rears his bike out on the road in a symbolic salute to the thrills of any motorcyclist pushing the envelope, the famous motorcycle "edge" run on a canceled insurance policy—a bravura piece of writing widely admired—dashed off "about twenty minutes after coming back from doing it,"[53] his face bristling with tears from the wind, so deliriously high that he pointedly captured the rush of an adrenalin high. This passage became the model for Tom Wolfe's thrilling depiction of Chuck Yeager's attempt to break the Russian altitude record with the E66A, a delta-winged fight plane described in *The Right Stuff*.[54] Here Wolfe surpassed his model in this passage, re-creating the first-person experience from Yeager's point of view.

The book's postscript—on being roughed up by a few Angels—provides a mocking self-parody of a deranged journalist hack.[55] Thompson's exposé of journalistic exaggeration and misleading hype, as it is linked to violence, concludes with a brilliant tour de force. His comic mask undergoes a metamorphosis from outlaw journalist to the at-large "loser" he just mocked a few pages ago to a Conradian Kurtz-like monster uttering "Exterminate" (the brutes) like an alien television monotone Dalek from then-contemporary episodes of *Dr. Who*. The apocalyptic mask of Nazi Holocaust also comically completes the participant journalist theme: the ambitious and arrogant narrator becomes what he despises, a soul living in complete despair like a Hells Angel—after a wisecrack that earned him a good bruising. Sonny Barger, the leader of the Hells Angels, recalls:

He knows policy and procedure [i.e., never criticize or insult another Angel] and he says, "Only punks slap their old ladies and kick their dogs." [George had just done that.] And George says, "Well, I guess

you want some too" and started beating him up. We let George beat
him up for a couple of seconds, and then we stopped him. To hear
Hunter talk, he was beaten half to death. . . .Well, he left. And then
his book was a myth I had to live with. Of course he doesn't want to
admit that he set it up.[56]

Ironically, Thompson had previously ridiculed other journalists for
not knowing how to behave around the Angels. Yet, consciously or
unconsciously, Thompson imitates the neck-wound gunshot scene
undergone by his hero Eric Blair (George Orwell) in *Homage to Catalonia*. The beating plunges the narrator into an infernal abyss,[57] plunking
him into his appropriate niche as a fallen angel in hell. The sociological
theme of irrational violence in America gorges itself in parody: after
writing a book denouncing the nascent police state, the narrator not
only identifies with the police, but sports a verbal Nazi swastika with no
more iconic sincerity than any Angel who blazons a swastika merely to
grab attention and scandalize an audience.

An April 26, 1966, letter to Norman Mailer, prior to the book's
publication, describes the book as "a frontal assault on everybody involved or even implicated. Mainly the press. And the cops."[58] The postscript also functions as a goofy, freak-out downer from the ecstatic high
of motorcycle speed and its unlikely marriage to LSD, offering a bummer crash from a drug-transfigured monster escaping from the heart of
darkness and living to tell the tale after a nightmare experience, like
Edgar Allan Poe's narrator from his Gothic classic, "The Fall of the
House of Usher."

The high-jinx circus journalist retains a high-wire dignity—unlike
the mainstream media that puffs paranoia and violence, making much
of it up out of thin air, cynically knowing citizens will pay to be scarred
in a culture that operates as a circus freak show. Above all, Thompson's
book presents a meta-textual warning on the misuse and reckless danger of opportunistic journalism, while endorsing, like a fatherly Virgil
(that legendary master of ambiguity), enterprising efforts of individual
journalists to renounce cringing conformity. Thompson plunges into the
existential anthropological dangers of being a creative spy in the underworld, a slumming Dantean visitor (he removes his Palm Beach sport
coat when entering a bar on his first meeting with Angels) who enters a
curious cult circle in an urban inferno that mimics, in minor key, the

full orchestra of potential Wagnerian violence tuning up in the menacing police state.

Thompson found a temporary disciple in Tom Wolfe who embarked,
despite his elegant couture, on a sequel book about Ken Kesey and his
prankster entourage.[59] In Alex Gibney's excellent film documentary,
Gonzo (2008), Tom Wolfe appears as a blue-shirted talking head en-
thusing on Thompson's comic over-the-top postscript, quoting Conrad:
"The horror, the horror." Wolfe amusingly deployed the identical Conrad passage, "Exterminate the brutes," with a late-night student dorm
setting in *I Am Charlotte Simmons* (2005).[60]

When a high school student wrote Thompson about her difficulties
in doing a term paper on the Hells Angels in 1968, Thompson generously replied to her, explaining the difficulties he had in writing the
book and avoiding the pitfall of instigating criminal charges for anyone,
as well as avoiding legal lawsuits; he advises the student to go below the
book's surface and find the "additional" information that can't be published. He cites Hemingway, referring to this situation as "part of that
iceberg that floats beneath the surface, or something more or less in
those words."[61] Thompson also adds that he didn't see himself as a
courageous man, and if the student wanted an example of a courageous
man, she should look to Martin Luther King.

The intricate rococo quality of the book with its labyrinthine ironies
evokes the Argentinean novel tradition associated with the antecedents
of Jorge Luis Borges and his circle. In retrospect Thompson recalled:

> But this subject was so strange that for the first time in any kind of
> journalism, I could have the kind of fun with writing that I had had in
> the past with fiction. I could bring the same kind of intensity and
> have the same kind of involvement with what I was writing about,
> because there were characters so weird that I couldn't even make
> them up. I had never seen people so strange. In a way it was like
> having a novel handed to you with the characters already devel-
> oped.[62]

Here sat the confounding hydra-headed New Journalism full blown:
participatory journalism that read like a novel with original subject matter, unusual and memorable characters, accomplished style (low-key
purple prose that exhibited a subtle lyricism) with casual cool riffs at
exciting moments that resembled soaring jazz solos, and enough archi-

tectural finesse to put even a good novel to shame. Although *Playboy* commissioned and paid for an Angels article,[63] it never published it, while *Esquire* ran with an excerpt from the book.[64]

Thompson remained annoyed that libel lawyers demanded the deletion of two names from the book: Neal Cassady, who taunted the cops in the buff at Kesey's party, and Thompson's neighbor, LSD researcher Dr. DeRopp.[65] George Wethern, who had assisted Terry the Tramp with dealing the LSD Terry acquired from LSD king Owsley,[66] and Vincent Colnett offered a harrowing but less well-written sequel to Thompson's book in *A Wayward Angel: The Full Story of the Hell's Angels* (1978). A more participant story of a biker gang, Mongol Nation (Southern California), burns rubber in William Queen's memoir *Under and Alone: The True Story of the Undercover Agent Who Infiltrated America's Most Violent Outlaw Motorcycle Gang* (2004). While the Hells Angels chapters in Oakland, San Diego, Phoenix, and Alaska enjoy monstrous reputations, apparently the distinction for the world's most violent and longest war between two rival motorcycle gangs from 1970 onward goes to the Rock Machine and Hells Angels in Quebec City, Canada.[67] By the 1980s American membership in Hells Angels chapters exceeded over 100,000, yet the Hells Angels Motorcycle Club had only been formed in 1948 and not incorporated until 1966.[68]

When Thompson's executor Douglas Brinkley read through Thompson's notebooks and correspondence from the early Sixties, he concluded that the central influences on Thompson's technique and style were Orwell's *Homage to Catalonia* and *Down and Out in Paris and London*.[69] The central irony exposed in Thompson's book—cultural behavior in America continues to possess fascistic tendencies under the banner of freedom. Corporate ideology (as illustrated by the media) and police behavior relish fascist methodologies. Just as in Orwell's *Homage to Catalonia*, where Orwell pointed out the extremes of fascism on the part of fascists, communists, and anarchists, Thompson records fascism at different levels of American society: upper (corporate), middle (police), lower (gangs). Thompson's enduring message is that despite patriotic rhetoric by all, the dream of freedom in America continues to be haunted by the specter of unthinking, collective fascism.

4

WHO'S DEPRAVED?

Champagne Powder, Sloppy Track

Look at your scales, your head is on all wrong.
I've got monsters on my brain.

—Piebald, "Fear and Loathing on Cape Cod"

Hell's Angels recorded echoing ironies about bikers and the news media amid the sociology of American culture, a niche market for exotic topics that might fill the far corner in a bookshop—not many readers will purchase a "fringe" book. Anthropological travel literature has an elite market of quirky readers, unpredictable in their tastes, who never drive best-seller lists. Nonetheless, *Hell's Angels* was a best seller even before it was published. Hunter went on a thirty-five day publicity tour, but few stores had the book in stock by the time he arrived.[1]

Jim Silberman at Random House had enthusiastically jetted Hunter to New York for the final editing of *Hell's Angels* where they met at Pete's Tavern in the Gramercy Park neighborhood. He furnished Hunter with two more contracts: a fiction contract to rewrite *The Rum Diary*, and a nonfiction contract for "The Death of the American Dream." Hunter eagerly signed without an agent; afterward, he felt victimized.[2] The vagueness of the latter project led to difficulties relating to focus and technique, yet Hunter knew much of the theme would concern the Horatio Alger work-ethic dream. In his September 1969 article for *Pageant* magazine Thompson, jokingly but somewhat incongruously, applied the Horatio Alger tag to test pilots at Edwards Air Force base, dividing the personnel into two classes of people: automaton fools who function like robots, and an outside-the-mold hero, Colonel Cotton, who opposed the Vietnam War while dispensing unconventional wisdom about life.[3] Yet the Horatio Alger obsession remained a high white note Thompson pursued without success.

With Thompson's coverage of the 1968 election over and a baby on the way, Thompson and Sandy moved to Colorado in 1969. Thompson turned to writing articles for immediate remuneration. He jumped at a chance to write an article for *Esquire* on the National Rifle Association, of which he was a member. But what was to be a brief article of approximately three thousand words ballooned into a whole book, about eighty thousand words, *The Gun Lobby*.

In Washington, DC, the NRA's headquarters, Hunter interviewed dozens of people. According to Douglas Brinkley, that book functions as the "bridge" book between *Hell's Angels* and *Fear and Loathing in Las Vegas*, but the explosive satire won't be available for about another five years.[4] The book contains traditional journalistic narrative but also exhibits the seeds of the creative split that flowers in *Fear and Loathing in Las Vegas*. Hunter fell into a funk when *Esquire* turned down the material.[5] He needed the money. Thompson could have published the book later in life, yet refrained—possibly because he felt conflicted as a gun enthusiast, or concerned about damage to his public reputation, or violent retaliation from gun fanatics or from the NRA itself.

Thompson's friend Bill Cardoso provided Thompson the opportunity to cover President Nixon's February 1969 inauguration for the *Boston Globe* magazine. A short Mittyesque fantasy appears at the end of the article entitled, "Memoirs of a Wretched Weekend in Washington," wherein Thompson abhors scuffling violence among demonstrators, becomes alienated from the desperation of the Peace movement, and is shocked by witnessing a single policeman being beaten and stripped by war protesters, concluding:

> Now on this Monday night in 1969, President Nixon was being honored with no less than six Inaugural Balls. I brooded on this for a while, then decided I would go over to the Hilton, later on, and punch somebody. Almost anybody would do . . . but hopefully I could find a police chief from Nashville or some other mean geek. In the meantime, there was nothing to do but go back to the hotel and

watch the news on TV . . . maybe something funny, like film clips of the bastinado.[6]

Thompson embraces in comic fantasy a more personal viciousness of medieval torture (bastinado being an extended upside-down beating of the soles of one's feet) than the scenario of mob action that he witnessed, citing the bastinado as the place where he fears press reporters will end up in a Nixon administration. Being a friend, Cardoso let Thompson get away with attitude and humor.

While there had been varied possibilities for Thompson to write for *Playboy* magazine, the only one that came through was the assignment to do a profile of 1968 Olympic and World Champion Jean-Claude Killy, who had retired at the age of twenty-six to shill advertisements with O. J. Simpson for Chevrolet in the United States. The article was scheduled for the March issue, but *Playboy* rejected it, probably because of Thompson's unconventional attitude, satiric innuendo, and evident disdain for Chevrolet, a magazine advertiser. The article, "The Temptations of Jean-Claude Killy,"[7] was eventually picked up in the first issue of a new magazine, *Scanlan's Monthly*,[8] a short-lived muckraking magazine (March 1970 to January 1971) edited by Warren Hinckle and Sidney Zion that became the first magazine to call for Nixon's impeachment; Nixon retaliated by having the magazine audited by the IRS, a procedure that Hinckle and Zion were ill-prepared for, and the magazine closed.

The arc of suspense that Thompson develops consists of whether he can penetrate the "bullet-proof" media carapace with which Chevrolet surrounds Killy. Is he a compliant robot? Can Thompson break through the official mask? Killy's Chevrolet managers become corporate enemies dedicated to presenting Killy as a cliché. Management appears to fear a sex scandal; while Thompson could care less about that, he attempts to penetrate Killy's personality. Thompson wants to puncture the mask and reveal Killy's real attitude toward the boring promotional venues Killy must shill when selling cars. Thompson describes Killy as looking like rich Jay Gatsby, but lacking Gatsby's personality.

The only time Killy lets down his guard occurs over the phone when he confesses he enjoys spending time in Hong Kong because he counts the police commissioner there as a friend and he can do whatever he wants when he visits. Subsequently, Thompson accidentally discovers

Killy had been engaged in sex during this only honest (45-minute) phone conversation. Thompson concludes that Killy really doesn't enjoy his selling job, America, or Americans, and that Americans tend to find the French to be inscrutably cool enigmas. Thompson judges Killy's tame acquiescence as pragmatic, soldierly, and the result of facing a terminal career, so Thompson humorously opines that "Now it's all downhill for the world's richest ski bum."[9] Killy went on to re-emerge successfully from retirement and ski to a championship, then switch to becoming a racing car star, moving to reality television shows in celebrity racing, and concluding his career with advertising for Moët champagne. But capturing the awkward cultural freeze between Americans and Frenchmen was not exactly a *Playboy* priority. Nor was Thompson's proletarian, insouciant attitude among the moneyed elite welcome.

McKeen cites the Killy article as nudging Thompson closer to the gonzo style, because Thompson indulges in satiric cartoon portraitures of football star O. J. Simpson and Chevrolet executive John DeLorean.[10] Thompson records—as if his musings are more important than the main story—his own thought process and casual journalistic methods in his efforts to write the article as he demythologizes his satiric targets, replacing them with his own self-mythology as the coolest journalist alive in opposition to Killy's manufactured corporate reputation as the coolest sex symbol (hence marketing vehicle) alive. Thompson even includes a parody of the marketing gossip mill that corporations employ to advertise for free their brand names in the business section of newspapers: "Speculation that DeLorean was about to sign Allen Ginsberg proved to be false: General Motors doesn't need poets."[11] The goof prank, popularized by Kesey and the Merry Pranksters, remained a favorite technique of hipsters.

Thompson reveled in Wolfe's *The Pump House Gang* (1968), for which Wolfe had supplied his own pen-and-ink cartoons for the hardcover edition. The humor of the savage cartoons and their intimate relation to the essays leaped off the page. Thompson was excited by Wolfe's performance and requested an illustrator for the Kentucky Derby assignment from *Scanlan's*. Giving the assignment to Thompson was a shrewd match: a sport-experienced journalist who had just supplied *Scanlan's* with a kind of offbeat attitude in the Killy article, which was well received by its audience; moreover, he was a local returning to his hometown. Thompson regarded the unpredictable one-eyed Hinckle as "the best conceptual editor I've ever worked with."[12] Yet Thompson was not at ease in returning home.

The assignment would test Tom Wolfe's concept of a rejected artist not being able to return home. The pairing with thirty-four-year-old Ralph Steadman from *Private Eye* magazine (cartoonist Pat Oliphant, Hunter's first choice, was unavailable)[13] to provide illustrations changed a speculative blind date into a phenomenally successful marketing marriage, the union of two sympathetic and comic surrealists working in parallel non-Euclidean worlds. They both shared an angry contempt for authority and a hilarious, exuberant humor, yet Steadman declared they were as different "as a moose is from a crab."[14] At the conclusion of his marvelous memoir on Thompson, Steadman wrote:

> For nearly thirty-five years I have endured, after unwittingly agreeing to meet him on his own home turf, one of the most wanton, rebellious, dangerous and perfect creative collaborators I could have teamed up with, and a God-awful lot more he should have answered for.[15]

Their marriage in art was a tortured storm of frustration and affection, misunderstandings and apologies, anguished exasperation and culminating wild success.

William Kennedy identifies Hunter's Derby piece as a story, a significant departure piece,[16] because the Derby effort was more a flight of fictive fancy than the sardonic journalism of a participant tourist tagging along, as was his previous essay for *Scanlan's*. Steadman sketched as the two drank their Rabelaisian way through the Derby ordeal, but Thompson left without a draft—only a few notes in a small red spiral notebook. The composition back at Aspen was fraught with angst and guilt; Thompson knew it was not what the magazine expected, fearing they would regard what he sent (past deadline) as what he lovingly labeled gibberish.[17] In a letter Hunter expressed his fear that his self-indulgent submission was "a shitty article, a classic of irresponsible journalism"[18] that would be summarily rejected.

A responsible piece of reportorial muckraking would involve investigating the paddock for the use of illegal drugs by trainers or jockeys; evaluating the length and nature of the pre-race training and warm-up; the quirky personality of horses, jockeys, trainers, and owners; behind-the-scenes off-track betting by the gentry; the scandalous cost of gentry couture and their private Derby parties, both before and after the race; the earth composition, texture, and subtleties in the condition of the track itself, factoring current weather in the race; and the breeding and performance history of the horses involved. Thompson had published a bemused article on the horse Kelso at Belmont racetrack, creating some mild comedy about appearance and reality while complimenting the racetrack as the favorite of jockeys and trainers.[19] Steadman notes the Kentucky Derby was a shopworn beat "written annually by armies of reporters since it had begun,"[20] thus a satiric approach would stand out as novel, appealing to *Scanlan's* nontraditional readers.

The magazine loved its irresponsible humor and caustic social critique, subjected it to some editing, and its success when published led to what was called the "gonzo phenomenon." Douglas Brinkley set the world straight on the origin of gonzo:

> The legendary New Orleans R&B piano player James Booker recorded an instrumental song called "Gonzo" in 1960. The term "gonzo" was Cajun slang that had floated around the French Quarter jazz scene for decades and meant, roughly, "to play unhinged." The actual studio recording of "Gonzo" took place in Houston, and when Hunter first heard the song he went bonkers—especially for this wild flute part. From 1960 to 1969—until Herbie Mann recorded another flute triumph, "Battle Hymn of the Republic"—Booker's "Gonzo" was Hunter's favorite song.[21]

Thompson's journalist friend Bill Cardozo, who jestingly called Thompson "gonzo" because he played Booker's recording so often when they covered the 1968 New Hampshire primaries together, responded to the publication of the Derby piece by complimenting Thompson: "you've changed everything. It's totally gonzo."[22] Booker's tune features percussion with a high-octave organ solo that sounds like a primitive flute. In Italian, *gonzo* can mean the effect of water warping wood, especially of a gondola in Venice.

The last chapter of Stendhal's *The Charterhouse of Parma* (1839), a satiric epilogue, features a preposterous comic character by the name of Signor Gonzo; he appears as part clown, wit, conversational provocateur, and awkward social climber with theatrical aplomb, who manages to entertain others by an embarrassing rudeness; he treasures the fantastic quality of insults as well as the compulsive habit of insulting others; despite his moth-eaten black plume, he manages to be tolerated at court for the mischievous amusement he conjures; and has himself followed by a footman "bearing an infinitesimal cup of coffee on a silver-filigree stem, and every half-hour a majordomo, wearing a sword and a splendid coat in the French style, passed around ices."[23] The character's name, Gonzo, could have become part of New Orleans Mardi Gras oral folklore because of its French origin and manifold satiric possibilities in carnival settings.

Like Thompson, Booker, a lifelong friend of the New Orleans musician Dr. John, walked with a limp, the result of his leg being broken in eight places when he was run over by an ambulance.[24] To Thompson's surprise, other journalists acclaimed the unconventional piece and his admiring friend Tom Wolfe later enthusiastically featured it in his anthology, *The New Journalism* (1973). Thompson had found the voice and character for which he would become famous. Thompson's first known description of gonzo was broadcast in a March 1973 radio interview (with Studs Terkel), where Thompson describes gonzo as "total subjectivity, out-front bias," saying that "participation is the key word, you are part of the story."[25] Eventually, the gonzo label became a brand signpost he wore, yet underneath it he worked hard to encode more serious reflection below its glib surface.

That voice remains essentially an irresponsible college sophomore who doesn't do his homework, but in his alienation as an outsider, Thompson offers a keen critique of American mores and customs, much as Mark Twain offered adolescent innocence as a foil to expose hypocrisy, greed, corruption, and irrational behavior in American society. In the face of prejudice and totalitarian inclinations, Thompson would offer the innocence of dropout incompetence and unhinged self-indulgence to provide comic reversal in the face of American shibboleths. In the American tradition of popular humor, from Bierce and Twain onward, the humorist remains a mischievous anti-intellectual on the surface while delivering an intellectual cultural and moral critique that subversively lurks beneath the surface of the narrative.

More important than the example of Mark Twain leers the subversive, Midwestern comedy and unhinged fantasies of James Thurber, who in his breakout book, *My Life and Hard Times* (1933), successfully mingled autobiography and fiction in such essay yarns as "The Dog

That Bit People," "More Alarms at Night," and "University Days," where he ridicules Ohio State University professors and dingbat student journalism. Thurber was to exploit the theme of glorious self-indulgent drinking in "If Grant Had Been Drinking at Appomattox," and neurotic self-indulgent anxiety in "How to Adjust Yourself to Your Work" as well as "Anodynes for Anxieties." Outlandish daydream fantasies figure prominently in "The Case for the Daydreamer" and, most famously, in "The Secret Life of Walter Mitty," where serial daydreaming fantasies of valor and martyrdom are unleashed upon a dreary conformist world by a man so distracted by these fantasies that he becomes comically embroiled by his inability to perform the common tasks of daily life.

Thompson was a Thurber enthusiast, as evidenced by a September 1963 letter to Clifford Ridley at the *National Observer*, where he acclaimed Ed Fortier, the self-published editor of *Alaska Hunting and Fishing Guide, 1961–62, vol. 2*, to be "the greatest comic writer since James Thurber."[26] Thompson's old Louisville classmate Fortier was at the time working as a hospital public relations and personnel director in Alaska.[27] Eventually, Fortier's literary ambitions carried him to publish a forty-one page pamphlet, *One Survived*, that cult Thompson fans have transformed into a rare collector's item.[28] In the 8 1/2" by 11" stapled Alaska guide, a few of Fortier's headlines run to the dryly amusing: "Resurrection Offers 12-Month Fishing," "Grizzly Fights for Recognition," "Women Threaten Male Role as Mightiest Hunters." Thompson's knowing prank reveals his own ambition to supplant Thurber—Thompson did become the greatest comic writer in America since James Thurber by incorporating elements of Thurber's technique into his writing, but with fantasies more unhinged than Thurber ever explored, more incisive social critique than Thurber ever dared, the use of animal motifs and, on balance, a more deliriously winsome paranoia than Thurber's curmudgeonly snarl at those who possessed two eyes. Thompson turned the handicap of his one short leg into a comic perception of the world, just as Thurber turned his handicap of having only one eye into a comic vision of those around him.[29] While Thurber began as Midwestern proletarian, "Ohio's gift to the oppressed and downtrodden of all nations,"[30] he concluded as an alienated Northeastern suburbanite. Thompson began as a disaffected sportswriter and dissident political journalist, but held fast with melding the hippie outlaw to the gun-toting, freedom-loving cowboy.

The Derby yarn, though extensively cut for the magazine,[31] can be divided into five parts: (1) prologue setting; (2) satiric social critique; (3) the race; (4) post-race hangover; (5) self-parodying postscript. The piece opens with a fat old-boy Texan, a dedicated repeat customer of the Derby who appears to know little about it except for the availability of loose women, escaping on his yearly spree from his wife. The archetypal Texan presumes Southern bonding with a local Louisville boy. When Thompson orders a margarita, he's ominously warned it's a faggot drink, that he'd better drink bourbon—this being corn liquor country—anyone drinking such sissy drinks will most likely be rolled and beaten. Rather than being flustered by the incident, Thompson manages to cadge a double bourbon, then proceeds to put a devilish scare into the Texan racist, as if he injected a paranoia serum into his veins. He mocks the out-of-town rube at full tilt without raising suspicion of a con by the undercover local, all under the persuasive protection of his phony *Playboy* press tag as if the laminated illusion was some magical mojo talisman. He then struts away with entertaining wise-guy copy. This suave exhibition trenchantly displays Thompson's hometown credentials in dealing with impertinent fools as he preens his own triumphant ego.

Thompson anxiously frets like some opera prima donna about the outsider from London he has not yet met and will work with. His pride is on the line, for as a local he should have connections as well as heightened neighborhood lore, but he's working for a small magazine with no local reputation. Yet the magazine subsequently managed to make the cut of Nixon's blacklist. The Englishman, an "innocent abroad"[32] whom he jokingly passes off as an Irishman to the press box credential manager (making Ralph Steadman more mysterious and perhaps more prestigious because Irish horse trainers have reputations in the paddock), would naturally expect his host to have pulled the proper strings for the setup in advance. Steadman wasn't any better organized than Thompson, leaving his inks and brushes in a taxi; on the way to the airport Don Goddard, *Scanlan's* editor, stopped by his apartment so that Steadman could borrow his wife Natalie's Revlon lipsticks and makeup colors.[33] After being ominously warned by the motel clerk about the strangely bearded Englishman, and plagued by bizarre surrealistic images of grotesque ugliness, Thompson discovers his companion to be a refreshing, workable nutcase.

With thirty hours to go before post time and no real press credentials, Thompson works his outlaw con magic and miraculously appropriates the necessary passes (presumably acquired through the magic of
the phony *Playboy* pass or his persuasive rap), supposedly through a
Thurber-like interior monologue where he threateningly fantasizes
blunt bribery or the more violent alternative of using mace. Maybe it
was the bribe that worked. The Walter Mitty device of unhinged fantasies percolates through the narrative, appearing four more times: the
fantasy of "thousands of people fainting, crying, copulating, trampling
each other and fighting with broken whiskey bottles;[34] the fantasy of the
holocaust clubhouse fire;[35] "banshees on the lawn at night," etc.;[36] and
the goof fantasy of the foreigner Steadman being beaten with trun-
cheons in the granite dungeon of the Manhattan Tombs.[37] These five
Thurber-like fantasies enhance the surrealistic social tableau of self-
indulgent madness and hysterical chaos expertly painted by Thompson.

Thompson's satiric social critique in the Derby piece attacks racial
prejudice, paranoia about hippies (Woodstock), fear of women (loose
women and women assuming men's jobs—women jockeys), and depraved elitism among faux Civil War colonels. The narrator's hysterical
fear of chaos becomes a form or a reveling in the pleasures of chaos as a
liberating aesthetic.

While searching for the great symbolic face of the Derby, the narrator stumbles across a familiar high school classmate, a former football
star, ridiculing him for his "pimps's smile, blue silk suit and his friends
looking like crooked bank tellers on a binge . . ."[38] This symbolic smile
of local corruption offers a summary sketch that implies excellence
need not apply for a job at home, proof of the Thomas Wolfe theme
that an artist with ideals, talent, and aspiration cannot go home again. In
a letter to Carey McWilliams at *The Nation*, Thompson described the
Kentucky outing as "a [Thomas] Wolfean nightmare."[39] Thompson
feared the prospect of returning home in any public fashion.

By not covering the favorites, the race itself appears anticlimactic in
the narrative, even though it's the story of a long shot with the amusing
name of Dust Commander. This least memorable section, the actual
reportorial assignment, helps to background the race as an irrelevant
ritual to carnival boozing. In his memoir Steadman even surpasses
Thompson's caustic description, declaring that the genteel clubhouse
with human excrement scrawled on the bathroom walls "was worse than

the night I spent on Skid Row a month later."[40] The notation that Thompson's horse did not finish in the money provides one of the few realistic facts in the story. As one disappointed bettor at the rail who knew the track and horses well joked with me at the Saratoga Race Track when his nag down the stretch was nipped at the wire: "Luck is not enough, you need divine intervention!"[41]

The day after the big Saturday race presents a lacuna, presumably containing scenes and embarrassments too awful to remember—perhaps they just spent the day guzzling beer with bourbon chasers while removing gound from the corners of their eyes. The hair-of-the-dogma (Flann O'Brien's witty tag) cure for Monday morning hangover features a sweet malt drink, Colt 45, favored by teenagers; Steadman mutters that the beverage is awful, but continues his consumption unabated. In the mirror Thompson views his alcoholic visage with horror, identifying his face as the gorgon grimace of the mad, diseased corruption for which the un-noble knights were questing.

As in the postscript to *Hell's Angels*, Thompson dons his comic Kurtz mask. Struggling with shaking hands, Steadman concurs that the mythic beast is indeed them, thus rounding out the thematic irony of "We had come there to watch the *real* beasts perform."[42] It had been H. L. Mencken's program to "shake up the animals" by providing shocking commentary on complaisant preconceptions. Thompson's twist was to turn that perception inward in self-examination, and admit that much of the moral problem lies within the journalistic community itself, the real beasts who sold out to their corporate employers by writing what management expected them to write. The witty technique of appending comic morals like "If you live as humans do, it will be the end of you"[43] to whimsical satiric animal fables had been pioneered with great success by Thurber in *Fables for Our Times* (1940).

The animal theme also appears in J. P. Donleavy's *The Ginger Man* (first published by the Paris-based Olympia Press in 1955) when Marion contemptuously flings a postcard addressed to Sebastian Dangerfield from his friend Egbert which says: "WE ARE ALL FANGED ANIMALS." Marion declares: "That's what he is, a detestable animal."[44] They continue to bicker while Dangerfield daydreams of buying a sheep's head. He leaves the apartment thinking of when he will inherit money from his parents, so that he'll undergo a bright Ovidian transformation into a big golden udder. Dangerfield then strolls in the park with his baby daughter, recalling varied dreams of horses, bullocks, goats, and the capping funeral of a gombeen man (a shady usurer, often a shopkeeper). Dangerfield's response to his friend's postcard has sent him into a Rousseau-like reverie promenade, where he envies what he considers to be the uncomplicated life of animals that don't have bills to pay or wives who demand fidelity.

The theme of man as a fanged animal intent on money and sex resurfaces as the novel's main theme in the concluding pages of the novel. In the last paragraph, Dangerfield once more daydreams of horses, the last two sentences declaring horses to be "running out to death which is with some soul and their eyes are mad and their teeth out. God's mercy/On the wild/Ginger Man."[45] Donleavy bemoans the burden of men haunted by the nightmare of sex (a medieval theme where sexual torment visits men in the haunting images of running horses) and the consequent need for men to produce money for the support of children. The novel remains a classic as a bitter youthful lament ruing the repression and conformity society demands and the dilemma of the daydreaming bohemian with artistic ambitions to renounce art and work for money.

Charles Bukowski appropriated Donleavy's beast theme for his first published chapbook, the short story *Confessions of a Man Insane Enough to Live with Beasts* (1965), wherein he introduces ranting Henry Chinaski, the alter ego who made Bukowski famous from his series of novels employing that unruly, bohemian persona. Bukowski's Henry Chinaski was an outgrowth of John Fante's now legendary Arturo Bandini character from *Ask the Dust* (1939) and its sequels, yet the immediate provocation of Bukowski's short story may have been a reaction to one of Thompson's articles.

A metaphor for bohemian behavior, perceived as amusingly animalistic, first appeared in a *National Observer* article in 1964, "When the Beatniks Were Social Lions." The article recalls the heyday of the beats in San Francisco, noting the press or public no longer has any interest in them although small pockets still exist, most having moved to New York City, Europe, or elsewhere, dispersed in diasporas of resigned conformity. Thompson discusses a contemporary beatnik rent strike which attempts to improve housing conditions, while retailing an anecdote about a couple of beatniks who stole Thompson's home-brewed beer, consumed it, then painted the front of their own rental like a

Jackson Pollack canvas.[46] After seeing this blue-splattered horror, the landlord called the police, the police in turn called for reinforcements; the pair's mugshots were labeled in the press as "the Frankenstein flash."

Subsequently, the two beatniks indulged themselves in a small jail riot whereby they destroyed the toilet and sink, hurling chunks of debris at the police through their iron bars. The press had labeled the rowdy beatniks as "animal men."[47] The article plays both sides of the street, presenting the beatniks as impulsive eccentrics concerned for social welfare yet warning that they can be unstable lunatics who might be best locked up. While society has jailed the wayward pranksters, Thompson lets the rubbernecking public into the beatnik zoo his article creates. Since much of the article finds its authority in Thompson's autobiographical link both to the beat community and his acquaintance with these two characters, the piece remains an early example of the New Journalism.

While Thompson conveys to the reader a genuine delight in the adolescent rebellion of his acquaintances, his socially conservative stance finds justification at the minor wrong done to the participant journalist. The reader sympathizes more with Thompson's loss of his homemade beer than the inconvenience of the landlord having to re-paint the facade of his dingy rental. The emotional reader will laugh at the irresponsible behavior of the beatniks thinking, "Yeah, lock up all these nonconformist crazies," while an intellectual might consider that the landlord mishandled this situation—he could have held anger in check and waited to confront the miscreants (since he knew them) when they were sober and persuaded them to repaint the house, getting some free compensation from them. Maybe, he could have purchased them a few six-packs and had them repaint the whole house. Thompson's theme of angry escalation with everybody involved losing their heads over something small is a comic staple, but his questioning the recourse to police and jail retains an implied caveat well above the ceiling of any reader who doesn't twice read the adroit article about men who perform as comic beasts.

The main thrust of the article with its lion metaphor argues the decline of the once-influential beatniks from intellectual lions to angry, defeated emotional lions. For those readers familiar with natural history, some of the joke resides in the realization that happy lions live prosperously with a harem—these impoverished characters appeared to have failed as artists in their European excursion, daubers who have enacted out a stupid and incompetent public parody of what an accomplished painter does in the privacy of a studio.

Meanwhile, back at the Derby, Thompson consummately convinces the reader that this later comic duo have completed their Frankenstein transformation into the real beasts, yet this transformation into beasts itself reflects an ironic revelation disrobing the true beasts: the postscript radio announcement of continued bombing in Cambodia displays the true holocaust and the face of the real-life Kurtz, Richard Nixon, landlord of America, the bestial monster without clothes. The killing of students at Kent State completes the theme of paranoia surrounding youth and hippies; the image of Steadman bathing in beer while sitting shotgun in the bouncing and lurching car rounds out the comedy of the mace-spraying scene in the restaurant. After the mace incident, Steadman says he realized that Thompson was not an ordinary person but somebody who "does things with a paranoiac fever."[48] That fever operated as a satiric, microcosmic allegory for the obscene holocaust the country exported to Indochina.

As in *Hell's Angels*, the closing monologue offers parody of the main character(s) turning into the monsters described, thus satisfying the anti-intellectual, cultural requirement that those who provide social critique on American mores remain greater jerks than those criticized. As Kennedy indicated, the Kentucky Derby piece presents a satiric story about America, not an exercise in journalism. Thompson's Derby piece became the cornerstone of gonzo journalism—participating in a story rather than merely reporting or re-creating a story like Gay Talese or Tom Wolfe.[49] Partnership with Steadman was crucial. Thompson's biographer McKeen declares that "Whatever *gonzo* is, when it's dissected, Ralph Steadman's art is part of its core DNA."[50] Thompson's personal reaction to the success of his Derby article was: "Holy shit, if I can write like this and get away with it, why should I keep trying to write like the *New York Times*?"[51] The new methodology of improvising on chaos was born amid extenuating exculpatory circumstances. Mat Johnson explains: "Because the gonzo narrative structure is so grossly exaggerated, its unbelievability manages to exculpate its proponents."[52] Yes, but only in the pen of a master performer. We might recall that much of Melville's *Moby-Dick* (1851) swims in chaotic currents of rambling digression as the author presents both a fictional narrative I in Ishmael, and an authentic authorial I when, early in the book, Melville briefly pulls back the curtain to give the date of the novel's composition as 1850, when he jokingly dissents from Linnaeus classifying whales as mammals by supplying Ishmael's uneducated observations on the sociology of whales and sharks.[53]

The founder of the inaugural Kentucky Derby race (1875), the flamboyant, mustachioed Colonel Meriwether Lewis Clark Jr., conceived of what is now America's most famous race as an equestrian Mardi Gras that would put Louisville on the map as an important river city.[54] For Thompson to treat the race as a warped Mardi Gras was in keeping with the spirit of gun-brandishing Meriwether Clark. During his lifetime, Clark had been notorious for threatening people with a pistol—in retaliation for a threat, Clark had once been shot in the chest.[55] Thompson's theatrical intimidation with mace can be interpreted as an updated satire on the neurotic and belligerent behavior of the founder of the Derby (the concept of which was modeled on the English Derby), which is also why Thompson would naturally delight in bringing to his narrative an Englishman.

The only way Thompson could cope with the "Wolfean nightmare" was to employ satire—the Kentucky Derby had been depraved and decadent at its inception. Clark eventually went bankrupt and, fearing penury, committed suicide with a pistol. The gonzo mask of Thompson as journalist-narrator may be interpreted as a prankster, historical joke—his over-the-top persona imaginatively re-creates the drunken mania and megalomaniac bravado of the Derby's founder. Although a satiric presentation of the Derby, the ultimate effect of Thompson's peculiar essay contributes to memorializing the irreverent spirit that invented the Derby. Gonzo is the ribald child of Meriwether Clark.

"Strange Rumblings in Aztlan," published in *Rolling Stone* on April 29, 1971, offered Thompson's "most serious piece of sustained reportage."[56] The detailed drama about a deliberate police murder of the popular television journalist Rubén Salazar peacefully drinking in a café after an anti–Vietnam War demonstration was sensational; it was followed by a subsequent cover-up by the Los Angeles Police Department—this was the kind of exposé Thompson relished and excelled at, especially because it involved the repression of journalism, which he had prophesied in the *Boston Globe* article. Working in the ghetto was difficult for a gringo, so Thompson was aided by his friend Oscar Zeta Acosta, who wanted to do for Chicanos what Martin Luther King did for African Americans. Acosta acted as advisor, intermediary, and translator.

An excellent article in the New Journalism participant style, which Ralph Steadman claimed legitimized *Rolling Stone* as a journalistic outlet,[57] the piece led to difficulties and threats from gangs. Thompson felt unreasonably pressured (threatened by gangs in the barrio) and suggested they travel to Las Vegas via Woody Creek, so that he could finish the piece. A skewed version of Oscar became his fictional sidekick for *Fear and Loathing in Las Vegas*, a *roman à clef* surrealist novel disguised as journalism.

The use of a foreigner as sidekick for the Derby story led Thompson to realize the Don Quixote–Sancho Panza combination could be effective fiction in an American context, just as Graham Greene would later realize its reusable possibilities for satire on European politics and secularism with *Monsignor Quixote* (1982). While Thompson recorded the death of the hippie movement, Greene chronicled the simultaneous death of Christianity and communism in Europe. To somewhat disguise the Don Quixote–Sancho Panza comic duo concept, Thompson transformed Oscar into a more exotic Samoan. Samoa had been a long-running joke obsession of Thompson's going back to 1964 when he wrote the White House requesting to be the American ambassador to Samoa.[58] In Acosta's autobiography, there are numerous anecdotes of Oscar telling others that he's a Samoan when he doesn't want to reveal his true identity. These anecdotes predate Hunter and Oscar's meeting—for Hunter the joke was a whimsical fantasy, while for Oscar it appears to be a humorous disguise.

Oscar saw his caricature as a betrayal of their friendship, as well as a serious libel, and threatened to sue. Jann Wenner at *Rolling Stone* temporarily mollified Oscar by agreeing to publish Acosta's own memoir, *Autobiography of a Brown Buffalo* (1972),[59] less than a year after the appearance of Thompson's piece in the November 1971 issue of *Rolling Stone*. Acosta's breathless, manic humor, very much in the mold of Henry Miller's *Sexus* (1949) yet with greater family pride and a keener political mind, achieved some success with reviewers, but royalties, which usually arrive at least a full year after actual book sales, are not an income that provides a living unless a book makes the best-seller list. In that book Acosta personally gives Hunter the wooden San Blas Caribbean Indian idol at the end of chapter 15, while in a 1971 previously published draft of his autobiography Oscar bestows the idol on Hunter's wife, Sandy, at the Glenwood Springs bus station, forty-one miles north of Aspen, as a gift for Hunter in January of 1968 after Hunter wires Acosta $150.[60]

There breathes an exuberant genial honesty in Hunter and Oscar's correspondence before their troublesome falling out over literary matters, yet there are also signs that Acosta's personal difficulties, both debt and health problems, were severely mounting by January 1970.[61] Thompson genuinely admired the grim humor of Oscar's 1970 peasant short story, "Perla Is a Pig,"[62] as well as his visceral autobiography. Thompson expected that sales of Acosta's books would provide an income, which did not develop—not because of lack of merit, but lack of immediate sales. Yet since Acosta's death in 1989, reprints have found an audience, and his works remain in print.

A photograph depicting Thompson and Acosta was planned for the back dust jacket of the hardback edition of *Fear and Loathing in Las Vegas*,[63] but to avoid any legal problems Thompson allowed his friend Curtis Robinson to remove Acosta from the cover artwork, which depicted both Acosta and Raoul Duke seeing bats.[64] The removal presents a more literal version of the book because the attorney does not see bats in the novel.

After Wenner published *The Revolt of the Cockroach People* (1973), which recounts a slightly enhanced version of the Chicano Moratorium of 1970 (an activist group opposed to the Vietnam War) with Oscar's courtroom arguments on behalf of Chicano rights, Acosta, now broke and desperate, renewed his libel suit, claiming he had been blackmailed and had not given permission for film rights. Thompson was angry that the taint of a lawsuit killed the prospect of a film option advance.[65] Acosta and Thompson met for reconciliation at the Seal Rock Inn in San Francisco in the spring of 1974. Oscar asked Hunter to finance an "illegal business operation." Hunter refused, advising against the venture.[66] It is commonly thought that this was a drug smuggling operation.

Acosta presumably died at sea off the coast of Mexico under mysterious circumstances in the summer of 1974.[67] Thompson has continually mourned the passing of his loquacious friend and political ally.[68] In

March 1989, Thompson concluded his introduction to the reprint of *The Autobiography of a Brown Buffalo*:

> When the Brown Buffalo disappeared we all lost one of those high notes that we will never hear again. Oscar was one of God's own prototypes—a high-powered mutant of some kind who was never even considered for mass production. He was too weird to live and too rare to die. [69]

Thompson always thought of his lost friend as an immortal, and remained haunted by his life without Oscar.

5

LOATHING AT THE TEMPLE

Las Vegas, Part I

A kind of Horatio Alger story based on the successful $30,000 kidnapping in Kansas City of Miss Mary Elroy, who had a lovely time, whose abductors gave her roses and wept when she left.—James Thurber

Thompson had retreated to Las Vegas to complete "Strange Rumblings in Aztlan." Before Thompson had finished writing the Aztlan piece, Hunter had shown to his editor David Felton at his house in Los Angeles[1] handwritten pages on Mint Hotel stationery the beginning of his Vegas novel (the opening driving scene). Felton encouraged Thompson to keep it up, this new form of wacky personal journalism, because it contained real and amusing anecdotes, but those things only happened because the involved narrator provoked them—it was an entertaining equivalent of novelistic narrative.[2]

At the *Rolling Stone* office Thompson gave nineteen neatly typed pages to Wenner and those were later passed around the office with enthusiasm. Charles Perry recalled: "After reading it, nobody with a straight face could talk about psychedelics as being essentially a religious experience."[3] The office happily anticipated the satiric explosion. Through the preview Thompson had cleverly hooked both Felton and Wenner on his new approach, prepping them and whetting their appetite for whatever he would turn in next.[4]

After *Fear and Loathing in Las Vegas* was published, Thompson described the work as "a *failed experiment* in Gonzo Journalism," saying gonzo was "a style of 'reporting' based upon William Faulkner's idea that the best fiction is far more *true* than any kind of journalism—and the best journalists have always known this."[5] Oddly enough, many commentators have reported Thompson's humble self-satire as serious thought. The main point about gonzo style remains that it "is as much theoretical exercise for the author as it is for the reader."[6] Thompson remained ambiguous about the nexus between real journalism and what was fantasy in the work—he would not take the bait to demystify and castrate the work through tedious autopsy that would leave a messy corpse repellent to anyone with common sense. But that ambiguity is not the only mystery present. As with Fitzgerald, there breathes in their lives the mystery of how each achieved the appropriate stylistic eccentricities that created such sparkling magic.

Every great artist knows that he or she must retain some element of mystery to provide the magnetic aura of transcendent fascination. Thompson not only admired Fitzgerald's artistry, but also his outrageous, eccentric, prankish behavior. Joan Taylor, daughter of composer Deems Taylor, recounted the Paris anecdote of her father and Scott at Zelli's dancing club in Paris. When surrounded by whores, Scott and Deems agreed that they should get rid of the tarts, so Scott said: "I like only men. And this is my friend."[7] At one point Thompson even imitated Fitzgerald's drunken-night floundering in the fountain outside the Plaza Hotel in New York City.

While the category of "The Fear" had played a significant role in *The Rum Diary*, its first appearance as a public phrase crops up in *Hell's Angels* with regard to the *Examiner*, which, according to Thompson, "always viewed the Angels with fear and loathing."[8] Douglas Brinkley set the record straight on its origin:

> Hunter used to claim that the phrase "Fear and Loathing" was a derivation of Kierkegaard's *Fear and Trembling*. In actuality he lifted it from Thomas Wolfe's *The Web and the Rock*. He had read the novel when he lived in New York. He used to mark up pages of favorite books, underlining phrases that impressed him. On page sixty-two of *The Web and the Rock* he found "fear and loathing" and made it his. I asked him why he didn't give Wolfe credit. Essentially

he said it was too much of a hassle, that people would think he meant Tom Wolfe, his New Journalism contemporary.[9]

Before using the phrase "fear and loathing" in publication, Thompson had privately used it in a letter posted to William Kennedy on November 22, 1963, discussing his shock over the assassination of President John F. Kennedy. Thompson's distraught night letter confesses his inability to talk and the possibility he may go mad from *not* talking, being unable to communicate "the fear and loathing that is on me after today's murder." Thompson thought the rotten murder was more significant than what could be articulated in any magazine and that the country would "now enter the era of the shitrain" under President Johnson. Thompson saw the coming 1964 election as "the most critical in the history of man."[10] His humor runs uncharacteristically low-key as fear struggles to find a souvenir scrap of reasonable discourse. The letter to Kennedy was an attempt to communicate that fear and loathing—a palpable *frisson* derived from that phrase must carry the weight of deep personal angst.

The book title, *Fear and Loathing in Las Vegas*, resonates with epic force and achieves for American literature what F. Scott Fitzgerald accomplished in his portrait and epitaph for the excesses of the 1920s in *The Great Gatsby* (1925). Thompson's obsession with *The Great Gatsby* exhibits the fascination of local lore: Daisy grows up in white Louisville and discovers dashing officer Gatsby at Camp Zachary Taylor in Louisville, where they become young lovers.

Paul Semonin recalled how he and Thompson once read aloud to each other essays by Tom Wolfe. Semonin said that while Thompson admired the outsiders depicted in Fitzgerald and Kerouac, it was the outcast bohemian character from J. P. Donleavy's *The Ginger Man* (1955) that Thompson most admired, because Dangerfield "fit him like a glove."[11] In a 1960 letter to Donleavy, Thompson approvingly declared that *The Ginger Man* "had real balls."[12] Thompson attempted to combine a Kerouac road quest with an outsized hallucinatory bohemian character in a high style imitating the musical mode of the moment— rock, as opposed to the mellow jazz prose and elegiac waltzing cadences of Fitzgerald, with its contrasting references to music like the waltz "Three O'clock in the Morning," or the wailing saxophones of "Beale Street Blues," or the popular song "Ain't We Got Fun" when things were trending south at a party, or the Mendelssohn Wedding March, those portentous chords, floating through the classy Plaza Hotel suite when Daisy argues bitterly with her husband Tom.[13]

Although Thompson's book originates in journalistic roots, the first part covers the Mint 500 motorcycle race, a piece commissioned and rejected by *Sports Illustrated;* the second part on the Las Vegas drug convention provides material for a book on the "Death on the American Dream" promised to Random House and possibly to run in *Rolling Stone*.[14] Yet this didn't relieve Thompson's frustration that Random House was still sitting on *The Rum Diary*.[15] Ultimately, Thompson managed the double bill: to fulfill his book contract with Random House while getting paid for a first appearance in *Rolling Stone*.

In a previous letter to Jim Silberman at Random House, Thompson had uncertainly proposed the Raoul Duke approach, "essentially a very contemporary novel with straight, factual journalism as a background."[16] But the use of the name was nothing new, as biographer William McKeen explains:

> Raoul Duke began appearing in Hunter S. Thompson's writing back in the days when he was the sports editor of the *Command Courier*, the official newspaper of Eglin Air Force Base in Florida. It was the late fifties and when Hunter couldn't find a bystander or a source or an expert to say what he wanted, he quoted "Raoul Duke."[17]

Yet Raoul was also the hillbilly nickname or code name of the "co-conspirator" with James Earl Ray, the assassin of Martin Luther King,[18] but the name more likely may have been his schizophrenic double ego. Thompson's use of the name casts a sinister shadow that hints at identity confusion, a nasty streak, and crass opportunism, linking him to Algren's Linkhorns and Faulkner's Snopes family. Raoul Duke, a larger-than-life character, can possess the dark vision of a dedicated Nietzschean cynic or the buoyant laughter of an adolescent young man agog in Wonderland. This schizophrenic aspect of his character is hinted at in the mention of the drug adrenochrome, derived from the oxidation of adrenalin, which Hoffer in Canada was unsuccessfully experimenting with to cure schizophrenia.

In a March 1970 letter to Acosta, Thompson observes:

> Politics is, I think, far more than Politics. It may be the ultimate
> high . . . and maybe adrenaline is the real super-drug. I read Aldous
> Huxley's *Doors of Perception* and saw his comment about mescaline
> and adrenaline having essentially the same chemical base . . . which
> makes perfect sense.[19]

One of the motifs of mescaline in the novel (Acosta actually preferred LSD-25) is that it not only opens the doors of perception in a
political sense, but it bestows the energy equivalent to the adrenalin
high that politicians experience riding on the wave of their mass-ador-
ing support, something Thompson experienced when he "finally drifted
so far into activist politics that he finally found himself riding the crest
of an energy wave that he never knew existed."[20]

He thought perhaps mescaline could bestow on the populace at
large the adrenalin power to which politicians have access. In March,
Thompson was thinking along the same lines that Kesey, Owsley, and
the Brotherhood of Eternal Love had followed with LSD, yet by the
time he finished the first part of the novel, he realized that the practi-
cality of such a wave was an illusion because the fragility of sanity in
most people would not allow them to handle the nonaddictive drug—
another reason for the absurdity of its illegality. But politicians were so
paranoid that the very possibility the drug would empower a small
number of disenfranchised people like Thompson was reason enough
for its illegality.

In the novel Raoul says he removed the adrenalin gland from a living
doctor, and that it doesn't work if it is derived from a corpse. This is
sheer, if not silly, fiction as Terry Gilliam points out in the DVD commentary to the movie version of *Fear and Loathing in Las Vegas*. Adrenochrome acts as much a prank as joke, but the joke contains serious
content. Here the allegorical goof joke explicitly connects Raoul, a
schizophrenic, with the hillbilly assassin of Dr. Martin Luther King:
freedom (adrenochrome) doesn't work if the good doctor is dead. Another aspect of the mythic joke resides in the fact that the drug is not
even illegal, either then or now, and the drug is not even psychoactive.[21]
Freedom is for everybody. It was because of these convoluted hipster
jokes and wacky rap monologues that Thompson called his work "gibberish," something only known to hipsters, and he was bemusedly
astonished he could publish such and make a living from being a psychedelic comic. There was an opening and he seized it, yet where else

could such hip humor be published for money, other than in *Rolling Stone*? People working in the office were nearly rolling on the floor with laughter when they first read Thompson's fiction. The humor in the novel remains so broadly accessible that people who don't get the insider jokes continue to find the novel hilarious.

In the same letter, Thompson, when recounting he was more than halfway through the arduous manuscript, described his difficulty in writing about the death of the American Dream, which was originally to be set in Los Angeles in the aftermath of the August 1965 Watts riot,[22] as a millstone around his neck—that it kept striking a false note, awkwardly intruding into his narrative, forcing him to pontificate and lose his narrative grip—which for him recalled the pontification of Fitzgerald's early title for the Gatsby book: "The Death of the Red White and Blue." Thompson feared he was lecturing rather than writing creatively while presenting the terminal agony of the El Dorado dream and its replacement by Chance, as Borges would pessimistically write of the Assyrian empire in "The Lottery," with its shadowy, allegorical implications about how the psychology of the American empire operated on an international scale. Thompson's essays, "The Motorcycle Gangs" and "The Non-Student Left," both of which Carey McWilliams had originally published in *The Nation*, had appeared in a 1968 anthology, *The California Dream*, that featured "A Journey into the Mind of Watts" by Thomas Pynchon. Also included was a reprint of an Aldous Huxley 1939 essay wherein a fat Englishman makes a pilgrimage to Los Angles to examine a rare manuscript which an ignorant oil magnate has at his circus-like castle, replete with baboons.[23] The educated African American chauffeur functions as the narrator's sidekick. This Huxley essay, revealing an inner emptiness connected to the worship of money, functions as a symbolic, inspirational template for the novel's climax at the Circus-Circus.

What Thompson needed at this point was not thought but action in the narrative about his theme, the death of the American Dream, on which he had two years earlier accumulated a bulky manuscript that "amounts to almost 400 pages of useless swill"[24] about which Thompson felt a paralyzing desperation; he was searching for an Archimedes-like fulcrum to organize his theme and make it entertaining. In Thompson's letter to his editor at Random House, he registers fear of not knowing any precedent for this experimental Raoul Duke approach; he eventually opted for it, and to skirt editorial objections to this novel approach, Thompson, after five more arduous drafts in a nondescript Ramada Inn in Pasadena, California, took the unusual precaution of turning in a neatly typed, complete manuscript to *Rolling Stone*.[25]

Mittyesque fantasy remains a central technique in *Fear and Loathing in Las Vegas*. Yet something else is happening with that technique. Once Thompson understood how successful his "gibberish" technique was, he ran with it, melding the hip goof-rap popular in the Kesey camp with unhinged fantasy—that is, the fantasies would become self-conscious exaggerations and even put-ons to amuse the reader, becoming a central aspect of the main character, the gonzo persona Raoul Duke, the name also conjuring a schizophrenic cultural split between the first name of Fidel Castro's brother and the right-wing cowboy hero, John Wayne.[26] Thompson needed only to thread such goofy discursive monologues and extravagant fantasies into narrative pacing. Most of these surreal fantasies concern freedom, paranoia, and satiric jibes at the establishment, as well as deluded optimistic hippies. Having a lawyer as sidekick never had so many ironic possibilities; Thompson expertly exploited that comic situation full tilt—Oscar Acosta became the most unpredictable companion since Rabelais introduced Pantagruel and Panurge to a public hungry for satire against rigid and repressive institutions, whether Roman Catholic or Calvinistic.

The famous first line of the novel describes drugs taking hold of the characters in the desert while in a speeding car, yet Silberman in a letter quibbled about the drug theme: it was "absolutely clear" to him that neither Thompson nor Acosta were on drugs in the novel. Thompson replies: "All I ask is that you keep your opinion on my drug-diet for that weekend to yourself. As I noted, the nature (& specifics) of the piece has already fooled the editors of *Rolling Stone*."[27]

Thompson argues that the perception of having written the book under the influence of drugs makes the book all the more astounding to others. He has used his drug experiences to enhance the mechanics of gonzo journalism. Thompson concludes the discussion with a plea: "So let's just keep our personal conclusions to ourselves." Later that month Thompson informed Silberman that Jack Kerouac's sales of *On the Road* were modest before the obscenity bust of Allen Ginsberg for *Howl*. Only then did Kerouac become a media sensation and the spokesman for the Beat Generation, which led to the perception that

Kerouac offered a new way of writing akin to journalism.[28] As a marketing device, the paperback edition of Thompson's novel still sports the paradoxical classification "nonfiction" on the back cover.

The opening of the novel recalls (or repeats) an amusing image that concluded the Derby story: the car companion washing his hairy chest with beer as the car speeds along. Yet the reader quickly notices, between the bickering road buddies, that this is not a Whitmanesque open road trip full of brotherly love and smooth camaraderie, but a satire on that trope. The two men on the road for holiday fun enter a modern inferno with the vision of bats, evoking a reference to an ancient inferno—the famous opening of Book Twenty-three of Homer's *Odyssey*, where the souls of the slain suitors, described as swooping and screeching bats, descend into Hades:

> Hermes herded the souls with his staff,
> and the souls, like a flock of seething bats,
> flapped and squealed in a great black writhing mass
> down in the depths of a plummeting, bottomless cave.
> They followed the wand of Hermes the healer
> through damp, dripping passageways full of mold,
> until they crossed under the flowing stream of Oceanus,
> passing the great White Rock, then the gates of Helios,
> and descended through the chaotic World of Dreams,
> then arrived at the splendid asphodel meadow
> where countless *eidolon*, images of men
> who no longer walk in sunlight, have their dwelling.[29]

The Homeric allusion provides a subtle comic twist: Just what disastrous love stories are these two underworld characters fleeing from? Another twist: the asphodel meadow turns out to be a desert. Another twist: they are not incorporeal souls, but men so immersed in the flesh that they might appear to some to lack a soul. The "unearthly" duo will confront countless men who are less than men, shadows of those who were once free men; their visit will be plagued by the chaotic world of dreams. Their dwellings are transient hotels where many will spend sleepless nights of torment, rolling dice and playing slot machines, roulette, and cards. Instead of damp, moldy passageways, there will dust at the motorcycle race and disembodied voices in the Beckett-like radio play where the site of the vanished American Dream is located.

From the outset the reader realizes there is a romantic/satiric split in the personality of the narrator, much like the narrator of Nathaniel West's *The Dream Life of Balso Snell* (1931) wherein the narrator is half savage, a figure of eternal revolt, a split continued in *Miss Lonelyhearts* (1933).[30] This schizoid split of the rational narrator and the behavioral savage provides the comedic heart of Thompson's novel.

Suddenly a disembodied voice, for at this point we don't know who is speaking, cries out, "Holy Jesus! What are these goddamn animals?" We note with irony that the speaker must be the damned animal. Even the great epic poet Homer provides raw grist for Thompson's humor mill. Beginning his novel with this epic allusion alerts the educated reader that Thompson composes no ordinary novel—he aspires to write an epic that will endure as the Great American Novel.

Another aspect of the bizarre bats in the desert consists of imagining the effects of mescaline as hallucination. One does not normally hallucinate through mescaline (yet it is possible). One notes the extraordinary visual beauty of nature, the narcissistic nature of the human ego, a sense of time moving in slow motion; one becomes aware that such a wealth of information is available to the mind both from the senses and from our intellectual processing that we constantly repress information into a narrow bandwidth, admitting only the little we are comfortable with. The word psychedelic derives from the Greek, meaning to make the soul manifest, or to manifest the real nature of something.

Canadian Abram Hoffer employed the word *hallucinogenic* in 1964 to describe any drug that modifies the narrow bandwidth of perception people usually live with. The catchall word was popularized when Hoffer titled one of his books *The Hallucinogens* (1964). From the start, it was a propagandistic misnomer to call LSD, psilocybin, or mescaline hallucinogens, a word that terrifies people. Because the word became commonly used to describe psychedelics (due to the commercial popularity of Hoffer's book), hipsters politically conscious of the Orwellian nature of the word often made goofy jokes about seeing unlikely animals to ridicule the stupidity of the word *hallucinogenic* when applied to psychedelics.

These jokes were a common cliché in hipster culture of the late Sixties and early Seventies. Although Hoffer's research on niacin as a cure for schizophrenia has led to the beneficial use of niacin for those who can withstand high doses to reduce their cholesterol, his other speculative work in drug psychiatry has not led anywhere, but he has left his mark on the language by injecting into it a misleading and thoroughly useless, propagandistic, distorting word. The satire on the noted drug expert, Dr. Bloomquist, in part 2 of the novel is most likely directed at Hoffer.

The encounter with the young hitchhiker supplies a follow-up to an article Thompson published in the *National Observer* back in 1964. His article, "Living in the Time of Alger, Greeley, Debs" rubs elbows with the sociological material of Jack London and Jim Tully. Thompson notes that old-time boomers, roustabouts who wandered from one boomtown to the next upcoming boomtown, still hitchhiked about in the West, but were a breed of hearty workers on the verge of extinction, doomed by unions and the increasing pressure to hire locals.

Thompson, in one of the few *National Observer* articles printed whole without editorial castration,[31] profiles two boomers, a tramp digger and a wildcat trucker, but with his assignment complete and on the road out from North Dakota, he picks up a young "happy-go-lucky type from Pennsylvania" with a blue plastic suitcase, dropping him off just south of Pierre. While older boomers who have skills and know the arcane ropes of wandering and surviving may not have long to live, how will this young optimist survive in the coming age of automation when people are far more anxious about job security? Thompson says, "I hope I don't have to pick you up in ten years, when they've really tightened the screws, because the day of the boomer is rapidly coming to an end."[32] We last see the naïve hitchhiker, experienced in the intricate trade of hay hauling, coping with a small dust storm, his extended thumb pointed toward Los Angeles, expecting to achieve the wondrous riches Alger promised those with a desire to work hard.

Some years later this same hitchhiker, or a similar type, appears to be reincarnated in Thompson's novel. Thompson charts sociological changes. Those picking up hitchhikers are no longer curious journalists sympathetic to the Jack London lifestyle, but wayward druggies looking for the next high or mischievous laugh. Steadman sketches a long-haired dope with a small canvas traveling bag wearing a Mickey Mouse T-shirt, the pseudo-corporate logo bearing a fascist swastika. The hitchhiker doesn't even possess the Alger work ethic, but merely Alger-like optimism.

Duke informs the hapless hitchhiker that he and his lawyer are on a quest to find the American Dream and that the car is a torpedo they'll ride to their death, a comic tribute to Terry Southern's script for *Dr. Strangelove* (1964), which concludes with actor Slim Pickens astride a nuclear bomb, whooping like a cowboy as he rides the bomb to earth, thus triggering the Doomsday machine. The Great Red Shark, a 1970 Cutlass Supreme, will transport them to their Doomsday revelation.[33] As a humorous conversation opener, this appears to be a nonstarter.

The amusing part, for Thompson fans, is that the hiker is *leaving* Los Angeles, heading east, perhaps to Las Vegas. The West Coast is now so full of optimism programmed by cartoon propaganda that it has brainwashed a whole generation—it now exports lame Alger-like optimists to the East Coast where they have less chance of making it financially than locating a needle in a haystack. Declining drugs marks the hitchhiker as a potential informant, not us—one of them.

The fevered fantasies surrounding the inconsequential hitchhiker, whom Thompson admitted to an Australian audience in 1976 was a fictional device,[34] initially run the gamut from sympathy to contempt—sympathy for his naïveté (no car, never been in a convertible before) to contempt (he's afraid of the car's speed, afraid of drugs, lacks self-confidence, has nothing to say). Raoul Duke firmly establishes his character as volatile rapper, quick thinker, and quirky observer of foibles—building the legendary character of Neal Cassady, yet more sardonic, brashly adolescent, and drenched in irony.

The origin of rap goes back to early eighteenth-century England, where rap was slang for swearing a charge against a person leading to arrest; the accused was said to take the rap or beat the rap, the rap referring to the initial knock or rap on the suspect's door.[35] Beating the rap meant absconding before the police entered and, by extension, beating the charge once the arrest was made. A rap sheet became slang for a list of charges (not convictions) against a suspect. Prisoners on their way to arraignment before the judge would often (and still today) excitedly claim innocence, announcing how they will beat the rap. In America such tirades often featured "trash talk," goofy, doomed satire on the purer boasting form favored by accused innocents.

Neal Cassady had wasted much time in prison. After his release, he became famous among artsy Beats for his improvised raps on assorted topics, especially satiric, imaginary convictions of those in power, like cops, judges, and wealthy snots. The Beats embraced and evaluated rap, enhanced by speed and an expanding catalog of drugs, as a popular improvised street art form akin to jazz. In general, traditional Beat-rap monologues were based on the use of marijuana in conjunction with either alcohol or speed.

The earliest forms of trash rap derive from soldiers disillusioned about World War I, a war whose reasons were facetious. Sarcastic nonsense became an entertainment fad among soldiers. Hemingway has the character Bill in *The Sun Also Rises* offer a ruling-class Southern example to Jake:

> Listen. You're a hell of a good guy, and I'm fonder of you than anybody on earth. I couldn't tell you that in New York. It'd mean I was a gigot. That was what the Civil War was about. Abraham Lincoln was a faggot. He was in love with General Grant. So was Jefferson Davis. Lincoln had just freed the slaves on a bet. The Dred Scott case was framed by the Anti-Saloon League. The Colonel's Lady and Judy O'Grady are Lesbians under their skin. [36]

Paranoia was a central thematic element of trash rap before drugs other than alcohol fueled it.

The legendary Chicago emcee, Lord Buckley (1906–1960), who became a lifelong friend of Ed Sullivan's during their armed forces USO tours, made a series of comic recordings that popularized a programmed biracial rap form, merging New Orleans backroom jazz argot with literary classics. "Lord" Buckley employed a pseudo-aristocrat British accent and scat songs in his reductive parodies of Western literature; his amusing "hipsemantic" monologue performances were admired by Nelson Algren, Quincy Jones, and Norman Mailer, [37] as well as sophisticated suburbanites familiar with old-time burlesque runway raps.

Douglas Brinkley notes the general influence of Buckley in some of Thompson's letters. [38] Thompson invented new ways to work in that broad comic tradition, donning comic personas similar to Buckley's, except not on the stage but in correspondence and newspapers. In *Fear and Loathing in Las Vegas* Thompson emphasizes spontaneity amid paranoid fantasies, supposedly fueled by acid in tandem with a pharmacist's traveling kit of illegal substances. Buckley influenced others, like Bob Dylan in "Mister Tambourine Man," [39] a favorite Thompson song cited as epigraph to *Fear and Loathing in Las Vegas*, yet what Thompson invented in the chemistry of his beleaguered frontal lobes remains more conveniently labeled gonzo, a robust cousin to the many cocktail varieties of Gothic literature.[40]

Based upon a distinction found in the historian Oswald Spengler, Thompson, in a 1958 letter, divides great writers into two camps: action men and thought men.[41] He identifies Proust and Joyce as great *thought* men, while tagging Hemingway and Rabelais as real *action* men, implying he feels akin to action writers; he appraises his idol Fitzgerald "to some extent" as an action writer, but he ultimately judges Hemingway as the more comprehensive writer who approaches literature from both angles.[42] While there's no ostensible evidence that Mikhail Bakhtin's masterpiece *Rabelais and His World* (1968),[43] a compelling study of carnival in Rabelais, had any influence on Thompson, yet Thompson may have read the John Cooper Powys study, *Rabelais* (1948), a book recommended enthusiastically by Henry Miller,[44] and includes such chapters as "The Wisdom of Nonsense" and "The Gospel of Humor," stating:

> Real humor—when you've cut out that pustule, that abscess, that gangrene upon its sweet and friendly flesh which is called Satire— resembles Bakunin's Anarchism; that is to say, it needs no "dictatorship" of any class. It knows neither the "Privilege of the Collar" nor the privilege of "No Collar.". . . It is born in the person who discovers it as much as in the person in whom it is discovered.[45]

The world turned upside down was a signature Christos theme of Rabelais that he paralleled with the secular carnival spirit of unrestrained impulse—in the Abbey of Thelème, monks have no schedule: doing as they please, their only rule. Rabelais mystically equates drinking with thinking and philosophy, just as Duke will mystically equate drug ingestion with sociological and political analysis. Thompson had been aware of Rabelais and his achievement as a towering master of satiric comedy. Because Thompson didn't acquire a formal college degree, readers sometimes don't realize the voracious intensity of his self-education and subsequent sophistication subsumed beneath a veneer of popular diction and populist political activism. Among Thompson's many Ivy League–educated friends, Floyd Smith (Yale and Columbia) judged that Thompson was better read than anyone in their bohemian circle.[46]

The astonishing success of *Fear and Loathing in Las Vegas* is due to the outrageous atmosphere of carnival—what was the background story for the Kentucky Derby piece became foreground for the Las Vegas narrative. Carnival elements include: the creative insult at which Thompson was a well-practiced connoisseur, as his correspondence abundantly verifies; a general atmosphere of thriving chance (gambling replaces traditional fortune-telling); the suspension of normal time and traditional mores through intoxication (drink and drugs); a parade of grotesque caricatures (subsequently illustrated by Steadman); a panorama of parody and satiric excess; an otherworldly pandemonium of manic extravagance; the cornucopia of plenty available to participants; and, above all, the cathartic release of laughter in the face of adversarial doom. Thompson brought the exuberant New Orleans Mardi Gras spirit to a Nevada desert paved with gold in the daydreaming tradition of Horatio Alger, whom he cites early and repeatedly in the novel.

"The death of the American Dream" had been Thompson's long-running obsession for a novel throughout his letters of the late Sixties, yet he realized that a book by that title would not sell and he called his bleak obsession and contract for the book with Random House a millstone around his neck. To Silberman at Random House, Thompson proposes in a novel "to use Duke, like Gatsby, to illustrate the Death of the American Dream theme" which he sees as virulently alive in the West.[47] While he was testing his ideas with Silberman, Thompson would eventually seize upon Las Vegas as the place to realize his symbolism. Thompson's fixation on Fitzgerald went beyond style—the hot white note he so admired—to theme and period: "Because the '60s are going to go down like a repeat, somehow, of the 1920s; the parallels are too gross for even historians to ignore."[48]

Parallels between the 1920s and 1960s include heightened prosperity; alcohol prohibition versus growing drug prohibition, especially marijuana; the rise of gambling in sports and stocks; an explosion of popular music recordings (also true of the 1940s) fueled by racial blending and quirky dance fads; the rise of a wealthy self-centered elite that considered itself above the law; increased availability of inexpensive automobiles; low food prices and volatile social mobility; rising monetary inflation and a sensation-seeking press; growing crime rates and a spike in divorces; unusual clothing fads; and a cultural obsession with speed and intensity. While these parallels vary from the superficial to the profound, it remains difficult to find another two decades in American history with so much in common.

Back at the buddy road trip, the drugged-up attorney exclaims, "Man, this is the way to travel." The lawyer cranks up the radio volume to hum along with the song "One toke over the line," but what's the point of traveling if your mind cannot function well enough to see what you are traveling through—discerning differences, and exploring the new, remain the integral purpose of traveling. We are not reading a Pied Piper, but a savage ironist. The next song on the tape features the Rolling Stones' (this was, after all, being published in *Rolling Stone*) "Sympathy for the Devil": the reader is being asked whether any sympathy can be harbored for these two desert devils. In a late interview, Thompson claimed that during the composition of the novel, he constantly played the Rolling Stones' 1970 album, *Get Yer Ya-Ya's Out*, which contains the in-concert version of "Sympathy for the Devil," wearing out four tapes.[49] Certainly Jefferson Airplane's 1967 *Surrealistic Pillow* was another of those tapes; also, Bob Dylan's 1965 albums *Highway 61 Revisited* and *Bringing It All Back Home*, which, among its many surrealistic tracks, includes "Mr. Tambourine Man" (cited on the book's dedication page) as well as "Outlaw Blues."

Meanwhile, the Alger-like, optimistic hitchhiker appears catatonic. Thompson's obsession with Alger goes back to a comic passage in Hemingway's *The Sun Also Rises* where the protagonist Robert Cohn is portrayed as dazzled and misled by a W. H. Hudson book at the wrong time:

> "The Purple Land" is a very sinister book if read too late in life. It recounts splendid imaginary amorous adventures of a perfect English gentleman in an intensely romantic land, the scenery of which is very well described. For a man to take it at thirty-four as a guide book to what life holds is about as safe as it would be for a man of the same age to enter Wall Street direct from a French convent, equipped with a complete set of the more practical Alger books. Cohn, I believe, took every word of "The Purple Land" as literally as though it had been an R. C. Dun report.[50]

The book stimulates Cohn, who has never experienced passionate love, to pursue other women despite his overly possessive second wife. Hemingway converts the illusion of Alger-like methods to acquire riches to an overly optimistic obsession in the erotic arena. Thompson redirects the theme back toward riches, with an emphasis on the closing of the West, with lessening social and economic opportunity in America. Thompson notes how Hemingway takes a theme and twists it in another direction—that becomes a central technique in Thompson's writing.

Duke thinks his attorney has gone mad when the lawyer tells the hitchhiker they are his friends; Doctor Duke threatens to cure the attorney with leeches. Shifting to interior monologue, Duke thinks the forlorn and barren desert was last known to be a friend of the Manson family. The clearly scared hitchhiker refuses both beer and drugs, and the touring knights take offense at such rude behavior, this uncivil rejection of the offered communion with his hosts. Duke announces the main theme of the novel: they are on their way to find the American Dream—perhaps a bit like Dorothy and her companions on the yellow brick road (is not the desert that?), who will discover that life presents a cynical pageant without a heavenly God, merely a man behind the curtains manipulating a primitive computer, thus foreshadowing Thompson's atheistic outlook. If a reader had the faintest notion that this book offers a fable suitable for television, they are curtly disabused.

The reckless swerving of the car terrifies the hitchhiker, who grabs the lawyer's neck, the lawyer rebuking him with screams while Duke seconds the rebuke. The lawyer continues to goof on the hitchhiker, telling him they are on their way to murder a certain Savage Henry who ripped them off. Duke thinks this quite funny, and the frightened hitchhiker scrambles out onto the trunk and leaps from the car, presumably during a slow distracted cruise in Duke's erratic driving. The hapless hitchhiker didn't make the grade of being intelligent, emotionally grounded, or courageous in the middle of nowhere, and is left in the dust storm of the car's speeding wheel. Having dispensed with the clueless hitchhiker—half cowardly lion without charm, half tin man without common sense, and half straw man devoid of sympathetic sentiment—we are suddenly transported in a time warp back to the practical and more mundane story of why and how the preparations for this unusual quest came about, the assignment to cover the Mint 400 motorcycle race.

The next chapter features a headline that satirizes sensational tabloid media: "The Seizure of $300 from a Pig Woman in Beverly Hills." Duke has stopped by an office to pick up a cash per diem allowance from his New York publisher; he's disappointed by the amount, and when he demands more than $300, she explains that's the entire amount the publisher sent. The tabloid headline promises a story that doesn't exist: no nasty behavior, nothing seized. Duke then joyfully exclaims that receiving the cash advance of $300 to cover expenses is itself the American Dream—the American Dream is about money, and they are going to perform the American Dream as "Horatio Alger gone mad on drugs in Las Vegas. Do it *now*: pure Gonzo journalism," yet this brief inset presents Thompson intrusively urging himself on, not Duke. Drugs are romantically described as a rejuvenating desert womb, a signal hint in praise of the rebirth qualities of peyote for those in the know.

Acquiring all the fabulous drugs proves easy compared to the arduousness of locating the proper car to cruise the desert, but they manage to nab the predatory Great Red Shark convertible. Maneuvering the rented car, suave Duke is so drunk he nearly totals it before leaving the rental lot. The lawyer muses about acquiring priest costumes as a convenient cover, but since no thespian stores stay open at that late hour, they sensibly refrain from burglarizing a church as the alcoholic poet Francois Villon had happily done without much scruple. They celebrate the conclusion of their preparations with mescaline (peyote) and a delightful midnight swim before nosing the drug-laden shark onto the Pasadena Freeway.

Duke thinks like an adolescent intent on scandalizing adults, yet arrives at poignant aphorism in the manner of Josh Billings, the great nineteenth-century humorist and aphorist: "Old elephants limp off to the hills to die; old Americans go out to the highway and drive themselves to death."[51] That sudden flip from adolescent mentality to sage sociological observation on the behavior of the elderly offers an unexpected change of tonal gears that a consummate writer can accomplish in comic narrative.

Asserting the need to hurry, Duke insists they must register at the hotel before the race begins or their expense account will not be honored. His lawyer nods agreement, suggesting that they forget about this American Dream "bullshit," truculently arguing "the important thing is the Great Samoan Dream." This comment indicates that the American Dream remains a colonial concept, dependent on crushing the dreams of unnamed victims, whether Samoans, Chicanos, or others.

The lawyer figure, based upon Oscar Zeta Acosta, sought to inspire the Mexican community in Los Angeles to fight for civil rights and political power in the manner of Martin Luther King to achieve the dream of equality and prosperity on a par with white citizens. Yet much of Acosta's Brown Power rhetoric remained more in the mold of Malcolm X—risking disbarment through brinkmanship confrontations with judges. John Lennon chanting on the radio, "Power to the People," popularized this sensibility in its March 1971 release. The lawyer dismisses Lennon as a punk who gets in the way of citizen rights by trivializing the issue as boutique, conscience-saving liberalism, irrelevant to legality. Duke/Thompson laments that the song arrived ten years too late, meaning that if that sensibility had taken hold earlier, the Vietnam War would have never happened. The lawyer says Lennon's a fool who should have stayed in England, a complaint that ultimately proved prophetic.

Lennon, when hanging out with Cambridge Marxists, had written the song in response to an interview he had done with journalist Tariq Ali. Lennon later confessed parts of the song to be "gobbledygook."[52] His self-deprecating assessment of his lyrics as gobbledygook parallels Thompson's self-deprecation of his own work as gibberish. Some years later in the early Eighties, Lennon, citing Thompson's remark in his posthumous *Skywriting by Word of Mouth*, ruefully agreed with Thompson's assessment that the song arrived ten years too late.[53] That whimsical miscellany with its scattershot satire and squiggly cartoons was influenced by both Thurber and Thompson, whose over-the-top humor Lennon appropriated in his chapter headline motifs and cynical social humor; Lennon was not above poking fun at Thompson: "*Fear and Loathing in the Vatican*, St. John Thomas' 19th book in the series 'Fear and Loathing Wherever I Can Find It.'"[54]

On the score of self-indulgent drugs, Thompson first offers self-parody with the bizarre mixing of drugs while driving to Las Vegas. Duke's attorney utters the comic line, "As your attorney I advise you to drive at top speed."[55] Such outrageous advice on the part of a sidekick is reminiscent of the occasional advice Panurge offered Pantagruel in Rabelais's third volume. Rabelais, master of outsized exaggeration and comic blasphemy in a Mardi Gras sensibility (as well as philosophical profundity) was the great master of comic long lists, but Thompson will offer shorter comic lists as a signature technique throughout the novel. The first such list occurs on the second page of the novel, where Duke recites a grotesque catalog of assorted and incompatible drugs, varying from the exotic to the trite, for casual consumption.

In the car Duke composes a short mental list of all they need to do, including the "official gibberish," the need to sheepishly conform. He then composes a comic list of fallen celebrities marking the end of the Sixties: Tim Leary a prisoner of Eldridge Cleaver in Algiers, Dylan clipping coupons in Greenwich Village, Owsley (the LSD manufacturer) folding napkins in prison, and Cassius/Ali thrown off his pedestal by Joe Frazier, a human hamburger. The counterculture had discovered an unlikely collection of disparate heroes now fallen upon hard times. Cassius/Ali, a Louisville hero in whom Thompson had invested local pride, had literally fallen to the floor. Thompson admired Ali not only for his boxing prowess and national success but also for his hometown wit, which was sometimes as mischievous as it was hilarious.

Owsley, hours after the California legislature made LSD illegal (and before the press could report it), was "preemptively" busted for manufacturing LSD, which had been legal when Kesey and the Pranksters were experimenting with it; now, when Thompson was writing, Owsley was forlornly folding napkins in the San Quentin cafeteria. After his release, Owsley, selling nostalgic Sixties memorabilia from folding tables, toured with the Grateful Dead and their deadhead fans.

At this point in time Cleaver, who was rumored to have murdered a seducer of his wife, had effectively made Leary a prisoner after a paranoid LSD trip. Cleaver thought a lowered sex drive under the influence of LSD (as contrasted with cocaine) was a secret plot to castrate African Americans—LSD provides such a visual experience that sexual fantasies are usually diminished as the ego dwindles while the brain's frontal lobes diminish control. Through pieces published in the *Berkeley Barb* and Thompson's editorial contacts at the paper, Thompson must have been aware of Dennis Martino's (the brother of Leary's son-in-law David, who was married to Leary's unstable daughter, Susan) cooperation with the FBI when Dennis was under indictment. The complicated legal web he was caught in would put Leary in a vise. Threatened with a life prison sentence, Leary buckled and gave the FBI the locales of nearly all the secret acid labs across America.[56] Leary continued to produce autobiographical goof nonsense books for a time. These books contained a peculiar psychedelic humor that has since waned, becoming obscurely impenetrable for those who attempt a literal reading. Not long thereafter Leary lost half of his soul, dignity, and sanity to guilt combined with psychedelic overuse, as he turned con man and Hollywood guru.

Dylan had retreated in anger from Woodstock, annoyed at his recent celebrity status as spokesman for the counterculture. Fans would seek him out merely to worship him and waste his time, so he fled to an anonymous Greenwich Village rental on MacDougal Street.[57] Dylan angrily denied he was a poster cliché for the counterculture or the spokesman for any generation. Some fans were angry that his friendship and association with Johnny Cash, as well as his 1969 *Nashville Skyline* album, which sold over a million copies and reached number one on the Billboard hit list, embraced commercial apolitical ideology. His Hollywood appearance in *Pat Garrett & Billy the Kid* (1973) furthered that perception. Yet, like Ali, victorious in his rematch with a less-than-gracious Frazier, Dylan was to re-emerge as the leading counterculture hero in an appearance at George Harrison's Bangladesh Concert on August 1, 1971, and especially later with his 1974 double-live album, *Before the Flood*, which blended country music with counterculture sensibility. Dylan, being an artist and not an ideologue, has been able to reinvent himself several times despite bouts of gloomy pessimism, producing music that transcends the partisan divides of politics, just as Thompson's satirical portraits of Americans transcend political prescription.

To cap off the list of fallen heroes: Thompson's hometown hero, Muhammad Ali, fallen to Joe Frazier, a man who lacked the civilized wit and eloquence of one of the greatest technical boxers in the history of professional boxing. This was a documentary list of the failed hopes of people who were the personification of cultural optimism.

Thompson's selection of fallen counterculture heroes spans not only varied parts of the country, but the Leary conundrum implies globalism. When Leary returned to Millbrook, New York, after his 1965 summer honeymoon in India with his third wife, the Swedish model Nena von Schlebrügge, Alpert had altered the research community of experimental scholars to a sexual playground for underclass street bisexuals from New York City, "using LSD for mischievous fun."[58] They claimed superior status based upon ego-tripping. Leary mistakenly thought Alpert had seduced his fifteen-year-old son, and the split between them became permanent.[59] The counterculture concept was to use LSD to sensitize people and enhance communal bonds, but no one can trip all the time, and bad trips enhance paranoia. Thompson saw the macroscopic picture from observing practically what happens in the microcosm of failed communal experiments, as well as the inclination for drug experimentation to devolve into ugly, deranged consumption.

Rabelais's comic dialectic features micro/macroscopic paradoxes and juxtapositions. After giving a macroscopic list of how the Sixties ended in doom, we are transferred to the hotel desk to discover a microcosmic petty doom: although they are on the hotel list, their room is not yet ready. Duke, half-incapacitated by drugs, becomes disorientated by this and begins to hallucinate, seeing carnivorous reptiles, blood seeping on the carpet. His lawyer notices his confusion and says he'll attend to lobbying for the room, while Duke should pick up his *Sports Illustrated* press credentials from the press welcoming table that he comically imagines to be out for his blood. At this point in time, many journalists were jealous of Thompson's fantastic success with the Derby piece as well as his getting away with having submitted such an outrageous story for a routine assignment. Thompson's original assignment was to write 250 words of captions for photographs on the Mint 500 motorcycle race. He submitted about 25,000 words.[60]

Duke, through the illuminating lens of mescaline, which would render him immune to the effects of alcohol, drinks at the hotel bar while ridiculing the middle-class press in the drunken figure of a *Life* reporter unable to keep up with his drinking. The reporter crouches comically on the floor to evade the clutches of a desperate lounge-lizard vamp trying to net him as if he were a fish to harvest. The reporter sprawls on the filthy floor, enjoying his groveling escape from the grasping viper lady, while an amused Duke half suppresses a good laugh.

The atmospheric strategy of the book induces in the reader a surreal hypergelastic state of laughter, something achieved by only the truly great comic writers, as in the good priest Francois Rabelais, Miguel Cervantes, Mark Twain, Jaroslav Hašek, and Mikhail Bulgakov. Here lies a caricature of the drunken press, a mere worm on the floor of life, while Duke, armed with the fortified strength and wisdom of peyote, can drink anyone under the table, since alcohol has little or no effect on someone tripping with peyote.

Once the motorcycle race in the desert roars off, the prospect of covering the race in any meaningful way becomes moot amid the swirling dust storm; the assignment itself becomes an illustration of futility and absurdity, which affords apposite opportunity for wayward humor and the self-indulgent vector of alienated commentary. While being mildly harassed by bored cops suspicious of East Coast press, Duke, performing populist guerilla theater, assures the skeptical police that he's a "friendly" Westerner—if they can catch him, they will have the golden opportunity to harass Joe McGinniss, author of *The Selling of the President 1968*, which introduced voters to the venue of stage-managed political campaigns, exposing some dubious tactics of Richard Nixon's during his 1968 campaign. The local police happily roar off on the red-herring expedition to search for the now-famous phantom "evil" egghead who was far away clucking his typewriter on his first novel, while the reader admires Duke's shrewd, spontaneous wisdom. Yet the passage also functions like an enthusiastic blurb, encouraging readers to chase down the McGinniss book.

Duke and his companion trudge over to the Desert Inn to catch Debbie Reynolds vamping the antiquated music of Sinatra and Presley as she prances with Fifties dance moves on stage. McKeen says she donned a silver Afro when she pranced about (satirically, I presume) to "Sgt. Pepper's Lonely Hearts Club Band."[61] In exasperation, Duke exclaims they've entered a time capsule; he turns cranky.

Thompson describes the dubious superiority of ether to alcohol, as "it makes you behave like the village drunkard in some early Irish novel."[62] This constitutes a jest, yet Thompson must be referring to the Anglo-Irish novel, the stage-Irish stereotype, or perhaps the American Jim Tully's *Shanty Irish* (1928). Duke's mumbling Orangeman rant of "Dogs fucked the Pope, no fault of mine" on the same page may, among Roman Catholics, be favored only by the limited number of Catholics who share Dante's moral preference for hurling predatory, fundamentalist, pernicious popes into the more colorful lower circles of his densely populated and highly personalized *Inferno*. The use of second-person monologue in that paragraph effectively emphasizes the schizophrenic perceptions of an inflated, etherized ego observing the circus of the disconnected self perform its own incoherent, rambling nonsense—a circus within a circus. Ether was widely overused in the medical profession at that time—it tragically often led to brain damage—and Thompson stakes the claim that even half-brain-dead druggies can easily comprehend the corruption and inanity of the circus that most people crave.

At Circus-Circus (one commentator identifies Circus-Circus as the equivalent of Gatsby's mansion)[63] the moralists invade the "Sixth Reich," twice as evil as Hitler's Third Reich (Thompson was later to label the George W. Bush's presidency as the Fourth Reich)[64] and the main nerve of the American Dream, that Great Nightmare where "reality itself is too twisted" to offer anything sensible for those whose minds have been illuminated by psychedelic drugs. Thompson momentarily puts aside the Duke persona and editorializes: "The Circus-Circus is what the whole hep world would be doing on Saturday night if the Nazis had won the war."[65] Thompson connects the tradition of fascism with the dictatorial penchant for distracting the masses through circus, a favorite distraction technique of the Roman Empire, which had not been able to invent virtual reality games.

Amid the varied spectacle of Korean Kitten acrobats, half-nude teenage girls being chased by a wolverine, and strippers in polar bear costumes, the animal theme of absurdity becomes amusingly ironic when the lawyer orders two more Wild Turkeys. The disorientating absurdity of the "bizarre shuck" becomes enhanced by the mescaline they have consumed. Amid this Alice-in-Wonderland fun house, we hear that for 99 cents, a computerized picture of anyone will stand two hundred feet tall on a mammoth screen in downtown Vegas with a short voice message—a feed-your-head-with-idiocy opportunity for the average street gawker.

Another way of looking at the giant screen symbolism may be derived from Oswald Spengler. When speaking of the atrophied soul of the city, Spengler observes: "By day there is a strange street traffic of colors and tones, and by night a new light that outshines the moon. And the yokel stands helpless on the pavement, understanding nothing and understood by nobody, tolerated as a useful type in farce."[66] Thompson has discovered an incarnation of Spengler's prophecy.

The lawyer begins to fear losing his sanity and wants to leave, saying this is serious. Duke astutely replies: "'George Metesky was serious,' I

said. 'And you see what they did to him.'"[67] Metesky was the notorious
gunpowder pipe bomber who terrified New York City for sixteen years
in the 1940s and 1950s by bombing libraries, theaters, offices, rest-
rooms, storage lockers, subways, the RCA building, Radio City Music
Hall, Penn Station, and Grand Central Station. Fifteen people were
injured. Metesky, a veteran and disabled mechanic whose lungs were
seriously scalded from a backfiring boiler, was angry at Con Ed for
summarily firing him and denying worker's compensation in court.
When caught and convicted, he was committed to a mental institution.[68] The irony and paradox here consists in the inhabitants of Circus-
Circus being crazier than those in a mental institution, but if the lawyer
leaves now, he may be in jeopardy of being committed to a genuine
mental institution, an inane but traditional "remedy" for those tripping
on psychedelics.

The owner of the Circus-Circus Casino was a once a boy who
wanted to run away and join the circus. Now the owner of a casino, he
stages every night a mock crucifixion of someone in a gorilla suit spinning atop a neon cross. The owner himself, an icon of the Horatio Alger
trajectory, becomes a parodic illustration of the Horatio Alger theme in
all its debauched and delusionary grossness. Once the dream is
achieved for oneself, one becomes a cynical exploiter of others, fleecing
them while entertaining them with inane and hallucinatory spectacle.

Despite the loathing of Mencken and Thompson, the Horatio Alger
myth still thrives within the business community today with awards,
honor lists, and philanthropic scholarships. Its hydra-headed endurance
appeals to something beyond the surface of the dime novelist's Midas-
like bromides:

> America has regularly manifested an ingenious propensity for dis-
> guising and updating the myths of ancient Greece to create more
> palatable cultural stories. Thus our version of Athena has characteris-
> tically been packaged under the name of Horatio Alger, whose he-
> roes embody the virtues and blessings of success through careerism.
> Alger's heroes were aggressive, individualistic, lucky, hardworking,
> honest enough to secure the trust they needed to succeed, and, of
> course, male. A casual reading of such scintillating novels as *Ragged
> Dick* and *Mark, the Match Boy* reveals how Alger created a virtual
> American mythology of success, the praise of which surely rivaled
> the hymns sung for Athena in ancient Athens.[69]

Alger appears to be a kind of Jungian archetype flipping coins in the *medulla oblongata* of the American psyche.

Speculative bemusement succumbs to "The Fear," which sets in with the attendant paranoia that time may be caught in an eternal loop of repetition, the terrifying yet typical hallmark of a bad acid trip, but also a religious conundrum with regard to historical time—the pagan myth of eternal return, repetitive cycles of human behavior from creative growth to apocalyptic collapse, from which both Jewish and Christian theologians seek an escape through communion with Yahweh or through Jesus. An awareness of this despairing cycle finds its trenchant articulation in both Aztec and German mythology and history.

Circus-Circus concludes with the cowardly narrator frustratingly comparing himself to Jesus in the temple wishing to expel the money changers and gamblers from the American Dream disfigured by "shooting galleries, money-changers, tattoo parlors, and cotton-candy booths."[70] This outlandish metaphor of Jesus and the money changers had been prepared by Thompson's previous mention of "Jesus christ" with correct lowercase archaic orthography—evoking Twain's amusing printer's devil's prank of Jesus H. Christ on a despised preacher, recounted in his autobiography—the ignorant confusion of nickname sobriquet with surname. The point of the allusion remains the futile feebleness of the deranged and incapacitated antihero, a fool—like Hašek's soldier Schweik—who so fears his own dysfunctional ineptitude that Duke, the superman driver and connoisseur of curves, requests his lawyer-companion to drive them back to the hotel where the underachieving narrator mockingly exposes his companion's crazed behavior about narcissistic sexual delusions and Lacerda, the magazine photographer in the hotel, giving assistance. Duke's cowardice in the temple, avoiding confrontation or imitating a false religion, follows Nietzsche's advice from *The Antichrist*.[71] In *The Antichrist* Nietzsche denies any salubrious qualities of guilt and punishment psychology, which Thompson applies to language and drug use. Thompson perceives both the new golden calf and religion as an identical continuum. Duke's general perspective on society runs parallel to Nietzsche's critique of the hypocritical decadence that the fictions of the Judeo-Christian tradition promote.

Another way of looking at Circus-Circus would be to picture the wry peasant entering the Big House, in the tradition of the Anglo-Irish novel. This tradition began with Maria Edgeworth's *Castle Rackrent* (1800), in which an old steward narrates the privileged excesses of decadent Rackrents through three generations. The decaying house, drunken antics, and class tension provide conflict and comedy. Such social satire was replaced by larger political implications in the work of William Carleton and others.[72] The symbolism of a big house retains a flexible *topos* and compact focus. Thompson's use of it blends social satire, sociological analysis, and political critique with his own brand of comic Gothic doom.

Spengler fixated upon central symbols for civilization: the Magian enclosed cave, the Egyptian arrow shot into eternity, the Greek nude freestanding statue, the Roman Coliseum where people were killed for entertainment, the Chinese wandering path, the unbound Russian horizon. Thompson/Duke performs a pilgrimage to the principal American shrine, the ultimate symbol of what American Horatio Alger aspirations have devolved into, a depraved belief in chance before the golden calf. Thompson was prophetic—today gambling has even entered the corner convenience store. Will future anthropologists eventually remember America as a civilization of a failed economy, symbolized by lottery tickets or the El Dorado legend of Las Vegas? For Thompson, the revelatory epiphany of the American Dream at Circus-Circus provides a crystallized symbol. He had first looked for such a symbol at the 1968 Democratic Convention, but the tumultuous and tragic events were too gloomy for even Thompson to use as a symbol. Discovering the desired symbol in Las Vegas fulfilled a quest of several years.[73] The adroit ambiguity between satire and serious critique remains an artistic signature that elevates this novel to the stature of a rare and savage masterpiece. The book becomes a circus fun house of relating and distorting mirrors, a theme Orson Welles made capital use of in *The Lady from Shanghai* (1947).

Circus memoirs and novels constitute a large and now largely forgotten genre in late nineteenth- and early twentieth-century American writing. For most people the notion of circus opens up a nostalgic and optimistic vein reflecting the joys of childhood, yet in the literary tradition this has not always been the case. For example, Jim Tully's *Circus Parade* (1927) roots into the seamy and savage backstage life of a traveling circus, grinding on the road from small town to city and back again, with dust-laden angers and bitter ironies in its exposé of performers cheated by sleazy management. The ending includes a murderous gang of men tanked up on heroin with an apocalyptic riot of blood, bullets, and mayhem. A slice from the deadpan epilogue: "Gorilla Haley's skull was fractured. He became insane. He later became a member of the Chicago police."[74] Perhaps he was the type of cop who nearly fractured Thompson's skull when Mayor Richard Daley dealt from the bottom of the deck by ordering a police riot at the 1968 Democratic National Convention at Chicago. Thompson's novel adopts and adapts that circus parade of citizens cheated at the brutal wheel of fortune.

Thompson's theme of standing on the main nerve of the American Dream parallels the conclusion of Donleavy's *The Ginger Man*. In London, Dangerfield encounters the American Dorothy Spendergold Cabot and her husband, Osgood Swinton Hunderington, two ninnies with upper-class pretentions and an accumulated lifetime of ignorance to fortify their empty lives. Dorothy (Dot) is a refugee from New York City, her family from upstate, and her husband owns a house in Cornwall, England, but she's not yet been to it any more than Dorothy from the *Wizard of Oz* has been to see the wizard.

They all share a taxi on Christmas Eve; Dangerfield grows nauseous and claustrophobic from the inanity of their conversation; he suddenly decamps the taxi for a laugh to clear his head, discovering he's been accidentally deposited in the banking sector of London, the financial capital of the world, near the Royal Exchange. This is the novel's climax: Dangerfield has found the center of the financial universe from which he has been excluded. He drinks a brandy in a male-only pub crowded with bankers. From a red telephone booth, he calls MacDoon at the Christmas party where they were headed. Dangerfield tells MacDoon he's lost his faith in courting the rich—they are mean beyond redemption. MacDoon replies that he's heard Dangerfield was rude to Hunderington, whom he ridicules as Lord Squeak, heir to legendary pigsties in Kent. MacDoon tells him Mary is at the party, ready to be reconciled with him, and if she's not, he has a backup girl who's interested in him. Dangerfield, sardonically claiming the banks have filled him with religious fervor, meets his mistress, Mary, in the library for their reconciliation. They argue about Mary working as a half-nude model; Dangerfield batters her about the face, they reconcile and leave the party. MacDoon cordially sends them off with a bottle of champagne.

The ending offers love banter, with Mary well aware of Danger-field's mean animal streak and Dangerfield haunted by the specter of his need to earn money for the support of forthcoming babies. The parallel between novels resides in the main characters realizing they are unbelieving outsiders and witnesses to the spectacle of chance that rules the financial world—in Donleavy, the reality of landed money and the speculative betting on stocks at the Royal Exchange; in Thompson, the Circus-Circus Casino where the perception of life in America is revealed as a zoo-like circus lottery where participants are relentlessly fleeced until death while entertained by animals. Both writers deliver a pessimistic analysis of the social spectrum, yet Donleavy's novel offers a grim hope that Thompson's Spenglerian doom denies. On October 6, 1967, the Diggers, in a street theater performance with the parade of a symbolic cardboard coffin, had produced the Death of the Hippie/Birth of the Free Man pageant in the Haight,[75] but Thompson was to pro-duce the Irrelevancy of the Hippie/ Death of the Free Man in his novel.

Concerned for the safety of his red shark convertible, Duke de-scends in the elevator at 4:30 a.m. on a Sunday morning to remove his car from the street and put it into the hotel garage. Duke rubbernecks a gross crowd surrounding a crap table still "humping the American dream." Making a losing "freak" bet with a Jefferson two-dollar bill to evoke the image of Jefferson's Platonic concept of a virtuous agrarian republic where all responsible voters would be free because they owned land (and would be voting participants in order to keep their owner-ship), he half convinces himself there's real pleasure in *losing* both money and his unfettered mind because he's merely a grubbing report-er covering a story, finding momentary consolation in running up his expense account by having his car washed and waxed.

As a reporter, he is analyzing the subconscious pleasure of the losers who flock to destroy their lives at the gaming tables, the antithesis of the Jeffersonian dream of free landowners. In real life this was the stealth moment Thompson, conjuring his invisibility cloak and sulking with an oversized suitcase, half carrying, half dragging it across the highly pol-ished marble foyer floors while attempting to assuage his paranoia about being nabbed by a bellhop or counter clerk, skipped out on the hotel bill of more than $2,000 that he and Acosta had accumulated with a swollen, gargantuan room-service tab.[76]

The climatic revelation from a two-dollar losing bet is not a fatality—it functions as a *surreal* construct in much the same way as it would in a story by Borges, like "Pierre Menard, Author of the *Quixote*" where solipsism, relativity, plagiarism, exact repetition, and the destruction of one's own writings become highly creative historical triumphs. In that story Borges, who first read *Don Quixote* in English, was paying tribute to his mentor, the oblique humorist Macedonio Fernández, about whom Borges later confessed, "I imitated him to the point of plagiarism."[77] In the preface to *The Museum of Eterna's Novel (The First Good Novel)* by Fernández, the British novelist Adam Thirlwell cites Alan Pauls' study, *The Borges Factor* (2004), and argues that for Borges "to lose is not a fatality but a construction, an artifact, a *work*."[78] While Thompson's humor is broader and more accessible than that of either Fernández or Borges, his satire on Didion and his numerous letters of comic invective often recapitulate many of the techniques discussed by Borges in his 1933 essay "The Art of Verbal Abuse," yet Thompson's humor has the *tabula rasa* stamp of an American populist, homegrown original, based upon a hipper update of the narcissistic fantasy vein found in Thurber's Walter Mitty character.

The splashy bathtub scene with the disorientated and drugged lawyer, accompanied by Duke's sanity-searching mace threat (augmented with musical allusions), exuberantly repeats the mace theme from the Kentucky Derby piece as Duke and the music-obsessed lawyer banter insulting trash talk. The bathtub setting evokes a contrast: the optimism of the 1950s, epitomized by such pop songs as the 1957 "Splish Splash" by Bobby Darin (Walden Robert Cossotto), conjures a playful world of innocent, alcohol-fueled partying, whereby the song's narrator placidly hopes "everything's all right" as he takes his ritual bath for the coming party. In contrast, we witness with horror the lawyer's drug-addled obsession with playing a haunting top hit of the sixties, "White Rabbit" by Grace Slick (Grace Barnett Wing)[79] in Jefferson Airplane's 1967 album *Surrealistic Pillow*. Nearly a decade separates the two songs, one a mega-hit on the East Coast, the other on the West Coast, giving the reader an East Egg and West Egg dialectic, as in *The Great Gatsby*—illustrating the change in American sociology from optimism to dangerous pessimism, along with the transition from alcohol to more dangerous drugs.

The story of "Darin" himself provides an appropriate submerged symbolism almost drowned in the scene: Walden Robert Cossotto, born in 1936 at the height of the Great Depression, grew up in an Italian Bronx ghetto in rock-bottom poverty (without a father, whom he later discovered to be his uncle); in the Fifties he became a huge Billboard and Hollywood success. His 1958 "Splish Splash" came about because he had boasted to his mother that he could write a hit song about anything. She told her daydreaming son if that was true, he should write a smash hit that began with the words "Splish splash, I was taking a bath." Darin (a whimsical stage name appropriated from a Chinese restaurant sign with the first three letters of "Mandarin Duck" missing) repeated the conversation to radio disk jockey Murray the K (Murray Kaufman). Laughing, Murray bet Darin money that he couldn't write a hit song that began with the nonsensical "Splish Splash." Darin had the last laugh, the song providing his first smash hit.[80] The story of the bet and the Horatio Alger motif in Darin's life neatly fits the scene. The contrast between Darin's playful, popular optimism and the despairing, pounding pessimism of Slick's full-throated lyrics sends a shiver down any sensitive music lover's spine.

The fierce and pounding disembodied contralto voice of Slick inhabits taunting lyrics of hypnotic delirium and ecstasy; "Feed your head" being the first commandment of the new dispensation and "Use your head" being the second, yet there's a subliminal awareness in the driving song that everyone's "going for a fall." The optimistic party of the Sixties has long ceased as the attorney contemplates committing suicide in a drug-induced nirvana. Slick, like Fitzgerald's Daisy, possesses a contralto voice, but Daisy's voice rings "sweet," while Slick projects a commanding apocalyptic harshness. Yet one might claim, in Fitzgerald's words, that for both contraltos, each change in song progression tipped out "human magic upon the air."[81] While Daisy's voice was full of money, Slick's voice was full of drugs—both mega-sirens seducing men to the rocks of doom. Slick's ethereal voice sounds like the anthem of pursuing Furies from Greek drama, via Lewis Carroll.

Since the lawyer was tripping on acid, the scene also functions as a satire on Timothy Leary, who propagandized the use of LSD as Tibetan prayer-death meditation. Perhaps Leary was inspired by hearing that Aldous Huxley had taken acid on the last day of his life. Leary's invention of a pseudo-religious cult with himself as its high priest was anathema to Thompson. Duke tosses a grapefruit instead of the radio into the tub, evoking the peasant tradition of tossing fruit at a bad stage performer.

The manic insanity of the lawyer's suicidal disorientation compares to Vincent van Gogh's cutting off his ear in a deranged fit of frustration. Duke presents himself a sane Gauguin, a primitive daubing realist amid the atavistic anthropological Wonderland that constitutes Las Vegas. But this dialectic remains a caricature. The "White Rabbit" song had special significance for Acosta, who had shown Thompson a rough draft of his autobiography in which he recounts not only a near-suicide, but a scene in the Daisy Duck bar where he first met Hunter. Acosta enters the bar, asking the barkeep if he knows Bobby Miller (Thompson's friend Michael Solheim). The bartender replies sit tight, his girlfriend will be here soon. Bobbi, as she's called, shows up—she's the cocktail waitress, a diminutive brown-haired girl in high heels. After a little while, she asks Acosta to dance. "White Rabbit" thunders from the jukebox. Acosta, a big man in construction boots and cut-up shirt, appears stunned. No woman has ever asked *him* to dance before. They dance,[82] although a different account of Acosta and Thompson's meeting appears in an earlier draft published in *Con Safos* magazine in 1972.[83] Thompson satirically conflates the theme of suicide with Acosta's favorite-memory song, while in Acosta's revised version he's careful to appropriate a casual, social, and romantic context for his love of the song. Acosta had freaked out when he read Thompson's manuscript, screaming to Thompson's editor, Alan Rinzler, "My God! Hunter has stolen my soul! He has taken my best lines and used me."[84] Those lines were on the tape recorder Hunter was running; Acosta felt betrayed and psychologically raped.

In a chattily humorous letter to Jim Silberman, in which Thompson defends his legitimate La Vegas expenses as "all in the interest of Journalistic Science" for the outing, he comically confesses that a few minor expenses were unreasonable, like "ordering two servings of 'Crab Louey' [*sic*, comic spelling] in the Flamingo, then sending them back, uneaten, but covered with broken light-bulb glass." The name Louis itself refers to the sun's light, Louis the Sun King being a tautology for those who have forgotten etymology.

Thompson had whimsically proposed adding a third Las Vegas section to the sequence, a section that would focus on Circus-Circus "where I finally found the American Dream."[85] While Thompson had discovered the vacant heart of the American Dream early in the novel, American Express, which had refused to accept any partial payment, had canceled Thompson's card for not paying his Las Vegas bills.[86] The crushed lightbulbs present a symbol not only of unenlightened food preparation at Circus-Circus, but by extension, the American tradition of cooking. Thompson would have been quite familiar with a quality version of the dish, the King of Salads as it's sometimes called, since it originated in San Francisco during the early 1900s.

The Crab Louey theme alludes to the song "Louie Louie," a popular rock 'n' roll standard written by Richard Berry in 1955. Set to the tune of "Amarren Al Loco" ("Tie the Crazy Guy Up") by Cuban band leader Rosendo Ruiz Quevedo, its style presents a first-person Jamaican ballad telling the tale of a sailor's return home to his beloved. Berry first recorded the West Coast hit 1957 song with Flip Records in San Francisco with his band, the Pharaohs. The Kingsmen, a Christian gospel quartet from North Carolina, covered the song in 1963, making it an East Coast hit.[87] Subsequently, crabbies in the FBI during the mid-Sixties conducted a two-year investigation into the possibility of obscenity in the song, but the investigation was deemed inconclusive.[88] Once again the polarity of East and West Coast musical styles delineates contrast, with the implication that West Coast music achieves a superior cutting-edge authenticity.

While it may appear that Duke acts like an ordinary reporter attempting to pad his expense bill, or that he's a common citizen anxious about leaving his car (it's only a rental, yet it's an open, screaming-red convertible) out on the street as a temptation to thieves or spoilers when many people may not be around at 5:00 a.m. on a Sunday morning, that's not what's really happening—all this occurs not on some deserted street, but in gonzo land. While a bus driver in New Orleans is merely a bus driver to the occasional tourist passing through on a weekend, his friends may know that he's not just a mere bus driver, that underneath his city bus–driver's blue uniform he's really Big Chief Whoever, leader of the Flying Eagle Plumes funk-stepping down the street on Mardi Gras day like a freakishly beautiful god come to visit amazed mortals. Likewise, Thompson becomes transfigured into Duke or the Doctor, musical sobriquet stage names—Duke deriving from the trickster-grafter character "Duke" in Mark Twain's *The Adventures of Huckleberry Finn* (1884).

Behind the excess of transformation, there's method in the seeming madness. Gonzo goes further, goes against the limits, turns the ordinary into perpetual carnival, a maelstrom of living on the edge and tipping over into an Otherworld of transcendence where anything remains possible, including decoding the savage heart of the American Dream in a casino or hotel room in Las Vegas. Afterward, there's a hangover, some aching bones, and some excess in expenses like crushed lightbulbs.

The revelation occurs at the Temple of Chance—the savage heart of the American Dream consists of *losing*, not winning. There can be no point in chasing out the money changers from the Temple of the Dream because no hope exists; the Temple of Chance functions as a symbol much like the ironic billboard eyeglasses in Fitzgerald's novel, symbolic of blindness amid the ash-dump wasteland. As with Nick Carraway in *The Great Gatsby*, the dream is "already behind him," yet in Fitzgerald it remains a dream of love, a dream of life with Daisy.

The only consoling revelation in Las Vegas is that one may momentarily swim solo against the tide and acquire an offbeat freak pleasure in *not* winning anything, which ironically presents an ascetic desert imperative—ultimately, that is what all the drug ingestion conjures, the stoic desert hallucination of cenobite celibacy with sex as a tempting hallucination, an asceticism Gustave Flaubert satirized in the luridly beautiful prose of *The Temptations of St. Anthony* (1874).

But Blaise Pascal's witty gamble of cynical hope does *not* apply in this godless universe, nor does love. In Las Vegas there's nobody to love. At the heart of the Dream lies loveless monetarism, a robotic emptiness in the clattering of dice or the clicking of the roulette wheel where algorithms bloom in the desert. While *The Great Gatsby* revealed that Americans value money above love, Duke reduces the possibility of love to narcissistic fantasy—his companion's imagined love in an elevator, love as a pulsing acoustic wave fantasy as articulated in the acid rock of Jefferson Airplane.

Ironically, the desert discipline implicitly advocated by Duke remains peculiar: endure the onslaught of varied drugs while retaining a far-out window to sanity—the drugs offer sublime revelations about unveiling the depraved depths of the nightmare, the comic inferno of lizards and bats fluttering about, if you can open your eyes and see reality for what it is beneath its hypocritical mask. Thompson's stoic attitude was probably the result of coping with his first bad acid trip on June, 9, 1969, where he records wrestling with his paranoia.[89] Unfortunately, the hoi polloi of hippies illuminated by LSD, peyote, or psilocybin were not up to the rigors of traditional desert asceticism—many lost their heads to the unforgiving Red Queen of overindulgence with bad drugs, another forceful aspect of Thompson's pessimistic, prophetic perspective.

Thompson may have picked up the occasional yet effective wave imagery employed by Oswald Spengler throughout *The Decline of the West*, especially the lines that "the great Cultures accomplish their majestic wave-cycles. They appear suddenly, swell in splendid lines, flatten again and vanish, and the face of the waters is once more a sleeping waste."[90] Like an evolutionary biologist, Spengler noted the erratic flux of such cultural waves and their fleeting impact on history.

Henry Miller adapted Spengler's wave imagery to the smaller canvas of personal enlightenment, of "sudden seeing" when the mind is flooded at once by multidirectional insight, yet he believed that capturing the *waviness* of the wave as the essence of art.[91] The wave functions as the central theme of Jack Kerouac's *roman à clef* novel *Big Sur*, the memoir of a writer who retreats to a cabin in Big Sur, owned by Lorenzo Monsanto (Lawrence Ferlinghetti). Kerouac goes there to dry out and commune with nature.[92] Upon arriving at night, waves appear terrifying in the dark as they crash against boulders. In contrast, waves at the beach offer a lyrical interlude of romance with Billie Dabney (Jackie Mercer). Jack, immersed in himself, his writing, and backsliding drinking, realizes that he's not really in love. Billie has a young child and when the romance goes sour, she speaks of suicide. The waves become a symbol of danger and ultimately of death:

> I suddenly remember James Joyce and stare at the waves realizing All summer you were sitting here writing the so called sound of the waves not realizing how deadly serious our life and doom is, you fool, you happy kid with a pencil, don't you realize you've been using worlds as a happy game—all these marvelous skeptical things you wrote about graves and sea death it's ALL TRUE YOU FOOL! Joyce is dead! The sea took him! It will take YOU![93]

In Joyce's *Ulysses* (1922), the sea finds description not as mother but as "snot green" and "scrotum tightening," irreverent images of cold adolescent restriction to young Stephen. Joyce's small bohemian community of housemates at the Sandycove Martello Tower likewise disintegrate amid acrimony. Kerouac feels guilt about the failed love affair with Billie, yet compensates by picturing himself rescuing Billie from the thrashing waves (like Holden Caulfield in *The Catcher in the Rye*) as she attempts in his freewheeling imagination to drown herself.

Wave after wave of haunting paranoia afflicts Jack, who feels like the artist crucified on the cross of life,[94] unable to cope with the community of drifters he has embraced in this summer idyll. All he wants to do is groove and party as in Henry Miller's *Big Sur*, yet nightmare hangovers overwhelm him and threaten his sanity. The community that was to unite around the rural lyricism of the splashing wave disintegrates. The novel unexpectedly concludes with a lyrical *l'envoi* of Jack taking a porch nap, waking up in blissful sunshine, daydreaming that the long nightmare is dispersed by golden sunshine. Jack will return to the city and then his mother's home, where everything will be okay.

Thompson spent time in Big Sur, hoping to meet Kerouac, wanting to chat with him and Henry Miller. The fantasy of a communal free-spirit wave enveloping others through good vibes and good drugs and expanding across the country had its seed in Beat bohemia and flowered in the hippie bloom. On the one hand, the idea that a tsunami wave of brotherhood and sisterhood would travel from the West Coast eastward appears ridiculously naïve, yet on the other hand, Thompson buttresses its fleeting reality with memories that validate the nostalgic possibility of hope, now lost. No communal wave of hip solidarity will ever splash mob-infested Las Vegas.

While Thompson admired Kerouac's *On the Road* and *The Dharma Bums*, his admiration didn't extend much further.[95] In a December 1, 1962 letter to his friend Paul Semonin from Rio de Janeiro, Thompson admits he's reading *Big Sur*, a "stupid, shitty book," which makes him feel murderous toward the author in a Dostoyevsky-like manner.[96] Kerouac's book, in the vein of F. Scott Fitzgerald's attempt to confront alcoholism in *The Crack-Up* (1940), portrayed what Kerouac "could not face in real life: the fact that he was drinking himself to death."[97] Thompson's over-going of Kerouac's wave metaphor functions as a "murderous" displacement, designed by comparison to obliterate the pathos of Kerouac's narcissism.

Thompson and Acosta, who first play like childlike porpoises in the Los Angeles waves under the influence of peyote, had fled to Las Vegas with the idea of getting work done—real writing—but amid the surreal nightmare of the gambling world, they stumbled upon a parallel to the paranoid nightmare limned by Kerouac's fantasies. Yet this nightmare was real, not mere fantasy. What Thompson did with Kerouac's wave metaphor was to transform it from a personal tragedy and invest it with a broad sociological sweep. The journalist as social artist replaces the self-indulgent lyricist.

After fleeing Los Angeles, there were rumors that Acosta and Thompson were not safe in the Aspen area, but why would they choose Las Vegas as a refuge destination? Thompson had been there before with Sandy to cover the Sonny Liston–Floyd Patterson fight on July 22, 1963, but when Liston summarily knocked Patterson out in the first round, Thompson did not file the story for the *National Observer*.[98] Tom Wolfe's first essay in *The Kandy-Kolored Tangerine-Flake Streamline Baby* featured casinos, tourists, and people working there, concluding with a visit to the county asylum—the essay implied the city was completely crazy, so perhaps they would check out what Wolfe wrote. . . . And the city did have the advantage of a large police force to protect tourists from out-of-town militant crazies who had threatened to kill Acosta or biker gangs after Hunter.[99] William Stephenson analyzes Wolfe's Raymond as a prototype of Thompson's Raoul.[100]

The next chapter (chapter 8) offers a digression on drugs and San Francisco at its peak in the mid-Sixties, a scene Thompson ably covered for the *New York Times Magazine*, May 14, 1967, where he quotes Country Joe and the Fish's band manager: "If the hippies were more realistic they'd stand a better chance of surviving."[101] In a 1986 interview Thompson grew nostalgic:

> The whole definition of the drug culture was that we were in it together. If you got something nice, the instinct was to share it. You could live a million years in this country, or any other, and you would never have as much fun as you would have in San Francisco in the middle sixties. The sixties were a time when the clouds broke.[102]

That communal ethic, the heart of a generous reform impulse, created the wave that never quite swept the country, but some other parts of the country did feel the flecks of its splash for a little while, especially in music. The novel offers an elegiac summation, born of lived experience at that magic peak of good drugs and music: Thompson sees that "highwater mark—that place where the wave finally broke and rolled back."[103] This is that shock of recognition prefigured by the schlock Art Linkletter quotation (rather than its literary formulation by the critic Edmund Wilson in the title of his two-volume anthology of American literature published in 1943) sardonically cited as the chapter headline.

A catalog of pleasant and offbeat San Francisco memories afflicts Duke/Thompson as he recalls the epoch of hope that contrasts so vividly with the current scene of desert despair. Linkletter was once a hobo (his 1980 autobiography was titled *Hobo on the Way to Heaven*), a Horatio Alger figure become a beloved national icon of humor and wisdom. Linkletter, a personal friend of Walt Disney's, fiercely opposed the counterculture. At the time of the window-jumping suicide of his twenty-year-old daughter Diane, a student at University of California–Berkley, Linkletter was touring the country with an antipermissiveness lecture, speaking that day in Colorado. He publically claimed, on information of her brother Robert, that Diane committed suicide as a result of either an LSD trip or an LSD flashback,[104] yet the autopsy showed no evidence of any drugs. Thompson cites this episode and Linkletter's public crusade (he later met with Nixon) as an example of television media faux propaganda that turned the tide of the nation against the San Francisco scene by vilifying it, blaming an innocent young girl's suicide on the counterculture rather than her identity problems of living in the shadow of her father, and making of Diane a sainted martyr poster child for right-wing extremists.

In this chapter Duke contrasts his own first reaction to LSD at the Filmore West Auditorium, which demythologizes the lore heard from a psychiatrist he had consulted. The psychiatrist had described himself as running naked down the street and confessing to crimes he did not commit. This scared Duke. Later, Thompson claimed he first took acid at the Hells Angels party with Kesey and the Pranksters,[105] an anecdote he repeats in 1990, saying he had heard stories about the dangers of LSD-25 that had put him off from trying it. In *Hell's Angels* Thompson mentioned he had a limited experience concerning LSD, a half-dozen trips, but that his best experience had been at Kesey's La Honda party with the Pranksters and Hells Angels.[106] He had weapons around and his name *was* Hunter, but when he took acid at the Prankster party, he had a wonderful time: "I thought, aha, I've gone to the bottom of the well here and the animal's not down there, the one they said was there."[107] That was also the point of Duke's autobiographical Filmore anecdote—Duke concludes his reminiscence by ridiculing those who play it safe by never trying LSD. Thompson's point is that people have varied reactions to acid, but that some of the sensational stories circulating in the news media may be merely inventive propaganda.

The moral: the schlock of recognition triumphs over the shock of recognition, which was the theme of Tom Wolfe's essay, "The Shokkkkkk of Recognition," in *The Pump House Gang*. Wolfe satirizes the naïve whimsy of Natalie Wood, a beloved movie star, with regard to her impulsive appreciation of painters, poking fun at her narrow view of contemporary art. The extra five ks offer play on the idiom culture shockkkkkk. In this Warhol-like essay, Wolfe hammers the irony of a current media icon being ignorant of contemporary pop art while being a living incarnation of it.

This short chapter displays an artful link with the previous chapter, which had ended with the hissing of white noise on the television—that noise links up with an LSD pseudo-expert recalled in anecdote, the doctor humming to block the narrator out, just as the white noise television becomes a symbol of noncommunication for Duke and his lawyer to block each other out (microcosmic personal metaphor to macrocosmic national symbol), much like the way the discourse on drugs by the government "expert" was transformed into a stumbling block as the government criminalized all the good drugs, creating a moral muddle: prohibition criminalizing what is good or harmless. The anecdotal interlude about the era of marvelous music sits bracketed in recollected nostalgia framed by the menacing hiss for Duke's Sunday morning sermon on the moment when "the energy of a whole generation comes to a head in a long fine flash."[108] As impromptu historian, Duke finds the two situations, so-then and so-now, five years later, bleakly baffling—but it's clear the book nails the epitaph of the Sixties.

The wave moment crystallizes a retrospective, backward look. Fitzgerald saw this Western backward look as the secret of Twain's success: "Huckleberry Finn took the first journey *back*. He was the first to look *back* at the republic from the perspective of the West. . . . And because he turned back we have him forever."[109] Yet Thompson's Western perspective was that the new optimism for reform and renewal never moved successfully out of the West into the rest of a country more set in its conformity as well as in its fear of the future. Like most novels, *The Rum Diary* had been situated to relate a story of the past that looked toward the future. Thompson was handling the situation from his ideal of attacking the problem from both angles: thinking as well as action.

Duke/Thompson's diagnosis tags the tide: exploration has collapsed into the need for self-preservation. In his early life this danger was ever clearly on Thompson's mind as a danger that he sought to avoid, especially since he saw the economic structure of America as rotten because the country was "buttressed from within by moneyed fear. . . . The enemy is any man who is willing to take the necessary steps to protect his own short-term interests—now or later, often never admitting it even to himself, rarely understanding his own implications, and always a little too human for any moral censure except in the name of fate and expediency."[110] This perception roughly accords with Jean-Paul Sartre's concept of engagement as an aspect of social justice. The book's chapter 7 provided the *action* climax of part I, while chapter 8 analyzes the post-coital *thought* meditation on what actions have happened.

Chapter 9, "No Sympathy for the Devil," referring to the Rolling Stones mega-hit, identifies a lack of mercy in the legal system for druggies. It opens with a complaint about Sidney Zion from *Scanlan's* not honoring his expenses as well as about the hotel room-service bill (as if Duke had caught a social disease). Duke itemizes a litany of preposterous tourist gewgaws that he purchases for no apparent reason other than to squander money for which he may (or may not) be reimbursed.

Duke then dumps the symbolic hoard of stolen hotel soap into the convertible, cramming the soap into every crevice, including the glove compartment, chanting to himself "it's all mine," yet it was his lawyer who bribed the hotel maids to steal the 600 bars of soap. Duke asks himself how Horatio Alger would handle his situation, but Horatio Alger supposedly never indulged in petty theft—only hard work, the basis of the myth. This incident offers satire on the commonplace of people appropriating towels, soap, and linens from hotels.

In a monologue to an imaginary cop, Duke rationalizes his possession of a .357 Magnum: "It's *mine*. My risk, my gun." He has stolen the

gun from his attorney, having told Dr. Gonzo that he had sold the gun
back in Baker. This section provides a rather loose and improved version of what had happened in Las Vegas: "Oscar had left me there with
a pound of weed and a loaded .357 and some bullets in his briefcase."[111]
Acosta had forgotten his briefcase. This offers another instance of doubling in the novel: the cheap blue plastic suitcase of the hitchhiker
stuffed with innocence as opposed to the dangerous metallic case with a
felonious supply of drugs, gun, and bullets. But so much for the much-
vaunted arsenal of drugs in the car . . . and yet it appears that on the
road to Las Vegas they stopped in the desert to pick peyote pellets.

Raoul explains to the imaginary cop who stops him for speeding that
it was a little bearded fellow who gave him the gun in the desert,
offering to carve an X on his forehead in memory of Lieutenant Calley.
Charles Manson appeared in the courtroom as his own lawyer with an X
carved on his forehead. The bearded fellow, obviously Manson,
presents the murderous domestic equivalent of Calley. At the Sharon
Tate rental, the chief murderer was Manson's henchman Tex Watson,
who introduced himself to the household as the devil: "I am the Devil
and I'm here to do the Devil's business."[112] Beside these murdering
devils, Duke's petty thieving devilment appears to be small potatoes,
and his nervousness registers as amusing as his solipsistic self-justifica-
tion. The source of Raoul's insecurity appears to originate in the fear of
meeting a Manson Family member or imitator while he's traveling solo
in the desert where the Manson Family lived.

At this point in the narrative Raoul becomes unhinged by his loneliness, which his paranoia effectively dramatizes. In reviewing J. P. Donleavy's *A Singular Man* (1963), Thompson had declared Donleavy a
first-rate author because he "writes about loneliness with a deep and
tough-minded conviction."[113] The book achieves a brilliant balance between bantering camaraderie and haunting, solitary introspection.

The "Sympathy for the Devil" allusion also refers to the 1968 documentary movie of that title wherein the director, Jean-Luc Godard,
poses the argument that the only way to become a revolutionary is to
reject being an intellectual. This was the sort of clever idiocy that ap-
pealed to future Weathermen types but Thompson found solipsistic,
barbaric, abhorrent, and as a satirist, ripe for ridicule.

Jean-Luc Godard's film on the Rolling Stones' recording sessions for
"Sympathy for the Devil" features witty but tendentious (and some-

times obnoxious) satire akin to the themes of Thompson's novel. In the satiric documentary *Sympathy for the Devil*, Godard attacks Western propaganda, Stalin, Mao, the papacy, the Vietnam War, publishing, an obsessive flair for sensationalizing cultural violence, and the robotic junk rhetoric of the Black Panthers. The repeated attempts to record the song in the studio operate as a refrain: the lyrics cite varied historical incarnations of the devil with little reference to the present (except for the satiric comment that you are responsible for JFK's murder). In the film's most amusing sequence, "All About Eve," a reporter interviewing an actress declares: "It's impossible—psychologically impossible—for America to get out of Vietnam." The actress agrees. Godard asks the viewer to understand the Vietnam War as a devilish reincarnation of Nazism, a theme explored in the previous chapter of Thompson's novel.

Switching identities, the good "doctor of journalism" realizes that mid-Sixties optimism had been a delusion. Whitmer comments: "The Woodstock generation had been maimed, lost forever, because the LSD-induced optimism, the visions of a better world were erroneous."[114] Thompson shifts to documentary mode by assembling newspaper cuttings on the danger and depravity of drug misuse by social misfits with the attendant war anxiety that pits demonstrating youth against police, illustrating a further social breakdown. The first exhibit consists of a murdered woman overdosed on heroin, her body crudely stuffed into a refrigerator. The second, purportedly an AP wire, supplies a summary of House Subcommittee hearings on drug overdoses among soldiers that concludes that upper-echelon officers are involved in the drug trade. The third entry discusses American soldiers using torture. Congressional witnesses testify, describing the execution of prisoners by tossing them out of helicopters.

The documentation of such war crimes supports Thompson's motif of Nazi revival in America—the image of prisoners falling through space links up with the air-tumbling trapeze performers at Circus-Circus. The anecdote about the casual slaying of a Chinese translator working for the Americans targets racism—why the bother of an investigation, asks an officer: "She was just a slope, anyway."[115] This entry recalls the chapter subheading "Newsmen Tortured?"—it's "torture" for newsmen to expose and discuss in gruesome detail the use of torture by Americans.

Chapter 9 concludes with the heroic example of Muhammad Ali being sentenced to five years in prison for refusing to kill "slopes," a capsule anecdote that indicates the racial underbelly of the Vietnam holocaust. Ali understands what is happening, but racist generals do not. The third chapter subheading, "Flight into Madness," finds fulfillment with the example of Ali's reasonable and eloquent conscientious objection compared to the government's irrational and punitive decision to imprison the famous boxer—another example of torture, but this time domestic. Yet most Americans remained unconscious of the nightmare in which they sleep comatose. The "No" in "No Sympathy for the Devil" indicates no sympathy for those people unconcerned about atrocities, as well as no minor work of art in the vein of Godard's ponderous *jeu d'esprit*. Reminiscing about Godard's documentary, Keith Richards observes: "I think somebody slipped him [Godard] some acid and he went into that phony year of ideological overdrive."[116]

Chapter 10 begins the bridge to part II, the special drug convention for cops. Plagued with paranoia about doing a long stretch in prison for possession of an arsenal of drugs, Duke retrieves his car for departure only to learn that in the wacko lottery of journalism, he has scored a second assignment. This information leads to an aimless drive on the outskirts of the city while he absorbs and digests the unlikely shock of good Lady Luck in the whimsical game of journalism, concluding with the understandable dire need for an early morning Sunday beer to celebrate his new assignment. At a desert bar he does a mildly meditative paranoid riff on Bob Dylan's 1966 "Stuck Inside of Mobile with the Memphis Blues Again" from the *Blonde on Blonde* album (1966).

Thompson's friend Tom Wolfe had evoked that same song when he concluded his final essay, "Sliding Down into the Behavioral Sink," in *The Pump House Gang* (1969), which lamented the "bombed out" condition of Manhattan Harlem fallen into ugly and treacherous dilapidation. In a letter to Silberman, Thompson had even suggested "whacking out a Thompson version of *The Pump House Gang*."[117] Thompson lays out a considerably more extended riff on the Dylan theme than Wolfe, yet to put Wolfe's essay next to Thompson's leaves a reader with a dual diptych of sociological and moral decay on both the urban East Coast and rural West Coast. There existed something of a mutual admiration society in the genial correspondence between Thompson and Wolfe.

Duke resolves to scream back to Los Angeles at 120 miles an hour in order to find out who won the Mint 400 race and to deliver the carload of Neutrogena soap to Malibu, then return to Las Vegas. Driving a flashy red car out of Las Vegas on the only road to L.A. with weed and a stolen gun, while passing the huge billboard at the city limit that says "Attention, 20 years for marijuana," stokes Thompson's real-life paranoia.

The concluding monologue parades a stock confession of guilt to the Lord on a Sunday morning, as if a backsliding Raoul has suddenly converted to Roman Catholicism (he wants a *priest*) or has succumbed to frontier revivalist fever. In a hysteric moment of prayerful blasphemy, the Lord is called "an evil bastard!" If Raoul's prayer is not answered, then God will have to answer to him! This trash-talk parody-rap as prayer depicting the satirist as succumbing to what he satirizes reprises the concluding strategy of the *Hell's Angels* postscript.

Chapter 12, as if there are twelve testimonial raps with attendant miracles included, cites Kesey's Bible—"Tune in, freak out, get beaten."[118] This aphorism is another goof, there being no Kesey Bible. Thompson jokingly references Herman Hesse's novella, *The Journey to the East* (1932), the sacred text of the Merry Pranksters on their cross-country journey to the Eastern states. Thompson had no use for Eastern spirituality any more than Western religion, consistently denying psychedelics had any relevancy to religion. Tom Wolfe's *The Electric Kool-Aid Acid Test* (1969) eloquently chronicled Kesey's holy fool antics on his cross-country bus trip, culminating in a prison stretch, which was the reason why Duke had prison so obsessively on his mind.

The epilogue features a dubious, speculative, psychological lecture on how to deal with highway cops from a man with wide experience in the field, and highlights Duke's chronic demented paranoia. "Highway 61" in the chapter heading refers to Bob Dylan's 1965 song, "Highway 61 Revisited," on the Legacy label, referring to the highway connecting Duluth, Minnesota, where Dylan grew up, to New Orleans. Five verses describe the surreal plight of several African Americans as God's children, absurdly harassed on the highway of life by persecuting police; between each verse Dylan blows on an imitation police whistle.[119] The chapter heading alludes to this musical motif; the reader should imagine riffs from Dylan's siren whistle as background noise to Duke's discursive monologue while he travels Highway 15 between Las Vegas and Los Angeles fearing police harassment and possible imprisonment.

Duke gives a nod to the Great Magnet as if he were a drifting piece of metal detritus in the great desert. He manages to reconnect with his "Samoan" lawyer by phone, and takes a break in another bar. Duke feels inspired to order a better choice of beverage in Ballantine ale, a favorite of both Hemingway and Thompson, described as "a very mystic long shot," rather unknown west of Newark, hoping to embarrass the bartender and put him on the defensive, a well-known tactic to prep an apologetic barkeep for the much-coveted future free round. Ian Ballantine, founder and president of Ballantine books, had taken a long shot "mystic" hunch on financially backing Thompson for his book on the Hells Angels.[120] When the bartender quickly serves up the ale in a matter-of-fact manner, Duke interprets this as a sign that his luck has definitely changed for the better—that on a second trip to Las Vegas, he will be coasting coolly and not sweating in paranoia. After Ballantine's backing Thompson's luck had changed, launching him on the path of a lucrative career, although that book did not at first prosper.

While there is no hope in praying to God or hope of redemption from the implacable law, there lies a smidgen of hope for personal redemption in the precarious grind of journalism, where the next random bartender will magically function as ersatz seer—a Thompson motif now serialized in Current TV's *Bar Karma*. The earnest and dull lawyer Duke converses with while in the bar admiringly assures Duke of his coming good luck, and then modestly confesses he's the local county prosecutor. Duke's good fortune ironically receives the seal of official confirmation as he pictures himself as criminal druggy with a carload of illegal drugs, casually chatting with the official opposition, the enemy who would clap him in jail, as was done with Thompson's friend Ken Kesey.

Thompson posted a draft of the book's first part to his friend Tom Wolfe, boasting that "Raoul Duke is pushing the frontiers of 'new journalism.'"[121] Thompson also confesses to attempting to find some "academic-type justification for the Mind-Warp/Photo approach."[122] This indicates that Thompson, like Wolfe, was intent on developing new techniques as well as encoding message layers for an academic audience (in addition to the populist audience he was intent on building), which somewhat accounts for his overly repetitious name-dropping of one

Horatio Alger throughout both sections of the novel. Wolfe had included a hortatory Horatio Alger motif in "Bob and Spike" from *The Pump House Gang*: a true "folk heroes" tale of an impoverished taxi driver and his devoted wife, who collect offbeat modern art (Jasper Johns and others), becoming multimillionaires as well as achieving the unlikely social status of being Manhattan stars famous for their trendy, slightly bohemian soirees. In his letter Thompson makes clear his intent to blur the line between journalism and fiction as much as he can, a technique fundamental to the book.

Justifying the book as a novel continues to be easier than accepting the book as a work of journalism, even under the lame rubric of "New Journalism." The blending of fact and fiction in either memoir or autobiography presents nothing new, as memoirs and autobiographies have often sought to mythologize authors, friends, or social periods. A teasing blend of fact and fiction in an American novel that prefigures the approach of New Journalism can be found in Jim Tully's populist *Blood on the Moon* (1931), the emotional story of an orphan who becomes a prizefighter and then writer, where embroidery enhances a novel based on bedrock autobiography, similar to the way Carlos Fuentes's novel *Diana, The Solitary Hunter* (1994) handles autobiography that fictionalizes the author's affair with actress Jean Seberg, the star of Truffaut's film *Breathless* (1960). Life has always intruded upon fiction, but when the blend becomes sensational, controversy arises. Thompson's biographer William McKeen cites Henry Miller's *Tropic of Cancer* (1934) as the stylistic model that Thompson adopted for his own blending of fact and fiction.[123] Miller's later version of those same years, portrayed at greater length and verbosity in *Sexus* (1949), contains episodic passages of effective, absurd humor, but the book ultimately fails precisely because of its banal accuracy in its depiction of sordid events.

In *The Pump House Gang* Wolfe articulated four rubrics of the New Journalism, although he disapproved of the label, since anything new grows old. The traits are: (1) a clear scene-by-scene construction rather than general narrative; (2) a point of view that should emanate from a character's consciousness; (3) allowing extended dialogue develop character; and (4) journalistic detail in manners and the itemization of milieu, as one finds in novels of realism. For Wolfe many of those details revolved around status signals. Yet Wolfe might well have added a fifth rubric—his sense of outlandish, ironic wit, an endearing quirk he

shared with Thompson and Norman Mailer. Thompson's Mind-Warp/
Photo offers his tag for trait one. The Mittyesque monologue insertions
apply trait two. The sidekick, functionary, or random interaction with
someone covers trait three. For the fourth trait Thompson substitutes
the façade of journalistic work as it combines with the surrealistic novel,
rather the novel of French and American Realism that Wolfe so admired and was to revive in his Savonarola-inspired *Bonfire of the Vanities* (1988), *A Man in Full* (1999), and *I Am Charlotte Simmons* (2005).
Thompson was more comfortable and familiar with the novelistic tradition of South American surrealism, first inspired by Lautremont's prose
poem *Les Chants de Maldoror* (1869), which featured the wandering
manic rants of its hysterical narrator.

The paranoia about a possible drug bust firmly links the two halves
of the novel, the second half beginning: "About 20 miles east of Baker I
stopped to check the drug bag."[124] He proceeds to shoot at nothing in
the vacant desert and imagines a comic interior monologue interview
with a highway patrol cop. The loss of hope and love in the American
Dream in the first part of the novel will now shift to a focus on guns and
violence in America, the darker side of what that loss will lead to. After
an imaginary interior monologue by a druggist from whom Duke purchases booze and ether, he steals a journal. An article about someone
under the influence of PCP (an animal tranquilizer) who has plucked
out his eyes while in jail is reproduced. The article on lost eyesight
illustrates that the culture itself functions inherently along paranoid
lines, because the victim was arrested for walking in the nude. For that
most heinous crime, he was locked up by a paranoid society; under the
depressing confines of jail with the assistance of bad drugs, he went
temporarily insane, with the result that he lost his eyes. The prospect of
legally categorizing any "unconventional" forms of erratic behavior to
be a prison offense offers anthropological evidence of cultural insanity.
No medical assistance is given to a person in need of it, but after the
self-mutilation doctors attempt a futile operation to restore sight, the
victim now becoming a medical guinea pig. Yet the larger irony squints:
the culture (and probably the readers of the article) lumbers blind to
the institutional insanity it inhabits—that insanity resembles a monstrous prison madhouse.

Duke offers no commentary other than throwing the journal away,
but the lack of verbal commentary supplies an effective technique for

drawing attention to the symbolic cultural decay of the barbaric society described in the anecdote. Did this happen in Borneo? While Duke may be impatient and disgusted with what he sees around him, as well as being a manic, boasting narcissist, he's not half as intelligent as Thompson. This journal article supplies pseudo-documentary—the piece may as well have been written by Jorge Luis Borges, so deep are the artful ironies in this carefully contrived fiction that appears as a toss-away off a drugstore rack in the middle of a desert. It's a good example of an aristocratic Italian Renaissance form—*sprezzatura*, the art of appearing effortlessly casual as one performs a difficult task. As with the case of really good fiction, it summarily describes reality better than mere reporting.

Duke swaps his rented red shark convertible for a sumptuous white Cadillac convertible. The cultural depravity of Las Vegas conjures a Charles Manson theme: mass murderers would be happily welcome in the city if they have plenty of money. Duke has no money, but back in the old days (before the instant intrusiveness of computer servers) his canceled credit cards worked at both the car rental and the Flamingo Hotel, which turns away prepaid registered cops due to overbooking, yet Duke's bankrupt American Express gold card works its mojo magic as he conspires with the hotel clerk to insult the prepaid cops. Fraud works even better than prepaid cash.

Boasting that his credentials to the drug convention are fraudulent, Duke repeats the Derby clubhouse theme, neither claim being true. Duke had received a telegram from his lawyer giving him the assignment, yet in a letter to Lynn Nesbit Thompson, he says that Jann Wenner has no idea that he's doing the drug convention, but he thinks it's safe to *assume* that *Rolling Stone* will accept such an article if he submits it.[125] Wenner may have been noncommittal because of possible expenses, but it was Felton at *Rolling Stone* who had informed Thompson of the police drug Convention, suggesting that he might be interested in covering it in order to expand the Vegas story into a book: "We weren't trying to get him to write a novel," said Felton. "It just came together naturally."[126] This fantasy telegram indicates that his so-called Samoan lawyer is mostly a fictionalized element of Thompson's ego, although Oscar's grotesque dialogue in the novel was literally derived from tape recordings Thompson secretly made during their Las Vegas trip—another blur in the line between fiction and journalism.

When Acosta's son Marco read the novel, he found it difficult to put his father in context because he couldn't see "how it was any different from reality."[127] Since Oscar's speech and behavior were on the tapes, any lawsuit would have been a humiliating circus, which is why Oscar had so quickly come to an agreement with Wenner, although even after the settlement when he saw the astonishing success of his friend's book, he continued to bitterly harbor fantasies of a lawsuit based upon the idea of coauthorship.[128]

The chapter functions as a reply to Wolfe's "The Automated Hotel" from *The Pump House Gang*. In that satiric sketch Wolfe ridiculed how computers had turned hotels, traditionally reputed to be based on the rapport of personal customer service, into impersonal machines. Thompson's hotel check-in chapter exposes a flaw in that new mechanized system—the story of how Duke evades the system with his savvy and charm, but such computerized delays on the health status of credit cards are now as distant as the dust clouds of Western Union horse messengers.

Duke declares the difference between the two reportorial assignments: the Mint 400 was an *observer* assignment, reflections on events and environment; the drug convention would be a *participant* gig, a comment that announces a change in technique and style, especially a shift from the muted pastels of interior monologue to a more phantasmagoric surrealism with a bolder painter's palette. Nick Carraway in *The Great Gatsby* operates as an observer narrator as opposed to an action narrator, say, in Conrad's *The Heart of Darkness* or the active, engaged narrators of Hemingway's novels. From Scribner's, Maxwell Perkins wrote to Fitzgerald after receiving the manuscript:

> You adopted exactly the right method of telling it, that of employing a narrator who is more of a spectator than an actor: this puts the reader upon a point of observation on a higher level than that on which the characters stand and at a distance that gives perspective. In no other way could your irony have been so immensely effective, nor the reader have been enabled so strongly to feel the strangeness of human circumstances in a vast heedless universe. In the eyes of Dr. Eckleberg various readers will see different significances; but their presence gives a superb touch to the whole thing: great unblinking eyes, expressionless, looking down on the human scene. It's magnificent![129]

That wan Lucretian-inspired gloom floating through music, parties, empty conversation, and billboards conveys powerful understatement that narrative distance supports. For the spectacle at Circus-Circus, Thompson achieves a reverse-distance equivalency to the billboard advertisement of T. J. Eckleberg, optometrist: looking upward without glasses at the flying trapeze performers offers to the naked eye a dazzling, glittering perspective of flesh and wealth that makes the viewer feel small and confused in the "stadium" amphitheater offering a cacophony of sounds (boisterous conversation, roulette wheels spinning, screaming at dice tables, etc.) and disorienting spectacle centered on lust and gambling, the new entertainment equivalent of the Roman Coliseum at the heart of the American Dream.

While Fitzgerald satirizes the burgeoning vacuity of the Madison Avenue approach to achieving the American Dream, Thompson ridicules the empty emotional spectacle in the marriage of lust and money—a crass and gross attempt to ground the American Dream in the vices satirized by Dante in his *Inferno*, a nightmare that in its fiscal depravity and hollow spectacle remains stubbornly antithetical to civilized reflection, as well as oblivious to art.

6

FEAR IN THE NATION

Las Vegas, Part II

They've all come to look for America.—Simon & Garfunkel

In the first half of *Fear and Loathing in Las Vegas*, Thompson underwrites, offering nuanced subtlety, musical allusions, symbolic happenings; the second half of the novel will feature the action narrator embroiled in the immediacy of emotion, immersed in overstatement rather than understatement, caught not in the plight of his daydreaming but in the closing brass vise of a greater political tragedy, the coming doom of an Orwellian police state that functions as a machine without knowing what it's doing. The lawyer and Duke will be mocking representatives from the drug culture, to bear living testimony, as if they were near-psychoreligious proselytizers intent on self-satisfying witness performance through merely being their disoriented and dysfunctional drug-addled selves.

Duke discovers young Lucy, "one of the more manic and frightening sections of the book,"[1] with his lawyer in the room, the antithesis of "Lucy in the Sky with Diamonds" (a popular acronym for LSD from the Beatles song, yet that acronym is not apparently the origin of the song): "Lucy's a mute Jesus freak sporting a famous boxer's square chin." Duke entertains the idea of turning Lucy into a prostitute,[2] offering a fantasy rap of selling her to the cops for fifty dollars a head so they can beat her and gangbang her. This somewhat nasty joke will become apparent (or meanly amusing) in retrospect only when the reader discovers who Lucy represents, as an allegory.

Duke fears Lucy to be a potential prison ticket and engages in colorful trash-talk to make it clear she should leave. Repelled by her pretensions to sketch, Duke prevails by arguing possible kidnapping or Mann Act charges (which indicates that she's under eighteen, as this act was most commonly used to prosecute men with underage girls), leading to the horror of disbarment for the lawyer, which was close to the truth because Acosta was up on drug charges for possession of about thirty amphetamine pills in connection with a speeding ticket.[3]

One might initially conjecture that the Lucy episode presents a satire on Vladimir Nabokov's *Lolita* (1955), yet Thompson appears to have held the work in awe as mere journalistic autobiography,[4] not understanding the book's deep European roots or Russian aristocratic disdain for Freud.[5] While Nabokov loathes driving automobiles on roads, Thompson revels in gunning the engine anywhere. Nabokov exhibits a comic horror for middle-class motels and hotels, which "victimize" Humbert with their shabbiness, while Thompson appropriates working-class pride while performing a con job on the most expensive resorts and thoroughly trashing their rooms. Lucy is a runaway waif, not an adopted daughter. Duke ridicules his lawyer's lust, mentioning the Mann Act, about which Nabokov famously declared in *Lolita*: "I deplore the Mann Act as lending itself to a dreadful pun, the revenge that the Gods of Semantics take against tight-zippered Philistines."[6] Although there's a red convertible in *Lolita*, the one technical ingredient they have most in common is the use of interior monologue within a Jekyll-and-Hyde dialectic that expands into ironic innuendo.

But Thompson's satiric target is not Nabokov, who detested symbols and allegories.[7] While Robert Louis Stevenson's employment of the drug theme charts the tragic decline and degradation of a middle-class drug indulger, Thompson's underclass heroes offer a comic drama of how drugs enhance and enlighten users, yet just as the good-evil dialectic of schizophrenia in Jekyll-Hyde leads to individual suicide, the schizophrenia of the parasitic and symbiotic (good-evil) relationship between the government and underworld gangsters (who control the drug trade) will lead to collective suicide for the nation.

This episode of a wayward teenage drifter looking for random sex somewhat resembles the episode of "Stark Naked" in chapter 6 of Tom

Wolfe's *The Electric Kool-Aid Acid Test*, wherein the Merry Pranksters discover they have a lunatic runaway on their hands and that LSD offers no assistance. According to Wolfe, Stark Naked departs from the Pranksters into the night desert; in contrast, Thompson's Lucy doesn't want to leave the hotel room. The physical description of Lucy appears to be the antithesis of Barbra Streisand, of whom Lucy ineptly sketches charcoal portraits from television; Stark Naked had an abandoned child, while Lucy slinks underage and single. Thompson does not satirize Wolfe, but runs parallel.

The portraits of Barbara Streisand with "teeth like baseballs, eyes like jellied fire," a verbal cartoon, evokes the horror of bad drugs as much as incompetent drawing and links with Donleavy's Dangerfield metaphor of men like horses with mad eyes and fanged teeth. The horse motif relates to the conclusion of the first chapter, in which a man was arrested for walking nude; he had put out his eyes when on both and LSD and PCP (commonly called angel dust, a tranquilizer for horses developed by Parke-Davis). Thompson highlights this mad, arbitrary mixing of drugs in cocktail fashion as a future sociological nightmare.

The nightmare continues today with ever more insane cocktail mixtures, often labeled designer drugs—*krokodil* (crocodile), a mixture of codeine, gasoline, iodine, paint thinner, hydrochloric acid, and red phosphorous, currently ravages Siberia.[8] Thompson has updated Donleavy's metaphor of men like crazed horses to include women, expanding on Donleavy's cynicism and sociology. At the conclusion of *The Ginger Man*, Mary willingly accepts Dangerfield as a crazed and dangerous man, prepared to risk her life for him, desirous of children by him at the conclusion. In Thompson's novel the possibility of love and children does not even rate the fevered desperation recorded by Donleavy.

We may assume that this Lucy episode presents Thompson's fiction as a friendly comic over-going (in the Renaissance sense of improving on the work of others) of Wolfe's fiction. Larry McMurtry claims Stark Naked fled his house in the nude and neighbors called the police; McMurtry bailed her out, took care of her, and sent her back home.[9] Wolfe's fictional version underscores the dangerous sociological epidemic of unstable daydreamers searching for alternative authority figures in the counterculture to guide them out of whatever family impasse or slump they find themselves caught in. For Thompson, this theme nicely dovetails into his double mention of Charles Manson (*Rolling Stone* had won a 1970 National Magazine Award for its Manson coverage) who had a group of such disoriented young girls in his fateful entourage. This extended anecdote with Lucy adds amusing melodrama, yet its excitable presence offers another indication that the book sails as a novel posing as journalism.

Ken Kesey followed Wolfe and Thompson in offering a symbolic journalistic essay on the menace of drugs and underclass criminal opportunists in the immediate aftermath of 1970 Woodstock, amid his reflections on the death of Neal Cassady in a 1979 *Esquire* article, "The Death of Superman,"[10] which belatedly sounded an alarm as it portrayed two menacing drifters and the near-allegorical story of how Cassady, the legendary natural Nietzschean *Übermensch* of the Beats, died as a nihilistic egomaniac counting railroad ties, suggesting that there were in fact limits to the self-creating power of the will. Kesey was agreeing with Thompson that the Woodstock spirit was definitely stillborn and that the criminalization of marijuana, hashish, and psychedelics was preposterous, yet objecting that the Nietzschean philosophy behind many Beats was a form of moral bankruptcy—that the cynical individuality of bad ego-fueled drugs leads to a relativism that dispenses with all philosophy as well as religion, inhibiting the necessary hope of artistic creativity. Thompson was not interested in either religion or philosophy, but merely in being a Superman character delivering moral critique rooted in effective mocking irony. In terms of philosophy, Thompson was a thorough disciple of Lucretius, believing only in the possibility of personal love and the reality of chance—hence his lifelong obsession with sports and betting.

The Lucy episode mildly supports the nightmare hippie vision from chapter 6, where Duke imagines dozing in the Mint Hotel while outside his window a vicious Nazi drunkard appears screaming "gibberish at the world: "*Woodstock Über Alles!*"[11] This hallucination presents a self-caricaturing cartoon that projects Thompson's own impossible subconscious fantasy that the Woodstock spirit would rule the world through fascism—that is, Woodstock idealism would in time disintegrate into its own vicious caricature and endemic violent intolerance, just as all idealism eventually degenerates into its opposite.

As with Fitzgerald,[12] a Spengler-like pessimism of apocalyptic cycles permeates Thompson's view of history. Duke confesses that ascetics who practice the ongoing art of continuous drug hallucination are brave veterans at coping with even greater nightmares like "seeing your dead grandmother crawling up your leg with a knife in her teeth."[13] The comic hallucination of possible castration by one's grandmother contrasts with the lawyer's predatory indulgence in seducing the under-age girl attracted to Broadway stardom (just as Broadway had corrupted West Egg in *The Great Gatsby*)—it was this concocted fictional scene that must have most angered Acosta, yet there was the matter of his upcoming drug trial for amphetamines and the depiction of extravagant drug consumption in the novel.

Duke taunts his attorney over a speculative charge of kidnapping Lucy, saying he would get the gas chamber like Caryl Chessman, a presumed serial rapist and petty robber in San Francisco who was charged with kidnapping for pulling a seventeen-year-old girl a few yards from her car to demand and receive oral sex; consequently, he was charged with kidnapping, which made him eligible for the death penalty. Chessman, who under coercion that he called torture, had signed a brief confession, but even on his last day before execution he denied being the infamous "Red Light Bandit," and wrote several books while he lingered on death row. He was convicted in 1948 and brought to the San Quentin gas chamber in 1960.[14]

The lawyer asserts he was only trying to *help* her. Duke smiles, replying "That's what Fatty Arbuckle said, and you know what they did to him."[15] Arbuckle, who Caruso said had the second greatest singing voice in the world, worked as a silent comedian, one of Hollywood's highest paid actors. In 1921 he hosted a raucous party at the St. Francis Hotel. At the party a minor, actress Virginia Rappe, became ill, dying a few days later. Arbuckle was later accused of raping and murdering her. After three sensational trials he was acquitted, but his career was ruined. The jury took only six minutes to acquit him, yet five minutes were spent writing an apology to Arbuckle for the absurd charges brought against him. Between court costs and Prohibition fines for serving alcohol, he was ruined, losing his house and car. He was banned from making films, but toward the end of his short life made a brief comeback.[16] The attorney doesn't follow the reference to Arbuckle, but

Duke briefly sketches what an average jury would think after finding out that he gave Lucy backrubs under the influence of LSD.

His counselor suddenly agrees, saying, "Shit, it doesn't pay to try to help somebody these days,"[17] thus reluctantly coming around to Duke's Nietzschean prescriptions on Judeo-Christian morals, which he had previously eschewed as decadent and nihilistic, a perspective antithetical to the Christianity espoused by the comic duo in *Don Quixote*, whereby Cervantes ridicules absolute idealism but implicitly argues for the wisdom of a moderated, practical idealism.

Joan Didion's 1970 novel, *Play It as It Lays*, achieved notable literary success as well as becoming a best seller. Antiheroine Maria Wyeth, a schizophrenic *player* (an actress and model in the game of men), suffers from severe mental instability after an illegal abortion (from which she expected to die) and the stress of coping with a four-year-old daughter hospitalized for acute spinal problems with "a chemical in her brain." Maria lives a promiscuous and nihilistic life, seeing life through the lens of her father, a larger-than-life gambler. She's made two films: an art film and a commercial success, *Angel Beach*, in which she plays a young girl gang-raped by a certain motorcycle gang in a film that satirizes upper-class slumming and sensationalizes underclass behavior. This scene alludes to the Carolyn Cassady toolshed gangbang at Kesey's famous shindig, depicted in Thompson's *Hell's Angels*.

In a novel of fast-paced slices from her upper-class life, we watch Maria (pronounced Mar-eye-ah as in the song about the wind) popping pills, career through the desert at seventy or eighty miles per hour in a Corvette with the radio on, playing with her life, yet not intent on suicide like her part-time homosexual lover, BZ, who overdoses deliberately on the drug Seconal while he's with her. Drunk driving, haunting nightmares, and a symbolic Las Vegas, the new Babylon, are plot highlights. Maria's estranged husband is shooting a movie near Las Vegas. When he takes the completed movie to the Cannes Film Festival, Maria stays in Las Vegas. She doesn't gamble but, too listless to leave the city, contemplates the life of her gambling father. Las Vegas is also part of her truant adolescent memories of running off with wild boys.

Maria has difficulty reading road signs: it's clear she's on the apocalyptic road to nowhere land. The giant red T sign for a Thriftimart, in whose parking lot she meets the abortionist doctor, allegorizes as a synthesis of Hawthorne and Fitzgerald: the tall red T standing for trollop, as in Hawthorne's adulterous red A; the visual T for reproductive tract where the abortion will occur functions as a sign of sterility, like the Dr. Eckleberg optometrist sign in Fitzgerald, referencing Eliot's *Wasteland* theme. That same wasteland theme occurs in part I of Thompson's novel with the monstrous, blinking neon sign outside their Vegas hotel room. The sign blocks the view of the mountains. Duke describes it as a big machine in the sky, some kind of electric snake coming at them, and his lawyer advises him to shoot it. Duke calmly replies he wants to study its habits first. His lawyer requests that Duke must stop talking about snakes, lizards, and that kind of stuff.

William Stephenson analyzes this passage as a reversal riff of Franz Kafka's 1915 story "The Metamorphosis." Instead of internalizing the insect metaphor, Thompson externalizes and multiplies it. The world, not the subject, becomes monstrous. Rather than repressing alienation like Gregor Samsa, Duke externalizes it through an acid hallucination, the favorite form of hip counterculture humor. Immersed in paranoid terror, Duke aggressively babbles to the hotel clerk: "Unlike Samsa, a classic salaryman, the ex-hippie Duke wants to, but cannot, reject his place in society." Samsa's problems are primarily intimately familial, while Duke's are impersonally social—the anonymous hotel, not one's bedroom, becomes the scene of the horror.[18]

When the female clerk informs Duke that his room is not yet ready but someone is looking for him, then hands him an envelope, Duke's paranoia explodes: he says he hasn't done anything *yet* (perceiving himself guilty as a habitual "criminal" because of his use of drugs), then sees the clerk transformed into a moray eel with fangs. Lunging back in frightened horror, the lawyer grabs Duke and accepts the bland envelope which has a note from Lacerda, Duke's assigned photographer for the bike race.[19] It's an amusing comic scene—satire on paranoid bad trips became a chronic staple of hippie humor: the lesson was always to keep your cool and not overreact to anything that happens, not to prejudge others through projection. Yet it was the pseudo-guilt derived from the use of an illegal drug that made such terror possible—it's an anecdote about cultural persecution, not familial, as in the case of Samsa.

The scene illustrates the improper approach to acid by allowing the acid to victimize the user. The follow-up scene in the hotel room depicts Duke overcoming his paranoia and correctly coping with acid by being mellow and cool. This was the use concept behind Aldous Huxley's vision of a utopian society mellowed by the use of psychedelics in his novel *The Island* (1962). Here the lawyer and Duke reverse roles as the electric-snake sign becomes a cultural sign that must be decoded, obviously as the snake in the garden, neon commercialism being the snake. The tawdriness of the neon sign also evokes the title of Algren's great collection of short stories, *The Neon Wilderness* (1948), about down-and-out drifters (often drug-addicted) in a rooming house. The literary allusion places the reader's expectations in such an inferno.

Thompson doubles the sign motif by referring to a second sign that causes fear and near-panic in both halves of the novel. The sign announcing the possible lifetime penalty for possession of marijuana (twenty years was the minimum sentence) had a second over-sign with black background and white letters reading: "Don't Gamble with Marijuana." The sentence sign sported a vibrant red background. This sign points to the Wasteland theme of a senseless war on drugs that continues today, especially with the banning of medical benefits of marijuana, which provides important therapy for glaucoma sufferers, millions of cancer victims, and those tragically burdened by dementia.

As in *The Great Gatsby*, music in Didion's novel offers glancing allusions or contrasts to the novel's plot: Les Paul and Mary Ford's "How High the Moon," Cole Porter's "I Get a Kick Out of You," Jo Stafford's "You Belong to Me," Dusty Springfield's "Son of a Preacher Man," Roger Miller's "King of the Road," and the Blood, Sweat, and Tears hit, "Spinning Wheel," evoking fickle Fortuna. The last three, more current songs point to a rootless world anchored in chance, while the earlier three songs register more social stability and a more romantic morality. Thompson replies to this East–West timeline dialectic in terms of highlighting East Coast Fifties optimism as against current prophetic hip pessimism circulating on the West Coast.

Influenced by Nathaniel West's *The Day of the Locust*, Didion's novel portrays Hollywood as a false idol, an amoral Wasteland, echoing T. S. Eliot and F. Scott Fitzgerald. The understated, bleak satire of the realist painter Andrew Wyeth, who painted rural farms and tragic families in the Northeast and Midwest, receives desert hues in this imagistic novel built on snippet monologues and a montage of scene-swerving slides. The novel bounces back and forth between New York and Los Angeles with an East Egg, West Egg rhythm of recollected anecdotes.

While the main character is schizophrenic, a lost soul in the wilderness in need of religious direction, we may sympathize with her plight but not identify with her; she becomes an advertisement for all the ills of secular culture, especially the disintegration of marriage and family values. Nonetheless, Maria continues to be committed to playing the game of life, whatever its consequences, believing all consequences to be wantonly irrational. In the second part Duke drives a Cadillac Eldorado, as does Maria's alienated husband, Carter. There are many parallel themes between the Didion and Thompson novels. Thompson's brand of nihilism remains not far from the restless highway traveled by a disenchanted Maria, yet Didion displays none of Thompson's Rabelaisian spirit.

Even the first sentence of Thompson's part II evokes the town of Baker, which finds citation in Didion's novel. The comic lizard phobia that afflicts Duke provides a parody of Maria's traumatic snake phobia in the opening pages of *Play It as It Lays*. The lizards are "loaded with poison." Didion describes the two glands of neurotoxin poison in coral snakes on the first page of her novel and tells the story, purportedly published in the Los Angeles *Herald-Examiner*, of two Detroit honeymooners discovered dead in their camper outside of Boca Raton. Didion's journalistic parable symbolizes how the serpent of promiscuous sex had destroyed contemporary marriage. Thompson would have dismissed such a moral appeal as nostalgic Puritanism—the shooting of the lizards offers Thompson's parody of Didion's Edenic parable, a phallic destruction of Didion's corny sex symbols. Perhaps this highly visual, literary yet metaphoric "shooting" of Didion's novel planted the conceptual seeds of what Thompson later called his Gonzo art collection, the framing of political campaign posters after they were blasted in Jackson Pollack fashion by his shotgun, selecting only the most arresting scatter-shot patterns for public sale.

While Didion's austere demotic style daubs in the traditional representative tradition with a postmodern minimalistic brush, Thompson's response to Didion's satire on rich, emancipated women remains boisterously comic in the tradition of male adolescent humor. Didion numbers her chapters, the numbers remain meaningless, as is fitting for the novel's aesthetic and philosophy, merely an aspect of Maria's claim that everything leads nowhere; Thompson doubles or triple-headlines his chapters, playing with nuance and the sensational tabloid heritage. One reason for this may be that in the newspaper business journalists don't compose headlines—it's something left to specialists—yet as a writer Thompson fought for his own headlines, so each chapter contains multiple submission titles.

Both Thompson's and Didion's novels chart the desert as the world of chance, a feverish mirage where the shimmering horizon deceives and promises prospective gambles that may not be what they at first appear. Memories become debatable artifacts laden with solipsistic nuance. Pursuing sunshine, enigmatic silences, and fiesta, Maria, while considerably less sane, resembles both Hemingway's Lady Brett as well as Fitzgerald's Daisy, a synthesis with a Western twang. Thompson perceived Didion as an upper-class literary rival and a representative of the Hollywood circle that Thompson at the time was excluded from, unable to get his 450-page screenplay for *The Rum Diary* into production,[20] both unpublished novel and unproduced film script depicting his own contemporary version of a Hemingway-Fitzgerald synthesis of a heroine from the upper-class East Coast in the character of Chenault.

Play It as It Lays was serialized in *Cosmopolitan* in 1970 and published to acclaim later that same year. There was ample opportunity for Thompson to read the trendy novel by a fellow West Coast practitioner of the so-called New Journalism. And it's clear from the satire in the second chapter of Didion's novel that she had read *Hell's Angels*. Thompson probably took this as a challenge to be answered.

Just as Karl Kraus's satiric play *The Last Days of Mankind* (1915–1918) gains focus from depicting a famous narcissistic reporter by the name of Alice, Thompson's novel creates a greater sociological radius through his satire of Didion.

In the title essay of *Slouching Towards Bethlehem* (1968), Didion profiles the meaningless lives of teenage runaways in the Haight-Ashbury district: "This was not a traditional generational rebellion. At some point between 1946 and 1967 we had somehow neglected to tell these children the rules of the game we happened to be playing."[21] She appears shocked that high school dropouts are not articulate intellectuals. Complaining about the erratic behavior of teenagers, as well as their casual drug use, Didion never consumes any drugs (nor, apparently, has ever taken peyote or acid) with the stoned people she interviews; she manages to work in an anecdote about irresponsible hippies giving LSD to their five-year-old daughter and concludes her nightmare essay with the story of a three-year-old who starts a fire and then chews on an electrical cord.

Amid the ubiquity of the rootless drug culture, Didion continually laments all the bad acid trips people experience,[22] yet admits she composed her essay on a diet of gin and Dexedrine, the drug of choice by upper-class women, because it keeps off body fat. Unlike Plimpton, Thompson, or Wolfe, as a New Journalist, Didion is not a *participant* journalist and not even, as she admits in her preface, a camera eye (referencing Dos Passos). Her success as a reporter resides in being "temperamentally unobtrusive, and so neurotically inarticulate that people tend to forget that my presence runs counter to their best interests."[23] This posits the wallflower approach to the New Journalism. While reading Didion, the reader is made acutely aware of both her message and her arduous efforts in composition; Thompson disguises and hides his work as an artist with dazzling surface comedy, making close reading a decoding of amusing puzzles.

Didion's doldrums and despair derive from an acute awareness of atomization in recording these meaningless lives (as she acknowledges in the book's preface), hence the reference to Yeats, yet Yeats was an erratic mystic theist, not a Christian. Thompson was a true follower of Lucretius—discovering liberation and joy in the realization of atomization, while Didion found it disturbing and confusing. Thompson has ironically profiled Lucy as one of the young, irrelevant, hippie runaways Didion described in her essay, "Slouching Towards Bethlehem."

John Gregory Dunne, Didion's husband, cowrote with his wife a 1971 screenplay for *Play It as It Lays*. The 1972 movie starred Tuesday Weld, with Anthony Perkins as BZ. Dunne later (with Frank Pierson) wrote the script for *A Star Is Born* (1976), featuring their friend Barbra Streisand, who also starred in the 1981 movie made from John Gregory Dunne's novel *True Confessions* (1977), for which Dunne, once again, wrote the screenplay. While Streisand is never satirized, the Lucy satire may be read both as a friendly joking reply to Wolfe and a savage satire directed at Didion. The gender dialectic rivalry between Didion and Thompson may be perceived by some as adolescent: Do you want to cry with the girls or laugh with the guys? Depicting Episcopalian Didion as a young Jesus freak remains nearly too true to be satiric. Can you imagine the civil rights activist Oscar Acosta having Joan Didion as his secret mistress? Lucy must be dispensed with immediately . . .

After transferring Lucy to the Americana Hotel, via a decoy run to the airport where they turn the "drunken" girl over to a cabby, they happily dispense with her, paying in advance for her night at the hotel. They celebrate by chewing peyote pellets near sunset on the way back to the city.

Lucy has left a message at the desk for them to call her. She's in room 1600. Why 1600? 1600 Campus Drive, Los Angeles, is the address of Occidental College's most famous graduate, Richard M. Nixon. This type of trenchant, detailed satire sometimes makes people angry. Both Calvin and the Pope unsuccessfully hired assassins to eliminate the good priest Rabelais, who had satirized them, yet Cardinal du Bellay and his extended family successfully protected him. Arthur Schlesinger Jr., in a brief meditation on enemies, notes:

> The attacks by Joan Didion and her husband John Gregory Dunne also derive basically from their hatred of Kennedy. This dreadful couple has moved to New York, and we run into them from time to time. Didion is a viperish, whispering little creature, and in my view, a breathy faux-sensitive writer. He is a sour Irish drunk. Like O'Brien [Conor Cruise] and Hitchens [Christopher], they manage to find ways of insult in wholly irrelevant contexts.[24]

That was February 20, 1993, yet by December 10, 1997, Schlesinger and Didion were able to kiss and make up.[25]

Duke says he feels like Othello, with Dr. Gonzo as the villain Iago in the classic tragedy. Dr. Gonzo again vomits from the peyote, expressing the feeble wish that peyote should be cut with Rolaids or something. (While Acosta's vomiting appears as a joke, he'd had a serious ulcer condition since he was twenty-one that caused him to vomit frequently. Acosta refers to this condition in his autobiography,[26] and he was later hospitalized for ulcers in San Francisco in the spring of 1974.[27]) Duke, who has not vomited, cheerfully replies that Othello (Duke) used Dramamine (also a joke about Shakespeare's maritime Othello using Dramamine for his attacks of seasickness when making vigorous love to Desdemona). Duke is not making love to anyone, yet he regards Dr. Gonzo's sneaky attempt to redirect Lucy's sexual attraction to him as a monstrous conspiratorial betrayal.

They wash their hands of Lucy through a trash phone conversation, telling some preposterous lies to get her off their backs. The rootless and deceptive nature of these trash conversations parody Didion's style of dialogue in the protracted noncommunication conversations between husband and wife (Carter and Maria) depicted in Didion's novel, where each marital member remains ensconced in his or her own private world. Here Thompson also manages to impart an amusingly cynical leer to his tonal textures while he's parodying Didion's theme of social anomie, displacement, and marital lies with a bemused, supercilious irony. Thompson appears to judge Didion's social critique to be puerile, her style boring, and her upper-class milieu irrelevant. The Great Red Shark eats Corvettes in the desert dust. When a masterpiece employs allegorical satire, the work it antithetically ridicules glows fitfully with the firefly status of lesser immortality.

Duke conducts a ridiculous goof put-on with the hotel clerk, who tells Duke that the woman who called (Lucy) sounded very *disturbed*. Thompson tells the clerk that Lucy is their special *case study*, but he needs to get back to the real news where people are being killed on television (there was some astonishing live television coverage back then that had the effect of turning people against the Vietnam War), and please send the ice up for his Chivas Regal. Acosta complains that there's been no interesting news for the past three hours. Thompson's final dismissal of Didion consists of the critique that at a time of war, the established literary community hails a novel about social anomie among the privileged elite. For Thompson such an ivory-tower academic exercise in the face of war and the national assassinations of political leaders constitutes an ultimate symptom of deranged cultural decadence.

Like Thompson, Didion, although with a different tone, had thrust herself into the narrative of the story, chatting with people and sharing her personal thoughts. When she wrote her Points West column for the revived *Saturday Evening Post*, one of her columns, "I'm Going to Be a Movie Star," empathetically profiles a young Los Angeles actress-waitress with a Horatio Alger complex named Dallas:

> In certain ways I had happened that afternoon onto a time warp, into a place where girls are still disappointed at not being chosen cheerleader, still get discovered at Schwab's and meet Clark Gable later at the Mocambo or Troc, still dream of big houses by the ocean and carloads of presents by the Christmas tree, still pray to be known. I hoped for Dallas that she would be known, and I hoped even more

that it would not turn out to be one of those prayers better left unanswered.[28]

Play It as It Lays dramatized that prayer answered as nightmare, but the sympathetic and condescending sentimentality of the magazine piece's tone, style, and content in hoping for an affirmation of the Alger-like daydream must have grated on Thompson's sensibilities, especially the prayer element. Didion's 1967 maudlin essay, "Slouching Towards Bethlehem," which attacked hippies like Thompson in the Haight-Ashbury neighborhood, was published three months before the summer of love; she equated the hippies with Yeats's apocalyptic view of Russian Bolsheviks. The Lucy theme illustrates that the Horatio Alger story in literature is still possible, but only at the level of collusion with the Establishment: "[John] Wayne had been Didion's embodiment of the frontier man of action, the hero of her young dream life."[29] In 1971 Thompson had written a letter essay on John Wayne's movie-hero image as the country's chief "hammerhead" that held the whole American Dream in his fists and beat those who were not white into "bloody, screaming hamburger."[30]

The southern California writer, writing about Southern Californian people and landscapes, that Thompson admired most was Carey McWilliams, author of *Southern California: An Island on the Land* (1946, 1973) and *California: The Great Exception* (1949). He was *The Nation* editor who gave Thompson his first writing assignment on bikers, and Thompson would have known about John Fante, a Mencken discovery, from McWilliams, who prized Fante's writing, flecked as it is with realism and a marvelous autobiographical humor. McWilliams was Fante's drinking buddy and best friend.[31] One of McWilliams's favorite southern California novels was Fante's *Ask the Dust* (1939). Another reason Thompson would know of Fante's irreverent anti–Horatio Alger novels: Fante cowrote the script for the 1962 film version of Nelson Algren's *A Walk on the Wild Side* (1956), a novel Thompson worshipped, although the film disappoints.[32] A proletarian writer of grit and earned sentiment, Fante, too, was influenced by Nietzsche and Spengler.

Thompson was also a fan of Nathanael West's novels and discussed them frequently with William Kennedy when they were in Puerto Rico.[33] A loose political parallel to the satire on Didion comically brightens West's *A Cool Million*—Calvin Coolidge's biographer, David Greenberg, comments:

> Coolidge survived not in weighty biographies but tucked away in novels like Nathaniel West's 1934 gem, *A Cool Million*, which parodies Coolidge as the former president Shagpoke Whipple, whose Horatio Alger–style platitudes, in the desperation of the Depression, curdle into fascism.[34]

Thompson would have judged Didion's work as an incipient form of fascism, yet when the Watergate scandal arrived, Didion's sense of justice turned fiercely on Nixon, validating Thompson's critique of the California crook backed by Prescott Bush.[35]

The subsequent silly phone comedy with the anxious clerk in the hotel most represents a transmogrification of the memorable con job Thompson and Acosta pulled on the *Rolling Stone* office. Thompson telephoned Felton, demanding an emergency $500 be wired immediately, while Acosta broke dishes and screamed obscenities in the background. Hunter kept yelling into the phone that Oscar was out of control. Felton surmised it was probably a prank but sent the money anyway. Wenner later had it deducted from Thompson's pay.[36] There was other financial squabbling over bills, yet Thompson requited his revenge in this dispute by selling the novel's book rights to Random House (which would give the book better distribution), which picked up his hotel bill and expenses—not Wenner's Straight Arrow Books imprint.[37]

The comic Lucy monologue functions to build up dramatic suspense before the drug convention. It also conveniently disposes of the subject of sex, usually deemed essential for a novel ever since Madame de La Fayette's *Le Princess de Clèves* (1678), the first Western novel, which focused on nuances of psychology yet did not consider national politics. In a political novel the comedy of scandal usually supplies the sexual element. Since everyone in the novel lives without a history within the anonymity of commercial mobility, Thompson's approach appears sensible and effective.

With the Lucy event behind him, Duke calms down, justifying what they've done as self-preservation because sooner or later *she* would be scandalized by their drug intake and probably turn informer. Duke indulges in another goofy monologue on what he might have said to the cops about his carload of drugs if arrested: "These experts have testified that the drug cache in the possession of these defendants at the time of the arrests was enough to *kill* an entire platoon of United States Marines."[38] Thompson and Acosta did consume a great quantity of drugs, but what consumption is real and what is fiction remains an irrelevant aside. When Charles Perry interviewed Hunter, in his response to the question of whether they consumed that many drugs, Thompson replied with an adroit "Maybe. . . . You figure it out."[39] But nobody worries about how many drinks or cigarettes are consumed by a writer when composing a novel, unless boasting takes center stage, and no novelist should ever confess that his story was in any way a literal transcription of what transpired while encouraging that illusion.

The opening of the Third National Institute on Narcotics and Dangerous Drugs begins with awkward technological incompetence that enhances the depersonalizing effects on the audience: the antiquated, defective speaker system and awkward seating arrangement, which transmits an atmosphere that conveys ominous authoritarianism. A lack of technological competence becomes prophetic for the absence of any real information on various drugs and their effects—"knowledge" becomes blunt propaganda with attendant confusion and gross misinformation even extending to language incompetence: "The reefer butt is called a 'roach' because it resembles a cockroach . . . cockroach . . . cockroach . . . "[40] Duke's lawyer becomes disoriented by this absurd and preposterous declaration, wondering if the speaker is on acid or just plain insane to think in this manner. Such sinister, demonic, propaganda shocks us—gonzo comedy that is surreal! A reefer derives from nautical slang, referring to the rolling up of a sail to reduce its exposure to wind and hence speed when nearing a reef, so the pilot has more time to maneuver—the word *reefer* merely refers to a properly tight-rolled tube that doesn't bulge awkwardly with matted marijuana or crumble apart when smoked. The word *reefer*, probably originating in the Orient with sailors, suggests marijuana will slow down your sense of time and permit you to think about more about what's happening. Toke, meaning to puff, derives from the Spanish *toque*, a hit or turn for a hit. One toke over the line means you've lost the ability to reason quickly or clearly.

The government's deliberate creation of such diabolic pseudo-etymology, attempting to reconstruct popular language for propagandistic disinformation as often practiced in warfare, thrusts the reader into the nightmare pages of George Orwell's *1984*. We have passed through the looking glass and we know that nobody will know what they are looking at or have the faintest idea of what they are saying (and perhaps doing) with this new "war" on drugs, which will create a countrywide boon for law enforcement agencies and a soon-to-be burgeoning prison industry that will incarcerate a higher percentage of its citizens than any other country in the world or in the history of civilization itself. Duke comments: "It was clear that we'd stumbled into a prehistoric gathering."[41] For the second part of the novel, the biting satiric influence of Orwell will replace the more subtle influences of Fitzgerald. After the introduction, the distinguished author of the cockroach theory promotes the fearsome myth of the acid flashback theory, which soon thereafter became an overused sardonic joke among hippies. This well-known expert turns out to be an associate clinical professor of anesthesiology. Thompson briefly quotes ridiculous passages from his book, comparing the knowledge, style, and witty sensibility to the wisdom of locker-room postings in police stations on how to bludgeon dangerous marijuana smokers to a pulp before they turn on you.

Thompson opens the next chapter by declaring it was easy to sit in the room with a head full of mescaline listening to this gibberish. There was no risk: "These poor bastards didn't know mescaline from macaroni."[42] Thompson scores a fierce argument: Who will you believe? Those who have investigated drugs, or those who know only rote propaganda that is not only misleading but ridiculous?

After fleeing the talk, they descend to the bar to prank a cop from Georgia in the same goof style as Thompson pranked the heavy Texan before the Kentucky Derby, by lurid stories—murderous blood-drinking vampires in Malibu—reeking of wild paranoia: the Manson group was just the tip of the iceberg, we shouldn't talk about these things with the press around, and so on. Duke and his lawyer have provided an amusing revenge-trash-talk goof-rap in reply to government bullshit, but this presents posture, disgust, and the armor of mockery in the face of cynically manipulative bureaucrats and an ignorant army of armed police who have no idea what they are doing or are about to do.

The next chapter, fittingly in the face of terror, offers comic relief. Duke notes the Caddy doesn't accelerate as quickly as the Great Red Shark, but once it hits eighty or more, it rides quite smoothly and luxuriously in its upholstered leather. On page 105 of the Modern Library edition there are black blobs of print. Similar blobs appear on page 154 where Duke inflates the rear tires to fifty and the front tires to seventy-five pounds of air pressure when the manufacturer recommends thirty-two in the rear and twenty-eight in the front. At first I thought these blots were Jackson Pollock–type drip blobs, or rubber tire marks from a dangerously careering car, or possibly an advertisement for Thompson's shotgun art, but when I asked myself why they occurred on those particular pages, the answer appeared. In both cases, these are comic slapstick oil drips for Duke's car to skid on, as in a television cartoon. The excessive provocations by his lawyer of the rich Oakies (in contrast to the impoverished Oakies of Steinbeck, oh how times have changed!) in the plush car running parallel on the road may be a typical adolescent prank with its carnival of insults, yet this version refurbishes the cliché with vigorous sociological humor.

Duke breaks in the Whale, as the white Coup de Ville is now called. In Las Vegas gambling lingo, a shark is a hustler while a whale is a hustler who has made it so big that he has uncounted millions to toss around at whim—even if a whale loses a big bet, he has so much money, it doesn't affect his finances. (Unlike a shark, a whale is also an intelligent mammal, not a fish.) Duke boasts about driving with tires pumped nearly fifty pounds over the limit of manufacturer recommendations as if it compares in danger to driving a motorcycle at top speed in the midst of pouring rain. The white Whale (*The Whale* was Melville's original title) itself enjoys the perverse game of pushing limits, as in the war between captain and whale, alluding to Melville's creature, the animal Ahab plots to revenge himself on. Duke plots his revenge on credit card companies, rental agencies, and in an extended fantasy goof, the St. Louis Browns. Duke has momentarily become a guerrilla Ahab at war with the financial system, mocking the Puritan society (like Melville) that disapproves of pleasure. Ahab attempts to kill the whale in a misguided attempt to fight evil and becomes evil in doing so; "Duke" rides the whale for pleasure, boasting of the thrill. In Melville the sperm whale became symbolic of all that's natural and free, what's lost to repression and civilization built upon acquiescence to narrow and arbitrary social codes. Thompson appropriates Melville's prophetic mantle for the second half of the twentieth century.

Thompson wants to ride the whale of liberty, economic and political, around dangerous curves at top speed, mocking conformity and humorless sheep in his adolescent joyride that defies ignorant authority. Just as Melville satirizes Ahab for turning Christianity into a quest for revenge and the exercise of hatred, Thompson ridicules Dr. Bloomquist for perversely transforming nonaddictive drugs into a demonized hunt to put inquisitive, innocent people behind bars. And just as Melville pokes fun at fundamentalist ideas and an inappropriate style of speaking rooted in the King James Bible (as when Ishmael and Queequeg enlist on the Pequod as the Quaker regales them with his silly gab), Thompson mocks the Orwellian language of the corporate police state with its vapid and lying sloganeering that clots brochures and flyers. Like the deaf-mute in Melville's unfinished novel, *The Confidence Man* (1857), Thompson wants to practice charity and sanity on the subject of drugs, but society in its cynical hatred and lack of self-confidence perceives only a world of cynicism and danger when an appeal for sanity is made—both the deaf-mute and Thompson are labeled as lunatics by a society brimming with hatred.

The conclusion of Burroughs's *The Ticket That Exploded* (1962), a novel that opens with two men on the road contending venomously with each other, in a passage written by Byron Gysin, intones: "marijuana marijuana why that's deadlier than cocaine it will turn a man into a homicidal maniac he said."[43] Both Burroughs and Thompson knew all too well that laws making drugs illegal created the permanent marriage of the Mob and the State in a war against average citizens. And what more symbolic locale in America is there for that corrupt marriage to be commemorated than Las Vegas?

To counter the faux lecture on the dangers of marijuana by the so-called expert, tourist Thompson offers an excellent ad-hoc lecture on the bizarre phenomena of the 1950s time warp of Vegas. He scores poignant comments on the depressing sociology of Vegas neighborhoods, as well as the psychology of tourists and marooned natives. Some of this commentary arrives in terms of critiquing the content policies of national newspapers. Duke and his lawyer ingest some mescaline (peyote) pellets with ritual jokes about vomiting. Past the queasy stage, they go to a diner for coffee, a rather strange thing to do at this point because peyote would alert anyone to the wonders of nature all about him and most people would admire sand, stones, cactus, or the horizon.

Duke steals a newspaper, not for its worthless content but for the sports statistics as he proceeds to make fun of college sport recruiting programs, the boasting of future victories by dimwitted coaches, and the political ambitions of retired lunk-headed football players who harbor outsized political ambitions.

The narrative in the diner about the attorney's pass at the busty 48EE waitress (a nonexistent, laughable bust size), followed by the prank "purchase" of a lemon meringue pie at knifepoint, reads like an impromptu *Saturday Night Live* skit, but it casts a backward glance to Didion's portrait of the Hollywood waitress, as well as providing a vitriolic satire on John Fante's temperamental waitress, Camilla Lopez, in *Ask the Dust* (1939)—but a portrait of sultry Camilla as a "burned-out caricature of Jane Russell,"[44] who twenty years earlier might have qualified as a spectacular Hells Angels mama.

Duke's sociological lecture reads, ironically, like a calm version of real-life Acosta's political analysis, and the lawyer's behavior in the diner presents the reverse of that political sensibility—the moral being that we can often see what's wrong with society, but it's something else to change people's erratic and compulsive behavior. There's minor comedy about the great driver Duke being lost on the road, driving in futile circles much like the aimless comic driving of Thurber's Walter Mitty.[45]

Chapter 9 presents a one-act play on the theme of the American dream on the outskirts of Boulder City, featuring parody on American fast food, lost tourists, and the American Dream being located on Paradise Boulevard at a defunct psychiatric club where young people hang out to deal drugs—sure proof that alienated youth doesn't buy American Dream propaganda. The Psychiatrist's Club, as it was called, had formerly been a nightclub called The American Dream. The dream has vanished; even the psychoanalysis of what the dream had been has gone up in smoke. It's now a dead slab of concrete. We live like ghosts in the ruins of our history.

This chapter offers a reply to Hemingway's short story, "A Clean Well-Lighted Place" (1933), which James Joyce thought a masterpiece. Hemingway's Manichean story of darkness and light, set at a small café at closing time, addresses hope and despair in a dialectic manner with one worker being a dreamer, the other being an atheist as they discuss the suicide of an elderly regular customer. In Thompson's play the characters are incapable of even thinking, much less seeing, life in terms of good and evil. Since the play is purportedly a defective tape in the mode of a Beckett one-act play, we hear disembodied voices at night like ghosts speaking about what they don't know—the waitress and owner of the greasy spoon appear to be bland, humorless automatons without flesh or any desire to affirm life. They yammer as specters working the underpaid nightshift of the lost American Dream in the middle of nowhere, confused about places, names, and their own small lives, which appear to have no significance. In an epilogue we are told that the comic duo finally locate the "Old Psychiatrist's Club," but it's a burnt, cracked shell of blackened concrete amid tall weeds. This scorched apocalyptic epilogue vividly contrasts with the snug vitality depicted in "A Clean, Well-Lighted Place" where the café will always be a locale ready to debate with honesty the ultimate dialectical questions about life and death. Hemingway's café serves decent wine or brandy, not stale American coffee that has decomposed to acid. The old man's suicide in Hemingway's story serves as prophetic prelude to the grander project of American collective suicide, for which the Psychiatric Club serves as a weird omen.

Despite the pathetic and abysmal simplicity of its two late-night dinner characters, the play presents a haunting portrait of the American Dream as a nightmare that should be forgettable but exists as a specter. The play has a forceful impact because it presents a slice of daily life that carries the shock of recognition, in the literary sense that Edmund Wilson employed. In the European context a debate about the meaninglessness of life or its potential meaning remains possible, while that debate cannot exist in America, which inhabits a limbo of terminal boredom and destructive use of bad drugs. Mocking ourselves offers forlorn entertainment, not a cure. Art has no value for Americans. The artist tinkers with defective equipment, a metaphor for words, but the artist can only identify the nihilistic emptiness of a society that has lost its way in the desert. In a 1997 interview discussing this chapter Thompson glumly commented: "I went out there to reaffirm Horatio Alger. I knew what was happening."[46] The lost tribe may build a glittering false idol (Las Vegas) in the desert, but the American Dream that was conceived in the late 1940s postwar optimism has turned to rubble, as if the nuclear destruction it invented by creating the atomic bomb had psychologically vanquished the psyche of the nation.

The American Dream offered a sublimated psychiatric distraction in the late Fifties, but by the late sixties it had disintegrated. The audio play remains a haunting masterpiece, a worthy reply to Hemingway, illustrating how much has changed since America thought itself the optimistic young kid who was going to remake not only America, but the globe in the template of Horatio Alger, for the betterment of humankind, the ideal of JFK's Peace Corps.

The wacky shenanigans of putting the lawyer on the plane provide needed comic relief. The prelude to that event features an autobiographical flashback epilogue to Thompson's stint in Peru with the *National Observer* when he was their South American correspondent.[47] The anecdote recounts the journalist missing a plane while jawing with a cocaine dealer. He attempts to board a jet while the engines are running, the police tackle him and beat him unconscious, thus saving him from being sucked into an engine. Anxious about making his plane, the attorney is not amused by this story. Thompson boasts that if you're in trouble, you can always send a telegram to the Right People. Acosta sarcastically replies that some asshole with shit for brains once wrote a poem on that subject, a reference to Thompson's only published poem, "Collect Telegram from a Mad Dog."[48]

The extended anecdote about the arrest and imprisonment of an innocent and genial hippie drifter from an Aspen passerby supplies a sociological anecdote, illustrating the arbitrary, unreasonable, and careless way in which the judicial system exploits those who don't have money. Absurd "Justice" incarnates the living nightmare of the American Dream, but if you have money, you walk free. The central point of the anecdote identifies the money "ethic"—the corruption that Vegas lives and breathes functions no differently from the way justice most commonly operates in America. The Bob Zimmerman–like wanderer investigating varied sociology in America ends up in jail because freedom is not tolerated in the temple of the American Dream. Here the testimony of the true-life anecdote substantiates the veracity of Thompson's symbolic one-act play (fiction).

That anecdote also works as a foil for Duke to assess his guilt over drug possession as he compares an extensive catalog of his felonies to the charges faced by the innocent drifter. A further Mittyesque fantasy has him buying his way out and dragging several publishers into tedious lawsuits. He realizes that his fantasy lacks sanity, but asks "what is sane . . . in this doomstruck era of Nixon. We are all wired into a survival trip now."[49] He attacks Tim Leary as an elitist who was narcissistically interested in consciousness expansion rather than politics, a group of peace-loving acid heads who could purchase peace through selling cheap acid and not realize the central fallacy of their thinking: that acid offered some kind of hope that people would change how they live in a materialistic system based upon exploitation. Such blind faith has failed in the past: churches, reformist generals, gurus, even God. Faith remains useless without deeds—a central Protestant maxim yet wedded here to cynical atheism. Thompson, dropping his persona of Duke, writes an op-ed column attacking Sonny Barger of the Hells Angels for introducing the first schism in the reform of the Youth Movement by pitting longhairs against greasers, students against workers.

In his memoir, Barger boasts that he and the Hells Angels saw the peace movement as composed of left-wing creeps—he deliberately set out "to fuck with them."[50] Barger went on to attack Jerry Rubin in order to take away the ring Rubin claimed was forged from an American fighter plane downed in North Vietnam (typical hippie goof rhetoric). The cops seized Barger and beat him with nightsticks. Other Angels came to his assistance, freed him, and the riot was on. Barger claimed that as a veteran, he was "sticking up for America"[51] and that the country needed to win the Vietnam War. Barger issued press releases and wrote a letter to President Nixon. Advisor and speechwriter Patrick Buchanan[52] noted the incident and letter; he thought Republicans could win by dividing lower-middle-class workers, who tend to be conservative, from the newly educated young liberals who customarily don't bother to vote. This gratuitous nastiness on the part of Barger opened a chasm that was subsequently exploited by Patrick Buchanan,[53] Ed Rollins, Lee Atwater, Karl Rove, and Sarah Palin—these actors in divisive culture wars defined the political landscape for the next several decades.

Laura Nyro[54] singing "Save the Country" (1969) or the Grateful Dead jamming "Keep on Truckin'" (1970), which memorialized the drug bust of the whole band in New Orleans, could never topple Wall Street, land owners, multinational corporations, the banks, or the Pentagon. The failure of the Youth Movement lay to some extent in its subsequent naïve success in ending the Vietnam War—that's when self-preservation gripped a generation eager to get on with their lives and raise a family. A plague of unenlightened drugs wrought havoc, steering the next reactive generation away from psychedelics, as well as any hope of changing society—for that generation, as a whole, saw no need for change and was successfully persuaded by faux government propaganda that psychedelics were harmful—and, typical of dialectical history as Hegel had formulated, did not want to partake of the previous generation's obsessions, ideals, or goals, and in this situation what they rationally deemed vices. Ultimately, it was the *criminalization* of psychedelics (which began in California) that doomed psychedelics. While most people could handle psychedelics and benefit greatly from them, it's true that a small portion of the population cannot handle them, yet if an accusing finger were to be pointed to anyone on this matter, it should be directed at politicians and physicians who thought it better to seize power or avoid the controversy.

The comic trailer to Thompson's meditation on what went wrong with the peace movement (where his exclusive West Coast perspective appears limiting) features vomit, nudity, a trashed suite, and the tackled chambermaid, whom they accuse of working for drug dealers. They recruit her as a spy—her name is conveniently Alice. She tells them she *hates* dope, announcing just the kind of ignorance they can manipulate. They will put her on the payroll and call the hotel every day. Duke will just ask the desk clerk for Alice, as in Grace Slick's song. The chapter concludes with an image of the suite door—when the door closes with her departure, a reader may recall what the doorknob said.

After the carnival list of physical destruction and negligent physical abuse in the hotel room, we are treated to a casual catalog of drugs sprawled about the room, a boast of consuming nearly every serious drug known to mankind since 1544, the year of Henry VIII's third and final invasion of France when the Duke of Suffolk besieged and took Boulogne to punish the French for aiding the Scots. After the victory, Henry (who preferred to drink Italian Frescobaldi wine) briefly visited. The use of the French word *montage* in the next sentence confirms the reference to grossly corpulent Henry, England's greatest king of sexual and culinary excess, who at this late point in his life consumed an encyclopedic medley of fascinating drugs for his terminal ailments when he wasn't enjoying the lolling lilt of cranes and winches to heft his royal tonnage onto and out of boats—much less onto or off of beer-fed workhorses with girths as wide as a captain's full wheel. Not since the

glorious reign of Herod Antipater had a great sovereign been flattering-
ly distinguished by so many enigmatic afflictions, skin eruptions, and
apocalyptic quack remedies. The implied comparison to Duke's attorney falls several centuries short of compliment.

When Duke returns to Circus-Circus, he receives the courtesy magic of his drug conference badge in the same mode of his success with
Thompson's *Playboy* bag tag at the Derby. High on mescaline, at Circus-Circus he converses with Bruce Innes, who had told Duke he knew
a man who had a housebroken trained ape. Thompson had really tried
to purchase an acrobatic ape from the Flying Wallendas.[55] Duke
wanted to purchase it, but the ape had just unpredictably bitten a customer at the casino when a rube threw a mug of beer in the ape's face.
The cops have taken the ape. Duke considers bailing the ape from jail.
Bruce convinces him that would be futile if not impossible. From the
point of view of pure circus, this ape is the real act. In the context of
faux circus, a genuine housebroken trained ape cannot function or exist.

Duke informs Bruce that he's leaving because his job of finding the
American Dream has been completed; they are sitting on its main
nerve. Bruce agrees that the owner of the casino has the right model of
the American Dream: both a circus and a license to steal. Duke grins
and sarcastically comments: "It's pure Horatio Alger, all the way down
to his attitude."[56] The American Dream of hope toward progress and
social mobility has reverted to a systematic scam under the big circus
tent. Thompson comments that the casino owner's executive secretary
told him to f— off: "She said she hates the press worse than anything
else in America." Unlike the humble and ignorant cleaning lady who
harmlessly hated drugs, the secretary symbolizes a wall of entrenched
wealth that despises the right of people to know what's happening in
the world. Jefferson had put his trust in a free press, yet Thompson
records the limits to that aspiration.

The entertainer Bruce Innes was a folk-rock guitarist, vocalist, and
songwriter, a member of the Canadian band Original Castle. They sang
folk songs in a style similar to Peter, Paul, and Mary or the Mamas and
the Papas. Thompson says that if the management listened closely to his
lyrics, Bruce would have been tarred and feathered. Thompson probably alludes to Innes's "One Tin Soldier," a folk-rock number written by
Dennis Lambert and Brian Potter (both of whom later worked with
Dusty Springfield), which was recorded in 1969. The anti-war parable

tells the story of the valley people who hear of a treasure marked by a stone on a mountain. At first the valley people demand to share the stone, which is fine with the mountain people, but the valley people decide to take the stone by force, exterminating the mountain people, only to discover that the treasure is a stone bearing the inscription "Peace on Earth." This ironic El Dorado allegory with biblical language and apocalyptic conclusion neatly fits into Thompson's theme of the lost American Dream in the context of the Vietnam War. The song includes the satirical lines "Go ahead and cheat your neighbor, Go ahead and cheat your friend." Jinx Dawson of the band Coven did a cover version of the song for the sound track of the 1971 movie *Billy Jack*. So it's amusing when Bruce registers his astonishment that Thompson, of all people, has *found* the American Dream.

Thompson concludes the chapter with an Aspen anecdote about Innes that counterpoints the Circus-Circus revelation, linking the two episodes. When a drunken astronaut walks over to Thompson's table and curses out Innes for singing anti-war songs at an Aspen bar, threatening to have the Canadian foreigner banned from America, Thompson summons his local "hash-bouncers" to quell the astronaut for hassling him and the musician. As the bouncers grab the astronaut's arms, he asks Thompson for his name. Thompson replies Bob Zimmerman, the name behind the stage name of Bob Dylan, and calls the astronaut a "bonehead Polack." The astronaut flips out, cursing Thompson and his table, shouting "You don't *represent* this country." Yet the anecdote is ironically that: a representation of the cultural divide over the Vietnam War. On the surface the incident illustrates the muscle of freak power, the protected enclave of the counterculture. Thompson was the counterculture hero who nearly became the sheriff of Aspen in 1970. The local hero on his own turf pulls rank on the national astronaut hero. While amusing, this anecdote of temporary victory offers further nostalgic evidence of the cresting wave of reform that failed in local and national elections. Under the surface, in hindsight and remembrance, the event presents an elegiac lament of what *could* have been.

The second part of the time warp insert employs an omniscient narrator. A fourteen-year-old boy at a restaurant requests the astronaut's autograph on a piece of paper, tearing it up when obliged, and declaring "Not everybody loves you." The corporate vacationers at the table are at first astonished then enraged, their collective mug shot looking like someone had sprayed them with "shit-mist." This episode recalls the restaurant mace-spraying Thompson indulged in when covering the Derby. Once again, Thompson the teenager has been left out of the circle of power, revenging himself on the exclusive elite. Although it reads like reportage, this anecdote furnishes a flight of fantasy.

Thompson concludes the chapter with an op-ed paragraph in the style of a casual casting director for a Hollywood movie. He opines that in an ideal world the re-elected Nixon would have made the perfect mayor for Las Vegas, a crook in his own element of petty power, bags of cash shuttling back and forth with couriers between his office, the casinos, and the airport. Gruff and detached John Mitchell would be right for the corrupt and sadistic role of sheriff, while Agnew could put his aphoristic talent for eloquence to exemplary use as the Master of Sewers.

Chapter 13 features an amusing identity goof about Hunter S. Thompson being Raoul Duke working as a cop for the government, and *not* that Hunter S. Thompson journalist, a really vicious crazy man who works for that notorious rag, *Rolling Stone*. Duke flashes his "gold" Police Brothers Association badge, a bought item like the *Playboy* bag tag from the Derby piece. Duke convinces the bouncer he's an undercover cop.

Thompson describes the death of the Whale, its electrical circuitry shorted out—its nerves gone, an overload metaphor for the country being brain-dead. Duke had ridden the vehicle to death in a joyful effort to escape paranoia, which cannot be done. The Cadillac, its upholstery stained and shredded, quirkily manages the run to the airport where Duke dumps the exhausted rental. Duke, an Ishmael who has survived the paranoia that the drug convention induced in him, becomes hysterical in the airport terminal lobby, surrounded as he is by cops departing the convention.

At the airport a jukebox plays "One Toke Over the Line" while Thompson, not Duke, listens with acute boredom, wishing the jukebox would play Dylan's "Memphis Blues Again," once again conjuring a parallel conclusion to Tom Wolfe's *The Pump House Gang*. The jukebox then plays Mick Jagger's 1969 eloquent cover of Robert Johnson's melancholy "Love in Vain," about a man bringing his beloved and now lost love to a train station—this irony glumly plays off Duke's grim situation of being surrounded by a sea of cops and district attorneys. Yet the theme of love lost also evokes the conclusion of *The Great Gatsby*, leading to a wandering reverie on bummer days when everything appears in vain, the kind of reverie that Dangerfield constantly indulges in *The Ginger Man*.

Thompson picks up a newspaper to read the obituary of the navy captain who had years ago rejected him from ROTC because one leg was slightly shorter than the other: the commander of the U.S.S. *Crazy Horse* was killed and dismembered in Guam. This gruesome Mittyesque fantasy provides the kind of goof journalism Raoul Duke would be capable of committing. The Crazy Horse is the name of a notorious strip club in Guam frequented by sailors, as well as the name of a Federation Starfleet battleship in *Star Trek*.[57] The grand doctor of journalism proceeds to rant obscenely about how newspapers have descended into printing the worthless trash fantasies of his daydreaming alter ego. Melville had once let his persona Ishmael playfully imagine himself as a journalistic headline:

> "*Grand Contested Election for the President of the United States.*"
> "Whaling Voyage By One Ishmael."
> "Bloody Battle in Afghanistan."[58]

Some headlines are so archetypal they refuse obsolescence. Melville also employed pseudo-quotation, identifying himself as "an old writer."[59]

Fitzgerald in his days at Princeton had published a story about cannibalism in the college humor magazine *The Princeton Tiger*.[60] The piece presented a satire on James Fennimore Cooper wherein the ol' b'ar hunter Davy, a grass eater who sported a fishskin hat and packed bloody scalp trophies, was after combat eaten by two American Indians who did not enjoy the tough old bird. Davy's trusty Eskimo cheesehound sits out the fight. The fantasy obituary mimics the mode of Fitzgerald's satire.

Just as *Hell's Angels* had concluded with harsh self-parody, so does *Fear and Loathing in America*. Journalism, even the New Journalism, is to be feared and loathed—after all, writing is really hard work. When Thompson had applied unsuccessfully to the *New York Times* back in 1958 for a job in response to a want ad, he listed his three strengths as: (1) the adverse effects of an ignorant public on the commercialization of literature and jazz, (2) an analysis of the bourgeois roots of the Beats, (3) a study of the decline of real journalism among young scribblers.[61]

The concluding epilogue plays with the postmodern dual identity of the writer as social observer and fiction creator. "Farewell to Vegas" alludes to Hemingway's *A Farewell to Arms* (1929), which contrasts personal injury against the impersonal tragedy in the great machine of war that has killed so many. Thompson will contrast the personal tragedy of the struggling reporter trying to make an honest living, as he did in *The Rum Diary*, against the impersonal tragedy of a nation dehumanized by puerile propaganda. Thompson tears off his laminated Raoul Duke Special Investigator tag: "The gig is finished . . . and it proved nothing."[62] Thompson assesses his work as futile because taxpayer dollars are still being wasted in funding films about the dangers of LSD, mescaline, and marijuana, featuring the triumph of the Lie. He laments the new trend of bad drugs like horse tranquilizers (still popular today in rural high schools) that reduce instead of expand consciousness. This fad in depression parallels the depressing incumbency of President Nixon, an administration that bars hope from the negotiating table—of war, drugs, and racial equality.

The secondary chapter title quotes Dangerfield's daily motto from *The Ginger Man*: "God's Mercy on You Swine!" While Donleavy directed that caustic blessing on those with inherited money or workers on the corporate-financial gravy train, Thompson fires that sardonic quip at the military machine and those who participate in it like mechanized robots. After the plane ride, Thompson cons a box of amyls at the airport drugstore with his correspondence school Doctor of Divinity (Universal Life Church) discount card. He opens a capsule, inhales, and reels into the corridor, just to see two Marines at whom he shouts a godly blessing as he skewers them as swine. His consciousness receding and dimming, he feels like a reincarnation of the Puritan Horatio Alger, the Harvard-educated daydreamer who believed that poverty and hard work led to riches, but Duke's confidence now resides in drugs that shrink perception to pusillanimous narcissism.

At the novel's conclusion, as in *Hell's Angels*, the narrator has transformed himself in self-parody into what he has so eloquently satirized—he's an Alger monster consumer on the move, hoping not so much for more riches, but more drugs to sedate himself from the burgeoning police state of Pigs at the government trough. Even the personal tragedy of a single irresponsible addict pales in comparison to the corruption and addicting power of corporate media manipulating government, based upon impersonal marketing projects that deceive millions through Madison Avenue and Disney techniques. There's a mathematical abyss between the tragedy of self-deception and the deception of a whole country.

Thompson wrote two other chapter conclusions for the novel, but these have never been published. In a late interview with Douglas Brinkley he stated that the printed version is not a proper ending, yet the inclination for self-denigration in Thompson remains strong. If and when those two chapters, which appear to be afterword musings, are published we might comparatively evaluate the endings, yet the picture of Duke as an Alger-like monster offers effective comedy that points to the enduring persistence of the American Dream. One of the unpublished chapters depicts Duke buying a Doberman pinscher to protect himself—Raoul on the road to becoming a suburban Nazi.[63] Yet that idea occurs in fantasy in the text, as we have Thompson following up Raoul's fantasy with the observation that Denver functions as a national clearinghouse for stolen Dobermans.

For a June 1970 issue of *Scanlan's Monthly*, Raoul Duke (Master of Weaponry) enthuses: "This book [*How to Defend Yourself* by George Hunter] is invaluable to anyone who fears that his home might be invaded, at any moment, by rioters, rapers, looters, dope addicts, niggers, Reds or any other group."[64] Thompson had proposed to Hinckle that *The Police Chief* become a regular advice column reflecting the rudeness of the age with Raoul Duke acting as "a virtual clearing-house for information on all forms of violence. Answer all questions, dispense strange advice of all sorts."[65] Raoul Duke remains one of the greatest satiric characters in Western literature.

When reading *Fear and Loathing in Las Vegas*, it's important to keep in mind that Duke usually harbors sharp practical observations, while Raoul furnishes the darkly scheming opportunist inclined to evil. Similarly, the other narrator, Thompson, has a split personality: the high-strung prankster, con man, and self-satirizing "good doctor of journalism" versus the more temperate sociological and cultural analyst by the name of Thompson who dispenses prophetic wisdom. These comic antagonists continually clash, swerve, and morph into each other, warping the narrative in a slightly bewildering multiplicity of directions.

The concept of warping in Thompson's work remains a fascinating subject. In *The Rum Diary*, he employs literary templates, bending them to make new statements. In an April 20, 1971, letter to Tom Wolfe, after Thompson completed the first half of *Fear and Loathing in Las Vegas*, he speaks of the Mind-Warp/Photo approach.[66] As a literary concept warping was extensively employed in the medieval anti-war Irish epic *The Táin* (The Cattle Raid), which had recently been rendered in a superlative English version by the poet Thomas Kinsella in 1969 (paperback 1970) with famous ink-blot illustrations by Louis le Brocquy, daubed with his left hand because he had broken his right arm. The work is a satire on war in which both the pagan and Christian elements become warped into satiric self-parodying commentary; the central hero, Cú Chulainn, the Warped One, a multilayered character, undergoes such magical adrenaline transformation that his presence expands in an explosion of pointillism across the battlefield, as if the writer has gone mad. The humor and satire work somewhat like *The Iliad* meets Aristophanes. Sometimes events are described in two different versions: there's an extensive satire on a powerful and treacherous queen, and druids accurately foretell great doom but no one pays them any attention. Thompson would have loved both the epic's approach as well as the arresting illustrations, yet I don't find any explicit mention of *The Táin* among his letters. Thompson had a natural tendency to warp things in different directions, and if he came across that comic epic of fantastic exaggeration with warping as its central technique, it may have confirmed his inclinations and bestowed self-confidence in its execution.

Even Neil Young, in his Thompson-inspired lyrics to "American Dream" concerning Gary Hart's failed Presidential bid of that year (the Donna Rice scandal), embraced the media smear of Hart. Perhaps Hart was America's last chance for a noncorrupt politician, but Hart was brought down by the intelligence community, which feared Hart's distrust of the CIA and especially its secret connections with Italian and Jewish mobsters. Hart also wanted to reopen the JFK assassination investigation. Santo Trafficante was forthright: "We need to get rid of that son of a bitch."[67] No real investigation of what happened in the boat incident was mounted at the time and subsequent investigation has revealed it to be a mob frame-up. Hart, who had wanted to destroy the mob, was doomed because of his so-called mob connections. Had Hart survived the false innuendo of the media, he would have been removed by the mob, anyway, just like Bobby Kennedy.[68] Hart never had a chance—Thompson's weary cynicism stems from his political knowledge.

Whether the literal events of the novel's plot provide an accurate, exaggerated, or invented version of what happened in Las Vegas might be debated, yet much of the book's appeal and enduring popularity consists of two elements: the literal, emotional appeal of its populist humor, and the metaphoric and philosophic nuances that lie embedded under the populist surface. An iceberg analysis reveals impressive oceanic depths and currents below the laughs and slapstick. The literary allusions contained in the novel are not window dressing, but detail important sociological shifts in American society since the writings of Fitzgerald, Dos Passos, Hemingway, and Donleavy. Thompson's friend Tom Wolfe effectively adopts this technique of topical sociological contrasts in his masterpiece, *I Am Charlotte Simmons* (2005), which chronicles the decline of American colleges into a debased rictus of political pap amid amoral conformity.[69]

If Thompson did not succeed in penning the Great American Epic, then he certainly created an enduring masterpiece equaling or exceeding his admiration for *The Great Gatsby*. Thompson's satire may, in its surface literal interpretation, understate the reality of Thompson's daily life, but it certainly remains the central text that records the ending of a popular artistic movement dedicated to consciousness expansion. Fitzgerald wrote an elegy for lost love in the jazz age, while Thompson's gallery of observer-participant Mind-Warp/Photos (along with Steadman's glorious gonzo illustrations) not only offers an ironic summation of the sixties, but provides the Southern answer to Norman Mailer's much-vaunted East Coast ambition to write the Great American novel. Even if many of the old-timey Fifties Beats fled old San Francisco, the fact that Fitzgerald wrote his masterpiece on the East Coast almost dictates that its companion reply would arrive from the West Coast, that its narrative techniques would not evolve out of the traditional European novel, but would exhibit the disruptive, chaotic esthetic of the West Coast, which faced the closing doom of America's westward expansion.

The book provides a seismological shiver—if not the great California earthquake dramatized by West and Fante—that opens a wide crack in the American realist tradition and in the end indicates apocalyptic affinity with the South American fabulist novels of Roberto Arlt, Jorge Luis Borges, and Julio Cortázar, whose use of interior monologue may have been as influential on Thompson as Thurber's daydreaming Walter Mitty. In a 1963 letter from Woody Creek to his close friend Paul Semonin, Thompson confesses that his chief vices are "top-volume monologues and midnight shooting."[70] *Betrayed by Rita Hayworth* (1968) by Manuel Puig (who died in 1990 from a botched gall bladder operation) also analyzes society through the sociological lens of mass culture and its effect on the nuclear family in a South American context, providing a severe critique of both religion and the state through his clever use of montage. One might register the claim that Thompson's surreal comedy thrust the American novel into the broader international arena where surrealism became the leading satiric voice of authors—Mo Yan's *The Republic of Wine: A Novel* (1992; translated into English, 2000) being a good example—longing for a better and saner world.

Beyond the comedy, some readers remain disturbed by the gonzo pursuit of what they might perceive as dangerous drug activity described in the novel, yet this supplies an adolescent fantasy and functions primarily as a joke, similar to Rabelais' conflation of drinking with philosophical thinking, often translated as "trink." A similar public reaction, with regard to realistic depiction of sexual activity, afflicted establishment reaction to Henry Miller's *Tropic of Cancer*. Norman Mailer's comment on Miller's novel is as appropriate to Thompson's: "It's because there is honor in the horror, and metaphor in the hideous."[71] That reflects a sentiment and judgment that Mary Godwin (Shelley) and Anaïs Nin would agree with, although feminists who grumble about the lack of women's themes or the single representation of a forlorn waif have a point, but not all novels—or even all masterpieces of art—may fit the social profile of political correctness because such a consideration or criteria relating to gender remains irrelevant to great art, an observation that both Shelley and Nin would most likely second and third.

Because of his South American travels, Thompson penned reviews on books about South America, including a couple of book reviews on South American novelists for the *National Observer*: one on the Venezuelan Arturo Uslar Pietro's 1931 novel, *The Red Lances*, when it was translated into English in 1963; also, Jorge Amado's 1961 novel, *Home*

Is the Sailor, in its 1964 English translation. The literary sensation of 1970 was the appearance in English of *One Hundred Years of Solitude* by the Colombian Gabriel García Márquez. At the end of that eloquently witty novel the glorious city of Macondo, a city of illusion, vanishes in "a fearful whirlwind of dust and rubble being spun about by the wrath of the biblical hurricane."[72] This masterpiece of magical realism presents an allegory of Spenglerian glitter and doom that traces the cyclical rise and fall of families and empires as legendary archetypes in the fable of humankind's foibles. Alerted to this work by his friend William Kennedy, who wrote a glowing 1970 review of the novel for the *National Observer*,[73] Thompson would have taken note of this mesmerizing literary success, yet Marquez exerts no influence other than a broad parallel.

The satiric, surreal comedy of Kurt Vonnegut's *Cat's Cradle* (1963) and *Slaughterhouse-Five* (1969) may have exerted a more immediate influence on Thompson. The former describes a government intent on wielding death by the hook for practicing the religion of Bokonism, a lunatic mysticism wherein people commune by touching the soles of their feet—an obvious allusion to China's state persecution of Christians, yet Vonnegut offers no sympathy for religion in general. The latter novel argues that a belief in green aliens who resemble a plumber's helper (a snake) offers more functional sanity than living with the memory of the Holocaust and the subsequent carpet bombing of Dresden during World War II. Vonnegut's theme of absurdity trumping reality as he blends autobiography and historical fact broke new ground, encouraging Thompson to push further the autobiographical angle as applied to drugs and government propaganda, while satirizing "objective" journalistic conventions or employing techniques like op-ed articles in the middle of a novel that shifts gears so often with such Homeric speed during the cultural divide the Vietnam War supplied.

While there is nothing new about the blending of fact and fiction—it's as old as Homer's *Iliad*, which Thucydides attacked in his famous preface to *The Peloponnesian Wars*, acclaiming fact over fiction—Thompson's blending of fact and fiction remained "new" because of its contemporary journalistic convention. Those roots wallowed in the established triumph of William Randolph Hearst's ideal of impartiality in news. Thompson advocated overturning Hearst's model—reverting back to the older tradition of advocacy journalism that denied the possibility of objectivity. Without any pretense of "objectivity," Thompson provided a dense "kitchen sink" approach that veers off in a multitude of directions.

One aspect of Thompson's technique and popular attraction lay in the hip allusions to music and literature in chapter titles. In-culture references to popular music, that anyone who listens to the radio would know, jostle with more obscure literary allusions. During the huge boom of recently educated college students, this was a novel and attractive way to validate the signposts of contemporary popular culture as contributing landmarks of enduring value that would follow the trajectory of their lives. Yet this technique, when combined with exaggerated drug use, also had the reverse effect of inhibiting a serious critical literary evaluation among academics.

Most contemporary reviewers of the novel were either baffled by the book or wrote unenlightening chatter about chemical highs. Thompson's big break came in a place he may not have expected—Crawford Woods at the *New York Times Book Review* gave the novel a glowing review. Woods, while being amusing himself, caught the echoing ironies, depth, and especially the humor: "a trendy English teacher's dream, a text for the type who teaches Emily Dickinson and Paul Simon from the same mimeograph sheet . . . a custom-crafted study of paranoia . . . a desperate and important book . . . the funniest piece of American prose since *Naked Lunch*."[74]

Thompson's use of staccato bursts of thought and observation crystallizes his concept of the Mind-Warp/Photo.[75] Yet such a practice was first introduced by William S. Burroughs in *Naked Lunch* (1959, Paris; 1962, United States based upon an earlier draft). Like Thompson's novel, *Naked Lunch* is a satire based on drug jokes with the addition of arcane same-sex humor. Both novels owe a debt to the style of the novelist Celine. While the extreme raunchiness and obscurity of Burroughs's novel have to some extent minimized the popularity of the novel as well as its academic appreciation, Thompson's panoramic and often paradoxical irony combined with his adolescent humor—as well as the political and sociological critique—has endured because of the novel's accessibility. While Burroughs remains a disdainful if perceptive elitist political critic, Thompson offers broad populism in a style rooted in journalistic clarity aided by comic redundancy, cartoon characters, and "the idiopathic anger of the righteous outlaw."[76]

Blurring the line between fact and fiction in the novel was not itself the point as some commentators appear to think: the practice does maintain a high-wire tension while the reader is challenged to discover why the shift has taken place. The warped shifting to another register introduces different themes, ironies, and perspectives. Such warping is anything but gratuitous and perfects the meta-textual innovations Thompson explores in *Hell's Angels* and pushes the envelope further. The writing offers intuitive nonlinear perspectives that mimic reality— the reverse of fundamentalist romanticism that wishes to freeze truth.[77] In the epic letter to his editor Silberman, Thompson hints at the rococo nature of his shifting technique for his new novel:

> It's the idea of emphasizing *my own involvement* with these various scenes to the extent that I become the protagonist—somewhat in the style of Frederick Exley's *A Fan's Notes*. The problem is one of perspective and control.[78]

Exley's 1968 "fictional memoir" abruptly shifts moments in time while it comically exaggerates incidents during a meditation on the failure of the American Dream in the narrator's life wherein he becomes a ghost witnessing his own doom. The excessive burden of drugs and alcohol fuels the memoir. Writing his friend Bill Cardoso, Thompson said of Exley's book: "It's a terrible fucking book—breaks every conceivable rule, etc.—for some reason it's one of the best things I've read in years."[79] Although an entertaining comic work of genius, Exley's memoir becomes circumscribed by the narrator, who remains an exceptional yet frustrated intellectual rather than an ordinary person.

A similar phenomenon occurred with Norman Mailer's *An American Dream* (1995), in which Dostoyevsky-like Rojack, dwelling in an underground netherworld symbolic of the American nightmare, did not connect with society—neither the literary world nor the world of popular readership. The main character, an obvious incarnation of the Horatio Alger theme until the murder of his high-society wife, becomes too far removed from ordinary experience, the murder being too alienating to evoke sympathetic identification.

In contrast, Thompson's novel appeals to both intellectuals and the average reader through its adroit combination of populist humor and iceberg allusions. Among novelists, Thompson acts like the popular jazz player in a band who suddenly shifts into a different key, leaving some members of the band baffled, challenged, and in awe of the progression. Thompson was able to *synthesize* many of the fugitive experiments of the late Sixties into a format accessible to any reader.

Fear and Loathing in Las Vegas presents a broad satire on the cultural and political self-destruction of America (rather than merely one character, as in Exley) through the lens of a self-destructive, schizophrenic character, Duke/Thompson, who embodies the best and worst of America. The self-destructive cynicism contains immense appeal for young readers who live at the economic and political margins of American society, fearing they will never make good. The novel confirms their worst fears about adult society and enables them to laugh at their own monsters, a noted Rabelaisian cure for the mind. Yet more happens in that slim novel than young readers imagine.

Chapter headings in the novel function as road signs and billboards. Not all road signs have significance for the driver, while billboards are of just passing interest. Some of the headings provide information on how to read the map encoded in the chapter while others point to itinerant themes outside the story, yet function like newspaper headlines to announce events or social symptoms, as one discovers in the *U.S.A.* trilogy (1938) by Dos Passos. The teasing pleasure of the headings consists in figuring out which leads provide important clues on how to read the chapter—some chapter headings are just the visible tip of the "iceberg" in the desert. A populist sensibility allows the reader to choose which heading the reader finds most relevant, humorous, or most arresting.

Thompson's sly use of poignant allusion opens up deep references and contrasts with the work of other writers and music, inciting incendiary commentary, both timely and prophetic. The submerged "iceberg" architecture employed earlier in *The Rum Diary* achieves dense sublimity that blooms, provoking close rereading. Carnival lists, whether absurd fantasies, casual insults, or self-parodying self-abasement, enhance the fabulous banquet of surreal absurdity.

The novel also features a plethora of journalistic modalities and techniques, as well as a cascading anthology of fictional techniques. While the surface psychology of the novel may be impishly adolescent, even hillbilly populist, the social critique, political commentary, and cultural analysis retain adroit sophistication that exhibits contemporary relevancy and enduring artistic excellence. While the novel documents both the optimistic humor of the late Sixties as well as their febrile collapse under Nixon, it attacks the Quixotic fabric of American corporate life; the novel endures as more than entertainment, offering a complex testimony of American schizophrenia as it relates to the myth of El Dorado and its incarnation in the delusionary optimism of Horatio Alger. Douglas Brinkley zeroed in on Thompson's general intent with the novel: "Thompson considered *Fear and Loathing in Las Vegas* a 'political statement' against Nixonian authoritarianism and the Vietnam War."[80] Yes, in juxtaposing the decadent glitter of moneyed waste while people die from the carpet-bombing, first proposed by Samuel P. Huntington,[81] the novel succeeds as that and so much more by surviving the temporality of its intent to become a prophetic, classic work that retains its relevance by dramatizing the period when the seeds of political oppression first created the nightmare that Americans, especially the young, still identify—consciously or unconsciously—with a shock of recognition and laughter that cannot be stifled. Thompson was well aware that a society at war, whether a city-state like Athens or a nation like England during World War I, begins unconsciously to act against any of its citizens who display freedom of thought.

The speedy pacing of Thompson's novel, on the surface, exhibits Duke's desire to travel at top speed and outrun the police, just as the noted surface speed of Homer's *Iliad* imitates the speed of a war chariot racing across a plain. The rapid pace, this epic *energia*, permits Thompson to convey the excitement of the imagination at play. The space for imagination to play and instigate the uncontrollable laugh defies the government's role to repress speech and make it conform to authority and its official representative, the dictionary, which fixes elite discourse, allowing governments and corporations to corrupt the freedom that sometimes inheres in language. The language of government in the novel remains but comic fraud, laughable nonsense, transparent to anyone with half a brain left after its assault by Orwellian government and corporate propaganda. The book races in demotic dialect, comic fantasy paranoia, and forbidden drug argot, rather than a high literary language—what we might call outlaw language. The music of the language resembles speedy yet lyrical guitar riffs—like Keith Richards in good form. While the book demythologizes the official language of both the state (historically, a military machine) and highbrow literature, it does not offer any mythology to replace what it criticizes—both Raoul and

Hunter have their dark sides: while Duke dispenses laughter, Thompson editorializes with wisdom.

Yet Thompson's Spenglerian gloom, like Lucretian atheism, offers liberation in the realization that the state (or a deity) does not own anyone's mind and that the human mind functions at its best when freely laughing at the edge of the Lucretian void, even if that vision be merely a temporary comingling of circumstances, or the twisting of language into satire and parody. Young people, most of Thompson's audience from generation to generation, respond to the instinctive imagination of freedom. Thompson illustrates that backwoods hillbilly distillers of literature know that real freedom remains something to be lived and not merely offered pious lip service—the theme of his first published essay by the Louisville Athenaeum club.

The theme of life lived as freedom remains the central tenet of Henry Miller's *The Books in My Life* (1969), a recently published book from a writer Thompson considered a literary hero, the writer "whose iconoclastic forthrightness he [Thompson] admired above all others."[82] Exfoliating literary templates and numerous references to varied books in Thompson's novel was most likely inspired by Miller's book, wherein he praises both known classics and obscure books he has read, enlivened by comic Rabelaisian anecdotes. Miller's rambling (seemingly spontaneous) meditation supplies Thompson with an iceberg ur-template, the "bottom" of the "berg," its bookish boot for a cornucopia of books whose influence he succinctly synthesizes—much as Robert Burton's *Anatomy of Melancholia* (1621) provided the template for Holbrook Jackson's *Anatomy of Bibliomania* (1930). All of these books are books about books that remain obsessed with a high style of writing. Miller's iconoclastic spirit and his organic innovations provided intellectual inspiration for Thompson.[83]

Yet all these influences on *Fear and Loathing in Las Vegas* may be peripheral to the central conceptual influence: *The Skin* (La Pelle), written by the journalist Curzio Malaparte (Kurt Erich Suckert). The book was available in an inexpensive Avon edition that went through several reprints in the late Fifties and early Sixties. Published in 1949, that book recounts the American occupation of Naples during World War II in 1944. The account emphasizes the surreal degradation of Italian culture at the hands of first the Germans, then American soldiers, who cannot comprehend the debased situation.

As in Thompson's novel, each chapter of the book functions more like a separate essay while adhering to a narrative that appears as surreal continuum. Each chapter employs neo-Platonic dialogue—the narrator speaking to a companion—although in Malaparte's reporting, which often indulges in fantastic exaggeration, the character spoken to is sometimes a different person. Both Malaparte and Thompson win the trust of the reader through humor, realistic honesty, and righteous rage. An emotionally wounded narrator employs aggressive insult to help the reader understand the humiliation of the people of Naples, just as Thompson's alter ego insults police and authoritarian figures of complacent privilege. As in Malaparte, the reader's sole link to the distorted story arrives through the brash perspective of the narrator, the reader's only reference; also, "observation takes second place to a reaction."[84]

Malaparte has a deep understanding of history and Italian culture, just as Thompson has a deeply populist understanding of American character and history when he analyzes the degradation of American culture from an unjust and unwinnable war on drugs. In both books the narrator's anger becomes a window of illumination amid a surreal landscape; anger and sarcasm become a plea for reason, the process of Plato's dialogues.

Thompson may have become aware of Malaparte from Jean-Luc Goddard's 1963 film, *Contempt* (*Le Mepris*), based upon an Alberto Moravia story but set in a house on Capri that Malaparte built after World War II. In the film with Bridgett Bardot and Jack Palance there swims a postwar Homeric allegory that even encompasses Godard's own failing marriage. The film was much acclaimed for its multilevel allegory, as well as its cinema construct, by French and American intellectuals at the time; its reputation has held. While the influence of Malaparte's reporting technique pervades *Fear and Loathing in Las Vegas*, Thompson's adaptation of that technique remains embedded in American culture.

While Thompson's dense epic synthesizes a plethora of literary and musical influences, it retains its reputation as *the* masterpiece in a large shouting corpus of hip literature, as well as the masterpiece of a particular era in which freedom of thought and action did not border on criminal activity. The tradition of comedy remains by definition and practice primarily the performance of extreme outsiders or comfortably embedded insiders. In summing up her classic study of American humor, Constance Rourke opined:

> Humor has been a fashioning instrument in America, cleaving its way through the national life, holding tenaciously to the spread elements of that life. Its mode has often been swift and coarse and ruthless, beyond art and beyond established civilization. It has engaged in warfare against the established heritage, against the bonds of pioneer existence. Its objective—the unconscious objective of a disunited people—has seemed to be that of creating fresh bonds, a new unity, the semblance of a society and the rounded completion of an American type. [85]

Thompson created art through a form of collage, blurring the borders between journalism, autobiography, and fiction. Perspective shifts "like a stunt driver, steering with the skids so that the most improbable intentions result in the smoothest maneuvers, the attitude of having one's personal craziness pale before the ludicrousness which passes for the normal in contemporary American life." [86] Thompson created a new populist identity with his writings that fortified unity in the hipster community by giving that community the proud identity of an epic, yet great epics from the *Iliad* to *Don Quixote* chart failure—they retrospectively attempt to win the war of words and legends, not the dismal parade of murderous history. Such epics partake of the godly vision that records the inability of humankind to achieve the freedom and love they imagine to be possible.

For Thompson, the Horatio Alger success dream had been possible in the past, but not after the assassination of President Kennedy. The final death knell of the dream arrived with the assassination of Dr. Martin Luther King and the subsequent criminalization of what remains an implacable reality of life: the use of drugs. Thompson provided the subversive hope of the outcast: humor in the absurdity of the dire situation in which the dream of Jean-Jacques Burlamaqui to wed liberty to pleasure, encoded by Jefferson as the right to "life, liberty, and the pursuit of happiness" in the Declaration of Independence, [87] was discarded in favor of criminalizing large swaths of the populace in order to promote jobs for politicians defending propagandistic lies, dutiful police, and depressed jailers who possess little idea of why they are participants in jailing a higher percentage of citizens than any other country in the history of world. In the face of that bleak prospect, laughter and witty defiance constitute the civilized response to organized barbarism.

It took a Southerner to understand fully Lincoln's dictum that a divided country (in a state of permanent war with the world) could not endure for any great length of time and that the practice of Jeffersonian freedom remains predicated upon trusting individuals and the press to be reasonable and responsible. But make no mistake—Thompson was no library liberal who idealized freedom—he lived freely as a practical libertarian, an opponent of liberal clichés as much as mind-numbing conservative slogans, while his behavior teetered on the hilarious abyss of absurd anarchism; out of that he created an artistic form of performance humor we now call Gonzo.

The book itself became, its title plainly alluding to the Gospel of Mark, the Peyote Gospel of the freak generation, revealing and exposing how drugs were about to ruin the American Dream: through futile police enforcement that would criminalize many innocents, and through cultural self-destruction whereby the best minds of his generation would be destroyed, not merely by conformity as Ginsberg had proclaimed in *Howl*, but through overindulgence in a pharmaceutical explosion that would lead to debilitating addiction for a large percentage of the nation's population.

In Mark Twain's *The American Claimant* (1892), the Gadsby was a splendid but doomed Long Island hotel burned down in a fire, while in Fitzgerald's novel *The Great Gatsby*, Nick Carraway the character is doomed; *in Fear and Loathing in Las Vegas*, American civilization is doomed in the personification of Las Vegas as a symbol.

7

MYTHIC ENIGMA

The Curse of Lono

*"Bad! Bad! What? Does he not—go back?" Yes! But you misunder-
stand him when you complain about it. He goes back like everyone
who is about to make a great spring.*—Friederich Nietzsche

In terms of concept and style, *Fear and Loathing in Las Vegas* is a
postmodern novel that incorporates many of the minimalist techniques
of modernism, especially the notion that the surface of the text only
hints at the possibility of networking complexities that lay beneath. *The
Curse of Lono* retains that approach as it plunges further into postmodern quandaries of identity.

The Portuguese poet Fernando Pessoa (1888–1935) assumed multiple identity masks for the echoing closet-drama of poetic perceptions in
"his" life. Being a modernist, Pessoa kept a rather strict demarcation of
these approximately eighty different identities until his legendary later
work, which anticipates postmodernism by blurring the *figura* of the
writer with his text. Like Pessoa's later work, Thompson's fiction will
echo and blend various alter egos of the author: all characters in *The
Curse of Lono* will be Virgilian shades of the author in a cosmic echo
chamber of divine irony. This remains Thompson's most difficult book,
not only because of its peculiar loose plot construction and intense
intellectual irony, but because the book presents a philosophical portrait of the artist imprisoned in a postmodern hell.

The plot of *The Curse of Lono* appears less accessible to the reader than *Fear and Loathing in Las Vegas* because its picaresque elements coalesce around literature and philosophy as much as the candied surface of comic episodes. The shifting of literary templates under the novel's surface resemble continental plate tectonics, although they are fewer in number than the radiant proliferation of American novels that appear under the surface in *Fear and Loathing in Las Vegas*. Thompson's literary assembly canonizes Melville, Twain, and Hemingway, elevating these great American writers to the more universal context of world literature that includes Homer, Virgil, Nietzsche, Joyce, and, finally, Thompson himself. The book's ambition creates an opaque lens. Because of the episodic nature of the book's plot, I will examine sequentially Thompson's process of thinking in composing the chapters, including his use of philosophy and allegory.

The Curse of Lono (1983), Hunter's most enigmatic book, was his last attempt to complete a major literary project. The effort was both encouraged and thwarted by his publisher. The book began as further development of an article Thompson wrote for *Running* magazine. The magazine's editor, Paul Perry (Thompson's future biographer), flew to Woody Creek in the early summer of 1980, hoping to persuade Thompson to cover a twenty-six-mile marathon in Hawaii. Thompson's divorce from Sandy had nearly been finalized, and he was living with Laila Nabulsi. With Perry, Hunter played hard to get, yet he was ready for a new project. Once he persuaded Steadman to join him for the Christmas vacation, the expedition was on, and Steadman decided to bring along his wife and children. Hunter completed the first draft of "Charge of the Weird Brigade" within a week,[1] yet had taken two more months before the burnished final copy was ready. Armed by advice from Ralph Steadman, Paul Perry kept Hunter on track by cajoling him with drugs, music, flattery, jokes, conversation, and bouts of extended insomnia. Thompson was still constantly playing the Rolling Stones and Bob Dylan as background fuel.[2] Perry claims to have provided Thompson with the basic idea for an extended book, yet he doesn't explain what that involved.[3]

Alan Rinzler, the former chief of Straight Arrow Books (which had folded in 1975), had spotted the published article in the April 1981 *Running* magazine; he wanted Thompson to write for him, despite the history of an aborted book on Ronald Reagan that Thompson never delivered for Straight Arrow after he had taken an advance. Rinzler persuaded Thompson to pitch a book based upon his *Running* magazine article. Bantam Paperbacks, a subdivision of Random House (where Rinzler now worked as president), promptly concluded a deal for a travel book. Yet despite help from Laila Nabulsi (doing research on Hawaii, Mark Twain, and Captain Cook), and novelist Tom Corcoran aiding to link chapters together, Thompson dawdled. He was attempting to explore new terrain as he searched for brilliant conceits and the seductive rhythms of writing musical "highs." But his working habits had seriously deteriorated after his divorce, and he was easily distracted by political news or friends. Biographer Peter Whitmer whimsically derides him at this time as being preoccupied more with cocaine than writing.[4]

After Random House had waited longer than the customary one year for manuscript completion, Rinzler arrived in good humor at Woody Creek to prod Hunter into completing the book. During this first of several visits, Thompson feigned reluctance to produce the masterpiece Random House expected; he claimed his contract called for a mere *jeu d'esprit*: "it was supposed to be 'Postcard from a wrong Vacation'—not 'Dr. Thompson rides again.'"[5] This protest displays self-frustration and offers another glimpse into Thompson's angry, self-satirizing irony. Rinzler returned once more in the fall of 1982. After three days of around-the-clock "work" amid the distracting chaos of Hunter's phone constantly ringing with offers for speaking engagements or friends wanting to chat, Hunter fell asleep. Rinzler seized the opportunity to scoop up the manuscript and appropriate a few fugitive fragments written on napkins and paper bags, shoving it all into a shopping bag, then speeding to the airport.[6] This theft was probably rationalized by the fact that Hunter himself had previously stolen *The Rum Diary* manuscript from Random House when there were disputes about its editing. Rinzler dutifully photocopied and returned all materials, although he frankly admitted "that was basically the end of our relationship."[7] To most readers *The Curse of Lono* looms as an aberrant decorative enigma in the form of a coffee-table book.

The oversized blue paperback appeared in November 1983, in time for the Christmas season (something satirized in the novel), nearly three years after the Honolulu marathon event. With his ties to Random House severed, Thompson characteristically nursed bitterness yet

quickly moved on to his next project, which was covering the sensational Pulitzer divorce trial in West Palm Beach for *Rolling Stone*.

Two epigraphs preface *The Curse of Lono*. The first, from Rudyard
Kipling's *The Naulahka; A Story of West and East* (1892), comes from a
novel Kipling coauthored with Wolcott Balestier and strikes an enigmatic note of anti-imperialism.[8] The second, from Mark Twain's *Letters
from Hawaii*, looms as a cautionary, comic warning.[9] Twain pokes fun
at Hawaiian legend surrounding the god Lono, sardonically observing
that instead of being worshipped in America, Lono would have been
made a postmaster—a forecast of Twain's famously popular 1870 satiric
essay "The Late Benjamin Franklin," in which Twain makes fun of his
(or anyone's) inability to live up to the talents, methods, and achievements of Franklin, the great giant in the American pantheon, whose
role was most crucial in the creation of America. The citation of Twain
signals that Thompson will warp the young Twain's joking, paternalistic
colonialism into something quite different, endowing Twain's humor
with a sinister retrospective glow, and effectively demythologizing
Twain's humor, just as Twain's obtuse, literal reading of Franklin demy-
thologized Franklin's understated, dry wit. Like a compulsively competitive athlete, Thompson usually wanted to compete only with the best.
If he could not achieve that, then he would habitually give up and try
something else, in the manner of a musician taking up another tune.

In major ways the fundamental template for the book appears in
Paul Gauguin's 1901 diary, *Noa Noa: A Tahitian Journal*. In that diary
Gauguin boasts of turning native ("I was a true savage, I was a Mao-
ri"[10]), dwells on renunciation of the beloved, embraces island mythology, and like Thompson, concludes his narrative with a native poem in
translation.

The book begins as if it were a diary narrative, a genre pioneered in
English by James Joyce in *A Portrait of the Artist as a Young Man*
(1916). Joyce's narrative provides the overarching model for the book,
but Hunter is not a young man. While Kerouac's American attempt to
redo Joyce's approach in *The Vanity of Duluoz* (1968) had faltered
through lack of trenchant irony, Thompson's ironies remain so submerged that most readers experience bewilderment. Thompson's twist:
we have a portrait of the artist in mid-life crisis (as a divorced, middle-
aged drug addict), not a *bildungsroman*. For his first-person narrative,
Joyce chose the name of his brother Stephen as the hero of his autobio-

graphical fiction. Hunter's shadow multiplies throughout the novel, so that all characters present lesser-incarnated manifestations of the artist, a godly avatar apart from all others. Hunter's consciousness begins where Stephen arrives at the end of Joyce's narrative: utterly alone.

Rather than attempt a running parallel, as did Kerouac, Thompson composes an American sequel. After achieving illumination, Stephen is left with the question of where to go in his desire to flee the nets of nationality, acquaintances, and family that held him to the ground. Stephen wanted to fly like his namesake, Daedalus. Joyce fled to Trieste, then Paris, and eventually Switzerland, where he ran at the last moment from the Nazis. Thompson fled to Hawaii, as painter Paul Gauguin fled to Tahiti with an invitation.

At the same time Hunter was writing, Steadman, as illustrator, was creating a parallel autobiographical narrative in images. While Hunter flees America, Steadman's fleeing England becomes a major motif. The scenario of both artists running in tandem flight created competitive friction as each sought to impose their own autobiographical stamp on the project. That furnishes the explanation for one of Thompson's sardonic jokes: when things were not going well on the project, he called it "a Ralph book."[11]

The narrative begins in mid-air flight. In the ancient Daedalus legend, the artist builds his own wings, but the postmodern artist buys a ticket. Moreover, the plane will land in safety, unlike the semi-tragic ending of the Daedalus legend (with son Ikaros dying from flying too close to the sun)—that risk of hubris, Joyce's Stephen jauntily acknowledges he will take.[12] On the plane to Hawaii, the Daedalian "Thompson" character encounters the colorful blue-armed Ackerman, who has mysterious drug connections, his blue arm being the result of a lengthy and ultimately successful attempt to retrieve an item accidentally dropped into the chemical sink of the plane toilet.

In Herman Melville's *Moby-Dick* (1851), Ishmael awakes with his roommate Queequeg's tattooed pagan arm around him, as if Ishmael had been his wife. The arm "tattooed all over with an interminable Cretan labyrinth of a figure, no two parts of which were of one precise shade,"[13] fascinates Ishmael. Melville's following hilarious scene, in which Ishmael watches Queequeg don his beaver hat, then slip under the bed with his trousers and boots to dress in mysterious privacy beneath the bouncing bed, provides the comic template for the oddly accoutered Ackerman and his blue arm attending to his private business in the claustrophobic toilet closet of the plane.

After breakfasting with his harpoon as substitute for knife and fork, Queequeg smokes contentedly his tomahawk pipe. Before the plane landing, Ackerman slips Thompson a small bottle of liquid and advises that he drink it in the tiny toilet, since he wouldn't want to be caught carrying illegal drugs at customs.[14] Just as Melville leaves the reader to imagine what was in Queequeg's pipe mixture (most commercial pipe mixtures of the day contained ten or twenty percent marijuana), Thompson as author leaves the reader to wonder what was in the little bottle Ackerman gave to the character Thompson. The little bottle that makes you short or tall may have been magically transported from Lewis Carroll's *Alice's Adventures in Wonderland* (1865). Perhaps the bottle makes him large, because later on Thompson will grow much larger, as large as a god.

Melville describes briefly, with comic absurdity, the history of New Bedford, Massachusetts; Thompson—even more briefly because he's interrupted by the stewardess—summarizes from a travel book the absurd history of "Owhyhee," beginning with its "discovery" by Captain Cook. While Melville had doted on New Bedford's fabulous wealth, Thompson sensibly emphasizes Hawaii's scenic beauty from an aerial perspective, although he observes that its 500-foot cliffs look more like a welcoming tomb than a harbor. This meditation on tombs also follows in Melville's footsteps, for in "The Chapel," the next chapter, Ishmael surveys the church tombstones, reproducing several inscriptions, although he warns that they are described from memory and may not be exact. In Melville's novel, this scene functions as a prefiguring hint regarding the fate of the *Pequod*'s sailors. Enhancing the possibility of Captain Cook–like sea doom, Ackerman warns Thompson that as a rank outsider tourist, he will definitely need help—a sinister parallel to Melville's ridiculing of rural greenhorns who naively enlist on whaling ships.

Skinner, an exotic photographer with a shady background in Vietnam, meets the arriving crew at the airport. Skinner had first appeared in Thompson's previous attempt at fiction, *The Silk Road* (1980), an abandoned novel about drug smuggling in the Florida Keys. (Two anemic sample chapters, plus a book outline pitch, appear in the anthology *Songs of the Doomed*.) Thompson couldn't find a publisher for the proposed novel, yet he lured Jann Wenner into selling its companion movie treatment, *Cigarette Key*, coauthored by Aspen novelist Tom Corcoran, to Paramount.[15] With the prospect of President Reagan threatening to censor Hollywood for irresponsible films, the movie project was dropped like a hot potato; without the carrot of another paycheck, Thompson lost interest in completing the novel. When he meets Thompson at the airport, Skinner greets Thompson with the prodding challenge that he thought Thompson had retired from "this business" (writing fiction). Hunter rejoins that he had grown bored.[16]

While Melville describes how Ishmael and Queequeg become unlikely bosom friends because of Queequeg's pagan superstitions and peculiar habits, Thompson describes how, in Vietnam he and Skinner, despite Skinner's visceral hatred of journalism, had become close friends over the mutual experience of leisurely smoking at Mr. Hee's opium den in Saigon. The cynical and viciously bigoted Skinner functions as a replacement for the dark side of Raoul Duke. Thompson considered Skinner a new mirror for the times, an antihumanist indifferent to the fate of others.[17] While Ishmael considered himself to be an upstanding member of the "infallible Presbyterian Church," Skinner notes that he and Thompson are *criminals*, drug fiends after the next high. This is, of course, a joke—no one accuses any writer who ever wrote of being a criminal for consuming alcohol, and no scholar accuses Coleridge, Baudelaire, or Poe of being criminals for having indulged in certain substances. Queequeg gives Ishmael a shrunken head as a gift, while Thompson will give Skinner an aspirin bottle of unnamed drugs that Thompson has surreptitiously smuggled in the luggage of the unknowing Steadman.

Much as Melville in "The Chapel" reproduces a folk song about the terrors of whaling and the need to call upon God for deliverance, Thompson reproduces a short excerpt from a Warren Zevon song about hula hula boys that blares from the car radio, the chapel of the current world. The song appears to tell a story about promiscuity—a girl leaves her boyfriend to run off with two native Hawaiians. When compared with the sermon about Jonah and the whale Ishmael hears in the chapel, this song functions as a telling register of how Puritan times have changed.

Just as Queequeg retails stories of his native island and family, as well as local tribal customs, Skinner informs Thompson about Hawaii. Both anecdotal performances emphasize cultural difference and cultural misunderstandings: Queequeg tells of the comic *faux pas* of a visiting captain obliviously violating cultural sensibilities, while Skinner relates a gruesome story about a whole family (children included) from San Francisco who were raped after dark on the beach by a gang of Koreans, as well as other tales of atrocity immured in bigotry. To a disbelieving bartender, Skinner makes the facetious claim that Thompson was a former governor of American Samoa.

Ralph Steadman replaces Acosta as Thompson's sidekick in the novel. In real life tensions arose between them because Steadman insisted they were equals. Instead of vomiting from mescaline like Acosta, Steadman vomits from scotch. A surfeit of Samoan jokes, some quite funny, flutter through *The Curse of Lono* like a flock of blind bats. These porpoise-frolicking jokes function as a tribute to the plentitude of Samoan jokes in Acosta's autobiography. Over-the-top social disasters find quick remedies with Thompson's improvised social wit. The entertaining *Running* magazine piece, with its inventive insults to marathon runners and health nuts, is reproduced in its full glory: Thompson and Steadman witness modern savages, "the doomed generation," perform their barbaric public ritual to the ruthless and merciless health god. Some runners are injured, or martyred, in the process. The fad of narcissistic masochism receives opportune ridicule, and Steadman's illustrations nearly leap off the page in comic acrobatics.

One aspect of the running event that fascinates Thompson is that people participate to *lose* rather than win. Hunter sees this as a novel and healthy development in American subculture. Losers finally have a place of pride in a monolithic culture blindly dedicated to "We're number one!" inanity. Runners merely receive a modest gray T-shirt announcing they've completed the marathon. The commemoration of victory in defeat also relates to the history of Pearl Harbor's bombing by the Japanese, yet the irony that half of the eight thousand runners are Japanese somehow seems surreal, since the Japanese appear to be honoring their own defeat or protesting the absurdity of the Japanese militarism that led to the absurd attack.

Hunter roots for the losers, yet he admires the genial eccentricity of the winner, Duncan MacDonald, a local who has a reputation for irregular training and weekend boozing. Thompson boasts that *he's* the real winner because he doesn't even have to run—he's being paid to *watch* the spectacle unfold, being a participant in the news that people placidly and unthinkingly consume on television. Eyeing the other journalists covering the event, Hunter prophesies indigence for future journalists—a brutal Darwinian crunch, especially for freelance journalists (who need to cover their own expenses) not enslaved by large corporations that demand mindless copy. The odds against Thompson's own Horatio Alger story of success in journalism appear to be much greater than the odds against a double-chinned couch potato winning the grueling marathon.

Thompson's marathon coverage includes an amusing and political tirade that confirms his announcement in *Fear and Loathing in Las Vegas* that hippies will abandon their romantic idealism:

> Run for your life because that's all you have left. The same people who burned their draft cards in the Sixties and got lost in the Seventies are now into *running*. When politics failed and personal relationships proved unmanageable; after McGovern went down and Nixon exploded right in front of our eyes . . . after Ted Kennedy got Stassenized and Jimmy Carter put the fork to everybody who ever believed anything he said about anything at all, and after the nation turned *en masse* to the atavistic wisdom of Ronald Reagan.[18]

Harold Stassen (1907–2001) was a former governor of Minnesota (1939–1943) who became a perennial Republican candidate for U.S. president, seeking the office twelve times between 1944 and 2000, five of those times *after* the publication of *The Curse of Lono*. Sitting instead of running, Thompson takes the opportunity to attack all those who have abandoned their idealism. This sensibility of this passage suggests Melville's weary comment on Captain Bildad of the *Pequod*, an idealistic Quaker pacifist who had romantically turned to the sea to make a living: Bildad "had long since come to sage and sensible conclusion that a man's religion is one thing and this practical world quite another. This world pays dividends."[19] Bildad began his career as a lowly cabin boy, working his way up the ladder, Horatio Alger-style, to achieve his glorious status as hiring manager under bloody Ahab. The process of selling out to the establishment has never changed during the course of history.

In the episode of Steadman's injury on a coral reef while swimming, Thompson draws a parallel with the fate of Captain Cook. Nature, not the natives, strikes back at the imperial Englishman, providing an environmental theme, the thread of which is later picked up in the fishing expedition: "The water all around us was littered with floating debris: beer bottles, orange peels, plastic baggies, and mangled tuna fish cans. About ten yards off the stern was an empty Wild Turkey bottle with a piece of paper inside."[20] Ackerman had tossed the bottle overboard with Thompson's message scrawled on free Kona Inn stationery: there "ARE no fish" in the ocean.[21] The frustration of fruitless fishing with the image of the ocean as a desert appears on the first page of Ernest Hemingway's *The Old Man and the Sea* (1952).

This predicament stands in direct contrast to Melville's estimation in *Moby-Dick* that over 260,000 sperm whales were killed off the American Atlantic coast every twenty years, and yet in his opinion, this number would not deplete the "immortal" whale.[22] Thompson makes the point that evolution in the ocean operates in reverse due to human overfishing. Like an artful silent-film comedian, Thompson was often capable of transforming a situational cliché joke like the message in a bottle into a revitalized laugh. Hunter's lifelong obsession with official stationery goes back to his beginning *Fear and Loathing at Las Vegas* on Mint Hotel stationery, yet reaches even further back to his stealing stationery at *Time* magazine, and from sundry other employers, to type his early efforts in fiction.

As a shaman "Doctor," Thompson performs a comic resurrection of Cook/Steadman with pulverized aloe plant, a three-hundred-year-old Samoan war club (perhaps inspired by Queequeg's comic use of his harpoon at breakfast, or the use of a war club to kill tuna as recorded by Paul Gauguin in his Tahitian journal, *Noa Noa*[23]), and enough flowing booze and erupting vomit to send a dozen sailors to the hospital emergency ward. Half-cured, Steadman teeters around the hotel "walking like a stroke victim"[24] with bent back and sketchbook, dazed by the overdose of valerian root that the good doctor inflicted upon him. A stranger leads Ralph away and advises him to depart for the leper colony at Molokai. Thompson notices the stranger giving Ralph a hard time and arrives to support him. The stranger, apparently a cranky marijuana drug dealer charging exorbitant prices, lashes out at Thompson with his razor-sharp cleats, but Thompson defeats him by mashing a lit cigarette into his face. Others restrain the stranger while Hunter and Ralph depart stylishly in their waiting limo.

The inspiration for this unlikely incident may be the episode of Iros from Book 18 in Homer's *Odyssey*, yet this will only be apparent on a second reading, because more specific allusions to the *Odyssey* appear only later in the book. Thompson inverts the situation in Homer, in which Odysseus, the stranger, appears in ragged disguise as a beggar. The raucous suitors manipulate a beggar's brawl for their entertainment, placing bets with varied odds, the favorite being the local alcoholic, Iros. Here, the stranger is the local pusher, but Hunter, neither the hometown native nor owner of the premises, is the real stranger at a hotel where he's merely a temporary guest.

Unlike in Homer, there's no betting on the fight, nor are there many spectators. Ducking and weaving from missing blows, Odysseus defeats his opponent with a single punch on the ear that cracks the skull, rendering his opponent unconscious and seemingly rendering Iros an utter idiot. Hunter parodies Homer's single punch with the thrust of a cigarette, but unlike Iros, the drug dealer is not hurt. Odysseus hangs around as a beggar without a place to go (although his son offers him the courtyard floor), while Hunter lounges in the back of a cushy limo on the way to a luxurious hotel, as Ralph finds himself wracked with spasms in the car as if he has just endured an arduous fistfight. Hunter had previously employed the one-punch knockout—Yeamon's clocking of Lotterman—in *The Rum Diary*, which had lightly cavorted with themes relating to the *Odyssey*.

Thompson and Steadman's family board a plane out of Honolulu to the Kona Coast, the fishing capital of Hawaii. The chapter "Why Do They Lie To Us?" brings changes on and twists the theme of lying into self-parody. It was Rinzler's favorite chapter. Workers in the tourist industry lie to clients; island natives lie to outsiders. Mr. Heem, their realtor,[25] lies to Hunter and Ralph about the size of the house they've rented. The car he arrives with at the airport is too small to accommodate them. Hunter doesn't care about such details, because Mr. Heem is so agreeable that he runs off to get a special package for Thompson, who lies to Steadman about why Heem has disappeared, leaving them stranded at the airport. Hugging his young daughter to his side, horrified Ralph says that what Hunter is doing is worse than outright perversion. Going native, Hunter has lied to his friend, in order to fulfill his "habitual needs." This confessional self-satire about drugs becomes amusing because of Steadman's hysteric exasperation with the irony of Steadman so closely hugging his daughter, as if he were the pervert.

Captain Steve arrives to transport them in a larger vehicle. He assures them they will catch fish in Kona. At the first red traffic light they come to, there is a garish bevy of transvestite prostitutes loitering under a banyan tree, hoping to catch "big fish" on vacation. Melville's *Redburn* (1849) had featured a whole chapter on the world's "Booble-Alleys," depicting the whorish trafficking sections of merchant ports as lurid Sodoms and Gomorrahs: "The pestilent lanes and alleys which, in their vocabulary, go by the names of Rotten-row, Gibraltar-place, and Booble-alley, are putrid with vice and crime; to which the round globe does not furnish a parallel."[26] While Melville waxes a wrathful Puritan sermon on the topic, Thompson treats the scene with comic brio.

One of the prostitutes, Hilo Bob, once worked as a mechanic for Steve (*hilo* is Hawaiian for "twisted").[27] After his sex-change operation, Bob appears at the boat's helm with his bare ass hanging out of his jeans. When Japanese tourists protest and riot at the sight of Bob's outfit, Bob is injured. The tourists file a lawsuit. Bob sues Steve for firing him. The satire on outlaw dressing, deviant sexuality, and the wild fracas recall Thompson's Hells Angels days. Hunter worries, What kind of place have they landed in?—a mild "flashback" acid joke that only old hippie fans will get. Steve casually informs Hunter that many of his tourist clients eat only cocaine for lunch. The upscale tourist industry catering to the very rich finds itself memorialized as dangerous cultural slumming. Hilo Bob's profession recalls that of Ralph "Sonny" Barger, the Hells Angels gang leader, who was a cycle mechanic. This wispy "floating iceberg" allusion continues the never-ending feud between Barger and Hunter.

Thompson's view of the Hawaiian tourist industry was jaundiced. He indulged in quixotic trash talk, telling Perry: "I am going to devote the rest of my life to the destruction of the tourist industry in these fucking islands."[28] Hunter saw the big lie stamped on all discourse directed at outsiders—viewing sports offers the only truth in television.

Arriving at an isolated house, Thompson and Steadman endure a week of relentless lashing rain, their only picture-postcard view being the steadily booming surf threatening to engulf them. Steadman's illustration features a monstrous wave of blood, an ecological motif that addresses the extinction of ocean life at the bloody hands of fishermen.

As a gesture of island hospitality, Steve ruefully retails his most macabre boat-accident tale, involving a sudden great wave, just to leave the visitors with something to think about. The recollection of a sudden great wave that ended in disaster conjures up the great hippie wave cited in *Fear and Loathing in Las Vegas* that concludes in disaster: "If the surf doesn't kill you, the Surge will, and anybody who tells you anything different should have his teeth gouged out with a chisel."[29] Hunter's metaphor turns primitive: the surf metaphor signposts drugs, one of the central iceberg motifs of the chapter. The "surge" coyly alludes to the danger of overdose.

A quarter of the chapter laboriously practices classic stichomythia (Acosta had effectively used stichomythia to describe a Mexican court scene with a judge in his first amusing letter to Hunter)[30] concerning the fickle art of weather forecasting and the infantile desire to deny reality: excitedly declaring the threat of a coming storm that is not a storm, in the manner of weather forecasters who (with a dose of hysteria) subscribe to the safe rather than sorry approach for their speculative science. Kona, on the leeward (dry) side of the island, possesses the distinction that "there is no other place in the world that so consistently bears the brunt of other people's weather,"[31] and this uncomfortable reality apparently leads to "institutional" insanity within the weather forecasting profession. Thompson did experience a Big Storm shortly after arriving at Kona, complaining in the aftermath that his cigarettes bent like limp rubber and his paper was so wet he needed waterproof pens to write, while boulders the size of television sets were cast into inhabitant's bedrooms. Cranes had to be hired to lift rocks from swimming pools.[32]

Following Twain's example, "Tits Like Orange Fireballs" mocks the folklore surrounding the female goddess Pele, the "randy Volcano goddess . . . who danced naked on molten lava with a gourd of gin in each hand, and anybody who didn't like it was instantly killed."[33] English gin in this archaic context provides amusing topical inference. Thompson relates that the historical King Lono, who accidentally killed his wife with a fatal blow, was *not* made in the same mold as Jesus, yet islanders subsequently elevated him to godhead during the Good Old Days before white men arrived.

The accidental death of the spouse appears, in its contemporary innuendo, to be a satiric reference to William Burroughs's accidental

murder of his wife Joan Vollmer, at a bar in Mexico City during a
drunken party exhibition of a "William Tell" game of shooting a drink
glass off her head.[34] The inference to be drawn? Thompson's drunken
behavior toward Sandy, whatever it was, pales in comparison to the
actions of the Beat celebrity Burroughs, whose family money got him
off the hook and out of Mexico without trial. (Burroughs later claimed it
was his guilt that motivated him as a writer.)[35] Yet this barb directed at
Burroughs, plus momentary self-satire, dims in comparison to the extended satire on Joan Didion that Thompson included in *Fear and
Loathing in Las Vegas*.

Thompson satirizes the brutal battles and acrimony between himself
and ex-wife Sandy.[36] Like Lono, a fertility god who failed to lift the sky
from the earth to provide more space for plants to grow, an angry
Thompson departs for foreign lands, vowing to return.

Christmas Eve, immersed in warm curling swirls of fog, finds celebration with traditional Hawaiian fireworks in honor of Lono. Memorializing an episode at Woody Creek in which Hunter was singed by an
explosion, Hunter manages to explode a surprise monster fireworks
bomb on a luckless neighbor's house, as if Thompson were a reckless
imperialist invader of Hawaii, like the Japanese at Pearl Harbor. Hunter's "bombs" consisted of five thousand fire crackers woven together
into a belt that was rolled up into a disk more than a foot across and
wrapped in bright red paper.[37]

The idea for a bomb episode probably originated as an effort to
outdo an anecdote about Hemingway in Bimini, where he employed a
tommy gun to shoot sharks (and taking pictures of the bloody mess) in
an article published in the July 1935 issue of *Esquire* entitled "The
President Vanquishes."[38] This type of over-going remains typical of
many artists. Hemingway was inspired by Zane Grey's excellent book on
tuna fishing, *Tales of Swordfish and Tuna* (1927), one of eight books
Grey wrote on fishing.[39]

Thompson proceeds to mock the sentimentality of an English
Christmas, a feast that coincides with the feast of the fertility god Lono.
Thompson notes that Dickens depicts the season accoutered by nostalgia for light snow, with a starving, shivering family huddling around
burning coals in "A Christmas Carol." In that story Dickens depicted
and popularized the idea of a white Christmas in England, an event that

rarely occurs in that climate, but remains iconic for the northern states in America. Dickens biographer Peter Ackroyd observed:

> In view of the fact that Dickens can be said to have almost single-handedly created the modern idea of Christmas, it is interesting to note that in fact during the first eight years of his young life there was a white Christmas every year; so sometimes reality does actually exist before the idealized image. [40]

Christmas Day was also the unlikely date that Melville's *Pequod* cast anchor with bawdy sailor songs, "some sort of chorus about the girls in Booble Alley." [41] On that day Thompson professes to be astonished that "nobody has lied to me for three or four hours." [42] Thompson perceives Christmas to be the Big Lie, a northern colonial myth of limited universality.

Steadman's family experiences Christmas marooned in a wooden shack, estranged from anyone they ever knew, surrounded by people who don't speak the King's English. They long for the snow and slush of Britain, a country that does not appreciate the television seasonal onslaught of football, an American game they neither appreciate nor understand.

For his Christmas illustration, Steadman offers an ink-splattered quill pen that commemorates the Hawaiian King Kamahameha the Great (c. 1758–1819), who conquered the Hawaiian islands, unifying them into single kingdom. He was famous for the "law of the splintered oar," which protects noncombatants in warfare. [43] The top of Steadman's leaking quill paints a splintered oar. The implication of Steadman's patriotic drawing is that Thompson pranked the wrong target with his explosion—perhaps Thompson should have targeted a foreign slum landlord for his fireworks experiment instead of the nearest house at hand (owned by a genial Hawaiian). The illustration dovetails with Hunter's text, celebrating Christmas from the Hawaiian perspective rather than the British perspective.

In "South Point," the narrative turns to domestic diary, haunted by the theme of why the news lies to people and why natives lie to tourists. Hunter explains that England would have controlled the whole Pacific if only the Earl of Sandwich was not distracted by his continuous orchestration of orgies. More jokes about corrupt lawyers give way to endearing sentiment that features Thompson cheerfully and dotingly fishing with son Juan, an episode that runs parallel to the opening pages of *The Old Man and the Sea* in which we are told that the charming young boy enjoys idyllic fishing with the old man, even when nothing is caught, as is the case with Juan and Hunter. In Hemingway's case this was an autobiographical reflection of a visit by his sons in Bimini,[44] or rather an inspired, fatherly imitation of Hemingway's diaries because, in his memoir, Juan recollects that his best memory of the trip consists of father and son golfing rather than fishing, since the weather was so awful.[45]

Juan departs on the plane. The bout of paranoia Thompson undergoes in the boat with Ackerman and Captain Steve in "We're All Equal in the Ocean" recalls a sudden bout of paranoia experienced by Ishmael on Nantucket Island. In the dark, searching for highly recommended lodgings, Ishmael dredges up a list of ominous symbols: his previous innkeeper's name, A. Coffin; the tombstones at the whaler's chapel; and a gallows specter, which are merely trees, he imagines fearfully in the dark.[46] After being nearly tossed overboard by a wave, and in the process losing Ackerman's vial of China White heroin, Thompson wonders if *both* Ackerman and Steve are junkies, reflecting that he doesn't know either very well, that you can't trust junkies: here he is, trapped in a small boat in the middle of nowhere with darkness descending.

"The Land of Po" refers to the fishing waters of Western Australia. Among the horrors encountered: a lethally poisonous sea snake; rough seas that threaten to douse Thompson's hibachi; an overdose of Dramamine for Ackerman, which renders him unconscious; the loss of an anchor, retrieved by scuba diving; a case of the bends; a scuba tank smashing Ackerman's foot; and a serious storm. Steadman was infuriated that the small boat they inhabited did not have a single rope aboard to toss to another boat when they ran out of kerosene and had to be towed.[47] This concludes Ralph's boating.

The futile fishing expedition finds mild comic interpretation as an adventure in imperial hubris, the defeated warriors slouching back with wounds as if they had been ambushed by armed fish. Ackerman suggests finding relief in the City of Refuge, an ancient sanctuary where no one may be arrested. Instead they retire to Hunter and Ralph's rental, only to discover Steadman's departure note: he and family have fled to the airport. Terry Southern, in his *New York Magazine* review of the book, jibed that the book's subtitle might have been "The Dismantling of Ralph Steadman."[48] Rupert, the dog that Thompson gave as a gift to Ralph's daughter Sadie, is bequeathed to Hunter for care. The two content themselves with drinking, smoking marijuana, and swapping storm observations at Ralph's abandoned balcony as they listen to the Amazing Rhythm Aces, a blues-inflected country rock band from Tennessee.

Thompson and Ackerman check into the hotel. The hotel clerk has noticed that Steadman and family have left the hotel and demands a new signature for the bill. Hunter cons the hotel by having Ackerman, who conveniently walks in at just the right moment, to sign the register in under the name of Rupert (as Rupert's dog manager); the clerk does not realize that Rupert is the dog. The dog has an acute case of fleas; the hotel clerk becomes queasy:

> Those goddamn things carry germs!" he shouted. "Red fleas are worse than rats! They carry smallpox! They carry cholera! They carry syphilis!"
> What about room service I asked.[49]

There are no red fleas—dog fleas are either black or brown, although they can appear red if covered with blood from excessive scratching or biting by the dog—this supplies a contemporary equivalent of Thomas Nashe's invention of the humorous red herring in *Nashe's Lenten Stuffe* (1599). While Nashe facetiously sang the praises of the red herring, Thompson characteristically inverts the joke into a feverish fear-rap. Distraught and hysterical, the hotel desk clerk supplies the con duo anything they wish, similar to the incident with the desk clerk in the Vegas novel.

Ackerman quickly signs the register, because he could care less about the hotel bill—he has just harvested his marijuana crop and is about to stuff the suite with at least a dozen black, bulging garbage bags of grass, which Hunter plans to mail to a near-abandoned farm outside of Houston for his cut of a profitable wholesale transaction. Ackerman has arrived with several flea collars for Rupert, who has such an acute case of fleas that the unnerved hotel clerk's fretful hysteria allows the scam to proceed smoothly.

Thompson catalogs various woes, including a triple wasp sting in the eye under his sunglasses, for which he's plotting with the Korean lawyer to sue the hotel. While on the surface this incident appears to be frivolous fiction, it's also likely a redramatization of insect stings Thompson experienced in his South American reportorial tours of duty.

The dog needs a new alias so that he won't be connected to the hotel bill; he is renamed Homer. In Homer's *Odyssey*, on returning as a beggar to his palace at Ithaka, Odysseus spots his old dog Argos, covered with fleas. His faithful dog Argos, whom Odysseus fondled as a puppy, recognizes his master. Despite his misery as a neglected outcast, faithful Argos, unable to bark even, expires on a pile of refuse, happy in death to have seen his master return home.[50]

Rupert, now "Homer," is the warped antithesis of Argos in terms of fidelity and behavior. Moreover, he is a puppy, not an old dog. He lounges in the lap of luxury, not on a pile of manure; he does not die, but magically grows grotesquely misshapen and large, presumably as a result of the various drugs Thompson and Ackerman feed him, an accelerated living Darwinian example of isolated island evolution. Dr. Ho, the visiting vet (who also treats Hunter for the wasp stings, since Hunter is just another animal), makes out an affidavit that the dog's name is Homer, yet he declares the dog a medical monstrosity before fleeing the Gothic horror show in a well-timed comic scene. Rupert begins to devolve into a mythological crossbreed between dog and dinosaur, as if he's turning into legendary three-headed Cerberus, the guardian hound of hell who will protect the underworld drug hoard. While indulging in creative myth making, this allegory presents evolution in reverse, questioning presumptions that biological changes are necessarily beneficial.[51]

The theme of reverse evolution in literature had first been pioneered by that charming and rebellious Scot, Robert Louis Stevenson, in his novella *Strange Case of Dr. Jekyll and Mr. Hyde*, which satirized the notion of the English gentleman that had been invented by Sir Walter Scott in his novel *Ivanhoe*. In Scott's novel the main character is not a superhero like King Richard—he's a stalwart and upright man who combines the best virtues of Anglo and Norman heritage; he's vulnerable, often physically wounded, yet always makes the correct moral decision with regard to politics and chivalry.

Stevenson's novella presented a parable: Jekyll remains a Victorian gentleman as long as his supply of exotic colonial imports sustains his upper-class lifestyle. Once a single drug ingredient essential to his demeanor, sanity, and gentlemanly equilibrium falters, he reverts to his primitive apelike origins as Hyde.[52] Underneath the placid propriety of the English gentleman lurks barbaric Hyde, who in London's Hyde Park de-evolves into his primitive Tudor origins.[53] Hyde Park was created (for hunting) by that larger-than-life monster, Henry VIII, who had confiscated the land from the canons of Westminster Abbey in 1536. Stevenson's fictional use of drugs as the transformational motif of his satire offered the thematic path and precedent for Thompson's island fantasy.

In the concluding fishing expedition, Hunter snags his trophy marlin. In the chapter, "We Killed as Champions," he exclaims deliriously in his "King Kong shout," "I am Lono." The chapter provides a parody tribute to Hemingway. Steadman says Thompson "was going out there to be Ernest Hemingway in *The Old Man and the Sea*."[54] The killing of a marlin by clubbing was the small fisherman's traditional way of killing a marlin, as Hemingway notes in *The Old Man and the Sea*. But the old man does not club the marlin; in one of the novella's best scenes, he clubs the many sharks devouring the marlin attached to his small boat.

Characteristically, Thompson warps Hemingway's parable of man against nature: Thompson's boasting furnishes the opposite of the humility prized by Hemingway. The triumph of ancient barbarism (the killing of the marlin with the ancient Samoan war club) comically proves Thompson's primitive divinity. Being victoriously divine, Thompson enters the legendary pantheon of nature.

Whereas the struggle of Hemingway's Santiago concludes with only the skeleton of the marlin as evidence of his epic battle, Thompson, without much struggle, except for previously enduring a storm while huddled over the coals of a hibachi during a fruitless outing, eventually possesses the whole huge carcass of 308 pounds,[55] with tangible photographic proof for a memento rather than the ghost of mere memory, as in Hemingway. Moreover, there is a crowd to witness his opportunistic triumph, even though there is the comedy of the pagan Thompson/Lono's divinity being scorned like Jesus of Nazareth's. The clubbing of the marlin by the "god" Lono satirizes the sadism of Christian theology, wherein the incarnated son discovers martyrdom. The physical viciousness of the clubbing also encodes the horror of the public exhibition of violence as social spectacle, memorializing Thompson's own clubbing (and the clubbing of other reporters) in the nationally televised footage of the Mayor Richard Daley's 1968 Chicago police riot. The superior technology of the rented boat makes incompetent, amateur fishermen victors over nature, erasing the heroic nobility of sweating and struggling humanity in the semi-defeat Hemingway had valorized. How times have changed.

Hemingway's parable presents a reification of Christianity, but Thompson, inversely, presents an allegory attacking Christianity. While Hawaiians remain notoriously superstitious, Hawaiians who literally worship Lono remain in short supply. If someone today were to boast that *he* was Jesus in his return incarnation, announcing his Second Coming, he would either be pelted with stones or carted to a mental institution. The superstitious locals appear crazy with intolerant prejudice. When Thompson yells "I am Lono," this functions as an allegory for Thompson's disdain for Christianity. Thompson shares this perspective with Yeats's poem, "The Second Coming," wherein Christianity is perceived as a historical nightmare.[56] While Joan Didion had applied Yeats's nightmare vision to Haight-Ashbury hippies, Thompson now invokes himself as the apocalyptic avatar of Lono to proclaim the exploitative conformity of the Anglo-American empire as the new global nightmare.

Thompson's Lono lifts a leaf from Nietzsche's concept of eternal return to enter the flux of becoming,[57] yet in execution, the theme becomes more notional appropriation under the surface than active development. The use of an allegory, a literary modality the modern world sometimes finds difficult or obscure, toward the end of Thompson's travelogue novel, instigates the abrupt shift that enhances the fragmentary feeling of discontinuity, especially since this shift occurs in personal letters to Steadman included at the end of the book. Such great leaps are the signature of the postmodern literary world, yet that very letter technique in a story about drugs had been done before: Stevenson's *Strange Case of Dr. Jekyll and Mr. Hyde* concludes with the indiscreet publication of three private letters explaining some of the more obscure aspects of the story, including the comic, satiric, swooning death of that gentleman, Dr. Lanyon, who died from shock at witnessing the physical transformation of Hyde into Jekyll.

Another aspect of the "I am divine" conjures up both Nietzsche and Rousseau. While Rousseau did not invent or idolize the "noble savage,"[58] he cast more complexity on the notion of childhood innocence, endowing it with self-love, self-worth, and a desire for self-respect, compassion for others, the power to choose, and discrimination of thought. For Rousseau, childhood was the root of morals and politics (the relations to others).[59] He identified this natural goodness as "amorality rather than any basic awareness of right or wrong. Yet if humankind is naturally good, how do we account for the degeneration of things at the hand of man?"[60] Lono's enigmatic distance from others, even within his own tribal culture, signals an otherness at odds with politics, the traditional situation of the artist devoted to cultivating the garden of art.[61] Like Rousseau in middle age, Thompson led mostly a private rural life with forays into the political arena, but in philosophy he remained closer to Nietzsche, who sometimes reverted to parable.

In *On the Genealogy of Morals* (1887) Nietzsche speaks of several necessary ideals for the artist as an instinct that enables conditions for intellectual development (the artist being the womb of his work). (This was an argument Thompson employed in his divorce settlement in order to maintain his residence at Woody Creek.) Nietzsche criticizes artists in general as being not independent enough, declaring they often resort to philosophy to justify their ideals in art. Rather than construct their own philosophy from scratch, they wear ready-made clothes off the rack. Nietzsche proceeds to analyze Wagner in terms of Schopenhauer's influence. If there is any ready-made philosophical clothing in Thompson, it comes from the mercurial workshop of Nietzsche.

Thompson landing the oversized marlin offers a fishing parable to counter the fishing theme of the Christian gospels and Hemingway's novel. Lono is a fisher of fish *for* the uncomprehending crowd at the dock. He's not about to proselytize—make men fishers of men. No disciples come forth. Thompson/Lono stands tall as a silent enigma. The huge marlin, which can feed masses, is presented as a miracle: the fish comes from a more primitive age when the ocean exhibited fecund fertility, and the political innocence of humans permitted individuals to transcend tribal structures. This pre-tribal dignity of the individual was an innocent communion with the divine in nature and within the self. From this perspective, Christianity appears as a barbaric, degenerative apparatus of the corrupt state that blinds people to the divine powers inherent in humanity.

In *Beyond Good and Evil*, Nietzsche charges philosophy with blindly accepting the Judeo-Christian tradition, arguing all religion to be but a form of "neurosis."[62] Just as Nietzsche finds Judaism more acceptable than Christianity, Thompson finds the pagan Lono more acceptable than the Christ of Christianity—the Lono versus Christ feast *agon* and the contrasting style of traditional celebrations valorizes Lono as being free of hypocritical moralizing. Nietzsche also criticized the British philosophers Bacon, Hobbes, Hume, and Locke for their construction of a stultifying, mechanical world model, a debasement of philosophy that Hegel and Schopenhauer had to refute.[63] Thompson follows the example of Nietzsche's attitude toward England when, in his discussion of Charles Dickens, he mocks the debasing sentimentality and excessive moralizing of English literature in Dickens's most popular piece, "A Christmas Carol."

While Rousseau attacks unexamined legal customs and precedents, Nietzsche analyses morality as accumulated tribal prejudices, casting his vision back 10,000 years to the pre-moral period of humankind, when actions were judged merely by their consequences. Such an amoral perspective, free of "civilized" blinkers, permits a clearer description of science, habits, society, and even morals. *That* is also the Lono perspective: the comic de-evolution of the dog Rupert relates to Nietzsche's point about science and the overly optimistic idea of progress. Nietzsche's arrival at this liberating amoral, or pre-moral, insight leans on Rousseau's notion of childhood's innocent amorality and the corruption of the child by social mores and customs, though Nietzsche is loathe to acknowledge the Frenchman. He praises in general only the sixteenth- and seventeenth-century philosophers of France, thus referencing the skeptical Pyrrhonist tradition[64] and silently snubbing the revival of French philosophy and mathematics under Descartes, while tossing a brief nod of literary approval to Marie-Henri Beyle (Stendhal).

Imitating Robert Louis Stevenson's comic travelogue, *Travels with a Donkey in the Cévennes* (1879), Twain had toured Hawaii in comic misery with a spavined donkey. Thompson, however, gleefully races a car (actually, a yellow Volkswagen convertible) on the Saddle Road in the rain at over one hundred miles an hour on straight stretches and over fifty miles per hour on mountainous S-turns. Thompson (according to the book's letter dated June 1, 1981, letter to Steadman) had completed that Saddle Road drive passage by then. The perfunctory speed run presents a pale reprise of the famous edge-cycle anecdote in *Hell's Angels*. The announcement that Thompson will attempt a speed record with a yellow Ferrari presents a substitute for Hemingway's record tuna catch in Bimini.[65] Steadman's illustration for the speed run, "It was *not* Rupert I saw on the Saddle Road—it was merely an apparition hitching a lift," might be interpreted as a ghostly portrait of Oscar Acosta rather than a random hallucination.

To avoid distraction, Hunter and Laila had retreated to Fairhope, Alabama, with Tom Corcoran to finish the book, yet they returned to Woody Creek with the manuscript unfinished.[66] Steadman, however, had completed his work for the book. Ian Ballantine, now a consulting editor for Random House, was exasperated that Rinzler had already disbursed the second half of Thompson's advance (a total of $90,000). Ballantine, who was convinced that Thompson was brain-damaged by an excess of drugs,[67] made several diplomatic visits to prod Thompson, demanding that Thompson cease any drug use. Thompson agreed,[68] although Ballantine's formal decorum, pompous manners, childlike elf-in smile, and conspicuous effort to appear professionally well dressed alienated Thompson, who lived with an informal Western sensibility. After all, Hunter was accustomed to running around half naked in bare feet at Woody Creek. Random House was anxiously expecting a companion masterpiece to his peculiar *Iliad*, *Fear and Loathing in Las Vegas*, yet Ballantine made it clear to Thompson that writing was about making money, that Random House would not be exploited. After such lectures, Thompson would head for the liquor cabinet and ferociously gulp down beer and vodka. Ballantine fled, fearing what Hunter would do if he was drunk.[69]

The concluding chapter, "Rage, Rage Against the Coming of the Light," appears to have been written when Rinzler arrived to extract more copy. That chapter title offers a satiric play on a line from Dylan Thomas's villanelle, "Do Not Go Gentle into That Good Night," changing Thomas's "Dying" to "Coming." Thomas, at his father's deathbed, implicitly promises his father, a high school Shakespeare teacher, that he will make their family name famous, "rage" being the first word of Homer's *Iliad*. Thomas's high rhetoric promises Homeric immortality, lamenting his father will die like Achilles before their family name achieves renown through the poems of the Welsh Homer.

According to Steadman's memoir, Thompson frequently ranted on the subject of that headline: the rant was directed at the future menace of a computerized world wherein "Every mindless little screwhead can pour his sickest thoughts into this new machinery, twist it a degree out

of normal and send it back out as wisdom."[70] That is an apt description
of the current Internet blogosphere and the vitriolic inanity of national
politicians—just what Thompson had foreseen once politicians directed
their minions to put their mitts on computer keyboards.

Without relevant text, that chapter headline pulses like a neon sign
blinking on an empty street at night, devoid of meaning because it
displays no connection with the following narrative. The chapter features a tape recorder gone amok, offering a parody of television commercials in the repetitive blaring of slogans about ice cubes, a favorite
health advertisement theme of Thompson's. He often reminds readers
that if you drink, the easiest and most pleasant way of avoiding dehydra-
tion is to ante up on cold cubes and dilute the alcohol running in your
veins while enlisting your kidneys to work overtime.

Thompson recycled the chapter title, "Yesterday's Weirdness Is Tomorrow's Reason Why," for a brief 1990 interview with biographer
William McKeen, reprinted in *The Kingdom of Fear*, wherein Hunter
laments that the decade will be known as "The Gray Area": by the end
of the nineties, "no one will be sure of anything except that you *must*
obey the rules, sex will kill you, politicians lie, rain is poison, and the
world is run by whores." The chapter title casts a backward look, acclaiming *Fear and Loathing in Las Vegas* as a masterwork that identified the nexus of repression which would unfold upon the country.
Hunter confesses, "I warped a few things, but it was a pretty accurate
picture." He boosted his masterpiece as "good as *The Great Gatsby*,
and better than *The Sun Also Rises*."[71]

The photo that fronts the chapter, with Thompson by the hung 308-
pound tuna, recalls the iconic photograph of Hemingway and his 381-
pound record tuna catch published in the Sunday *New York Times* on
June 6, 1935.

The conclusion features letters, plus historical quotations from Laila's research. As printed, "Yesterday's Weirdness Is Tomorrow's Reason
Why" does not offer the why to what. Possibly that title belongs to the
concluding chapter, which was probably to feature a conversation with
Skinner about what happened the day before with the bathing girls.

"A Dog Took My Place"[72] should depict the comedy of the unfaith-
ful and now vicious dog, "Homer," snapping at security guards, peeing
and puking on the first-class carpet as he soars out of Honolulu with a
hundred yapping snarls on Thompson's personal return ticket. Thomp-

son may have contemplated adding more scenes: perhaps a dispute at the airport with an official that would provide an opportunity for a comic chase to arrest Thompson, who would successfully flee to the hotel. As it is, the dog Argos merely occupies Thompson's hotel room and provides an insulting caricature dis against Sandy's current lover.

Accompanying his June 21, 1981, letter to Steadman, Hunter sent a photo scrawled over with "We Killed Like Champions." This was certainly not intended by Thompson to be part of the book. As noted in the letter to Steadman, that chapter was tentatively titled "How to Catch Big Marlin in Deep Water."[73] Thompson's boast of killing fish resembles in its dark humor one of the funniest passages in Twain's narrative, wherein he facetiously argues for the virtuous propriety of tourists appropriating human arm and thigh bones from an ancient battlefield for the proper safekeeping of the trophy relics.[74] Twain was undoubtedly mocking Lord Elgin's appropriation of the Parthenon fragments (1801–1812). Thompson alludes to Twain's passage from his 1867 *Letters to Hawaii* with an amusing line in the letter: "Why won't Norwood return my calls about sacking the gravesites?"[75] That was Thompson's comic version of his frustrated request for permission to visit the sacred grave sites.

The book's letter to Steadman reads: "I was forced to flee the hotel after the realtors hired thugs to finish me off. But they killed a local *haole* fisherman instead."[76] A *haole* indicates a white fisherman. Among native Hawaiians, a gang of high school students might casually get together and celebrate "Kill a Haole Day," which could be Christmas, Sunday, or any day of the year—by beating up someone from the American military base, usually a white soldier.[77]

Skinner might have driven Thompson out to the base of the City of Refuge to tell Thompson that he was now a marathon runner and must run for his life. After a comic run uphill with police sirens gaining on him, Thompson would breathlessly make the gates of the City of Refuge. There would be, however, no ancient priestly class residing there to welcome him, only a solitary and bored park ranger.

The custom of asylum was once nearly universal in the pagan world and played an integral role in Egyptian, Greek, and Hebraic culture, but in practice its observance depended on the arbitrary granting of mercy, which was not always given—Hector's father Priam was said to have been slain at the altar in Troy, and after the fall of Athens to Sparta under the reign of the Thirty Tyrants, leading citizens were murdered in temples.[78] In medieval Europe, church sanctuary was observed as often as it was not. Even Dante, who received asylum from various nobles, puts the asylum of Limbo in the first circle of his Inferno as a place of refuge for pagan authors such as Homer, Ovid, and Lucan, a master of violent description. Descartes sought asylum in Holland; both Voltaire and Rousseau sought political asylum in England for a time. England had a long legal tradition of asylum, the most famous violation in medieval times being the murder of Thomas à Becket in Canterbury Cathedral. England and the United States offered asylum to Jews and dissidents from Nazi Germany. The United States was once the Country of Refuge, a giant political asylum for the globe, but Thompson presents that history as shriveled to an archaic corner, forgotten by amnesiac Americans. Today, England and Western Europe appear to have abandoned the tradition of political asylum, as illustrated by the notorious case of Julian Assange. In the United States, the Occupy movement quickly discovered that public space no longer offers asylum, despite the fact that the country's origin derives from the free use of public space and the concept of international asylum. The appearance of asylum in the postcolonial world that Thompson describes poses a challenge to the sensibility of contemporary readers, who tend to think mercy and asylum archaic irrelevancies.

Asylum for the innocent, or those caught in dubious situations in times of turmoil, retains the vital principle that all human life is sacred, especially the just. Thompson employs asylum in an ironic manner—it is not the writer who is insane, but society, driven by insatiable greed that creates predators and victims. As a personal matter, Thompson had been concerned about retaining his home "asylum" after his divorce from Sandy (who initially claimed half the house and property). A young writer may wander the globe and scribble, but a mature writer usually requires a refuge base, as a practical and psychological mechanism to work in solitude.

Finding that refuge remains problematic for any artist, but the character Thompson momentarily achieves a symbolic refuge, unlike the ambiguous but hopeful conclusion for Stephen Dedalus in Joyce's *Portrait of the Artist as a Young Man*. The refrain in Joyce of "Alone, quite alone,"[79] echoes in Thompson's book title. *The Curse of Lono* depicts the ragged plight of the mature artist, who must necessarily be a critic of society, someone who stands alone: "A good writer stands above movements, neither a leader nor a follower, but a bright white golf ball in a fairway of wind-blown daisies."[80] Thompson's conclusion is tragicomedy: comic for the author who risks all (although tinged with memories of loss regarding Sandy and Acosta), but tragic for civilization which will always suspect that an artist's honest social critique remains a suspicious criminal enterprise.

"Yesterday's Weirdness Is Tomorrow's Reason Why," the final chapter, displays Thompson's paranoia and ecstatic comic self-delusion: Thompson had turned into Lono, but no one recognizes him in his Odysseus/divine identity except the native park ranger, who appears to change into a porpoise. This "miracle" confirms Thompson/Lono as divine. He embodies one of those drug reincarnation memories that members of the Rainbow Tribe loved to natter about in the late 1960s. In a coded way, the porpoise swim of the park ranger presents a hagiographical memento of Acosta, recalling when Hunter and Acosta frolicked in the Pacific Ocean like two porpoises after having taken peyote (as recorded in *Fear and Loathing in Las Vegas*). Now there is only Lone Hunter and his memory of his dead companion, represented by the Samoan park ranger. There will be no Second Coming of anyone like the real Acosta, any more than there will be the Second Coming of the 1960s. The park ranger declares the sharks in the ocean are his uncles; in common slang, a shark is a lawyer. As a lawyer who devoted his career to *pro bono* work for the impoverished, Acosta had to swim among many sharks.[81] The swimming of the Samoan park ranger back to Samoa provides another trope of reverse migration because Hawaiians are the historical descendants of Samoans, linguistically and genetically.

This quite memorable conclusion to Thompson's book may have been inspired by Francine du Plessix Gray's 1972 penetrating sociological meditation, *Hawaii: The Sugar-Coated Fortress*. The book's final paragraph about a native Hawaiian begins:

> I have a memory of Tom then diving into the sea and gamboling in it for hours, frolicking with an animal persistence and a religious veneration. He let himself be tossed and beaten by the surf, his black hair floating on the tide like that of a drowned man, and then he turned again to court the waves, arms outstretched, with a kind of weary devotion, like a man making love to a woman for the sixth time.[82]

Gray's book offers a concise and empathetic guide to the troubled history, politics, and attitudes of native Hawaiians; it is a nuanced book Thompson must have read.

While living in Key West as a bachelor redux, Thompson's pick-up line to single women he took a fancy to was, "Come live with me and we will live like dolphins."[83] Swimming had always been Thompson's luxurious pleasure, yet the humorous oceanic variation on Christopher Marlowe's poem, "The Passionate Shepherd to His Love" with the opening lines "Come live with me and be my love/And we will all the pleasures prove," might have been lost on some Jimmy Buffett groupies.

The porpoise imagery also relates to Thompson's association with poet and novelist Jim Harrison. In the late seventies, they fished together in Key West.[84] Harrison frequently employs porpoises in his poems. A poem in *Letters from Yesesin* (1973) contains a line about Janis Joplin as a porpoise: "There is some interesting evidence that Janis was a porpoise and simply decided to stop breathing at a certain depth."[85] The prolific Russian poet Sergei Yesenin, who committed suicide in 1925, offers a parallel: both Sergei and Janis, who died in 1970, were populist rebel troubadours whose impulsive behavior, combined with erratic binge drinking, put their lives on the edge. Before hanging himself, Yesenin wrote his last poem, "Goodbye, my friend, goodbye," with his blood. The metaphor of a porpoise appears appropriate for a natural, exploratory innocence that can't survive long in a world of sharks. Their "noble savage" character attributes identify Yesenin, Joplin, and Acosta as belonging to the brilliant naïve porpoise tribe of those who die young.

In "The Banshee Screams for Buffalo Meat," which Thompson had teasingly freighted with libelous humor in order to draw out Acosta, if he was still alive,[86] Thompson records the anecdote of a drug dealer, Drake, telling a story: when ambushed in the Florida Keys, he turned coward, but Oscar took the wheel of the boat when the captain was killed; he steered the damaged boat out of gunfire range, and then grabbed the small suitcase they had picked up in Bimini and dove overboard, disappearing.[87] Thompson replays that disappearing dive at the end of the novel.

The overall architecture of *The Curse of Lono* combines a parody-tribute of the *Odyssey* with a parody of the Christian Second Coming through the Second Coming of Lono. Thompson replays a goof reincarnation rap, usually derived from a collective memory hallucination under the influence of mescaline or acid. Hunter has great fun with the god theme, spooking the natives who want to do away with him for his blasphemous boast, as they did with Captain Cook—or with Jesus and St. Stephen when the latter declared the spirit of Jesus was with him. While the concluding letters to Steadman from June and July of 1981 make a fairly effective ending to complete the plot, they were working-draft ideas, yet the spontaneity and geniality of the letters offer an upbeat, satiric conclusion.

In Hawaii there are no suitors to slay (only bottles), no estate to lay claim to (the divorce has made Thompson nearly bankrupt), no kingly office to hold (he lost that battle in Aspen)—no one but the Samoan ranger, who functions like Homer's Argos by acknowledging Thompson's hidden identity. The notorious superstition of the Hawaiian populace offers a parallel to the superstition in Christianity with Thompson/ Lono as a possible sacrificial scapegoat. We have the self-satirizing letter written to Steadman about Thompson's unrecognized divinity, yet its effectiveness remains diminished as it appears at the conclusion of a sequence of letters. The Nietzsche-inspired riddle of the conclusion presents Thompson's farewell to literature, since we have only the two surviving masterworks from Homer.

In September 1982, the end of the book consisted of the chapter, "Tits Like Orange Fireballs," to which Ian Ballantine objected, upset at the word *tits*.[88] Thompson kept the chapter and moved it, probably because he did not want to conclude the book on the note of self-pity that the last paragraph implies. He complained to Steadman that the book was already longer than the contract specified and that the publisher now appeared to allow Steadman considerably more than the 50/ 50 split of space agreed upon, with equal authorial billing, and that that arrangement should be carried over into their next book. Thompson was angered by that suggestion.[89]

The theme of a threatened Second Coming, the prefatory nightmare theme of Didion's title essay in *Slouching Towards Bethlehem*, does not quite rise to the intensity and importance of the American Dream theme. Are there really any second acts in America? Was Fitzgerald right? William Kennedy notes: "Scott Fitzgerald's line that there are no second acts in American lives was the sad, solipsistic truth about that wonderful writer's self-destructive career; but for those who take this as wisdom it can be a pernicious fallacy."[90] As in his other books, Thompson's conclusion points to oblique self-parody: Hunter as an irrelevant social icon, an antique celebrity god worshipped out of nostalgia for a past that no longer exists, wrapped in his public persona as a gonzo performer.[91] No one knows who he really is. The stranded Thompson/Lono figure re-enacts the Thomas Wolfe theme of the artist unable to return to his native home, adding the twist that the artist may not know exactly who he is because the practice of art's exploration precludes stable identity. Thompson's assertion of his pagan divinity appears to be a rather cloaked metaphor (like Odysseus speaking to the swineherd Eumaios) for himself as the unknown American Homer.

As we have the story, the Second Coming of Odysseus/Lono/Thompson remains incomplete. The appearance of the park ranger supplies a tall fish tale amid a comedy of narcissism, while both paganism and Christianity are perceived as equally out of date in the new technological world. The book hobbles, seriously weakened without the technological rant chapter that would have delivered the culminating political slam the narrative lacks. Yet this particular difficulty was not only a problem of plot, but inherent in the artistic philosophy Thompson had articulated in his "noble savage" allegory, which enunciated, via Hemingway and Nietzsche, an *artistic* rather than a political perspective. The political chapter would have difficulty in knitting plot and philosophy—it was probably the source of Thompson's writer's block that loomed like a wall in the final stages. Thompson could have given a lecture, but he was a satirist and needed to encode the political within the plot. The ultimate question was how to generalize from Hawaii to encompass both America and the globe.

One of the difficulties in reading the novel remains the self-referential compass of the book, as if the book is only written for devoted fans, the initiates in Hunter's way of thinking. The intent of the book appears to delineate a cultural change since the publication of Thompson's masterpiece in 1971. That seismic change has to do with selfishness: Thompson's persona and all the other personas—Steadman, Ackerman, and Skinner; the islanders, the visiting runners, the realtors, the fishing guides, the tourists—are all out for themselves. Everyone swims like a shark in the water, yet amid the allusive largesse of literary templates, Thompson's intellect appears like a whale. Ishmael adopts the outsider perspective of Pacific islander Queequeg; Thompson adopts the primi-

tive Hawaiian perspective on religion by becoming Lono, thus synthe-
sizing the varied sensibilities of Ishmael, Queegueg, and Thompson into
a Trinitarian avatar.

A tragic, haunting absence hangs over the novel (as if it were an
Argentine satire on the culture of money, about which everybody is
stressed and obsessed). The central fear running through the novel
remains the fear of not being able to pay one's bills. In that process of
being a slave to debt, people have lost the freedom to be playful. The
only joy left is to insult those whose delusions protect them in the age of
new economic slavery. While the American Dream is not overtly mentioned, the theme of pervasive greed connects *The Curse of Lono* to
Fear and Loathing in Las Vegas, just as the theme of the real estate
developers casts a backward glance to *The Rum Diary* and a forward
look to bankers of today. On the theme of real estate, Gray observed:

> No restructuring of Hawaiian society engineered by the Americans
> was more important than the division of land, or Great Mahele,
> which is responsible for the amazing centralization of real estate
> ownership that still prevails in contemporary Hawaii. As of now,
> some 80 percent of the privately owned acreage in the state belongs
> to twenty individuals or corporations. An equally significant statistic
> is that fourteen individuals or corporations control—through owner-
> ship or leasing—40 percent of all Hawaii land. [92]

Acquisitive greed is not as great a moral theme as senseless war.

The Vietnam War and the attendant cultural divide knitted together
Fear and Loathing in Las Vegas, but *The Curse of Lono* floats at sea in
the fog with the slightly smaller ship of demythologizing an epic home-
coming, the Second Coming, and the American economy. While there
are philosophic themes, they remain too submerged to attract much
attention for the average reader. The sociological theme of body fitness
and the exploitation of nature through technology, plus the future role
of technology in society, are rather disparate themes, except that people
who sit at computer keyboards for a working shift do need some form of
exercise. Yet it is the enslavement of individuals to large corporations
that presents the greater tragedy.

The fickle and sometimes incompetent fishermen Thompson encounters become, upon reflection, the real Hemingway heroes, who
live their improvisational lives outside the oppressive system. The pub-

lic spectacle of mass exercise conjures an implicit robotic conformity, as if people have become ants who remain selfish at the Darwinian level of self-preservation. The mass media covering an event becomes its monstrous mirrored double, just as the media became the mirrored double of police bulletins in *Hell's Angels*. While *The Rum Diary* offered the Spengler-like Conradian symbol of Miami as a whited sepulcher, and *Fear and Loathing in Las Vegas* provided Circus-Circus, the City of Refuge as a Spengler-like icon remains far too abstract and culturally foreign for most readers to absorb. In a postmodern profusion of disparate literary modalities, especially the use of parable and allegory, Thompson attempts to dramatize the confusion of the American zeitgeist with acquisitive greed, but in the end the book remains enigmatic to readers not accustomed to making such unexpected literary shifts or willing to accept the dour Puritan ethos from Thompson, the drug-champion legend. In Gauguin's *Noa Noa*, the narrator presents himself as an enigma, while ironically describing Tahitians as "enigma itself, or rather an infinite series of enigmas."[93]

Hunter's conclusion contrasts sharply with that of Homer's *Odyssey*, which embraces a more universal polity wherein the state is considered to be a large family where peace should prevail under the aegis of the gods. Athena's concern for her chosen family extends to all within the political hegemony of Ithaka under its favored king, Odysseus, restored to his people. At the end of *The Curse of Lono*, Thompson the god remains alone, a divine writer whom nobody understands, while his worshippers appear to ignore him as they are caught like writhing fish in a corrupt social network. Just as Thompson twists Odysseus's beloved dog Argos into a monster, he turns Homer's religious and political vision into its bleak antithesis.

The epilogue poem and prose about the thirteenth-century prophetess Waahia evokes Hunter as Lono lost to Waahia, who now lives alone on a hut in the valley, which appears to conjure an image of Laila Nabulsi, who lived in a separate cabin at Woody Creek. As with Lono in the poem, Hawaii cannot "break" Hunter. In the chant of Waahia, Lono has lost his knife. Like Nabulsi, Waahia negotiates a peace settlement and restores her king (Kuala) to his throne by producing a revered sword. According to the settlement, Kuala, to his wife's displeasure, marries the daughter of the enemy king (Kalauni) to ensure peace, but the inheritance of Kuala's Hawaiian kingdom will go to his first wife's only son.[94] Steadman's drawing of Thompson reproduces the high stone walls of the hut in which King Kuala was imprisoned.

The surface ending indulges in posturing comic apocalypse (unlike the genuine apocalypse in *Moby-Dick*), yet under the surface, the epilogue implies the hope that a peace treaty has been concluded (Thompson's divorce from Sandy) and that domestic peace may prevail. This wraps up and brings reversal to the chapter "Tits Like Orange Fireballs." The epilogue quotations obviously express a hope for peace similar to what Homer articulates at the conclusion of the *Odyssey*, where Athena intervenes in human history to demand peace from the warring parties. Odysseus and Telemachus had fought shoulder to shoulder. Thompson's twist on the Homeric template was for father and son to fish peacefully, shoulder to shoulder. This optimistic implication provides a personal comic vision brimming with cautious hope, although on the surface Thompson's public fears are cast as comic apocalypse.

The inclusion of excerpts from the historical epic by the last reigning monarch of Hawaii, King David Kalakaua (nicknamed the "Merrie Monarch"), offers the image of an Odysseus-like traveler, practical inventor, literary historian and poet, enemy of missionaries, composer of the state's song, reviver of the hula dance and surfing, as well as the martial art of Lua, a bone-breaking form of combat.[95] Like many epics around the globe, Kalakaua's historical, literary epic is written in both prose and poetry; he is Hawaii's native Homer.

About the book, Rinzler ruefully admits: "There are a lot of disparate elements. It was a patchwork, a cut-and-paste job. It doesn't quite make sense, but the language is really good."[96] One of the paradoxes of the book consists of the fact that Hunter boastingly mythologizes himself as a god in name but demythologizes his own celebrityhood and legend. Yet Thompson mythologizes the ordinary and personal: his relationships with Sandy, Juan, Acosta, and Steadman; friendship, Nature as a vengeful god, and the "monstrous" dog Rupert—as well as running a car at top speed around dangerous mountain curves, drinking at sunset, and the delicious detonation of fireworks.

Thompson demythologizes Lono, the Christian God, Captain Cook, Western imperialism, Mark Twain, Nature as a romantic construct, mass assemblies, the contemporary idol of health, the abilities of weather forecasters, tourist con operators and souvenirs, the "wisdom" and status of realtors, the professional competence of fishermen, the propa-

ganda of television news, and the myth of local bathing beauties. Overall, the book proclaims the intimate as the sacred in life as opposed to
the public pageant of the profane, which presents concatenating lies
vacillating between the tawdry and the obscene. Overall, the book
presents a descent into an *Inferno*, the antithesis of the travelogue
genre.

Steadman's penultimate illustration in black-and-white depicts
Thompson as King Kuala in a stone hut with a miner's headlight
beamed at his manual typewriter—Hunter writing at dawn with skulls
behind him, as if he's St. Jerome writing a sacred text. His hair stands
up like two hairy, white rabbit ears—a nearly bald Thompson as the
incarnation of Lewis Carroll's White Rabbit. Here Thompson finds depiction as "the mystic in a wild state."[97] In this state of refuge or asylum,
the artist creates a world where people can be transformed into porpoises, where the surreal can transform the ordinary, where the artist
has become the shamanic medium to the Otherworld. At this nodal
point, the artist can enter the empyrean.

The final illustration presents Thompson flying alone in a plane over
the globe with "Aloha Lono" on the tail wing.[98] The jet engines spurt
apocalyptic blood as Thompson/Lono waves good-bye to humankind
while he ascends into heaven. The visuals parallel a passage in Henry
Miller's *Big Sur and the Oranges of Hieronymus Bosch*:

> I lift up my arms as in prayer, achieving a wingspan no god ever
> possessed, and there in the drifting fog a nimbus floats down about
> my head, a radiant nimbus such as the Buddha himself might proud-
> ly wear. In the Himalayas, where the same phenomenon occurs, it is
> said that a devout follower of the Buddha will throw himself from a
> peak—"into the arms of Buddha."[99]

Miller's poetic mountaintop passage about watching a Pacific sea-
scape sunrise when gazing up the coast captures the weightless feeling
of becoming a mystical avatar in communion with the eternal.[100] Yet
Miller, another admirer of Spengler,[101] knows the transcendental experience is merely a temporary immersion, while Thompson's Lono avatar
experience presents an apocalyptic finale, both because this book is his
last work of extended fiction and because it projects his eschatological
vision of humankind's eventual doom.

The final irony argues that Thompson's claim of divinity appears in meditative retrospect as merely a sane delusion in a world that has institutionalized insanity in its pursuit of greed, producing a society that more resembles ancient barbarism than any civilized achievement. The Darwinian theme at work argues for contemporary aspects of reverse evolution: modern technology, processed and polluted food, and mass activity will make us more akin to ants than were our primate ancestors. One of the concluding letters to Steadman presents the theme of reverse evolution, using the term Cro-Magnon man (first early humans): "Few people are comfortable with this concept [reverse evolution], and fewer can live with it. Thank God I have at least one smart friend like you."[102] Like Spengler and the historian J. B. Bury, who denied the idea of progress, Thompson embraced the argument that perpetual human progress was a belief system, an optimistic delusion. Darwin himself had pointed out that evolution was experimental and that new designs in nature did not succeed in every case.

Many aspects of the book revolve around the theme of reverse evolution: the dog devolving into prehistoric monster; the overfished ocean devolving into an arid wasteland; journalism devolving into propaganda; a social tolerance for pranks and jokes devolving into political correctness; the financial system, which is ultimately based upon trust, devolving into rapacious greed; the need for the artist to drop out from the insanity of society (Joyce's theme) and connect with the more primitive wholeness of humankind's origins (Thompson's City of Refuge, his hip twist on Joyce). Thompson's skepticism remains firmly rooted in Bury, his optimism rooted in Joyce.

The idea of the City of Refuge more likely has its origins in *Noa Noa*, where Gauguin takes refuge in the forest mountain Aroraï, the place were God announced to men death, the place where demons dwell at night, so that no native dares to go there.[103]

The freak perspective proclaims that the wise use of good drugs can transform an ordinary person into an avatar, while the continued suppression of nonaddictive drugs warps people into compliant, unthinking robots. Jann Wenner said, "Hunter always told me that without the drugs, he would have had the mind of an accountant."[104] While that appears to be comic rationalization, drugs were a two-edged sword: they did help Hunter think in creative ways as well as distract him from work.

The Curse of Lono remains disparate, its thematic density bewildering: its aesthetic effect resembles that of a scattershot shotgun blast. For a close, traditional reader, the shock of the book being incomplete resembles the effect of standing next to someone who has unexpectedly fired a shotgun with the outcome not yet registered.

Another way of viewing the book's aesthetic is a fireworks show with a variety of exploding styles, yet when it comes to the climatic bursting bank, only a single beautiful bloom appears amid the nightscape, the remainder of the bank being sputtering duds lost in a downpour. A glance at the text focused on the lacuna of missing chapters makes the work appear like a rediscovered pagan classic, with concluding pages that have disintegrated. The pacing of the book permits disorientation, as if the reader is lost at sea in the lingering calm from a commonplace guidebook that dutifully records a vacation occasionally upended by rough, roiling waves of intellectual frisson, an evocation not far from the pacing of Hemingway's *The Old Man and the Sea.* Thompson attempted his ideal solution: to offer a book with both action and thought, "coming at it from both angles,"[105] as he had described Hemingway's achievement. Yet in the end there is more thought than action, which he had criticized as the limitation of Proust, Joyce, and Faulkner.[106]

Behind appearances, Hunter's Nietzschean iconoclasm levels all, but since this theme lurks below the surface, much like an iceberg, it circulates like an enigmatic oceanic current. The Ahab-like irony of an isolated atheist in the middle of the Pacific Ocean, claiming himself to be an immortal god while his anguished professional alter ego suffers from writer's block, may not be attractive to all readers, even if there are many good laughs on that road to deific tragedy and savage cultural critique.

Thompson was a perfectionist, yet the end result was an obscure masterpiece. If one is composing a masterpiece at the demand of a publisher, perhaps empathetic encouragement rather than aristocratic demand would have been wise. Rinzler obviously made a mistake by allowing friendship to interfere with the project—paying the second half of the advance before completion lessened Hunter's motivation. Rinzler ultimately lost a friend, while Random House had on its hands a disgruntled author who had scant motivation to fulfill the rest of his contract. Thompson shifted to Simon & Schuster.

To many readers the concluding chapter appears unacceptably un-satisfying, weirdly enigmatic—which is why many readers find the book's oblique density annoying and why the book received many nega-tive reviews, despite the miscellaneous vagaries of amusing comedy and poignant social critique skidding up to the obscure dénouement. Since the book began with the striking blue-armed Ackerman, many readers would prefer a more concluding resolution to the character than his merely disappearing to go to Bimini for the Tuna Tournament. Since Ackerman functions as a partial fictional double for Steadman (the blue arm recalling the woad dye of Welsh Celtic warrior bodies), Thompson may have not wanted to offend the Welsh Steadman in any serious way—after all, Ackerman, a heroine user, is a shady drug dealer provid-ing the novel's futile Ahab-like obsession: drugs and death. Like Stead-man in real life, Ackerman just drops out of the plot.

Yet like Ahab, Ackerman achieves his obsession—the mountain of marijuana that's pointlessly left piled in the hotel suite along with the dog Rupert. Like the revenge killing of Melville's white whale, the drug-dealing dream score has been achieved. The achieved goal means nothing in Melville or Thompson, yet the outcome is antithetical: in Melville the killing of the whale provides disaster for others; in Thomp-son's novel the abandonment of a drug score hurts nobody. In each case there remains a lone Ishmael who recounts the story. Ackerman, an aged hippie devoid of hippie idealism, has gone fishing, and Thompson has ascended into the pagan heaven, the City of Refuge. The plot's climax and focus remains on Thompson/Lono, and one cannot devote too much attention to a subsidiary character, yet the social significance of Ackerman's hollow quest for drugs remains a satiric theme addressed to a new generation partly destroyed by Ackerman's avidity. It remains unlikely most casual readers will see the brutally repetitive "get the drugs" theme as Homeric irony or as Melville-inspired satire. While the freedom to use drugs provided the comic answer that illuminated *Fear and Loathing in Las Vegas*, here the ability to acquire drugs can only lead to the tragic victory of money, the real Inferno of the novel being the greedy acquisition of money. The novel as collage appears enigmat-ic to many readers because they may not grasp either Thompson's deep Puritan roots or the complexity of his literary ambition and the depths of his allusive "iceberg" approach.

The thinly drawn character of Skinner might have undergone more development. Skinner could have recounted in detail his adventures in Vietnam as a photographer and subsequent adventures in South America. With more background, Skinner's history (more about his flying helicopters in Vietnam and other escapades) could have supplied the vehicle for the missing political slam, with Thompson/Lono delivering wise but minimal responsorial questions in the format of a racy Socratic dialogue punctuated with humor. Skinner's confessional narrative might have given "the weird fishhook in the story" that would have wrapped up the "they lie to us" theme, the levels of lies providing a Dantean indictment ranging from corrupt media to monstrous governments to venal tourist hospitality. Like Dante, Thompson eventually loses his Virgil-like sidekick Ackerman-Steadman in the Inferno when Thompson's own physical difficulties become more purgatorial; however, a scene with Skinner as sidekick was never completed. While at its conclusion Joyce's *A Portrait of the Artist as a Young Man* had devolved from autobiographical narrative into diary entries, Thompson's book devolved into diary letters, as in the *Strange Case of Dr. Jekyll and Mr. Hyde*.

The final letter to Steadman, dated July 1, 1981, supplies an epilogue. Like Nick Caraway, Thompson sees an ironic Green Light; but not a light on the shore of Long Island Sound. The Pacific allegorical Green Light affirms Thompson's avatar primitivism. He's happy as a worm in his isolation, crawling out at night to collect the superstitious detritus of coins and odd objects offered in homage to his divinity. He appeals for Steadman to send him money! But then there's a mysterious female voice at night that whispers "You knew it would be like this." Thompson shouts back into the night "I love you," only to hear no reply.[107] This ironic cry of pathos on the surface might appear to be addressed to ex-wife Sandy, yet this would be a misreading. Within the context of the letter, which functions as a working draft of a chapter, it was an ironic, self-satiric stance—Thompson/Lono had just been boasting that women were throwing themselves at him. The solitude Thompson/Lono wraps himself in at the City of Refuge recalls the "drunken" solitude (Thompson's drinking being more comically literal in the letter) of Nietzsche's Zarathustra. At the end of Book Three of *Thus Spake Zarathustra*, Zarathustra sits alone in his cave, with his followers outside, to encounter the final female love of Zarathustra's life, "For I love thee, O eternity!"[108] At the final conclusion of Book Four, Zarathustra achieves enlightened immortality through accepting his true identity in the ecstatic, pantheistic All where the soul expands into the widest sphere.[109] For Thompson, that eternity is represented by the vast, pagan Pacific Ocean, the land of Po, greater even than the symbolic Christian eternity of Hemingway's Atlantic Ocean.

For the reader who misses the philosophic iceberg, the apparent maudlin undertow of self-pity diminishes the thrust of Thompson's epic, which concludes in philosophic triumph rather than defeated self-pity. The larger problem posed is that most readers will see mere self-pity rather than either the intimate self-indulgent irony addressed to a friend or the potent philosophic subtext that alludes to Nietzsche. Yet what writer can abide an ending, based upon rough drafts, imposed by a publisher?

A Hawaiian reading of the cave of solitude would include ironic, hallucinatory delusion: just as "Thompson" begins his last letter as a crazed Ahab nearing his big catch (satirized by Steadman in his depiction of Thompson as the big fish strung upside down with shaved head, glasses, and cigarette holder), he also taunts "Steadman" ("who had already fallen in love with King Kamehameha"[110] and had fled to the big hotel of that name) with the bravado brag of his living in mobile Kamehameha-like promiscuity by picking up female hitchhikers and seducing them with gin.

Discussing the latter pages of the book, William Stephenson builds an intriguing argument around Thompson's use of the bullhorn with tape covering the on-off switch: Stephenson interprets the bullhorn as a political metonym within postcolonial contextualization.[111] While Stephenson's argument makes good sense in the context of postcolonial global theory, I see the bullhorn as a time-warp allegory. In its contemporary Hawaiian context the bullhorn offers a fiction satirizing the technology that Western society has employed to dazzle and trick less technologically developed cultures, but the bullhorn also commemorates Thompson's personal use of the bullhorn during his days on the Freak Power ticket when he ran for sheriff. At that time curious visitors occasionally would want to monkey with it when they stumbled across it in his compound.

Another political spur: the loud bullhorn could be also a memorializing of Hunter's first meeting with John Kerry (whose presidential bid

Hunter supported in 2004) in front of the White House in 1972. This was the first time that Thompson and Kerry met. Kerry "was yelling into a bullhorn, and I was trying to throw a dead, bleeding rat over a black-spike fence and onto the president's lawn."[112] Like Hawaiian natives, many American citizens did not comprehend at the time what protesters were saying or what really was going on in Vietnam.

The bullhorn also functions as another retro allegory: Aspen natives did not understand the godly message Thompson delivered in his campaign. The on-off switch masked by duct tape symbolizes the inability of Aspen natives to discern which parts of his political campaign were prank jokes and which elements were serious. While dazzling Aspen locals with his capering pranks, Thompson's wacky bullhorn campaign transmitted coded messages to other freaks, yet in such an individually artistic manner that other freaks were not able to replicate what he was doing. A "head" could acquire the trinkets or clothing accoutrements of the hipster, but mere trappings, however groovy, left such superficial freaks incoherent in speaking the inspired message that the political world required. Such people could not see the "godly" on-off switch one needed to push in order to function in the world of drugs and then switch back to the real world of mature work. Most hipsters either drifted off into the drug world and destroyed their lives, or reacted with vengeful anger at being opened up to a larger world they could not handle, returning to the "real" world as intolerant fascists dedicated to persecuting those who were illuminated.

Mark Twain abandoned his proposed 1884 novel about Hawaii, while he retained fond memories of his visit. Thompson abandoned his book in anger, but only at the wire. He certainly lost interest in the book after Rinzler's "theft-rape," which included much of the material Laila had gathered. Thompson complained to Steadman about the situation but was understanding of Steadman's cooperation with Random House, yet Thompson was never provided with galleys to correct, despite Steadman's moving plea for that to Ian Ballantine,[113] who appears not to have understood the book at all. The inclusion of Hunter's letters to Steadman in the book allowed publication, but the error on the final chapter heading, "Rage, Rage against the Dying of the Light," also reveals that even Steadman's advice and input were not taken too seriously.

Laila, whose efforts to salvage the project appear heroic, provided Random House with more bulk for the book by selecting passages from Richard Hough's *The Last Voyage of Captain Cook* (1979) that capture a suggestive frisson regarding neocolonial aspects of American culture and business, as William Stephenson discusses in his book.[114] Yet "the joke around Bantam was that Hough should have received a third of the royalties."[115] That joke may reveal a condescending and derisive mentality at an office that expected its employee, Thompson, to produce a work for posterity to marvel at. Thompson's Captain Cook theme connects to Duke's sardonic airport statement in *Fear and Loathing in Las Vegas* about the South Pacific fantasy of being sliced up alive "like pineapple meat in a brawl,"[116] as happened to Cook. The Hough insertions serve to heighten the narrative drama of Hunter's text. The supercilious mentality at the publishing office reeks of the patronizing colonial mentality of Cook's civil liberalism. The point of the Hough material consists of running a parallel about the contemporary exploitative speculation of the Hawaiian real estate market: "The bull market of the early Seventies is just another Hawaiian legend now, like the hubris of Captain Cook."[117] Thompson was satirizing the greed that produced an overpriced and overextended market, a problem that plagued the whole American nation by 2008. In the novel, realtors send out thugs to kill Thompson, as the novel dabbles in traditional noir territory.

What staff at Random House evidently did not understand was that Hunter was, in a conceptual way, working too hard in his perfectionist strain. Thompson's great achievement in *Fear and Loathing in Las Vegas* was to run simultaneous myriad intellectual threads in a synthetic manner made accessible to a large audience through its humor. The multithread perception that became his trademark has its roots in the experience of peyote, or as he often jokingly called it in *The Curse of Lono*, "organic mescaline" contained in a jar. Only a psychedelic initiate hears the rattle of peyote buttons in the jar and through the symbolic rattle hears a warning jingle that thought must trek in multidirectional latitudes. In *The Curse of Lono* those multithreads were running in a multitude of directions united in an archaic mythology, based on philosophy, cultural critique, and shifting literary templates. This appeared enigmatic to readers mired in the propagandistic mind-set of Western imperialism.

The hermetic iceberg below strives to render a deep yet wise complexity. Edward Said's comment that "everything about *Moby-Dick* as a stunningly created work of literary art—tells of someone always moving away from the expected or the known,"[118] equally applies to *The Curse of Lono*, which attempts a more postmodern collage technique buttressed by philosophic commentary than does *Fear and Loathing in Las Vegas*. While readers might have difficulty with symbolism in *The Curse of Lono*, F. O. Matthiessen's older comment on Melville also applies to Thompson's book: "The symbols in *Moby-Dick*, therefore, come with the freshness of a new resource, just as, in spite of its great length, the book is the most complex expression of Melville's enormous imaginative range."[119] Matthiessen compares the compactness of Melville's novel to that of Hawthorne's *The Scarlet Letter*, acknowledging that Hawthorne achieves a greater compactness of energy, yet the same concision may be weighed in favor of Thompson's achievement.

Thompson's use of literary templates resembles the manner of writing employed by the four canonical gospel writers—to use the traditional Torah as a template to invent contemporary myth and allegory as inspired illustrations of the divinity incarnated in the prophet Jesus of Nazareth. While the gospel writers wrote riffs off Jewish texts and the events in the lives of revered prophets, Thompson employed esteemed secular texts to run variant riffs: Melville, Nietzsche, Twain, Joyce, Spengler, and Hemingway. *The Curse of Lono* bears the burden of attempting a new freak synthesis: a "gospel" of secular social critique for illuminated freaks who share Thompson's perception of cultural impoverishment in American mythology. Thompson demythologizes traditional American commerce, religion, politics, and the accompanying myth of progress (which he had come to see as more pernicious than even the Horatio Alger myth), but he mythologizes his own illumination through mescaline, the transformative powers of cynical comedy, and the antique healing potency of primitive wholeness before the corrupt greed and clutter of the contemporary world. Yet only a hip devoted fan or academic geek could come to believe that Thompson was in some way the reincarnation of Lono, and laugh understandingly in the Rabelaisian peyote-goof sensibility.

Rather than accept the truncated Random House version, the resourceful reader might take up Steadman's memoir, *The Joke Is Over*, and swim in its parallel hilarity, yet there lingers a strong sense in which

Steadman's account (Thompson had made much fun of Steadman in the book) offers the competitive reply of a rival comedian, albeit with a tender and nostalgic empathy for Hunter and his absurd situation.

Ever self-critical, Thompson knew the book was not quite the masterpiece he secretly wished it to be, yet he self-defensively declared it was never meant to be a masterpiece. The text refutes that. In a moment of petulant depression Hunter wrote to Steadman in March 1983 that he would prefer to kill the book despite the prospect of his 2.5 percent royalty from book sales.[120] Midway through the book Thompson had grown depressed about the assassination of John Lennon, of whom he was fond. Whitmer rather preposterously speculates, without evidence, that Thompson lingered over the project in order to delay royalties that Sandy might collect,[121] but Thompson's feud with Ballantine appears to be far more important in this procrastinating delay. One other important consideration: Hunter may have been very reluctant to deliver a direct political slam in the Hawaiian context, because Hunter fell deeply in love with Hawaii. Another peripheral reason Hunter may have been reluctant to deliver the completed manuscript on Random House's schedule is that he loathed the thought that the book would become a mere Christmas gift item to be given to people who might very well never read it—it would become an unread coffee-table souvenir, mere bric-a-brac.

Thompson was finished with any *formal* long fiction. He expressed that fear in a letter to Steadman while objecting to pressure from Random House to turn what was to be a miscellany into a novel: "This thing [the book] has already put serious strains on our friendship, & if it festers much longer I might not survive it, as a writer. This is the Curse of Lono."[122]

Reviewers were either polite or confused, not appreciating probing literary depths from an author known for comic bravado. The book sold well,[123] but Thompson may have felt no one understood what he had been up to. Serious intellectuals didn't appear interested in his work. Like any writer, Thompson wanted to be understood rather than seen as quirky cipher or strange clown. *The Curse of Lono* presents an amusing yet ambitious frolic—an atomized, episodic collage-diary novel lit with philosophical fireworks and sometimes oblique allegories that furnish Thompson's farewell to fiction. The practical curse of Lono was to exile Thompson from the larger world of experimental fiction (in newspaper columns he occasionally resorted to tiny fables). Steadman, who attempted to be a peacemaker-arbiter, eventually commiserated that Thompson, calling the publishers scum, was, in the end, correct.[124]

Because of the way Thompson was treated by the publishing industry, as well as his crisis of self-confidence about creating accessible literary motifs, he lost interest in the demanding grind of further fiction. He contented himself with columns on politics and sports, despite the fact that he owed editor Jim Silberman at Simon & Schuster's Summit imprint another novel, for which he had accepted $125,000 as the first half of the advance. Paul Perry claims he came up with the idea for a nonfiction social satire book on physical fitness entitled *The Rise of the Body Nazis* that Hunter enthusiastically agreed to write, yet Silberman rejected the proposal, still hoping for another novel from Thompson. But the publication of another novel would, for marketing purposes, inevitably have become tied to illustrations from Steadman. Thompson may have decided that the only way Steadman and he would remain friends (and they did) was not to work on another long project together. (They did reunite professionally a decade later for "Polo Is My Life.") Silberman eventually accepted *Songs of the Doomed*, the anthology of *San Francisco Examiner* columns, as a substitute for the contracted novel.[125]

Some of the book's disparate themes and their relevancy to the contemporary world certainly could have been made clearer. Most readers today respond primarily to Steadman's marvelous illustrations, which may occasionally outshine Thompson's narrative in the lavish coffee-table book reprint of 2005 by Taschen, for which Steadman added additional drawings (the dust jacket portrays Hunter as an astonished yet perplexed squid punctuated with his cigarette holder). Yet a close meditation on Steadman's drawings provokes further reflection on Thompson's text.

Perhaps the principal problem with the book lay in employing too many *antithetical* literary templates that cannot approach synthesis. How does one reconcile the theism of Homer's *Odyssey* (the *Iliad* in its anthropomorphic sci-fi theogony appears to be atheistic through accretion), or Dante's and Hemingway's visions with Zarathustra's bold atheistic apotheosis, except by postmodern fiat? The varied literary templates offer trenchant illuminations, but readers remain uncomfortably lost at sea. If that state of being lost is considered mimetic for the current American condition of approaching apocalypse, there's a message in that tossed bottle, an irony deeper than any iceberg imagined by Hemingway.

In A. E. Hotchner's memoir on Hemingway, Hotchner tells the story of Hemingway declaring *The Old Man and the Sea* a double *dicho*: a statement that can be read forward or backward, declaring that "Man can be destroyed but not defeated" as the preferred reading of his ocean parable.[126] Thompson offers the inversion of the dicho: Lono can be defeated but not destroyed, which is also the message of Luke's Acts of the Apostles with regard to Jesus (Yeshua).

The Curse of Lono is the sequel to Thompson's Peyote Freak Gospel, *Fear and Loathing in Las Vegas*. Thompson as Lono has remained faithful to peyote revelations, while Ackerman represents those who have fallen away from Thompson's gospel into the temptation of self-destruction that Thompson had prophesied. Of course, Ackerman exhibits an aspect of Thompson himself, so the book itself marginally and often humorously inhabits the confessional genre.

Like Jonathan Swift's Gulliver, Lono is perceived as a threat to society and expelled. While Gulliver upon his return cannot adjust to domestic life in England, the reader is left wondering if Lono-Ishmael will be able to adjust to life in continental America.

8

LITERARY ADDENDA

Further Fictions

Literature is nothing when it bears no relation to life.—H. L. Mencken

ROXANNE PULITZER: "A DOG TOOK MY PLACE"

Since *The Curse of Lono* was snatched from Thompson without the intended political slam, Thompson was determined to deliver one as soon as possible. Jann Wenner asked Hunter to cover the impending divorce trial of Herbert Pulitzer and Roxanne Renckens Pulitzer. The trial ran from September 20 to November 9, 1982. The resulting article, "A Dog Took My Place," appeared in *Rolling Stone* on July 21, 1983, with an illustration by Ed Sorel, several months before the publication of *The Curse of Lono*. The use of the chapter title from the forthcoming novel is unusual.[1] Furthermore, the title doesn't, on the surface, relate to the article. The amusing-to-hilarious article satirizes the corrupt practice of lawyers with the concluding argument that animals, and people who behave like "animals," are morally superior to wealthy elites because they don't hire lawyers. Thompson was gunning for lawyers because he thought he and Sandy could have arrived at a more amicable settlement without the meddling intervention of expensive lawyers. Hunter appears to have disliked the "dog" who literally took his place when Sandy left him for another man after Hunter's numerous infidelities.

"A Dog Took My Place" offers Thompson's best social critique, attacking the legal system for allowing a person of wealth to be exempted from alimony law. At the Pulitzer trial, lawyers were permitted to employ unsubstantiated, vicious slander. The legal ruling suggested the mid-eighteenth century prejudice for landed nobility over aggrieved peasants: the trial was a circus resembling episodes recounted in Fielding's *Tom Jones*, rather than scenes from traditional American jurisprudence.

Making the case for American exceptionalism, Thompson jokes that the American Social Contract provides the antithesis of Rousseau's Social Contract: police exist to protect not the populace, but only the wealthy. Moreover, they perform criminal dirty work for the wealthy, if that is what is needed. The wealthy own the government, and through the government, they own the people—that is the current American Social Contract. Hunter observes that not all the "animals" who reject the American Social Contract live on the West Coast and that there are enclaves of free "animals" still alive on the East Coast. Brimming with irony, he exclaims at the conclusion: "Bestiality, is the key to it, I think."[2]

The conclusion that the upper class devolve away from organic origins revives an observation by Spengler, who discussed the sterility of "civilized man" in his latter stages, wherein the concern for progeny nearly vanishes amid the splendor of wealth. Spengler interprets this phenomenon as a mystical turn toward death because the abandonment of one's own children—a principal leitmotif of Thompson's Pulitzer essay in his depiction of how the upper class distantly "raises" children with nannies and servants—remains irrational on both the emotional and intellectual level. Thompson documents the frivolous crudity, corruption, and despotism of the Palm Beach jet-set that Spengler describes in the concentration of wealth among society's elites who, in Spengler's words, have lost any interest in their children because "intelligence at the peak of intensity can no longer find any reason for their existence."[3] It is this unconscious cult of death among the wealthy, who have lost interest in their families, that Thompson trenchantly ridicules.

In a way reminiscent of his high school–era apology to and befriending of the teenage couple he had participated in robbing, Thompson

eventually reconciled with self-promoting Roxanne Pulitzer. After unsuccessfully and repeatedly phoning the novelist for eight years to talk
about his article on the divorce trial that had chronicled her abusive
ordeal, she reconciled with him at his Aspen home in 1991, just before
the publication of her novel, *Twins* (1992). The two became lifelong
friends. While Thompson had reported a cornucopia of foul rumors
swirling around Roxanne (labels like slut, and so on), the perspective of
his article was rooted in their mutual working-class origins. Hunter
painted corruption in the courtroom, both of the judge and of Herbert
Pulitzer's underhanded lawyers, through the special privileges (and habitual virulent nastiness) extreme wealth often bestows. Roxanne's novels, rooted in her Palm Beach experiences, followed in Hunter's cynical
footsteps with melodramatic flair.

ALPHONSE KARR

While Thompson's *San Francisco Examiner* columns of the late 1980s
usually eschew literary motifs, there is one some readers may not be
familiar with. It concerns Alphonse Karr (1808–1890), the Parisian journalist, essayist, memoirist, aphorist, horticulturalist (devoted to dahlias),
and romantic autobiographical novelist. None of Karr's major books,
much less his journalism, have been translated into English. English
speakers nonetheless habitually quote his most famous aphorism, "*Plus
ça change plus c'est la meme chose*" ("The more things change, the
more they remain the same")[4] which appeared in January 1848 in a
satirical monthly pamphlet he edited (eventually collected as a book)
called *Les Guêpes* (The Wasps).[5] Yet for those in the know, Karr was a
forerunner of the so-called New Journalism movement by virtue of
writing heavily autobiographical novels that mingled fact and fiction.

In *Songs of the Doomed*, Thompson had included an early unpub-
lished short piece, "Dance of the Doomed,"[6] dated April 1975, from
Saigon, wherein he briefly reports the communist victory in Saigon.
Columns referring to Alphonse Karr were collected in *Songs of the
Doomed* (1990).

The first, "Let the Cheap Dogs Eat" addresses the abuse of dogs in
the queasy times we live in: after all, *Rolling Stone* magazine "now"—
that is, in the 1980s—disapproves of marijuana and our Irish President

(Ronald Reagan) has discovered that "in his heart he has always been a Nicaraguan revolutionary." As recounted in the *Denver Post*, the chief medical examiner of Connecticut had resigned after admitting that she had permitted her dogs to wander into the autopsy room and that the dogs sometimes snacked on human tissue. Other dog abuse stories are cited before Thompson shrieks about the barbaric gang of huge lapdogs from the University of Kansas, ranked number two in the nation, snatching victory from the Michigan State underdogs at the NCAA quarter finals, concluding with "Alphonse Karr was right,"[7] alluding to but not quoting Karr's famous aphorism. Yet there was no urgent need for Thompson to bark: Connecticut appointed a new medical examiner, while Kansas ultimately finished seventh, and underdog hometown Louisville triumphantly defeated Duke. Hometown Louisville could yip about its second national championship. Alphonse Karr was indeed correct.

"Dealing with Pigs" provides an op-ed review of the 1986 Meese Report on pornography and violence, which attempted to posit a definitive link between these two modes of behavior. Thompson attacks the front-page article in the *New York Times*, which "ranked with some of the worst and most baffling outbursts of utterly meaningless gibberish in English-language journalism since the days of Yellowboy Willis."[8] Yellowboy Willis? In Thompson's obituary for the *San Diego Union-Tribune*, Arthur Salm, while ridiculing Thompson as an interesting yet incoherent has-been, bemoans his own inability to unravel that obscure reference.[9] Salm's problem was his ignorance of European folklore, opera, or of Alphonse Karr, journalist author of "Les Willis" (The Fairies), a short story Giacomo Puccini transformed into *Le Villi* (1884), an opera ballet in two acts. (This ballet was preceded by *Giselle* [1841], a French two-act ballet, based upon a poem by Heinrich Heine, and featuring a similar plot.)

In the Karr-Puccini version of this European folk legend, the betrothed Roberto pledges his undying fidelity to Anna. He travels to Vienna to conclude an inheritance before the wedding. There he meets an older woman who seduces him, and they dally in a love tryst for nearly a year. Roberto returns home to find that Anna has died of a broken heart. Her father invokes the Fairies for vengeance and the Fairies, acting as Furies, angry at such betrayal of true love, appear to Roberto with Anna, who accuses him. He dances with Anna's ghost, dancing himself to death in a frenzy of hypocritical anxiety. This is the origin of the phrase "to get the willies," that is, to shiver in fear of the Fairies.

Thompson warns the *New York Times* that if they continue to publish such nonsense (affirming the spurious link between pornography and violence), the Furies will invoke the dance of doom and extinguish the paper for its hypocritical infidelity to truth. It was Hearst's flamboyant *New York Journal* that gave rise to the popular phrase "yellow journalism."

In "The Hellfire Club," a 1988 column on the Jimmy Swaggart sex scandal, Thompson nostalgically reminisces on the good old days when civilized men, who were not merely thugs, indulged in recreational orgies without any qualms. He cited the great impresarios of the Hellfire Club (a private club of politicians who met to mock religion) in the general mold of Caligula—like the Prince of Wales, Ben Franklin, the "crazed" Earl of Sandwich, and the Earl of Bute, the first Scot prime minister of England. These were real gents who enjoyed their sex orgies and no one was going to stop them, unlike the "whimpering mashers fouling our headlines today. Maybe Alphonse Karr was wrong."[10] The old gents knew proud and true decadence, while contemporary wimps only know petty, righteous scandal.

Thompson's book title, *Songs of the Doomed*, announces a Spenglerian moral sensibility couched in irony. Those who, like Thompson, sing the songs of the "doomed" will eventually be vindicated by the historical cycle that will overturn haughty and corrupt rulers. Well-composed songs or well-written books usually outlive their time.

SCREWJACK

A screwjack is a nut-thread device used to acquire leverage with minimum effort; the car tire jack is such a device. In 1991 *Screwjack*, labeled a collection of short stories, was published in a limited edition. These three pieces are less short stories than provocations; two shorts lead up to the title piece, which arrives last, like the celebrity dinner guest.

The first piece, "Mescalito," had previously debuted in *Songs of the Doomed* (1990) under the title "First Visit with Mescalito." It reproduced diary entries from February 1969 wherein Thompson describes his first experience with mescaline laced with speed, a gift from Acosta. The surreal description focuses on the heightened visual effects of synthetic mescaline. Cut with speed, it enabled Thompson to record his spontaneous wonder, paranoia, and bliss on his typewriter. The publication of the frank piece was intended to offend drug prudes—it acted as a screwjack.

"Death of a Poet" features the suicide of the poet F. X. Leach, a pseudonym of Thompson's. The "story" features crazed betting on a football game and a sexually frustrated poet who beats up two inflatable-rubber sex dolls as a comic substitute for beating his wife. Leach fears retribution from the Mafia for losing bets he cannot cover.

When his wife returns with police to have him arrested for physically abusing her, Leach plugs her twice like a Cagney gangster before taking his own life with a Magnum .44, the same gun with which poet and novelist Richard Brautigan and Thompson himself ended their lives—both writers being fierce admirers of Hemingway, who also committed suicide. Leach's manic personality and dedicated alcoholism may satirize Brautigan, but like the character Yeamon in *The Rum Diary*, it reveals a more bitter and agressive alter-ego of Thompson. This story is merely a slightly modified center excerpt from "Fear and Loathing in Elko," an amusing fantasy skit with colorful language and wise-guy attitude but, nonetheless, shallow until the arresting, digressive line: "That lone bullet on the stretcher in Dallas sure as hell didn't pass through two bodies, but it was the one that pierced the heart of the American Dream in our century, maybe forever."[11]

The title piece sports a huge black cat,[12] Mr. Screwjack himself. Thompson was a dog and bird man. When you raise peacocks, you don't want cats around. In the story Raoul Duke physically consummates love with the monstrous cat amid their love-hate relationship. William F. Buckley, in his August 1979 review of *The Great Shark Hunt* for the *New York Times*, had taunted Thompson with the preposterous speculation that Thompson had no interest in sex because he never wrote about it. Such provocation was undoubtedly intended to goad Thompson into publishing something Buckley could ridicule. After having this story read aloud to friends in his kitchen, Thompson reportedly laughed, "Let's see what Bill Buckley thinks about *that*."[13] The bizarre piece boasts satiric homoerotic detail and is clearly psychotic. As a satire on the sexual intimacy of petting animals, the piece is not about human sexuality. For his part, Thompson appears to want to goad Buckley or other writers into writing a response to it, but Buckley wisely ignored the bait on writing about bestiality.

In the piece Thompson takes a swipe at Norman Mailer, calling the cat "no better than that punk Norman Mailer fell for,"[14] alluding to Mailer's interest in freeing the criminal and murderer Jack Abbott from prison. Mailer had persuaded his publisher to bring out a book of letters between them, and he penned an introduction to Abbott's prison letters. Anatole Broyard wrote a favorable review of *In the Belly of the Beast* for the *New York Times Book Review* supplement, commending the book's "tender brutality reminiscent of Jean Genet."[15] To Mailer's chagrin, Abbott committed another murder on July 18, 1981. The *New York Times* ran a second favorable review of the book in the daily edition the very next day. Terrence Des Pres labeled Mailer's introduction romantic and refuted Broyard's literary assessment by declaring "Abbott is no Saint Genet," yet acclaimed the book as "awesome, brilliant,"[16] a compelling articulation of the American penal nightmare. Thompson subsequently employed the subheading "In the Belly of the Beast" for miscellaneous pieces, including the hilarious "Jesus Hated Bald Pussy" in *The Kingdom of Fear*. Thompson's ultimately successful interest in the Lisl Auman imprisonment case was likely instigated by an attempt to succeed where Mailer had failed, but unlike Mailer, Thompson fought a legal battle (moved by a deep emotional sense of justice) and not a literary crusade.

One might justly assert that some of Thompson's journalistic pieces, like his 1992 satire, "Fear and Loathing in Elko,"[17] on Supreme Court Justice Clarence "Long Dong" Thomas during Thomas's confirmation hearings, supply merely self-indulgent fantasy.

"POLO IS MY LIFE"

Originally contracted as a book, "Polo Is My Life" is a self-contained short story. Thompson twists the epigraph from *Don Quixote*, "Arms, my only ornament—my only rest, the fight" from Cervantes's satire of a delusional individual to indicate that his story provides satiric invective on class warfare. Thompson satirizes the ultra-rich, or as he notes, the top .00001 percent. *The Great Gatsby*, with its social and geographical setting on Long Island as well as the pool murder, provides the surface literary template. Steadman appears as illustrator, and Hunter's anecdotal humor soars in top form on "the sport of Gods and Kings."[18]

The story's gangster figure indulges in the pseudonym Averell Harriman, which conjures the respectable image of Averell Harriman, the wealthy, progressive Democratic former governor of New York State from 1955 to 1958. Before becoming Governor, Harriman had been heavily involved in owning thoroughbreds racing under the stable name, Arden Farms. This upper-caste identity parallels the peculiar college friend of Edgar Allan Poe's narrator in his 1845 masterpiece, "The Fall of the House of Usher," as well as its Poe-influenced progeny, "The Rats in the Walls," by H. P. Lovecraft.

In Poe's story the narrator, curious and intrigued by the eccentricity wealth bestows, becomes the unwitting accomplice to the murder of his college friend's sister. Thompson's narrator likewise begins with curious fascination and respectable admiration for the wealthy. From Lovecraft's story, Thompson appropriated the theme of the rat swarm living inside the walls of an ancient structure of legend, Exham Priory in England, which has been reconstructed after its destruction—here, the old Gadsby hotel on Long Island. Lovecraft's dramatic ending of reversion to an ancient form of genetic-linguistic atavism was influenced by the Kentucky writer and journalist Irvin S. Cobb from his 1923 story, "The Unbroken Chain,"[19] which, aside from the accident of its Long Island setting, does not relate to Thompson's story. Lovecraft's Delapore narrator has gone insane. In a concluding monologue, the hitherto excited but reasonable narrator begins to rant: he denies the cannibalistic crimes of his ancestors and what he has done himself, as he blames *rats* for his having eaten alive his companion, the plump Captain Norrys whose family, centuries ago, had once taken over the narrator's family estate, and with whom the narrator had lived while the ancient De la Poer estate was reconstructed after the First World War. The belated confession of insanity influenced Thompson.

When Thompson's narrative persona beats the bartender Hugo for accepting tips, he endears himself to the sinister gangster who employs the pseudonym Harriman. The bartender is named for the writer Victor Hugo, who was a populist champion of the underclass and common-sense justice. The thrashing of Hugo, presumably for pocketing tips to supplement his minimum wage, a modern-day equivalent to the stolen loaf of bread in Hugo's 1862 *Les Misérables*, cements the bond of upper-class solidarity between Thompson and the vicious "Harriman." The scene is a more clever variation on the thrashing of the bartender in "A Dog Took My Place."[20] Like Poe, Thompson dyes his story with rich ironies that appear only at a second reading: "I considered myself lucky to have stumbled on something no more dangerous than a skillful Averell Harriman impersonator instead of something much worse."[21]

We are informed of the "amusing" incident when Harriman played polo with a dead child's head, which was possibly the head of the aviator Charles Lindberg's kidnapped twenty-month-old son. The kidnapping, the so-called crime of the century in 1932, led Congress to pass the "Lindberg law" making kidnapping a federal offense if the victim was transported across state lines. Bruno Hauptmann, a German immigrant carpenter, plotted a phony ransom scheme, was caught for the scheme, and immediately sentenced to death. Admitting the blackmail scheme, he denied the kidnapping and murder for which he was convicted. Despite the New Jersey governor's offer of lifetime imprisonment if Hauptmann would admit to the murder, Hauptmann continued to assert his innocence, preferring execution to an admission of guilt.[22] Here Thompson "solves" the kidnapping and murder of the twenty-month-old child while, by implication, denouncing the class-hysteria media circus that had resulted in the conviction and execution of a lower-class innocent. Thompson fantasizes that a conspiracy of Lindberg's upper-class enemies kidnapped and killed the baby, keeping the head as polo ball trophy. It is true that all ball games, including baseball and hurling, evolved from primitive celebration games played with war trophies, skulls, or brains (which were mixed with lye). Today many judge that Hauptmann was convicted by the press rather than by any evidence. This aspect of the menacing story extends the thread of Thompson's "sins of the press" that appears in all his major works.

We discover that this Harriman character had murdered his former hotel partner, then burned down the hotel for the insurance money, rebuilding the hotel in its current luxurious incarnation. In Mark Twain's novel, *The American Claimant* (1892), a sequel to the more popular *The Gilded Age* (1873) and based on Twain's play, *Colonel Sellers* (1886), a luxurious Long Island hotel by the name of the Gadsby burns down.[23] To assure his readers that he speaks of that same hotel,

Thompson notes that the place is full of ghosts, many of which "burned alive in a series of disastrous fires that have plagued the hotel since it was built in 1874."[24] He also believes that Scott Fitzgerald himself probably once drank at the bar.

Harriman claims the bartender Hugo has been cheating him for years by accepting tips; he murders Hugo in the same vicious way he had killed his former hotel partner: having him eaten alive by rats and subsequently tossed into the hotel pool with the rats, as if Thompson was punishing jokingly Lovecraft's Delapore narrator. (In the original *Rolling Stone* magazine publication, Steadman had great fun illustrating this.) The dead, floating body invokes a parallel with Gatsby's dead body, but the twist is that the crime appears to have been committed out of a vicious whim by a rich man rather than by an aggrieved worker (Fitzgerald's auto-shop mechanic, Wilson). In Poe's story the narrator naïvely assists his friend in moving the coffin with his friend's sister in it (whom he either poisoned or buried alive), while in Thompson's story his narrator's beating of Hugo had encouraged Harriman to murder Hugo.

While noting that the disco floor has replaced the carriage house and that Joey Buttafuoco, a contemporary auto mechanic, has replaced Gatsby as the "resident celebrity manqué" (thus mixing fact and fiction), the one unchanging constant is that underworld gangsters still rule Long Island, just as they did in the 1920s, thus illustrating Alphonse Karr's most famous aphorism: "The more things change, the more they remain the same." The introduction of Joey Buttafuoco continues Thompson's long-standing joke about the sinister aspects of auto mechanics like Ralph "Sonny" Barger and Hilo Bob. In 1992 Amy Fisher, Buttafuoco's seventeen-year-old girlfriend, wearing a T-shirt advertising Joey's auto body shop, shot Joey's wife point-blank in the face, thus providing more evidence that Long Island culture both changes and does not change—the change being merely related to sex, another aspect of the Belinda theme.

The musical comedy *Les Misèrables*, based on Hugo's tragic novel, became in 1985 the longest-running musical in the world. The comic thrashing of Hugo by Thompson's persona might be seen as a satire on the musical version of the novel. The execution-style murder of Hugo points to incisive social commentary: the wealthy would prefer that Victor Hugo's populist novel had never existed. In Victor Hugo's novel, the hero Valjean at least receives a prejudiced, perfunctory trial, while Thompson's character Hugo undergoes summary execution by torture. While Harriman finds himself arrested and charged for the murder he undoubtedly committed, his wealth protects him and his trial receives an indefinite delay.

The celebration of the Aspen Club Polo victory takes place neither in Garden City, Long Island; Greenwich, Connecticut (where half the games are played); nor Manhattan, but in Amityville, Long Island, the site of the Amityville horror film series that began in 1979, based on the series of Gothic novels penned by Jay Anson about a house haunted by evil spirits. Thompson believes the homes of the rich to be de facto haunted mansions, but from time to time the demons need to get together and party at Horror Central.

The reference to the narrator's old Mexican friend Memo Garcia Jr., who "sits at the right hand of God," supplies another memorial tribute to Oscar Acosta. The notion that the city of Aspen fields a polo team is sheer silliness, providing an allegorical dig at upper-class pretentions in Aspen, revolving around the sport of skiing. The two Polo aces, the "ringers" on the Aspen team who deliver the tournament victory, present affectionate portraits of Thompson's son Juan and Acosta's son Marco.

The digression devoted to a discussion of the polo goddess Belinda, who appears as a four-eyed predatory goddess, offers a Belinda who is a raving antithesis of another Belinda, the embodiment of passive beauty, in Alexander Pope's mock-epic *The Rape of the Lock* (1717). The four-eyes constitute a wild jab at Pope's academic style. While Pope's ideal of beauty is so chaste, ethereal, and precious that the loss of a single lock of hair would comically damage Belinda's beauty in his satire, Thompson's Belinda is a dissolute, rapacious slut who takes bribes, peddling her influence over polo players. Thompson's satire illustrates the extreme degree in satiric conventions—from one excess of politely refined minimalism to an overly aggressive maximal crudeness—that has occurred in popular writing over the centuries.

The conclusion of Thompson's story provides another twist—to the Poe template. In Poe's story, the narrator flees in horror as the huge Gothic edifice literally crumbles before his eyes—Poe's passive spectator indulges in the hallucinatory fantasy of the ultra-upper class destroying themselves through madness, incest, and murder. Poe's fantasy vision would argue that the upper class is ultimately irrelevant to society, but time has shown that Poe was mistaken politically, although he shared Thompson's jaundiced view of the upper class.

Thompson's satiric epilogue, with the Caesarian epigraph *Veni, Vidi, Vici*, opts for a more entrenched and cynical irony. The narrator has approved of Harriman's lifestyle and now imitates him: "I am a polo person now, and I know the Polo Attitude. I smoke the finest opium, and I drive a Ducati 916. Birds sing where I walk, and my home is a magnet for children."[25] The narrator has morphed into a social monster like Harriman—he's an accomplished pedophile scooting about on his swank Italian motorcycle, asking underage children if they want a ride. The omission of what happens to the children only enhances the possibilities of horror. Members of the upper class retain their power by secretly colluding with gangsters, and they are still out there, preying on your children. This satiric monologue coda repeats the savage irony strategy at the conclusion of *Hell's Angels* where Thompson has been transformed into the kind of monster biker he has spent the book satirizing.

The narrator of "Polo Is My Life" has *learned* how to be a successful ghoul by aping the very rich. Thompson's story shows how the rationale of greed corrupts both thought and behavior. In hindsight, the story appears prophetic of the scandalous rampant greed that the coming decade would exhibit when wealthy bankers and investors who indulged in arguably criminal behavior received government bailouts. Thompson declares that "if there is any natural sport for the '90s in America, it is polo."[26]

In interviews Thompson frequently mentioned that "Polo Is My Life: Fear and Loathing in Horse Country" was to become a novel connected to the JFK assassination. Thompson thought the assassination was carried out by the Mob and covered up by J. Edgar Hoover,[27] a perspective subsequently explored by Lamar Waldron's book coauthored with Thom Hartman, *Ultimate Sacrifice* (2005). It's probable that after Mailer published *Oswald's Tale* (1996), Hunter decided not to compete on the assassination theme, just as he had decided not to compete with Mailer's 1975 *The Fight* on "The Rumble in the Jungle" in Zaire by not filing for *Rolling Stone*.[28] Likewise, Thompson may have never published his account of the 1968 Chicago Democratic Convention and Daley's porcine, baton-wielding thugs because of Mailer's magisterial and panoramic *Miami and the Siege of Chicago* (1968), or even Terry Southern's gripping account in *Esquire*.

George Plimpton competed with Mailer (and the Hemingway macho-bullfighting approach) in *Shadow Box* (1977), the last chapter concluding with three interviews: Thompson, along with Frazier corner men Archie Moore and Dick Sadler. Plimpton asked Thompson why he did not attend the fight and reported a complicated and comic entanglement of anecdotes about Thompson smuggling elephant tusks in public at a hundred miles an hour.[29] In Thompson's September 29, 2003, genially effusive obituary for Plimpton, Hunter acclaimed the departed as "about as good a friend as a man can have in this world,"[30] arguing facetiously for a life-size Manhattan midtown monument for this handsome wealthy scion from Harvard,[31] while disclosing genial George to have been a furtive but discriminating connoisseur of the finest Afghan hashish money can buy—that may have been Hunter's final fictive flourish.

About fifty unpublished short stories, written during the Sixties and Seventies, slumber neatly filed away in Thompson's bunker archive.[32] None of them are likely to be a chilling masterpiece like "Polo Is My Life." As early works, they would be in the Hemingway tradition of realism as in *The Rum Diary*. Yet when published, there may be a few iceberg surprises.

9

SHOT OUT OF A CANNON

Final Assessment

Methinks my body is but the lees of my better being.—Ishmael, in Herman Melville's *Moby-Dick*

While still capable of the prankish literary reference, Thompson had retired from literature, although in a 1990 interview with future biographer William McKeen, he admitted that he still possessed the ambition to write another novel.[1] Yet there appears to have been a failure of both ambition and imagination. Thompson's plots had been combinations of his autobiography and the irreverent twisting of literary templates. Speaking of Thompson's fiction, William Kennedy observes: "If Hunter left the traditional form, he created a new one, a fictional hybrid with his persona dominant."[2] Thompson's writing had been rooted in the experiences of his life, the literature he read, or analysis of political events. Subsequently, he energized his political and sports columns with the involved enthusiasm of a Grantland Rice, his own brand of memorable humor, and Mencken-like wit, while he grew more aloof about literature and participation in politics. Ralph Steadman commented:

> All his heroes like Joseph Conrad, Ernest Hemingway and William Faulkner wrote proper stories and then there was Hunter, this magnificent outlaw, with jangling silver spurs on a pair of Converse Low

basketball sneakers, whose prose style was peerless, but whose ability
to write a novel eluded him to the end. He was his own best story. [3]

But there was the one novel, *Fear and Loathing in Las Vegas*, for which
Thompson will be remembered as long as critics compose their favorite
top 100 list of American novels. In my opinion, it must be ranked in the
top ten.

Thompson's ambition had been to write novels as good as or better
than Conrad's *The Heart of Darkness*, Hemingway's *The Sun Also Rises*,
and Fitzgerald's *The Great Gatsby*. He fulfilled that ambition with *The
Rum Diary* and *Fear and Loathing in Las Vegas*. His unpublished book
on the gun lobby has yet to see the light of day, but when it does, we
will be able to assess how close it comes to competing with Conrad's
great masterpiece. There are about fifty unpublished short stories.
Some of them may be interesting, yet I doubt they can compete with
those of Hemingway, Fitzgerald, Faulkner, Flannery O'Connor, or Eu-
dora Welty, but there may be a few surprises.

William Kennedy, one of the few people who have been able to
combine journalism and fiction successfully, notes the precarious danger for the journalist:

> every day becomes for him, a tabula rasa. This is deadly. The fiction
> writer who puts little or no value on yesterday, or the even more
> distant past, might just as well have Alzheimer's disease; for serious
> fiction, especially novelistic work, has time as its essence and memo-
> ry as its principal tool. [4]

Immersed in the random chaos of unfolding events, it is difficult for
journalists to step back and reflect on how the past informs the present,
but Thompson managed to find that space for *Fear and Loathing in Las
Vegas* and more obscurely and enigmatically in *The Curse of Lono*.

Comparing Thompson's work to Twain's, Tom Wolfe points out that
Twain was subtle in the way he took dignified things and put them up
against a wall to show how idiotic they were, while Hunter wanted to
"just go *through* the wall. He was brilliant—there are very few writers
who could top him. I can't think of any humorist in the whole century
who could touch him." [5] Hunter's joking insult letters to Kennedy and
others became an intimate art form for his friends. These insults were
coveted, as if he were a tribal shaman bestowing blessings. Johnny

Depp recalls that one minute before he departed for Allen Ginsberg's 1997 memorial service in Los Angeles, Thompson faxed him a eulogy to read, calling Allen "a dangerous bull-fruit with the brain of an open sore and the conscience of a virus," and that Allen was now happy because he knew he could get into the grim reaper's pants.[6] Some letters written to mere acquaintances offer trash-talking hilarity through their satiric bite. The 1998 foreword that Thompson penned for Ralph Steadman's *Gonzo: The Art* analyzes Steadman's work as the result of terminal syphilis.

Thompson's overriding ambition has been to be a political commentator in the mode of H. L. Mencken. Thompson fulfilled that ambition with *Generation of Swine, Better than Sex,* and *Hey Rube. Hell's Angels* and *Fear and Loathing on the Campaign Trail* remain enduring journalistic landmarks. Thompson also wanted to cover sports in a dramatic manner, like Grantland Rice, and he fulfilled that ambition through his miscellaneous sports pieces. Hunter became a great Midwestern humorist, like James Thurber. Thompson participated as an active politician in Aspen, yet much of that was not open to public view. He dabbled in painting. Partying was a professional habit. Being a backwoods hunter was a habitual compulsion. Perhaps Thompson wore too many hats, yet his exploits will leave a folkloric legacy as large as Horatio Alger's. Like journalist Malaparte, Thompson wrote two reportorial novels of outrage. Malaparte's *Kaputt* (1944) may be considered his *Iliad*, while *La Pelle* (1949) may be considered his *Odyssey*.

Thompson's use of literary templates had been the habit of Western literature since Homer. Everyone attempted to riff off Homer, to equal or surpass him in their own way in other Greek epics. Then Latins attempted to displace him, from Virgil to Dante.[7] Chaucer rendered and modified in verse templates from Boccaccio. Just as Edmund Spenser attempted a Protestant moral over-going of nominally Roman Catholic Ariosto, Milton attempted a simultaneous Protestant moral over-going of Homer (syntax and Iliadic theogony), Virgil (shadowy nuance), and St. Luke (Christian mythologizing). Shakespeare appropriated templates from varied sources. Thompson was not a modernist who attempted near *ex nihilo* imaginative creation like Joyce (although Joyce casually used templates from Homer in *Ulysses*) or Kafka (who used the template of legal procedure in *The Trial*), but even though he was off the well-worn path, he worked in the more traditional methods of Western literature. Thompson consistently ran multiple template lines, transforming that technique into an original signature. That signature included simultaneous running lines that elevate *Fear and Loathing in Las Vegas* to the status of a masterpiece and *The Curse of Lono* to an unusual hermetic achievement. Thompson's practice of warping template may be rooted in his experience in Big Sur. His literary hero, Henry Miller, who wrote autobiographical fiction that Thompson admired, anonymously quotes a friend who characterizes the vagrant intellectual tendencies and behavior of Big Sur's bohemian denizens as: "They're all a bunch of morphodites!"[8]

Thompson's 1967 "The 'Hashbury' Is the Capital of the Hippies" observes that the Haight-Ashbury scene "is only the tip of a great psychedelic iceberg that is already drifting in the sea lanes of the Great Society."[9] In his commentary on this passage, William Stephenson emphasizes the mobility of this berg in society's shipping lanes as it conjures images of mercantilism and outlaw piracy,[10] but the concept of iceberg *mobility* also applies to the varied, exfoliating allusions to literary templates in Thompson's three works of fiction as they sail between the shelves of American and world literature.

T. S. Eliot exhibited an intense use of literary templates in *The Waste Land* (1922) by paraphrasing French poets and other writers in cornucopia of world literature. In journalism, riffing off literary titles evolved from book review headlines has now become fairly commonplace. Thompson was a master of the twisting headline riff, as anyone who has read his numerous witty columns knows.

In *Finnegans Wake* (1939) Joyce ran simultaneous lines around the relativity of multitudinous languages and songs as if he were multiplying loaves and fishes via Einstein, while Thompson applied simultaneity to plot and theme in a submerged "iceberg" manner that would draw in, on the one hand, a populist audience with the visible comic ice tip and (eventually), on the other hand, an intellectual audience with deep cultural themes that exhibited literary and historical themes like unexplored underwater currents.

Maybe Thompson did not fulfill his ambition to exceed Homer, Melville, Twain, Hemingway, Mencken, Thurber, and Fitzgerald all at once in his own carnival, but perhaps Thompson should be considered as having donned the illustrious antique laurel of being the American Juvenal who satirized Christianity and American government rather than paganism and Roman government, the satirist of politicians and businessmen who deluded people with the lottery of the American Dream, the champion of sanity who derided the corruption of government drug policies. It remains remarkable that scholars have paid minute attention and homage to the acid-head multiple threads in Thomas Pynchon's work while paying little attention to Thompson's literary achievements.

Most writers choose a narrow path and exploit that trail as an allegory for the situation of the world, often repeating themselves while ringing a few changes in their music under slightly different circumstances. Thompson's invention of gonzo, as a style and method, liberated his personality, but was wayward and scattershot from the beginning. Gonzo was an approach to the immediate vagaries of life, not a disciplined program to create a single vision or unified work of art. On the contrary, there was in its philosophy an aesthetic appreciation of chaos in the vein of Lucretius: "We are not a nation of honest men. Despite our love and trust of Sports and all the swill it pumps out. In our hearts we are circus people."[11] In that same spirit of chaos, when a journalistic or literary project did not immediately appear to work out, he put that project aside, moving on to another project. This is why there remain many unpublished efforts.

While Plato's *Republic* sought to demythologize Homer and popular democracy with a cynical intellectual elitism,[12] Thompson sought to demythologize the elitist Puritan mythology adopted by American moguls to justify the continued exploitation of the lower classes. Thompson's perspective was a Jeffersonian belief in the power of the press to hold government leaders accountable for bad policy, corruption, and inanity. Unlike Plato, Thompson believed that the general populace had the ability to recognize truth. Journalists, if they were responsible, had the power to ridicule political lies. People who met him were intensely moved by his manner. As Ralph Steadman put it:

> His hesitant way of expressing anxiety and rage, his certainty and his suspicion that what he was saying was and is right, drove a stake through the hearts of every red-blooded American who wanted to believe in some real American Dream. Even if the dream wasn't perfect, it represented the very most that any human creature searching for a Dream could realistically expect.[13]

Thompson was always searching for that Dream even as he exploded it in absurdity and irony. Like a doctor examining the body of an old man, he saw decay and disease, but he believed in life and its joy. While Rousseau saw Hume's belief in the progress of science and civilization as merely a delusion rooted in moral decay and even desperate despair,[14] Thompson's populist apocalyptic pessimism was inspired by Spengler and the Book of Revelation, from which he had "stolen more quotes and thoughts and purely little elegant starbursts of writing"[15] because as a traveling journalist or circuit speaker, the Bible could be found in any hotel-room drawer.

The theme of the American Dream, whether analyzed by Thompson or through his various alter egos, ultimately provides a flexible dialectic—its powerful presence finds acknowledgement before its cynical exploitation by others is detonated and demolished. In *Walden* (1854), two years after Horatio Alger graduated from Harvard, Henry David Thoreau opined: "I learned this, at least, by my experiment; that if one advances confidently in the direction of his dreams, and endeavors to live the life which he has imagined, he will meet with a success unexpected in common hours."[16] Emma Knight, 1973 Miss U.S.A. pageant queen, once lamented: "The minute you're crowned, you become their property and subject to whatever they tell you. . . . I was supposed to live it [the American Dream] their way."[17] On the other hand, successful Jann Wenner enthused: "I wonder if the American Dream is as ugly as Hunter Thompson says it is. . . . I've always gotten what I wanted."[18] The American Dream operates like a casino poker game: while most hulk out of the building as losers, there remain some spectacular winners who achieve the money shot of publicity and stardom.

As an identifiable voice Thompson stands out from the throng of American writers. Morris Dickstein notes that "in high gear Thompson paraded one of the few original styles of recent years, a style dependent almost deliriously on insult, vituperation, and stream-of-invective to a degree unparalleled since Celine."[19] Thompson's lyrical vernacular has a tone and cadence both uniquely his own and yet as close to common speech as the style of Twain spoken in his day. While not a poet, Thompson loved to read his work out loud like Mark Twain to help him capture both common rhythms of speech, nuances of humor, and the music of well-crafted sounds.

Fear and Loathing in America remains so appealing in its carnival humor nailed to the frontal lobes. This book may be the funniest novel in American literature, yet its humor is augmented by intellectual perspectives on social observation as well as innovative writing techniques, especially the warping of literary templates. Thompson's novel remains one of the most provocative and amusing novels in the American canon[20]—yet it remains accessible to any reader.

Not many writers have so stamped their identity into the language—*gonzo* has been in the dictionary and our daily discourse for some time. The tag phrase *fear and loathing* has become nearly a common cliché. While either segment of the phrase individually indicates tragedy, Thompson's compound now invokes comedy, a defensive reaction that attempts to turn threat into the optimism of laughter, the pleasurable rictus that indicates the tragedy will pass and the normalcy of random hope will return. In the face of disaster, Thompson offers that absurd and courageous levity that Nietzsche advises.[21]

Thompson loved literature, but he also loved life and its absurd collision with the spontaneous. He wrote two journalistic masterpieces, one major literary masterpiece and one minor hermetic masterpiece, and many columns that were sculpted masterpieces in the realm of sports, humor, and politics, often combining those sensibilities into a single column. While other humorists might be funny on stage, he made his life funny to everyone he knew. Anita Thompson says: "Hunter was fun. He never stopped playing and seeing the undercurrents of humor in every situation, weird or not."[22]

The critic's observation that Thompson could not portray women indicates his limits. With the exception of a few characters in *The Rum Diary* and Acosta (whom he surreptitiously taped) in *Fear and Loathing in Las Vegas*, it could be argued that fictional characters were exaggerated versions of his own alter-ego. But within those restrictions, he excelled.

One of the less publicized aspects of Thompson's life was his local activism, both political and environmental. Much of the character of Aspen as a city is the result of an outgrowth of Thompson's campaign for the toleration of individuality, no matter how weird. He valued friendship and loyalty above all; his household ran on the understanding that "*We* is the most important word in politics."[23]

Behind the scenes, Thompson acted as an effective mentor to many journalists and writers. His influence continues to fuel a later generation of journalists: Garry Webb, Thom Hartmann, the prolific Chris Hedges, Naomi Klein, Jeremy Scahill, Robert Scheer, and Nick Turse, all investigative journalists too serious to invoke Thompson's populist humor, but John Carroll Dolan in *Pleasant Hell* (2004) and Gary Brecher in *War Nerd* (2008) do not shy from that approach. With habitual irreverence, Mark Ames in *The Exile* (2000) and *Going Postal* (2005) reports cultural critique with satiric attitude.

Not without his own sense of humor, an investigative journalist in Thompson's footsteps has been Matt Taibbi with *Spanking the Donkey* (2006), *Smells like Dead Elephants* (2007), *The Great Derangement* (2009), and *Griftopia* (2011) and, with Molly Crabapple, *The Divide: American Injustice in the Age of the Wealth Gap* (2014). Founding *Granta* magazine editor Bill Buford's first book was inspired by Thompson's *Hell's Angels*. A study of English football (soccer) fanatics, their hooligan alienation and random violence, Buford's amusing *Among the Thugs* contains some wise observations on journalism[24] and concludes with Buford receiving a truncheon beating by police, yet the book lacks Thompson's signature *energia*, his mischievous edge.

Television personalities such as Jon Stewart and Stephen Colbert have built on the flair of Thompson's insouciant satire. The roving journalist appears in Ted Conover's *Rolling Nowhere* (1984), and the books of Pulitzer Prize–winner Charlie LeDuff, like *Work and Other Sins* (2004), exhibit the gonzo spirit. From a financial point of view, *The Betrayal of the American Dream* (2012) by Donald L. Bartlett and James B. Steele explains how the middle class in America lost the American Dream that so mesmerized the middle class.

Thompson's comedic writing has always been popular among those in the movie business. Important stars like Jack Nicholson, Margot Kidder, and Johnny Depp were close friends. In recent years his influence has become more visible with films like *The Rum Diary* (2011), *Beware the Gonzo* (2011), and *Butter* (2011). Much of Thompson's populist appeal resided in the perception that he was a singular libertarian "outlaw" fighting to preserve the liberties that intrusive government wanted to rescind.[25]

In addition to the marvelous intellectual letters Thompson wrote to those he knew, Thompson also wrote humorous letters to those he didn't know—corporations, publications, and government functionaries. The immediacy and accuracy of his spot-on laser style in letters, with its cocktail of honesty and humor, has recently impressed the literary world, and Thompson has in fact earned new accolades as a man of letters. Posthumously, Thompson is becoming one of America's Great Men of Letters. While literary connoisseurs might read Mencken's *Prejudices*, Edmund Wilson's *Diaries*, John O'Hara's *Letters*, John Cheever's *Journals*, or Jack Kerouac's juvenilia, they now read Thompson's witty and wily letters.

Students and other people disillusioned by the harsh economics of the contemporary world relate to Thompson's prophetic vision of economic enslavement. Although Hunter had evaded that harsh fate, his public image and success has always appeared to him as a peculiar quirk of chance, a fortuitous accident. He had seen the specter of the bugbitten itinerant end of journalism in South America. He was impoverished and barely surviving, both economically and in terms of his own intellectual freedom, outside of the conformist corporate mainstream. Hunter well knew his Horatio Alger–like success was a one-time achievement not available to others.

As an appendix to *Songs of the Doomed* (1990), Thompson began an Honor Roll list of those who "ride for the Gonzo brand." The names listed paid tribute to friends and those who assisted him in various ways. The list began with twenty-five names, and by *The Kingdom of Fear* (2003) comprised 105 names, a retrospective list of all those who played an important role in his life, whether in public or behind the scenes. While Thompson was an atheist, he was raised as a Presbyterian, a Christian community that places great emphasis upon establishing personal relationships amid a small fellowship of believers whose lives are united in the Christian faith and whose members support each other's endeavors with a shared loyalty. While Thompson was not a religious believer, he subscribed to a moral political outlook with an awareness that all organizations evolved into corruption. He believed in the capacity of individuals to make a difference and preferred to bond with people through peyote or drink.

A secular sensibility of communal hip solidarity became the bedrock of Thompson's life and the lives of those around him. Thompson was the secular elder of that community, urging his friends to go further in political action and laughter, speaking of social justice as if he were a humorous Calvinistic minister preaching doom, even when he was incapacitated, wheelchair bound, and crippled by pain.

An examination of Thompson's longer fiction reveals an interlocking referential web that incorporates not only major elements from Hunter's autobiography and various fictions, but also a humorous use of those erudite books on literature and history he thought central to an aware consciousness and of great importance to society. An aerial view of Thompson's technique resembles the construction of a Daedalian labyrinth to imprison a Minotaur: an attempt by a Jeffersonian journalist and creative writer to limit the sway and propaganda of abusive state power and devious religious chicanery over the peaceful loving citizens whom the imperial state condescendingly considers slaves or criminals, not unlike the situation of early Christians in Rome.

Discriminating readers and the populace at large, especially the young, still avidly devour *Fear and Loathing in Las Vegas* for both its durable humor (which time has made more absurdly riotous) and its prophetic sociological analysis (which recent events have made more relevant) of the fabled American Dream:[26]

> The enormous popularity of Thompson's work among young people gives them hope that reasonable action to correct society may be possible, just as Molière's comic stage bestowed that hope.[27]

That legacy of hope, along with its hilarious critique of abusive power, bumbling national incompetence, and moneyed corruption, secures his position in the pantheon of American letters, as well as his place as the author of an enduring, singular classic. The laughter that Thompson's work engenders—both literary and political—revives the courage to face contemporary problems that glare at us now with even more Spenglerian doom than when Thompson was alive.

NOTES

1. LOUISVILLE SLUGGER

1. For an analysis of the Freak Power symbol, see William Stephenson, *Gonzo Republic: Hunter S. Thompson's America* (New York: Continuum, 2012), 70–75.

2. Michael Cleverly and Bob Braudis, *The Kitchen Readings: Untold Stories of Hunter S. Thompson* (New York: Harper, 2008), 269–72.

3. Jay Cowan, *Hunter S. Thompson: An Insider's View of Deranged, Depraved, Drugged Out Brilliance* (Guilford: Lyons Press, 2009), 243.

4. Ralph Steadman, *The Joke's Over: Bruised Memories: Gonzo, Hunter S. Thompson, and Me* (New York: Harcourt, 2006), 1–2.

5. William McKeen, *Outlaw Journalist: The Life and Times of Hunter S. Thompson* (New York: Norton, 2008), 364. See also Juan F. Thompson, *Stories I Tell Myself: Growing Up with Hunter S. Thompson* (New York: Knopf, 2016), 259–265.

6. The city of Aspen would not let the cannon monument stand for more than a month, so it was dissembled and placed in storage.

7. Steadman, 1–2.

8. Hunter S. Thompson, "The Mailbox: Louisville, Summer of 1946," in *Kingdom of Fear* (New York: Simon & Schuster, 2003), 3–6.

9. Marc Weingarten, *The Gang That Wouldn't Shoot Straight* (New York: Crown, 2005), 125.

10. Hunter S. Thompson, "Grantland Rice Haunts the Honolulu Marathon," in *Better Than Sex* (New York: Random House, 1994), 159–63.

11. McKeen, *Hunter S. Thompson* (Boston: Twayne, 1991), 3.

12. Paul Perry, *Fear and Loathing: The Strange and Terrible Saga of Hunter S. Thompson* (New York: Thunder's Mouth Press, 1993), 18.

13. Ibid., 17.

14. Hunter S. Thompson, *The Proud Highway: The Saga of a Desperate Southern Gentleman, 1955–1967*, ed. Douglas Brinkley (New York: Random House, 1997), 436. For the process of how that book was done, see Thompson, *Stories I Tell Myself*, 232–237.

15. Ibid., 438.

16. Hunter S. Thompson, *Fear and Loathing in America*, ed. Douglas Brinkley (New York: Simon & Schuster, 2000), 724.

17. McKeen, *Hunter S. Thompson*, 4–5.

18. Robert Draper, *Rolling Stone Magazine: The Uncensored History* (New York: Doubleday, 1990), 154.

19. Peter O. Whitmer, *When the Going Gets Weird: The Twisted Life and Times of Hunter S. Thompson* (New York: Hyperion, 1993), 75.

20. Ibid., 79.

21. Draper, 157.

22. Thompson, *Kingdom of Fear*, 47.

23. Mikal Gilmore, "Hunter S. Thompson: The Last Outlaw," *Rolling Stone*, no. 970, 24 March 2005; reprinted in *Stories Done* (New York: Free Press, 2008), 237.

24. McKeen, *Hunter S. Thompson*, 6; Weingarten, 127.

25. P. Perry, 47–48.

26. Hunter S. Thompson, "Fleeing New York," in *Songs of the Doomed* (New York: Simon &Schuster, 1990), 60.

27. For an acidic account of this experience, see Thompson's first draft of the introduction to *The Great Shark Hunt* in *Fear and Loathing in America*, 723–30.

28. Hunter S. Thompson, "When the Thumb Was a Ticket to Adventures on the Highway . . . The Extinct Hitchhiker," *National Observer*, 22 July 1963.

29. A heavily revised version of this novel, which features a comic cameo of Ernest Hemingway, was published as *Changó's Beads and Two-Tone Shoes* in 2011.

30. McKeen, *Outlaw Journalist*, 57–60.

31. Draper, 158.

32. Thompson was probably attracted to Big Sur by Miller's *Big Sur and the Oranges of Hieronymus Bosch* (1957), which depicted a motley crew of artists and eccentric outcasts creating an informal community of friendly neighbors. That book became an iconic touchstone for the hippie movement. About Big Sur, Miller wrote: "The most important thing I have witnessed, since coming here, is the transformation people have wrought in their own being" (26).

33. P. Perry, 53.

34. "Who can blame me for whipping that paraplegic in the baths?" Thompson, *Songs of the Doomed*, 136. Presumably, a comic exaggeration of whatever happened.

35. P. Perry, 64–65.

36. Thompson, *The Proud Highway*, 351.

37. Whitmer, *When the Going Gets Weird*, 130–31.

38. Ibid., 134. Despite Walter Cronkite's opposition, Charles Kuralt successfully pitched a similar traveling-feature approach to CBS in October 1967. (The concept derives from the early columns of Ernie Pyle.) Ultimately, Cronkite and Kuralt became best friends. See Douglas Brinkley, *Cronkite* (New York: HarperCollins, 2012), 363–65.

39. McKeen, *Outlaw Journalist*, 61.

40. P. Perry, 124–28.

41. In Acosta's galleys Hunter was originally called Ramon Duke. See Thompson, *Fear and Loathing in America*, 476.

42. Whitmer, *When the Going Gets Weird*, 164–65.

43. Thompson, *Better Than Sex*, 236–46. Originally published in *Rolling Stone*, 16 June 1994.

44. McKeen, *Outlaw Journalist*, 120.

45. Thompson, *Fear and Loathing in America*, 42.

46. Draper, 164.

47. Peter Richardson, *A Bomb in Every Issue: How the Short Unruly Life of* Ramparts *Magazine Changed America* (New York: New Press, 2009), 140.

48. Whitmer, *When the Going Gets Weird*, 123–25. For an overview of that critical year, see James Witcover, *The Year the Dream Died: Revisiting 1968 in America* (New York: Warner, 1997).

49. McKeen, *Outlaw Journalist*, 138.

50. Thompson, *The Proud Highway*, 313–14.

51. Thompson, *Fear and Loathing in America*, 189.

52. McKeen, *Outlaw Journalist*, 128–29. It may still be years before it is published.

53. Ibid., 359.

54. Ibid., 132–33.

55. Whitmer, *When the Going Gets Weird*, 173–74.

56. P. Perry, 154–55.

57. Thompson, *Fear and Loathing in America*, 311.

58. Thompson, *Rolling Stone*, no. 67, 1 October 1970. Reprinted in *The Great Shark Hunt* (New York: Simon & Schuster, 1979), 151–75.

59. Thompson, *Fear and Loathing in America*, 208.

60. Thompson often said jokingly that ibogaine was a fictional drug, yet it was used for centuries by the Bwiti tribes of Gabon and Cameroon. See Stephanie Hegarty, "Can a Hallucinogen from Africa Cure Addiction?" BBC News Magazine, 13 April 2002, http://www.bbc.com/news/magazine-17666589 (accessed 14 April 2012). The joke had stunned the newscorps and Muskie's campaign because they had never heard of ibogaine.

61. Thompson, *The Great Shark Hunt*, 58.

62. Ibid., 299–339.

63. McKeen, *Outlaw Journalist*, 204.

64. McKeen says it was $30,000 (ibid., 238).

65. Thompson, *Songs of the Doomed*, 193.

66. Cleverly and Braudis, 42–49.

67. For details, see William McKeen, *Mile Zero Marker* (New York: Crown, 2011), 174–81.

68. McKeen, *Outlaw Journalist*, 264.

69. Ibid., 255–58.

70. Whitmer, *When the Going Gets Weird*, 247.

71. Cleverly and Braudis, 179–89.

72. Whitmer, *When the Going Gets Weird*, 208–12.

73. McKeen, *Outlaw Journalist*, 267.

74. E. Jean Carroll, *Hunter: The Strange and Savage Life of Hunter S. Thompson* (New York: Dutton, 1993), 217.

75. Anecdote furnished by Martha Leatherwood Moffett, *National Enquirer* chief librarian. In 1951, when I was four, my mother's father and I were watching the Brooklyn Dodgers on television. Jackie Robinson stole second base. He was clearly safe, yet the umpire called him out. My grandfather, who had made his living working in the complaint department of Abraham & Strauss for thirty-five years, exercising his great lifelong capacity for patience, got up from his chair in anger and plunged his foot through the television. My grandfather thought the call a blatant exhibition of racism; it was over a year before the television was replaced.

76. John Wilbur, in Jann Wenner and Corey Seymour, *Gonzo: The Life of Hunter S. Thompson* (New York: Back Bay Books, 2007), 399.

77. Steadman, 377.

78. McKeen, *Outlaw Journalist*, 341–57.

79. Hunter S. Thompson, *Screwjack* (New York: Simon & Schuster, 1991, 2001), 48–49.

80. McKeen, *Outlaw Journalist*, 361.

81. For Fuller's relationship with Hunter, see Juan F. Thompson, *Stories I Tell Myself: Growing Up with Hunter S. Thompson* (New York: Knopf, 2016), 96.

82. Matthew Mosely, *Dear Dr. Thompson: Felony Murder, Hunter S. Thompson, and the Last Gonzo Campaign* (Denver: Ghost Road Press, 2010).

83. See J. G. Merquior, *Rousseau and Weber: Two Studies in the Theory of Legitimacy* (Boston: Routledge & Kegan Paul, 1980), 77–86.

84. The Writer character, a composite figure who appears to be part Hemingway, Banks, and Thompson, dresses in a red and yellow Hawaiian shirt: "The Writer has a crooked smile and speaks partially from the left side of his mouth as if he may have suffered a minor stroke long ago and did not fully recover his speech." Russell Banks, *Lost Memory of Skin* (New York: HarperCollins, 2011), 352. Instead of doing actual research, the Writer mostly composes fantasies for a magazine called *The Outsider*, the title of a book by Colin Wilson, which once impressed Thompson. Thompson, *The Proud Highway*, 67.

85. See James E. Caron, "Hunter S. Thompson's 'Gonzo' Journalism and Tall Tradition in America," *Studies in Popular Culture* 8, no. 1 (January 1985), 1–16.

86. Steadman, 234.

87. Blurb on the cover of Thompson, *Fear and Loathing at Rolling Stone: The Essential Writing of Hunter S. Thompson*, ed. Jann S. Wenner (New York: Simon & Schuster, 2011).

2. PLAY IT AGAIN, HUNTER

1. Thompson, *Songs of the Doomed*, 47.

2. Hunter S. Thompson, *The Rum Diary: A Novel* (New York: Simon & Schuster, 1998), 50.

3. P. Perry, 43.

4. During spring of 1962 Thompson had read an early draft of *The Ink Truck*. He appeared to enjoy the book, complimenting Kennedy on the toughness of his writing, but he had misgivings about the book's penultimate scene, the bathhouse orgy, saying: "That scene with the guy taking off his clothes still bothers me." Thompson, *The Proud Highway*, 336.

5. Kennedy's masterpieces, *Billy Phelan's Greatest Game* (1978), *Ironweed* (1983), and *Roscoe* (2002), sit squarely in the tradition of American Realism; *Quinn's Book* (1988) and *Very Old Bones* (1992) limn the Anglo-Irish tradition; *The Ink Truck* (1969), *Legs* (1975), and *The Flaming Corsage* (1996) blend the Anglo-Irish tradition with symbolic surrealism from the South American tradition. See Philip Baruth, "Beyond Realism: William Kennedy on the Surreal and the Unconscious, the Religious, the Sublime, and the Gonzo," *New England Review* 19 (1998), 116–26.

6. Peter O. Whitmer, *Aquarius Revisited: Seven Who Created the Sixties Counterculture That Changed America* (New York: Macmillan, 1987), 99.

7. Thompson, *The Proud Highway*, 387.

8. Ibid., 411.

9. Bailey is also the name of the main character in Flannery O'Connor's famous 1955 short story, "A Good Man is Hard to Find," where the character's name recalls the song ballad's refrain, "will he [Bill Bailey] come home?"

10. For background on the contemporary literary scene in Puerto Rico, see Baruth, "Beyond Realism."

11. Thompson, *Songs of the Doomed*, 110.

12. Thompson, *The Proud Highway*, xvi. The late Irish poet James Liddy published a wickedly amusing chapbook of poetry on the subject of bowling, *In the Slovak Alley* (Milwaukee: Blue Canary Press, 1990).

13. Ibid., xx.

14. For a concise and brilliant overview of this genre, see Donald Keene, *Dawn to the West: Japanese Literature in the Modern Era* (New York: Holt, Rinehart and Winston, 1984), 506–55.

15. Thompson, *The Proud Highway*, 99.

16. McKeen, *Outlaw Journalist*, 40.

17. Ibid., 115–16.

18. Ibid., 109.

19. Thompson, *The Rum Diary*, 11.

20. Ibid., 60.

21. Thompson, *The Proud Highway*, 186–89.

22. Thompson, *The Rum Diary*, 80.

23. McKeen, *Outlaw Journalist*, 56–58.

24. Thompson, *The Proud Highway*, 399.

25. Thompson, *The Rum Diary*, 97.

26. Ibid., 102.

27. McKeen, *Outlaw Journalist*.

28. After decades of Puerto Rican protest, the U.S. Navy finally withdrew from Vieques in 2003; most of the land in question has become a wildlife refuge, although much unexploded ordinance lies below the sand and high cancer rates afflict the island. See Shannon Novak, "Vieques Cancer Rate an Issue," *Miami Herald*, 7 May 2004. Archived at http://web.archive.org/web/20070311075133/http://www.americas.org/item_14739 (accessed 17 April 2007).

29. Thompson, *The Rum Diary*, 13.

30. Ibid., 149.

31. Interview with Dana Kennedy at Skidmore College, 21 July 2011.

32. Marion Elizabeth Rodgers, *Mencken: The American Iconoclast* (Oxford: Oxford University Press, 2005), 532.

33. Ibid., 244–45.

34. At this point the n-word was removed from the printing of the full-length novel: "That filthy sonofabitch" (157) replaces "That weasel of a nigger" (106) from the excerpt in *Songs of the Doomed.* The repeated use of the n-word was also censored from Thompson's piece on the cult of running "Charge of the Weird Brigade." Thompson defended himself as just an all-around prick and not a racist. McKeen, *Outlaw Journalist*, 273.

35. Ernest Hemingway, *The Sun Also Rises* (New York: Scribner's, 1926), 222.

36. A. E. Hotchner, *Papa Hemingway* (New York: Random House, 1966), 49.

37. Ibid., 148. See Greg Forter, "Melancholy Modernism," in *Hemingway: Eight Decades of Criticism*, ed. Linda Wagner-Martin (East Lansing: Michigan State University Press, 2009), 55–73.

38. See Nancy R. Comley and Robert Scholes, *Hemingway's Genders: Rereading the Hemingway Text* (New Haven, CT: Yale University Press, 1994), 44–46.

39. Thompson, *The Rum Diary*, 183.

40. An obsession with Conrad's *Heart of Darkness* also appears in Thompson's friend Tom Wolfe, both in *The Bonfire of the Vanities* (1987) and *I Am Charlotte Simmons* (2004). See Kevin T. McEneaney, *Tom Wolfe's America: Heroes, Pranksters, and Fools* (Westport: Praeger, 2009), 118–20, 145–46. Wolfe's *The Electric Kool-Aid Acid Test* (1968) also contains a Bogart-like outlaw homage passage, 304. The outlaw theme remains central to both Thompson's *Hell's Angels* and Wolfe's *The Electric Kool-Aid Acid Test.*

41. Thompson, *The Rum Diary*, 103.

42. Introduction to *The Great Gatsby* (New York: Modern Library, 1934), ix; also reprinted in Mathew J. Bruccoli and Jackson R. Bryer, *F. Scott Fitzgerald: In His Own Time* (New York: Popular Library, 1971), 156.

43. Benjamin Barber, *"The Rum Diary*: An Introduction to Hunter S. Thompson's Esthetic Evolution," *Anthropoetics* 16, no. 1, 2010.

44. Jack Kerouac, *Big Sur* (New York: Penguin, 1962), 177.

45. The one-punch kill accidentally happened July 6, 2011, in Las Vegas. See "Police: Man Killed with One Punch at Casino, AZ.com, July 6, 2011, http://www.azcentral.com/news/articles/2011/07/06/20110706las-vegas-casino-beating-death.html (accessed 12 July 2011).

46. Thompson, *The Rum Diary*, 17.

47. Thompson had sold travel articles to the *New York Herald Tribune*, *Milwaukee Journal*, and *Baltimore Sun.* McKeen, *Outlaw Journalist*, 56.

48. William Kennedy, "Foreword," *The Proud Highway*, xvii.

49. Thompson, *The Proud Highway*, 236.

50. Published in *Rogue* magazine, December 1961. Reprinted in *The Proud Highway*, 264–77. This article remains heavily indebted to Miller's *Big Sur and the Oranges of Hieronymus Bosch* (1957) as it updates Miller.

51. Thompson, *The Rum Diary*, 134.

52. See Eleanor Coppola, *Notes on the Making of Apocalypse Now* (New York: Simon & Schuster, 1979).

53. Timothy Ferris, "Foreword," *Kingdom of Fear* (New York: Simon & Schuster, 2003), xvi.

54. Somber Kierkegaard had no inkling of Hebrew humor.

55. The most famous of which is man as a spider held over the flames of hell.

56. The phrase "fear and loathing" in a Thompson publication first appears as a casual description of *The Examiner*'s view of the Hells Angels in Thompson's book, *Hell's Angels* (New York: Modern Library, 1999), 54. When asked by Brinkley in the excellent *Paris Review* interview, Thompson jokes that he's been accused of stealing the phrase from Nietzsche or Kafka. See Anita Thompson, ed., *Ancient Gonzo Wisdom* (New York: Da Capo, 2009), 207. The phrase has casually appeared in various novels, like Mary Shelley's *Lodore* (1835) and Robert Southey's blank verse poem, "For the Cell of Honorius."

57. Thompson, *Hell's Angels*, 21. The quotation is from Kierkegaard's *The Last Years: Journals, 1853–55*.

58. The English translation of Arlt's *Mad Toy* sports a complimentary introduction by James T. Farrell, defining a classic as something that endures. Like *Studs Lonigan*, Arlt's novel deals with youth gangs.

59. Roberto Arlt, *The Seven Madmen* (Boston: David R. Godine, 1929/1984; trans. from 1958 edition), 6. The character Ernesto Erdosain reappears in fellow Argentinean writer Ricardo Piglia's novel, *The Absent City* (1992; trans. 2000); the story "End of the Ride" from Piglia's collection *Assumed Name* (1975), which satirizes the concept of originality, employs the device of the main character attempting to unravel the mystery of an unpublished manuscript by Arlt while indulging in many literary jokes about Arlt's work. See Ellen McCracken, "Metaplagiarism and the Detective's Role as Critic: Ricardo Piglia's Reinvention of Roberto Arlt," *PMLA* 106, no. 5 (Oct. 1991), 1071–82.

60. Naomi Lindstrom, "Introduction," *The Seven Madmen*, viii.

61. A. Thompson, *Ancient Gonzo Wisdom*, 126–27.

62. James Boswell, *The Life of Samuel Johnson* (London: Penguin Classics, 2009), letter of April 5, 1776.

63. Hunter S. Thompson, *Generation of Swine* (New York: Simon & Schuster, 1988), 10.

64. McEneaney, *Tom Wolfe's America*, for Conrad see 118–20 and 145–46; for Luce, 81–84.

65. The element of sociological absurdity amid personal conversation and anecdote was pioneered just after the First World War in Jaroslav Hašek's uncompleted masterpiece, *The Good Soldier Schweik*, yet the satiric pacifist novel remains closer to lampoon cartooning than anything resembling journalism.

66. Wolfe penned a witty and supercilious imitation of Malaparte's style in his introduction to Michael McDonough's *Malaparte: A House Like Me* (1999). Jean-Luc Goddard's early masterpiece, *Le Mépris* (Contempt, 1963) with Brigitte Bardot, was set at Malaparte's house.

67. McKeen, *Hunter S. Thompson*, 90.

68. McKeen, *Outlaw Journalist*, 339.

69. Beef Torrey and Kevin Simonson, eds., *Conversations with Hunter S. Thompson* (Jackson: University of Mississippi Press, 2008), 110.

70. Hunter S. Thompson, "Polo Is My Life," in *Fear and Loathing at Rolling Stone*, 529.

71. Thompson, *Kingdom of Fear*, 226–27.

72. See Kevin T. McEneaney, *Russell Banks: In Search of Freedom* (Santa Barbara: Praeger, 2010). In *Affliction*, Banks indirectly dramatizes Thompson's summation that the fictional lone bullet "found" on John F. Kennedy's stretcher "pierced the heart of the American Dream"; Thompson, *Kingdom of Fear*, 315.

3. ODDBALL JOURNALISM, UNDERCLASS CULTURE

1. Douglas Brinkley, with Terry McDonell and George Plimpton, "Interview," *The Paris Review*, Autumn 2000; reprinted in A. Thompson, *Ancient Gonzo Wisdom*, 270.

2. Craig Vetter, *Playboy*, November 1974. Reprinted in A. Thompson, ibid., 36.

3. Interview with Douglas Brinkley, 14 June 2011.

4. Thompson, *The Proud Highway*, 498.

5. Hunter S. Thompson, *Hell's Angels: A Strange and Terrible Saga* (New York: Modern Library, 1999), 55.

6. Jann Wenner and Corey Seymour, *Gonzo: The Life of Hunter S. Thompson* (New York: Back Bay Books, 2007), 81.

7. Reprinted in Arthur Veno, ed., *The Mammoth Book of Bikers* (Philadelphia: Running Press, 2007), 115–26.

8. Sonny Barger, with Keith and Kent Zimmerman, *Hell's Angel: The Life and Times of Sonny Barger* (New York: Morrow, 2000), 125.

9. Ibid., 127.

10. Thompson, *Hell's Angels*, 45.

11. Wenner and Seymour, 83.

12. Ibid., 104.

13. Carey McWilliams, *The Education of Carey McWilliams* (New York: Simon &Schuster, 1978), 236.

14. McKeen, *Outlaw Journalist*, 101.

15. Thompson, *The Proud Highway*, 516.

16. Reprinted in Thompson, *The Great Shark Hunt*, 343–45.

17. Thompson, *The Proud Highway*, 527.

18. Thompson, *Songs of the Doomed*, 115.

19. Barger, 53.

20. Thompson, *Fear and Loathing in America*, 23–24.

21. McKeen, *Outlaw Journalist*, 109.

22. See Douglas Brinkley, "Introduction," in Jack Kerouac, *Windblown World: The Journals of Jack Kerouac 1947–1954*, ed. Douglas Brinkley (New York: Penguin, 2004), xxiii–xxvi.

23. Douglas Brinkley, "Introduction," in Thompson, *Hell's Angels*, xi.

24. Thompson to Angus Cameron, *The Proud Highway*, 529.

25. Thompson, *Hell's Angels*, 40–41.

26. The best of American humor has always been sophomoric, from Mark Twain and Ambrose Bierce up to Hunter S. Thompson and P. J. O'Rourke, Jon Stewart, and Stephen Colbert.

27. Thompson, *Hell's Angels*, 64.

28. Ibid., 68.

29. Ibid., 111–12.

30. McKeen, *Hunter S. Thompson*, 28.

31. Thompson, *Hell's Angels*, 64.

32. Ibid., 70.

33. Ibid., 39.

34. Algren, in Thompson, *The Proud Highway*, 559.

35. Thompson to Algren, ibid., 558.

36. Thompson, *Hell's Angels*, 147.

37. Thompson, *The Proud Highway*, 567.

38. Russell Banks offers homage to Algren in an over-going on the Linkhorn theme with a geological twist at the beginning of *Continental Drift* (1985).

39. Barger, 171.

40. Thompson, *Hell's Angels*, 526.

41. Barger, , 103.

42. Thompson, *Hell's Angels*, 160–61.

43. Ibid., 152–54.

44. Ibid., 193.

45. Tom Wolfe imitates Thompson's bacchanalia in *Back to Blood* (2012). Instead of a remote state park, Wolfe paints a lurid party of privileged yahoos at a remote atoll off Palm Beach during a Columbus Day Regatta. See Kevin McEneaney, "Review: The Diamond Cesspool," *Millbrook Independent*, 21 November 2012.

46. Thompson, *Hell's Angels*, 194.

47. Ibid., 197.

48. Ibid., 216.

49. Deborah Dupre, "Rights Abuse: Riot Police Attack Students with Military Weapons," *Examiner*, 2 May 2011, http://www.examiner.com/article/rights-abuse-riot-police-attack-students-with-military-weapons-video (accessed 21 May 2011).

50. Whitmer, *When the Going Gets Weird*, 156.

51. Hunter S. Thompson, "The Distant Drummer," 1967, reprinted in *The Great Shark Hunt* (New York: Simon & Schuster, 1979), 99.

52. Thompson, *Hells Angels*, 253–54.

53. Thompson, *Songs of the Doomed*.

54. Tom Wolfe, *The Right Stuff* (New York: Bantam, 1983), 355–61.

55. See Gary L. Kleffner, "Myth, Reality, and Revenge in Hunter S. Thompson's *Hell's Angels*," *International Journal of Motorcycle Studies* 1, no. 2 (July 2005), n.p.

56. Wenner and Seymour, 146–47.

57. Sonny Barger later disparaged Thompson's involvement with the Angels as "all hat and no cattle," just another barroom yakker. McKeen, *Hunter S. Thompson*, 108.

58. Thompson, *The Proud Highway*, 567.

59. For a thorough explication of this event, see McEneaney, *Tom Wolfe's America*, 25–53.

60. Tom Wolfe, *I Am Charlotte Simmons* (New York: Picador, 2005), 94.

61. Thompson, *Fear and Loathing in America*, 54. The Hemingway "iceberg" reference derives from the first chapter of *Death in the Afternoon* (1932), wherein Hemingway discourses on the hidden textures and subtleties in music, wine, and bullfighting.

62. Thompson, *Songs of the Doomed*, 115.

63. The *Playboy* piece became the first and last chapter of the book. Thompson, *Fear and Loathing in America*, 367.

64. McKeen, *Outlaw Journalist*, 116.

65. Whitmer, *When the Going Gets Weird*, 270.

66. Stewart Tendler and David May, *The Brotherhood of Eternal Love* (London: Cyan Books, 2007), 88; see also George Wethern and Vincent Colnett, *A Wayward Angel* (Guilford: Lyons Press, 1978/2004), 85–89.

67. *Royal Canadian Mounted Police Gazette*, "The Hell's Angels vs. The Rock Machine," 1999, reprinted in Veno, *The Mammoth Book of Bikers*, 482–90. The Las Vegas shootout between the Hells Angels and the Mongols inside Harrah's Hotel in April 2002, left three dead bikers and sixteen (including bikers) others wounded. See Yves Lavigne, *Hells Angels: Into the Abyss* (New York: HarperCollins, 1996/2004), vi.

68. Lavigne, 1.

69. Douglas Brinkley, "Editor's Note," in Thompson, *The Proud Highway*, xxiv.

4. WHO'S DEPRAVED?

1. McKeen, *Outlaw Journalist*, 112.

2. Ibid., 114.

3. Hunter S. Thompson, "Those Daring Young Men in Their Flying Machines . . . Ain't What They Used to Be!" Reprinted in Thompson, *The Great Shark Hunt*, 406–13. Tom Wolfe would later select a hero pilot in John Dowd for his October 1975 *Esquire* essay, "The Truest Sport: Jousting with Sam and Charlie", while supporting the Vietnam War. Later, Wolfe would portray the test pilot Chuck Yeager and the early astronauts as national heroes in his 1979 epic, *The Right Stuff*.

4. Personal conversation, June 14, 2011.

5. McKeen, *Outlaw Journalist*, 128.

6. Hunter S. Thompson, "Memoirs of a Wretched Weekend in Washington," *Boston Globe*, 23 February 1969. Reprinted in Thompson, *The Great Shark Hunt*, 177–82.

7. Ibid., 77–95.

8. The magazine "was named after a little-known Nottingham pig farmer named Scanlan." Steadman, *The Joke's Over*, 6. The title of Steadman's memoir derives from *The Curse of Lono*, 107, where the following line is "It's time for the bomb," by which Steadman means Thompson's funeral.

9. Thompson, *The Great Shark Hunt*, 95.

10. McKeen, *Hunter S. Thompson*, 38.

11. Thompson, *The Great Shark Hunt*, 88.

12. Draper, 162.

13. Steadman, in Wenner and Seymour, 120. Peter Richardson, *A Bomb in Every Issue: How the Short Unruly Life of* Ramparts *Magazine Changed America* (New York: New Press, 2009), 155.

14. Steadman, in a letter to McKeen, *Hunter S. Thompson*, 145.

15. Steadman, *The Joke's Over*, 364–65.

16. William Kennedy, in Wenner and Seymour, 124.

17. Sandy Thompson, in Wenner and Seymour, 123–25.

18. Letter to Bill Cardozo, in Thompson, *Fear and Loathing in America*, 295.

19. Hunter S. Thompson, "Kelso Looks Like Any $1,307,000 Horse . . . A Day with a Champion," *National Observer*, 13 July 1963, 1, 7.

20. Steadman, *The Joke's Over*, 21.

21. Douglas Brinkley, in Wenner and Seymour, 125–26.

22. McKeen, *Hunter S. Thompson*, 149.

23. Stendhal, *The Charterhouse of Parma*, trans. Richard Howard (New York: Modern Library, 1995), 480. If Thompson read the book, he would probably have read the translation by Lady Mary Lloyd or George Scott-Moncrieff.

24. Booker played with Fats Domino, B. B. King, Wilson Pickett, and Little Richard and discovered and tutored Harry Connick, Jr. Booker, who taught Dr. John the organ as well as how to goose up his piano playing, sometimes played with Dr. John, who acclaimed Booker a musical genius. See Dr. John (Mac Rebennack), *Under a Hoodoo Moon: The Life of the Night Tripper* (New York: St. Martin's, 1994), especially 50–56, 206–10.

25. This interview was rediscovered, digitalized, and rebroadcast on February 22, 2016, at http://chicagoist.com/2016/02/22/exclusive_studs_terkel_interviews_h.ph.

26. Thompson, *The Proud Highway*, 396.

27. National Research Council, *The Great Alaska Earthquake of 1964*, vol. 1, part 2 (Washington: National Academies Press, 1970), 266–67.

28. Fortier's pamphlet *One Survived* (1978) now circulates on the rare book market for a phenomenal amount of money, currently selling for five or six digits.

29. Thomas Fensch, *The Man Who Was Walter Mitty: The Life and Work of James Thurber* (Woodlands: New Century Books, 2000), 233–40.

30. Frank Sullivan in *Books*, quoted by Fensch, ibid., 226.

31. About 4,000 words were cut. Correspondence from Thompson to Hinckle, in *Fear and Loathing in America*, 296.

32. Steadman, *The Joke's Over*, 20.

33. Ibid., 8.

34. Hunter S. Thompson, *Fear and Loathing in Las Vegas and Other American Stories* (New York: Modern Library, 1996), 272.

35. Ibid., 276.

36. Ibid., 277.

37. Ibid., 282.

38. Ibid., 278.

39. Thompson, *The Proud Highway*, 481.

40. Steadman, *The Joke's Over*, 25.

41. 20 August 2011.

42. Thompson, *Fear and Loathing in Las Vegas and Other American Stories*, 271.

43. James Thurber, "The Tiger Who Understood People," in *Thurber: Writings and Drawings* (New York: Library of America, 1996), 452.

44. J. P. Donleavy, *The Ginger Man* (New York: Dell, 1969), 53.

45. Ibid., 313.

46. For a marvelous selection of illustrations with a penetrating view of Jackson Pollack, see Donald Wigal, *Pollock: Veiling the Image* (New York: Parkstone Press, 2006).

47. Hunter S. Thompson, "When the Beatniks Were Social Lions," reprinted in *The Great Shark Hunt*, 394–98.

48. Steadman, in Wenner and Seymour, 122.

49. Craig Vetter, "Interview: Hunter Thompson," *Playboy*, November 1974. Reprinted in A. Thompson, *Ancient Gonzo Wisdom*, 47.

50. McKeen, *Hunter S. Thompson*, 167.

51. Vetter, in A. Thompson, *Ancient Gonzo Wisdom*, 47.

52. Greg Wright, "The Literary, Political, and Legal Strategies of Oscar Zeta Acosta and Hunter S. Thompson: Intertexuality, Ambiguity, and (naturally) Fear and Loathing," *Journal of Popular Culture* 43, no. 3 (June 2010), 622–43.

53. "But of my own knowledge, I know that down to the year 1850, sharks and shad, alewives and herring, against Linnaeus's express edict were still found dividing the possession of the same seas with the Leviathan." Herman Melville, *Melville: Redburn, White Jacket, Moby-Dick* (New York: Library of America, 1983), 935.

54. Meriwether Clark was the originator of many racing rules, including a uniform system of weights in handicapping as well as pioneering the stakes system. He also worked to develop a horse-racing industry in Kentucky.

55. See "Call to the Derby," Wayback Machine Internet Archive, n.d., http://wayback.archive.org/web/20081223235529/http://www.derbypost.com/churchill1.html (accessed 1 December 2015).

56. McKeen, *Hunter S. Thompson*, 159.

57. Steadman, *The Joke's Over*, 67–68.

58. Thompson, *The Proud Highway*, 456–57.

59. McKeen, *Hunter S. Thompson*, 175–76.

60. Oscar Zeta Acosta, *Oscar "Zeta" Acosta: The Uncollected Works* (Houston: Arte Público Press, 2006), 173. In a 1972 letter to Thompson, Acosta boasts that he wrote the autobiography in less than five weeks (yet a couple of variant version excerpts had been previously published) but that he spent over ten weeks on *Revolt* and it was nowhere near done (ibid., 105).

61. Hunter S. Thompson, *Fear and Loathing in America*, 272–73.

62. Ibid., 272. Reprinted in Acosta, *Oscar "Zeta" Acosta*, 125–45.

63. For the circumstances of the photo, see Thompson, *Fear and Loathing in America*, 407.

64. Interview with Curtis Robinson, June 18, 2011.

65. Thompson, *Fear and Loathing in America*, 476–77, 526, 542–43, 554, 561–62.

66. Carroll, *Hunter*, 190.

67. McKeen, *Hunter S. Thompson*, 230.

68. See "The Banshee Screams for Buffalo Meat," reprinted in *The Great Shark Hunt*, 495–516.

69. Oscar Zeta Acosta, *The Autobiography of a Brown Buffalo* (San Francisco/New York: Straight Arrow/Vintage, 1972/1995), 7.

5. LOATHING AT THE TEMPLE

1. Draper, *Rolling Stone Magazine*, 177.

2. P. Perry, *Fear and Loathing*, 160–61.

3. Draper, 177.

4. McKeen, *Outlaw Journalist*, 365; P. Perry, 160–61.

5. Thompson, *The Great Shark Hunt*, 106. Also reprinted in *Fear and Loathing in Las Vegas and Other American Stories*.

6. Mat Johnson, "The Literary, Political, and Legal Strategies of Oscar Zeta Acosta and Hunter S. Thompson: Intertexuality, Ambiguity, and (Naturally) Fear and Loathing," *Journal of Popular Culture*, June 2010.

7. Jeffrey Meyers, *Scott Fitzgerald: A Biography* (New York: HarperCollins, 1994), 142.

8. Thompson, *Hell's Angels*, 54. In a 1967 letter to Tom Wolfe, Thompson describes his loathing for his typewriter. See *The Proud Highway*, 653.

9. Wenner and Seymour, 128–29. In an interview with Brinkley, Thompson joked that he's been "accused of stealing it [the phrase "fear and loathing"]

from Nietzsche or Kafka or something." A. Thompson, *Ancient Gonzo Wisdom*, 207.

10. Thompson to William Kennedy, *The Proud Highway*, 420.

11. P. Perry, 32.

12. Thompson, *The Proud Highway*, 242.

13. F. Scott Fitzgerald, *The Great Gatsby* (New York: Scribner, 1925), 128.

14. Thompson, *Fear and Loathing in America*, 377.

15. Thompson to William Kennedy, *The Proud Highway*, 568–70.

16. Thompson, *Fear and Loathing in America*, 267.

17. "William McKeen," Hunter S. Thompson: A Learning Curve, http://hstforbeginners.com/william-mckeen (accessed 8 December 2015).

18. Hampton Sides, *Hellhound on His Trail: The Stalking of Martin Luther King Jr. and the International Hunt for His Assassin* (New York: Doubleday, 2010), 390–91.

19. Thompson, *Fear and Loathing in America*, 286.

20. Ibid., 423.

21. See "Adrenochrome," The Vaults of Erowid, http://www.erowid.org/chemicals/adrenochrome/adrenochrome.shtml (accessed 8 December 2015).

22. Thompson, *The Proud Highway*, 591.

23. Aldous Huxley, "A Journey Through Los Angeles" in Dennis Hale and Jonathan Eisen, eds., *The California Dream* (New York: Collier's, 1968), 234–50. The essay is reprinted from *After Many a Summer Dies the Swan*.

24. Thompson, *Fear and Loathing in America*, 205.

25. McKeen, *Outlaw Journalist*, 168.

26. Weingarten, 122–23.

27. Thompson, *The Proud Highway*, 406.

28. Ibid., 421.

29. For this and my subsequent translation, I am indebted to annotations in Joseph Russo, Manuel Fernandez-Galiano, and Alfed Heibeck, *A Commentary on Homer's* Odyssey: *Volume II, Books XVII–XXIV* (Oxford: Oxford University Press, 1992).

30. Jay Martin, *Nathaniel West: The Art of His Life* (New York: Carroll & Graf, 1970), 202.

31. Thompson, *The Proud Highway*, 458.

32. Reprinted in Thompson, *The Great Shark Hunt*, 378.

33. See Delia Falconer, "From Alger to Edge-Work: Mapping the Shark Ethic in Hunter S. Thompson's *Fear and Loathing in Las Vegas*," *Antithesis* 6, no. 2 (1993), 111–25.

34. "The Doc Down Under," The Great Thompson Hunt: Articles and Essays, http://www.gonzo.org/articles/litdfb4.html?ID=1 (accessed 8 December 2015).

35. Paul Beagle, ed., *Partridge's Concise Dictionary of Slang and Unconventional English* (New York: Macmillan, 1989), 363.

36. Hemingway, *The Sun Also Rises*, 116.

37. A sympathetic account of Mailer's involvement with Buckley appears by H. L. "Doc" Humes in Peter Manso's *Mailer: His Life and Times* (New York: Washington Square Press, 2008), 307–9.

38. Kennedy, in Thompson, *The Proud Highway*, xxiii.

39. H. Sounes, *Down the Highway: A Life of Bob Dylan* (New York: Doubleday, 2001), 181.

40. Gothic literature, often said to be invented by the liberal aristocrat Horace Walpole in *The Castle of Otranto* (1764), had its origins in excited ignorance and self-righteous prejudice, specifically rabid anti-Catholicism and the embarrassingly obscene practice of the Confessional. Puritans thought literature, not being the word of God, was the work of the devil—that by its nature a work of man's words illustrated the devil's idle imagination. After all, French literature focused on sociology, style, and sex, things that shouldn't cross the channel. The English re-invented literature in their own image: the Gothic, the detective story, and science fiction. Gothic was the first breakthrough: barbarian plot stories were fine if they were morally righteous in exposing works of the devil—most problems in society were caused by passionate lust run amok or by Roman Catholics, an illegal religion run by the Antichrist from Rome that was designed to thwart England's ambition to rule the world. The secret loves of priests and nuns became popular sensational topics. Anne Radcliffe's *The Castles of Athlin and Dunbayne* (1789) outlined the ruinous dangers of passion, while Matthew "Monk" Lewis's *The Monk* (1796) illustrated the demented deviations of Catholicism and still provides excellent tingles along the spinal cord.

Subversive Huguenot genes in Ireland eventually produced the 1872 short story by Le Fanu, "Carmilla," about an undead blood drinker, which influenced the Dublin-born Bram Stoker in *Dracula* (1897), a gut-curdling political allegory about absentee London landlords who sucked the lifeblood from their tenants. Despite Stoker's plodding drab prose, his invention of marrying an obscure species of vicious Mexican cave bats to eternally bored humans became immortal, and vampires now live and drink among us. In a similar fashion, Thompson was inspired by his own Kentucky Derby story and invented a kind of gonzo Gothic, an entertaining allegory about the monstrous Orwellian police state. Thompson's prose sails with more panache than Stoker's impish imagination, just as Thompson's obsessive stories about wayward guns remain more explosively enlightened than the blood-spattered victims of osculable vampires, as depicted in erotic fundamentalist interpretations of Stoker spin-offs paraded in movies and daily television with deodorant commercials after midnight.

41. Fitzgerald had read Spengler at the advice of his editor Maxwell Perkins; there are several references to Spengler in *The Beautiful and the Damned*.

42. Thompson, *The Proud Highway*, 128–30.

43. The manuscript was completed in 1941 as Bakhtin's doctoral dissertation, but Bakhtin was denied the doctorate due to its nonconventional, controversial content. The book, now regarded as a world classic, was finally published in his native Russian tongue in 2002.

44. Miller admits that the two writers he worships the most are Rabelais and Dostoevsky. Henry Miller, *The Books in My Life* (New York: New Directions, 1969), 138.

45. John Cooper Powys, *Rabelais* (New York: Philosophical Library, 1951), 306.

46. McKeen, *Outlaw Journalist*, 41.

47. Thompson, *Fear and Loathing in America*, 266–68.

48. Ibid., 343.

49. Thompson, "The Paris Review," Autumn 2000, with Douglas Brinkley. Reprinted in A. Thompson, *Ancient Gonzo Wisdom*, 274.

50. Hemingway, 9.

51. Thompson, *Fear and Loathing in Las Vegas and Other Stories*, 18.

52. Elizabeth Thompson and David Gutman, eds., *The Lennon Companion* (Cambridge, MA: Da Capo, 2004), 165.

53. John Lennon, *Skywriting by Word of Mouth* (New York: HarperCollins, 1986), 25.

54. Ibid., 103. The book also features a parody tribute to James Joyce's *Finnegans Wake*, 109–17.

55. Thompson, *Fear and Loathing in Las Vegas and Other Stories*, 22.

56. Robert Greenfield, *Timothy Leary: A Biography* (New York: Harcourt, 2006), 462–510.

57. Robert Shelton, *No Direction Home: The Life and Music of Bob Dylan* (New York: Morrow, 1968), 418–21.

58. Don Lattin, *The Harvard Psychedelic Club* (New York: HarperCollins, 2010), 116.

59. Ibid., 117–18.

60. McKeen, *Outlaw Journalist*, 164.

61. McKeen, *Hunter S. Thompson*, 53.

62. Thompson, *Fear and Loathing in Las Vegas and Other Stories*, 45. Ether was first approved in America as safe medical treatment by Boston

General Hospital in October 1846. There is a large monument commemorating this in Boston Commons.

63. Whitmer, *When the Going Gets Weird*, 181. For further analysis, see Robert Sickels, "A Countercultural Gatsby: Hunter S. Thompson's *Fear and Loathing in Las Vegas*, the Death of the American Dream and the Rise of Las Vegas, USA," *Popular Culture Review* 11, no. 1 (February 2000), 61–73.

64. Thompson, *Kingdom of Fear*, 332–34.

65. Thompson, *Fear and Loathing in Las Vegas and Other Stories*, 46.

66. Oswald Spengler, *The Decline of the West*, vol. II (New York: Knopf, 1926), 94–95.

67. Thompson, *Fear and Loathing in Las Vegas and Other Stories*, 48.

68. Charles A. Monagan created a musical, *Mad Bomber* (2011), based on Metesky's unusual life.

69. Harold Y. Vanderpool, "The American Success Syndrome," *The Christian Century*, 24 September 1975, 820.

70. Thompson, *Fear and Loathing in Las Vegas and Other Stories*, 50–51.

71. Friederich Nietzsche, trans. Walter Kaufmann, *The Portable Nietzsche* (New York: Penguin, 1954/1982), 565–655. H. L. Mencken, Thompson's literary idol, published in 1920 the first English translation of Nietzsche's 1895 essay *The Antichrist*.

72. The genre then entered the Gothic in works by Charles Maturin, Sheridan Le Fanu, and Charles Lever before becoming sociological in the work of George Moore, Somerville and Ross, and Elizabeth Bowen, where family isolation in the face of social change creates symbolic class tragedy. In the twentieth century, the convention has been employed by Sean O'Casey, Brendan Behan, and Brian Friel in plays; Molly Keane, Mervyn Wall, Aidan Higgins, William Trevor, John McGahern, and John Banville in the novel; and many others, like Sean O'Faolain in the short story. See Vera Kreilkamp, *The Anglo-Irish Novel and the Big House* (Syracuse, NY: Syracuse University Press, 1998), and Jacqueline Genet, *The Big House in Ireland* (Dingle: Brandon Books, 1991).

73. Thompson, "The Paris Review," 272.

74. Jim Tully, *Circus Parade* (New York: Albert & Charles Boni, 1927), 279. See also Paul J. Bruer and Mark Dawidziak, *Jim Tully: American Writer, Irish Rover, Hollywood Brawler* (Kent, OH: Kent State University Press, 2011).

75. Gilmore, *Stories Done*, 98–99.

76. Weingarten, 247.

77. Quoted by Margaret Schwartz, "Translator's Introduction" to Macedonio Fernández, *The Museum of Eterna's Novel (The First Good Novel)* (Rochester: Open Letter, 2010), xiv.

78. Adam Thirlwell, "Preface" to Fernández, v.

79. The unpredictable critic Lester Bangs once talked Slick into baring her breast for the December 1977 cover of *Creem* magazine.

80. "Session Notes: The Splish Splash Sessions," BobbyDarin.net, http://www.bobbydarin.net/sn_041058.html (accessed 25 June 2011). Darin's biography was stylishly captured in the film *Beyond the Sea* (2004).

81. Fitzgerald, 109.

82. Acosta, *The Autobiography of a Brown Buffalo*, 136.

83. Reprinted in Acosta, *Oscar "Zeta" Acosta*, 173.

84. Whitmer, *When the Going Gets Weird*, 183.

85. Thompson, *Fear and Loathing in America*, 382–83.

86. Ibid., 388–91.

87. Brooklyn-born Laura Nyro was inspired by "Louie Louie" to write her quite original hybrid song "Lu" for her 1968 album, *Eli and the Thirteenth Confession*. The last stanza of the song keeps the imagery of a boat captain returning home. Her debut performance was in San Francisco at the age of eighteen in 1966, the year she sold the hit "And When I Die" to Peter, Paul, and Mary, yet it was the cover by Blood, Sweat, and Tears that climbed the charts.

88. See Bob Greene, "The Man Who Wrote 'Louie Louie,'" *Esquire*, September 1988, 63–67.

89. Thompson to Acosta, in *Fear and Loathing in America*, 189.

90. Spengler, *The Decline of the West,* vol. I, 106.

91. Miller, *Big Sur and the Oranges of Hieronymus Bosch*, 94–95.

92. Curt Worden's 2008 documentary on the novel, *One Fast Move or I'm Gone*, is decent.

93. Kerouac, *Big Sur*, 158.

94. Kerouac wrote to Allen Ginsberg: "Did you see *Big Sur* novel which I had sent to you? And what do you think of the ridiculous denouement in THAT? All too true." In *Jack Kerouac and Allen Ginsberg: The Letters*, ed. Bill Morgan and David Stanford (New York: Viking, 2010), 472.

95. Kerouac's writing was rejected by brilliant academics like Wylie Sypher in *Loss of the Self: In Modern Literature and Art* (1979), while the imperious Jacques Barzun in his massive Spenglerian tome on Western art and literature, *From Dawn to Decadence* (2000), expressed great admiration for the artistic populism of Peter Finley Dunne's comic argot dialogues, but disdained to mention either Spengler or Thompson.

96. Thompson, *The Proud Highway*, 358.

97. Bill Morgan, *The Typewriter Is Holy* (New York: Free Press, 2010), 179.

98. McKeen, *Outlaw Journalist*, 84.

99. Thompson to Silberman, *Fear and Loathing in America*, 397.

100. Stephenson, *Gonzo Republic*, 57–58.

101. Reprinted in Thompson, *The Great Shark Hunt*, 387.

102. Simon Key, "Fear and Loathing: On the Trail of Hunter S. Thompson and Ralph Steadman," *T.O. Magazine*, November 1987, reprinted in A. Thompson, *Ancient Gonzo Wisdom*, 146.

103. Thompson, *Fear and Loathing in Las Vegas and Other Stories*, 68. Keith Richards says flower power died at the December 6, 1969, Altamont concert, and his account refutes the preposterous boasting lies contained in Barger's memoir. Richards, *Life* (New York: Little, Brown and Company, 2010), 279–82.

104. Arnold Mann, "Achievers: Preacher's Kid," *Time*, November 11, 2002, http://www.time.com/time/magazine/article/0,9171,1003636-1,00.html (accessed 28 June 2011) .

105. Vetter, reprinted in A. Thompson, *Ancient Gonzo Wisdom*, 33.

106. Thompson, *Hell's Angels*, 227.

107. Thompson, *Songs of the Doomed*, 121.

108. Ibid., 67.

109. Fitzgerald, at the bequest of the International Mark Twain Society, 30 November 1935. Reprinted in Bruccoli and Bryer, *F. Scott Fitzgerald*, 176.

110. Letter to Semonin, in *The Proud Highway*, 470–71.

111. Interview by P. J. O'Rourke, *Rolling Stone*, 28 November 1996; reprinted in A. Thompson, *Ancient Gonzo Wisdom*, 201.

112. Vincent Bughosi, with Curt Gentry, *Helter Skelter—The True Story of the Manson Murders, 25th Anniversary Edition* (New York: Norton & Company, 2001), 241.

113. Hunter S. Thompson, "Donleavy Proves His Lunatic Humor Is Original," *National Observer*, 11 November 1963.

114. Whitmer, *When the Going Gets Weird*, 183.

115. Thompson, *Fear and Loathing in Las Vegas and Other Stories*, 73.

116. Richards, *Life*, 252.

117. Thompson, *Fear and Loathing in America*, 266.

118. Thompson, *Fear and Loathing in Las Vegas and Other Stories*, 89. The phrase is now a 2006 song by Doctor Thrasher.

119. The album liner notes from Dylan's *Live 1966* record that drummer Tony Glover brought his Siren Whistle to the recording session. See Mark Polizzotti's *Highway 61 Revisited (33 1/3)* (New York: Continuum, 2006), and Colin Irwin's biography, *Bob Dylan: Highway 61 Revisited* (New York: Billboard Books, 2008).

120. P. Perry, 100–102. Subsequently, Thompson was extremely disappointed with "worthless" Ballantine: "They blew the Hell's Angels pb.[paperback] distribution badly." Thompson, *The Proud Highway*, 432.

121. Thompson, *Fear and Loathing in America*, 375.

122. Ibid., 376.

123. McKeen, *Outlaw Journalist*, 61.

124. Thompson, *Fear and Loathing in Las Vegas and Other Stories*, 99.

125. Thompson, *Fear and Loathing in America*, 377.

126. P. Perry, 164.

127. Whitmer, *When the Going Gets Weird*, 183–84.

128. P. Perry, 167–68.

129. Quoted by Thomas Flanagan, *There You Are* (New York: New York Review of Books, 2004), 73.

6. FEAR IN THE NATION

1. McKeen, *Hunter S. Thompson*, 54.

2. Thompson, *Songs of the Doomed*, 178.

3. P. Perry, *Fear and Loathing*, 167. In Thompson's May 1975 "Checking Into the Lane Xang," Lucy's is the name of the most disreputable whorehouse in Saigon.

4. P. J. O'Rourke, interview with Thompson in *Rolling Stone*, November 1966. Reprinted in A. Thompson, *Ancient Gonzo Wisdom*, 212. But this, too, might be a put-on, and Thompson may have known about the Sally Horner episode that inspired *Lolita*. See Alexander Dolinin, "What Happened to Sally Horner?: A Real-Life Source of Nabokov's Lolita," http://www.libraries.psu.edu/nabokov/dolilol.htm (accessed 11 December 2015).

5. For the little-known inside story, by a former *Paris Olympia* editor, on the literary pedigree of *Lolita* see Gerald Williams, "Lolita, Who's Your Daddy?," *Massachusetts Review* 47 (Winter 2006), 757ff.

6. Vladimir Nabokov, *The Annotated* Lolita, ed. Alfred Appel, Jr. (New York: Vintage, 1991), 150.

7. Nabokov, "On a Book Entitled *Lolita*," ibid., 314.

8. Simon Shuster, "The Curse of the Crocodile: Russia's Deadly Designer Drug," *Time*, 20 June 2011.

9. For commentary on Wolfe's exaggerated novelization of this event, see Larry McMurtry, "Bus Story #3: Stark Naked Gets Off the Bus," in David Stanford, ed., *Spit in the Ocean #7* (New York: Viking, 2003), 104–6.

10. Reprinted in *Demon Box* (New York: Viking, 1986). Kesey's technique here owes something to Tom Wolfe's portrait of Freewheelin' Frank at the beginning of *The Electric Kool-Aid Acid Test*. In *The Sweet Hereafter* (1991) Russell Banks offers a similar commentary with his characters, the Bong brothers.

11. Thompson, *Fear and Loathing in Las Vegas and Other American Stories*, 47.

12. Maxwell Perkins had highly recommended Spengler to Fitzgerald. For a brief discussion of doom in Fitzgerald, see Harry Salpeter, "Fitzgerald, Spenglerian," *New York World*, 2 April 1927. Reprinted in *Conversations with F. Scott Fitzgerald*, ed. Matthew J. Bruccoli and Judith S. Baughman (Oxford: University Press of Mississippi, 2003), 86–87.

13. Thompson, *Fear and Loathing in Las Vegas and Other American Stories*, 47.

14. Alan Bisbort, "The Curious Case of Caryl Chessman," Gadflyonline, 9 July 2001, http://gadflyonline.com/home/10/29/01/ftr-caryl-chessman.html (accessed 11 December 2015).

15. Thompson, *Fear and Loathing in Las Vegas and Other American Stories*, 117.

16. Denise Noe, "Fatty Arbuckle and the Death of Virginia Rappe," trutv.com. http://www.trutv.com/library/crime/notorious_murders/classics/fatty_arbuckle/2.html (accessed 13 July 2013).

17. Thompson, *Fear and Loathing in Las Vegas and Other American Stories*, 117.

18. Stephenson, 60, roots his discussion of this passage in Huxley's discussion of Kafka's negative vision found in *The Doors of Perception* (1959).

19. Thompson, *Fear and Loathing in Las Vegas and Other American Stories*, 23–24.

20. Thompson, *The Proud Highway*, 400.

21. Joan Didion, *Slouching Towards Bethlehem* (New York: Farrar, Straus and Giroux, 1968), 123.

22. Oscar Zeta Acosta describes a bad trip quite well: "There isn't much sense in trying to explain what a 'bad trip' is. You simply lose your marbles. You go crazy. There is no bottom, no top. The devil sits on your head and warns you of your commitment. You see for the first time what the bottomless pit is all about. And you hang on for dear life." *The Autobiography of a Brown Buffalo*, 183.

23. Didion, *Slouching Towards Bethlehem*, xvi.

24. Arthur M. Schlesinger, *Journals 1952–2000* (New York: Penguin, 2007), 745.

25. Ibid., 824.

26. Acosta, *The Autobiography of a Brown Buffalo*, 12, 126.

27. Chronology of Acosta's life in *Oscar "Zeta" Acosta*, xxi.

28. Joan Didion, "I'm Going to Be a Movie Star," *Saturday Evening Post*, 14 December 1968. This essay became part of "Notes Toward a Dreampolitik" in

The White Album (1979). That same essay includes a discussion of outlaw biker films and Didion, quite justifiably, delivers a feminist dis.

29. Weingarten, 123.

30. Thompson, *Fear and Loathing in America*, 437.

31. Stephen Cooper, "John Fante's Great Gift to Los Angeles," *Los Angeles Times*, 8 April 2009. Fante's selected stories, *The Wine of Youth*, is dedicated to Carey McWilliams.

32. In the late 1970s Charles Bukowski, who was greatly influenced by Fante, convinced Black Sparrow Press to republish Fante's work in 1980, with great success.

33. Thompson, *The Proud Highway*, xviii–xix.

34. David Greenberg, *Calvin Coolidge* (New York: Macmillan, 2007), 2.

35. When Nixon defeated Helen Gahagen Douglas—a Barnard College graduate, feminist, minor Hollywood actress, and third woman ever in the House of Representatives—in the 1950 California Senate election through an ugly smear campaign—calling her a pinko fellow traveler and printing attacks on pink paper flyers—I vividly recall my mother's mother, Gertrude Becker Monahan, the first ward boss in the Democratic party (Queens, New York), lamenting that the election of Nixon and the unethical, sleazy tactics employed by Nixon (she called them criminal) signaled the death of democracy in America when a politician so corrupt could enter the U.S. Senate, an analysis Thompson would have appreciated. I had just turned three years old at the time—it's about the only incident I can remember from that age, perhaps because her rants of doom on the subject were repetitive. Douglas gave Nixon the lasting moniker ,"Tricky Dick," but she was gone from politics; not even her affair with Lyndon Baines Johnson could save her.

36. P. Perry, 164.

37. Draper, 177.

38. Thompson, *Fear and Loathing in Las Vegas and Other American Stories*, 127.

39. Charles Perry, *The Haight Ashbury* (New York: Random House, 1984), 165.

40. Thompson, *Fear and Loathing in Las Vegas and Other American Stories*, 138.

41. Ibid., 138.

42. Ibid., 143.

43. William Burroughs, *The Ticket That Exploded* (New York: Grove Press, 1962), 216. Thompson paid tribute to Burroughs, valorizing him as the second man to be busted for marijuana (after the actor Robert Mitchum), declaring "He was my hero long time before I ever heard of him" (*The Kingdom Fear*, 341).

44. Thompson, *Fear and Loathing in Las Vegas and Other American Stories*, 158.

45. Robert Bly's "Driving to Town Late to Mail a Letter" (1962) satire on Robert Frost's "Stopping by a Snowy Woods" presents privileged Americans burning gasoline because they are bored with nothing to do but risk death on icy roads, while Frost pokes fun at the obsessive work ethic of Puritans who don't have time to dwell upon the beauties of landscape they traverse.

46. A. Thompson, *Ancient Gonzo Wisdom*, 239.

47. Two of these pieces about Peru are reprinted in Thompson, *The Great Shark Hunt*, 352–61.

48. The poem first appeared in *Spider Magazine* 1, No. 7, 13 October 1965. The poem presents a mediocre imitation of Charles Bukowski's work. Reprinted in *The Great Shark Hunt*, but with a typo: "and dawn," the second line, should read "*at* dawn." In *Hunter,* E. Jean Carroll's *Hunter*, states: "Danielle Steel will write like Emily Dickinson before Hunter turns out a good line of verse," 235.

49. Thompson, *Fear and Loathing in Las Vegas and Other American Stories*, 178.

50. Barger, *Hell's Angel*, 119.

51. Ibid., 121.

52. "I disagree savagely with at least 92% of Pat's political views—but I like the bastard and I intend to keep on drinking with him, from time to time, and anybody who doesn't like it can suck wind." Thompson to Garry Wills, *Fear and Loathing in America*, 550.

53. Invoking Spenglerian doom and growing aphoristic, Buchanan declared that "the rise of feminism spells the death of the nation and the end of the West." Patrick Buchanan, *The Death of the West* (New York: Thomas Dunne Books, 2001), 42.

54. A local Italian neighborhood singer-producer, Bobby Darin, attempted to take Laura Nyro under his wing when she was nearly sixteen by advising her to write a pop song like "What Kind of Fool Am I?" Laura returned to see Darin for a second and last time to play him a song she composed: "What Kind of Fool Are You?" See Michelle Kort, *The Music and Passion of Laura Nyro* (New York: St. Martin's, 2002), 22.

55. Weingarten, 246. In 1962 Hunter showed up at Copacabana Beach in Rio de Janeiro with a drunk monkey in his coat jacket pocket. The monkey eventually jumped from a ten-story balcony, a presumed victim of delirium tremens. McKeen, *Outlaw Journalist*, 73.

56. Thompson, *Fear and Loathing in Las Vegas and Other American Stories*, 191.

57. "USS *Crazy Horse*," Memory Alpha, http://memory-alpha.org/wiki/USS_Crazy_Horse (accessed 8 May 2011).

58. Melville, *Melville*, 799.

59. Ibid., 803, 1431.

60. F. Scott Fitzgerald, "The Old Frontiersman," *The Princeton Tiger* 27, 18 December 1916. Reprinted in *F. Scott Fitzgerald: In His Own Time*, 84–85.

61. Thompson, *The Proud Highway*, 120.

62. Thompson, *Fear and Loathing in Las Vegas and Other American Stories*, 201.

63. Brinkley, "Hunter S. Thompson: The Art of Journalism No. 1," reprinted in A. Thompson, *Ancient Gonzo Evenings*, 271. Before they were married, Hunter and Sandy had a Doberman named Agar.

64. Thompson, Hunter S., *The Great Shark Hunt*, 418.

65. Thompson, *Fear and Loathing in America*, 325.

66. Ibid., 376.

67. Roger Morris, *Partners in Power: The Clintons and Their America* (New York: Holt, 1996), 443. Also see DC Dave, "Gary Hart, Donna Rice, and the Real Monkey Business," 2 April 2000, http://www.dcdave.com/article3/000402.html (accessed 18 July 2011).

68. See Richard D. Mahoney, *Sons and Brothers: The Life and Times of Jack and Bobby Kennedy* (New York: Arcade, 1999).

69. See McEneaney, *Tom Wolfe's America*, 143–61.

70. Thompson, *The Proud Highway*, 410.

71. Norman Mailer, *The Spooky Art: Thoughts on Writing* (New York: Random House, 2003), 264.

72. Gabriel García Márquez, *One Hundred Years of Solitude* (New York: Knopf, 1970), 383.

73. Its lead: "*One Hundred Years of Solitude* is the first piece of literature since the Book of Genesis that should be required reading for the entire human race." William Kennedy, *Riding the Yellow Trolley Car* (New York: Viking, 1993), 243.

74. Crawford Woods, "Fear and Loathing in Las Vegas," *New York Times Book Review*, 23 July 1972, 17.

75. A parallel development in photography was Ira Cohen's marvelous Mylar photos.

76. Kennedy, from the inside jacket copy of *The Rum Diary*.

77. For a discussion of this theme see John Ralston Saul, *On Equilibrium* (Toronto: Viking, 2011), 204–12.

78. Thompson, *Fear and Loathing in America*, 266.

79. Ibid., 273.

80. Douglas Brinkley, "Johnny Get Your Gun," June 1996, Johnny Depp Zone Interview Archive, http://interview.johnnydepp-zone2.com/1998_06George.html (accessed 25 June 2011).

81. Samuel P. Huntington, "The Basis of Accommodation," *Foreign Affairs* 46, no. 4 (July 1968), 642–56.

82. Brinkley, "Editor's Note," in Thompson, *The Proud Highway*, xxiv.

83. When Thompson lived in New York City back in the mid-Sixties, he had written three short stories under the pen name Aldous Miller-Mencken. Thompson, *The Proud Highway*, 95.

84. William Hope, *Curzio Malaparte: the Narrative Contract Strained* (University of Leicester: Troubadour, 2006), 145.

85. Constance Rourke, *American Humor: A Study of the National Character* (New York: New York Review of Books, 2004, reprint of 1931), 231–32.

86. Jerome Klinkowitz, *The Life of Fiction* (Urbana: University of Illinois Press, 1977), 31.

87. For the layman, the best book on the subject remains Gary Wills, *Inventing America: Jefferson's Declaration of Independence* (New York: Doubleday, 1978), especially 207–55.

7. MYTHIC ENIGMA

1. P. Perry, *Fear and Loathing*, 238–39.

2. McKeen, *Outlaw Journalist*, 276.

3. P. Perry, 253.

4. Whitmer, *When the Going Gets Weird*, 260.

5. Thompson to Steadman, in Steadman, 265.

6. McKeen, *Outlaw Journalist*, 271–76.

7. Wenner and Seymour, 235.

8. An early novel, it is not much read today. Wolcott, the brother of Kipling's fiancée Caroline (whom Kipling married in 1892), composed the first four chapters, but due to his unexpected death from typhus in Dresden in 1891, Kipling completed the novel and composed some verses for it. Kingsley Amis, in his portrait *Rudyard Kipling and His World* (London: Thames and Hudson, 1975), thought well of the novel.

9. If Twain's newspaper letters had been published right away, they would have constituted Twain's first book, predating *Innocents Abroad* (1869). See Grove A. Day, ed., *Mark Twain's Letters from Hawaii* (Honolulu: University of Hawaii Press, 1966).

10. Paul Gauguin, *Noa Noa: The Tahitian Journal* (New York: Dover Publications, 1985), 22.

11. McKeen, *Outlaw Journalist*, 274.

12. James Joyce, *A Portrait of the Artist as a Young Man* (New York: Viking Compass, 1964), 247.

13. Melville, *Melville*, 820. It was Daedalus who constructed the Cretan labyrinth.

14. A similar funny scene from 1999 appears in "Ambassador to Cuba" in *The Kingdom of Fear*, 229.

15. Wenner and Seymour, 268–70.

16. Hunter S. Thompson, *The Curse of Lono* (Los Angeles: Taschen, 1983/2005), 33–34.

17. McKeen, *Outlaw Journalist*, 275.

18. Thompson, *The Curse of Lono*, 73.

19. Melville, 873.

20. Ibid., 935.

21. On May 14, 2003, the *New York Times* ran a page one story declaring that 90 percent of the ocean's big fish had disappeared.

22. Melville, 1286.

23. Gauguin, 61.

24. Thompson, *The Curse of Lono*, 59.

25. Same name as the hotel manager in *Fear and Loathing in America*, 78. *Heem* is a Dutch word, the English cognate being home, an appropriate satiric name for a hotel manager or realtor. On the other hand, *Heem* is the phonetic last syllable of Hebrew *Elohim* (God of gods), *him* indicating a minor god; the desk clerk, who has the power to allocate room service perks, is abusively derided as a minor deity in this novel and respected as a more important deity in *Fear and Loathing in Las Vegas*, the latter clerk being more indulgent.

26. Melville, 211.

27. Lloyd J. Soehren, "Hawaiian Place Names," Ulukau, the Hawaiian Electronic Library , 2010. http://ulukau.org/gsdl2.5/cgi-bin/hpn?l=en&a=d&d=HASHbe6bbaa7d9c7c80616c1b0 (accessed 14 September 2011).

28. P. Perry, 238.

29. Thompson, *The Curse of Lono*, 88.

30. January 31, 1968, in Thompson, *Fear and Loathing in America*, 30–31.

31. Thompson, *The Curse of Lono*, 88.

32. Ibid., 100.

33. Ibid., 95.

34. Rob Johnson, *The Lost Years of William Burroughs: Beats in South Texas* (College Station: Texas A & M University Press, 2006), 148–57.

35. William Burroughs, "Introduction," *Queer* (New York: Viking, 1985).

36. Juan F. Thompson, *Stories I Tell Myself: Growing Up with Hunter S. Thompson* (New York: Knopf, 2016), 97.

37. Ibid., 76–93.

38. See Paul Hendrickson, *Hemingway's Boat* (New York: Knopf, 2011), 223–26.

39. According to Grey's son Loren, Grey spent about 300 days of the year fishing, (see introduction to *Tales of Tahitian Waters* [1927]) while he wrote his nearly innumerable Westerns.

40. Peter Ackroyd, *Dickens* (New York: HarperCollins, 1990), 34. In his novella *City of Truth* (New York: Harcourt Brace, 1990) James Morrow has his main character say: "*A Christmas Carol* had entered history as one of the falsest fables of all time, a gift embodiment of the lie that the wicked can be made to see the errors of their ways," 66.

41. Melville, 902.

42. Thompson, *The Curse of Lono*, 105.

43. Norris W. Potter, Lawrence M. Kasdon, and Anne Rayson, *History of the Hawaiian Kingdom* (Hong Kong: Bess Press, 2003), 9–21.

44. See Hendrickson, 223–26.

45. Thompson, *Stories I Tell Myself*, 98.

46. Melville, 862–63; Thompson, *Stories I Tell Myself*, 98.

47. Steadman, 218–19.

48. Terry Southern, "The Curse of Lono," *New York Magazine*, 7 November 1983, 91–92.

49. Thompson, *The Curse of Lono*, 160.

50. The passage in *The Odyssey*, Book 17, 290–323, in my translation reads:

As they spoke, a dog that had been dozing
raised his head, pricking up his ears.
This was Argos whom Odysseus bred before leaving for Ilios,
but he had never gotten any work from the dog,
who once went out with the young men hunting
for wild goats, deer, or hares, yet now that he was old,
he lay neglected by the household, sprawling
on a heap of mule and cow dung by the stable doors,
until he was shoved aside when they needed dung for the fields.
His coat was covered with a thousand fleas.
As soon as he saw Odysseus standing there,
he dropped his ear flaps and wagged his tail,
but he could not get close to Odysseus because of the fence.
When Odysseus saw the dog lying in the yard,
a tear welled in his eye, but he didn't let Eumaios see it, saying:
"Eumaios, that looks like a noble dog there on the manure pile.
Is he as fine as he looks, or is he just a stray that comes round

begging for scraps and people tolerate him out of kindness?"
Eumaios replied, "That hound belongs to the owner who died
in some far away country, so far that no one knows what happened.
You should have seen what he was like when Odysseus left
for the fabled walls of Ilios—he'd show you what a real dog can do!
If he was on the scent of a wild beast, not one could get away from
him,
but now he has fallen on evil days, for his master is dead and gone,
and the women of the household don't take care of him anymore.
Servants never do their work when a master is not checking on them,
for Zeus takes half the good out of a man the day he becomes a
slave."

51. For recent scientific evidence confirming reverse evolution see Pavel B. Klimov and Barry O'Connor, "Is Permanent Parasitism Reversible—Critical Evidence from Early Evolution of House Dust Mites," *Systematic Biology*, 5 February 2013.

52. For background and the theme of the double, see Ian Bell, *Dreams of Exile, Robert Louis Stevenson: A Biography* (New York: Henry Holt and Company, 1993), 172–80.

53. In a letter to Stevenson, John Addington Symonds wrote of the novella that "The art is burning and intense. The Peau de Chagrin disappears and Poe's work is water. Also one discerns at once that this is an allegory of all two-natured souls who yield consciously to evil. Most of us are on the brink of educating a Mr. Hyde at some epoch of our being." Cited in *Encyclopedia Americana* under "Doctor Jekyll and Mr. Hyde" (New York: Grolier, 1935).

54. Steadman, 210.

55. Zane Grey's record catch was a 1,040-pound striped marlin near Tahiti on May 16, 1930. See Thomas H. Pauly, *Zane Grey: His Life, His Adventures, His Women* (Urbana: University of Illinois Press, 2005), 287.

56. R. F. Foster, *W. B. Yeats: A Life, vol. II: The Arch-poet* (New York: Oxford, 2003), 150–51.

57. See Paul E. Kirkland, *Nietzsche's Noble Aims: Affirming Life, Contesting Modernity* (New York: Lexington Books, 2009), 168–73.

58. Jacques Barzun, *From Dawn to Decadence* (New York: HarperCollins, 2000), 382.

59. Joshua Cohen, *Rousseau: A Free Community of Equals* (New York: Oxford University Press, 2010), 98.

60. Jean Starobinsky, *Jean-Jacques Rousseau: Transparency and Obstruction*, trans. Arthur Goldhammer (Chicago: University of Chicago Press, 1966), 20.

61. Kevin Inston, *Rousseau and Radical Democracy* (New York: Continuum, 2010), 17.

62. Friedrich Nietzsche, "Beyond Good and Evil," reprinted in *The Philosophy of Nietzsche* (New York: Modern Library, 1947), 55.

63. Ibid., 187–88. Nietzsche respected only John Stuart Mill, Charles Darwin, and Herbert Spencer.

64. See "Nietzsche and the Pyrrhonian Tradition," in Jessica N. Berry, *Nietzsche and the Ancient Skeptical Tradition* (New York: Oxford, 2010), 20–48.

65. Hendrickson, 234.

66. McKeen, *Outlaw Journalist*, 275–76.

67. P. Perry, 251.

68. Ibid., 250.

69. Ibid.

70. Steadman, 187–89.

71. Thompson, *The Kingdom of Fear*, 188.

72. Thompson later used this title as the *Rolling Stone* headline for his 1983 Roxanne Pulitzer article wherein he turns into a dog (or behaves like a dog) instead of a journalist. Retitled as "Love on the Palm Beach Express: The Pulitzer Divorce Trial," in *Songs of the Doomed*, 211–29.

73. Thompson, *The Curse of Lono*, 180.

74. Day, 60.

75. Thompson, *The Curse of Lono*, 174.

76. Ibid., 196.

77. Francine du Plessix Gray, *Hawaii: The Sugar-Coated Fortress* (New York: Random House, 1972), 17–18.

78. For dramatic rendering on the death of Theramenes at the hands of Critias (Plato's uncle) see Xenophon, *A History of My Times*, trans. Rex Warmer (New York: Penguin, 1966), 109–23.

79. Joyce, 247.

80. Thompson, *The Proud Highway*, 129.

81. In Orson Welles's *The Lady from Shanghai* (1948), Banister says to Grisby, "George, that's the first time anyone ever called you a shark. If you were a good lawyer you'd be flattered."

82. Gray, 144–45.

83. McKeen, *Mile Marker Zero*, 194.

84. Ibid., 256.

85. Poem #18. Reprinted in George Murphy, ed., *The Key West Reader: The Best of Key West's Writers, 1830–1990* (Key West: Tortugas, 1989), 96.

86. McKeen, *Mile Marker Zero*, 188.

87. Hunter S. Thompson, "The Banshee Screams for Buffalo Meat," *Rolling Stone*, 15 December 1977. Reprinted in *The Great Shark Hunt*, 495–516.

88. Steadman, 261. The line "Can you not say tits, please!" made its way into the movie *Four Christmases* (2008).

89. Ibid., 265.

90. William Kennedy, *Riding the Yellow Trolley Car* (New York: Viking, 1993), 66.

91. In 1984 Thompson worked the college circuit, delivering about twenty-six talks. P. Perry, 253.

92. Gray, 48.

93. Gauguin, 31.

94. David Kalakaua (King of Hawaii), *The Legends and Myths of Hawaii: The Fables and Folklore of a Strange People* (Honolulu: S.I. Publishers, 1995, reprint of 1888), 201–8.

95. See Helena G. Allen, *Kalakaua: Renaissance King* (Honolulu: Mutual Publishing, 1995).

96. Wenner and Seymour, 235.

97. Steadman, 202.

98. When asked what "aloha" means, a young Hawaiian student replies: "Hello, thank you, good-bye; mostly these days goodbye." Gray, 5.

99. Miller, *Big Sur and the Oranges of Hieronymus Bosch*, 95.

100. Miller refers to people like Arthur Rimbaud or Vincent van Gogh. Miller, *The Books in My Life* (New York: New Directions, 1969), 35.

101. *The Decline of the West* and Mencken's *Prejudices* appear in the list of a hundred books that influenced him the most. See *The Books in My Life*, 318. Miller defends his rationale for quoting Spengler at length in *Plexus* (1953) (*The Books in My Life*, 27).

102. Thompson, *The Curse of Lono*, 193.

103. Gauguin, 22–25.

104. Wenner and Seymour, 396.

105. Thompson, *The Proud Highway*, 131.

106. Ibid.

107. Thompson, *The Curse of Lono*, 197.

108. Nietzsche, 236.

109. Julian Young, *Friederich Nietzsche: A Philosophic Biography* (Cambridge: Cambridge University Press, 2010), 381–83.

110. Thompson, *The Curse of Lono*, 115.

111. Stephenson, 151.

112. Thompson, *Fear and Loathing at Rolling Stone*, 569.

113. Steadman, 266.

114. Stephenson, 148–51.

115. P. Perry, 251.

116. Thompson, *Fear and Loathing in Las Vegas and Other American Stories*, 200.

117. Thompson, *The Curse of Lono*, 166.

118. Edward Said, "Introduction," in Melville, *Moby-Dick* (New York: Library of America, 1991), xvi.

119. F. O. Matthiessen, *American Renaissance* (New York: Oxford University Press, 1941), 286.

120. Steadman, 267.

121. Whitmer, *When the Going Gets Weird*, 258.

122. Steadman, 262.

123. About 200,000 copies (P. Perry, 217). Bantam probably made close to a cool million from the book.

124. Steadman, 268.

125. P. Perry, 255–56.

126. Hotchner, *Papa Hemingway*, 73.

8. LITERARY ADDENDA

1. The title, "Yesterday's Weirdness Is Tomorrow's Reason Why," from *The Curse of Lono* was reused for a short 1990 interview with William McKeen. Thompson, *The Kingdom of Fear*, 187–89.

2. Thompson, *Fear and Loathing at Rolling Stone*, 462.

3. Spengler, *The Decline of the West*, vol. II, 104ff.

4. It was written in January 1849 as a sardonic comment on the fundamental nature of political revolutions following the populist Revolution of 1848 and its disappointing aftermath, which featured Louis Napoleon as president accompanied by a National Assembly stuffed with obese, rabid monarchists.

5. The poet Louise Colet, whom Flaubert used as the model for the doctor's wife in *Madame Bovary*, attempted to murder Karr with a knife for his scurrilous barbs, but Karr had anticipated her rage by donning an iron vest. Critics have generally embraced Karr's aesthetic and social critique of Colet's poetry. See Francine du Plessix Gray, *Rage and Fire: A Life of Louise Colet* (New York: Simon & Schuster, 1995), 79–84. Since Thompson had found Gray's book on Hawaii valuable, he most likely discovered Karr through Gray's subsequent book on Colet. Outside of France, Karr's first romance, *Sous les Tilleuls* (1832, *Under the Lindens*) continues to be popular in the Arab world.

6. Thompson, *Songs of the Doomed*, 176–77.

7. Ibid., 94–96.

8. Ibid., 129.

9. Arthur Salm, "Rest in Peace H. S. T. (and you too, Y. W.)," *The San Diego Union-Tribune*, March 6, 2005, http://legacy.utsandiego.com/uniontrib/20050306/news_z1v6salm.html (accessed 3 August 2011).

10. Thompson, *Songs of the Doomed*, 21–23. The book arrangement is not chronological.

11. Thompson, *The Kingdom of Fear*, 315.

12. This extra-large cat may have been Liz Treadwell's; an anecdote about the cat appears in Cleverly and Braudis, 75–79. Hunter shot the cat full of buckshot when it attacked his peacocks.

13. McKeen, *Outlaw Journalist*, 313.

14. Thompson, *Screwjack*, 57.

15. Anatole Broyard, *New York Times Book Review*, 20 June 1981.

16. Terrence Des Pres, *New York Times*, 19 July 1981.

17. Thompson, *The Kingdom of Fear*, 285–316.

18. Thompson, "Polo Is My Life," *Rolling Stone*, no. 697, 15 December 1994, 44ff.

19. Irvin S. Cobb, *On an Island That Cost $24.00* (New York: George H. Doran, 1926).

20. Thompson, *Fear and Loathing at Rolling Stone*, 456–57.

21. Ibid., 528. For this reprint some of the self-referential foolery in section headlines has been removed along with Steadman's illustrations.

22. "Hoffman Carries Fight to Critics; Insists Lindbergh Case Not Fully Solved," *New York Times*, 6 April 1936, 42.

23. Mark Twain, *The American Claimant* (New York: Charles L. Webster & Co., 1892), 72–74. Rudyard Kipling's early work, *The Story of the Gadsbys* (1888), a closet-drama satiric story, was heavily influenced by Twain's novel and play.

24. Thompson, *Fear and Loathing at Rolling Stone*, 524.

25. Ibid., 544.

26. Ibid., 521.

27. Matthew Hahn, "Writing on the Wall: An Interview with Hunter S. Thompson," *Atlantic Online*, 26 August 1997; reprinted in Torrey and Simonson, 124.

28. For Hunter's antics in Zaire, see Steadman, 115–36. Hunter attempted to arrange to sit next to President Mobutu during the fight in order to make Mobutu the comic center of his piece, supplemented by a back-channel investigation of corruption connected to the fight, but both efforts fizzled.

29. George Plimpton, *Shadow Box* (Guilford: Lyons Press, 1977/2010), 321–24.

30. Hunter S. Thompson, *Hey Rube: Blood Sport, the Bush Doctrine, and the Downward Spiral of Dumbness: Modern History from the Sports Desk* (New York: Simon & Schuster, 2004), 240.

31. Nelson R. Aldrich organized an anecdotal monument in *George, Being George: George Plimpton's Life* (New York: Random House, 2008).

32. Interview with Douglas Brinkley, 14 June 2011.

9. SHOT OUT OF A CANNON

1. Torrey and Simonson, 97.

2. Kennedy, in Wenner and Seymour, 331.

3. Steadman, 269–70.

4. Kennedy, *Riding the Yellow Trolley Car*, 31.

5. Wolfe, in Wenner and Seymour, 436.

6. Depp, in Wenner and Seymour, 362.

7. Both Virgil and Dante over-go Homer's Hades episode. Aeneas looks over the ship's bow and curses Ithaka (Nicholas Horsfall, *Virgil, Aeneid 3: A Commentary* [Leiden-Boston: Brill, 2006], 14.), the birthplace of his adversary Odysseus. Dante puts Odysseus in the eighth circle of Hell (fraud, as an evil counselor) based upon a Byzantine encyclopedia article that erroneously attributed a lost Homeric imitation sequel to Homer wherein Odysseus enlists others to follow him on a further expedition, thus abandoning their families.

8. Miller, *Big Sur and the Oranges of Hieronymus Bosch*, 75.

9. Thompson, *The Great Shark Hunt*, 393.

10. Stephenson, 40.

11. Hunter S. Thompson, "Introduction," *The Gospel According to ESPN* (New York: Hyperion Books, 2002).

12. Book 7 of the *Republic* contains "The Allegory of the Cave" which attacks Homer's pantheistic vision of truth in nature amid personal communion with the divine in Book Seven of the *Odyssey*. Plato maliciously caricatured Athenians, who accept the popular culture invented by Homer, as blind as the poet who invented democratic participatory government balanced by its corollaries of strong executive leadership and impartial judicial system.

13. Steadman, 143.

14. Robert Zaretsky and John T. Scott, *The Philosopher's Quarrel* (New Haven: Yale, 2009), 6.

15. Thompson, *Generation of Swine*, 9.

16. Henry David Thoreau, *Walden: A Fully Annotated Edition*, ed. Jeffrey S. Cramer (New Haven, CT: Yale University Press, 2004), 313.

17. Studs Terkel, *American Dreams: Lost & Found* (New York: Pantheon, 1980), 3–4.

18. Ibid., 400.

19. Morris Dickstein, *The Gates of Eden* (New York: Basic Books, 1977), 133.

20. Along with Mark Twain's *Huckleberry Finn* (1884), Stephen Crane's *The Red Badge of Courage* (1895), Kate Chopin's *The Awakening* (1899), Frank Norris's *The Octopus* (1901), Upton Sinclair's *The Jungle* (1906), Edith Wharton's *The Custom of the Country* (1913), Willa Cather's *My Ántonia* (1918), Theodore Dreiser's *An American Tragedy* (1925), John Dos Passos's *Manhattan Transfer* (1925), F. Scott Fitzgerald's *The Great Gatsby* (1925), Ernest Hemingway's *The Sun Also Rises* (1926), Sinclair Lewis's *Elmer Gantry* (1927), Jim Tully's *Blood on the Moon* (1931), James T. Farrell's *The Young Manhood of Studs Lonigan* (1934), John O'Hara's *Appointment in Samarra* (1934), Henry Roth's *Call It Sleep* (1935), Zora Neale Hurston's *Their Eyes Were Watching God* (1937), Henry Miller's *Tropic of Capricorn* (1939), John Steinbeck's *The Grapes of Wrath* (1939), Nathaniel West's *Day of the Locust* (1939), William Faulkner's *The Hamlet* (1940), Carson McCuller's *The Heart is a Lonely Hunter* (1940), Richard Wright's *Native Son* (1940), Robert Penn Warren's *All the King's Men* (1946), Norman Mailer's *The Naked and the Dead* (1948), Nelson Algren's *The Man with the Golden Arm* (1949), J. D. Salinger's *The Catcher in the Rye* (1951), Ralph Ellison's *The Invisible Man* (1952), J. P. Donleavy's *The Ginger Man* (1955), William Gaddis's *The Recognitions* (1955), Jack Kerouac's *On the Road* (1957), John Updike's *Rabbit, Run* (1960), John Barth's *The Sot-Weed Factor* (1960), Joseph Heller's *Catch-22* (1961), Ken Kesey's *One Flew Over the Cuckoo's Nest* (1962), Thomas Pynchon's *V* (1963), Jerzy Kosinski's *The Painted Bird* (1965), William Styron's *The Confessions of Nat Turner* (1967), Robert Stone's *A Hall of Mirrors* (1967), Kurt Vonnegut Jr.'s *Slaughterhouse-Five* (1969), Saul Bellow's *Humboldt's Gift* (1975), E. L. Doctorow's *Ragtime* (1975), Charles Bukowski's *Women* (1978), William Kennedy's *Billy Phelan's Greatest Game* (1978), John Kennedy Toole's *A Confederacy of Dunces* (1980), Don DeLillo's *The Names* (1982), Russell Banks's *Continental Drift* (1985), Madison Smartt Bell's *Waiting for the End of the World* (1985), Cormac McCarthy's *Blood Meridian* (1986), Toni Morrison's *Beloved* (1987), Amy Tan's *The Joy Luck Club* (1989), Rick Moody's *Garden State* (1992), Gish Jen's *Mona in the Promised Land* (1996), John Fante's *The Bandini Quartet* (2003), and Tom Wolfe's *I Am Charlotte Simmons* (2005).

21. Young, *Friedrich Nietzsche*, 283–84, 319.

22. Anita Thompson, *The Gonzo Way* (Golden: Fulcrum Publishing, 2007), 77.

23. Ibid., 65.

24. Bill Buford, *Among the Thugs* (New York: Norton, 1992), 70.

25. To combat populist humor and promote its own cultural agenda, the CIA now provides scripts and script doctors to Hollywood, as well as props, and even partners in productions—this was done for all three popular *Transformers* films. While the CIA invests in the heightened suspense of spy films or the heroic tragedy of war films, Thompson ridiculed corruption in finance and government, the delusion of empire. He presented dysfunctional skits dramatizing repressive elements of ordinary life as comedic therapy. This dialectical observation can be easily overplayed, yet its roots go back to the peace-versus-war cultural split that Thompson so eloquently charted in *Fear and Loathing in Las Vegas*. The military establishment recognizes that the cultural propaganda those old "hippies" began still remains a threat to the state's Orwellian script to hypnotize every teenager with the ghastly explosions that Thompson himself so loved to watch. It's a cultural war that the state believes it will win against individuals because it has the money and technology to make that happen.

26. Academic studies on the American Dream theme, like Andrew Delbanco's *The Real American Dream* (1999), Jim Cullen's *The American Dream* (2003), and Karen Steinheimer's *Celebrity Culture and the American Dream* (2011) don't mention Thompson's critique.

27. John Ralston Saul, *Voltaire's Bastards* (New York: Random House, 1992), 52.

BIBLIOGRAPHY

HUNTER S. THOMPSON BOOKS

Hell's Angels: A Strange and Terrible Saga. New York: Random House, 1967.

Fear and Loathing in Las Vegas: A Savage Journey to the Heart of the American Dream. New York: Random House, 1972.

Fear and Loathing: On the Campaign Trail '72. New York: Straight Arrow/Grand Central, 1973.

The Great Shark Hunt: Strange Tales from a Strange Time. New York: Simon & Schuster, 1979.

The Curse of Lono. New York/Los Angeles: Bantam/Taschen, 1983/2005.

Generation of Swine: Tales of Shame and Degradation in the '80s. New York: Simon & Schuster, 1988.

Songs of the Doomed: More Notes on the Death of the American Dream. New York: Simon & Schuster, 1990.

Screwjack. Santa Barbara/New York: Neville/Simon & Schuster, 1991/2000.

Better Than Sex: Confessions of a Political Junkie. New York: Random House, 1994.

Fear and Loathing in Las Vegas and Other American Stories. New York: Modern Library, 1996.

The Proud Highway: The Saga of a Desperate Southern Gentleman, 1955–1967, ed. Douglas Brinkley. New York: Ballantine Books, 1997.

The Rum Diary: A Novel. New York: Simon & Schuster, 1998.

Fear and Loathing in America: The Brutal Odyssey of an Outlaw Journalist, 1968–1976, ed. Douglas Brinkley. New York: Simon & Schuster, 2000.

The Gospel According to ESPN. Introduction by Hunter S. Thompson; ed. Jay Lovinger. New York: Hyperion Books, 2002.

Kingdom of Fear: Loathsome Secrets of a Star-crossed Child in the Final Days of the American Century. New York: Simon & Schuster, 2003.

Hey Rube: Blood Sport, the Bush Doctrine, and the Downward Spiral of Dumbness: Modern History from the Sports Desk. New York: Simon & Schuster, 2004.

Fear and Loathing at Rolling Stone: The Essential Writings of Hunter S. Thompson, ed. Jann Wenner. New York: Simon & Schuster, 2011.

The Mutineer: Rants, Ravings, and Missives from the Mountaintop, 1975–2005, ed. Douglas Brinkley. New York: Simon & Schuster, 2014.

SELECT SECONDARY BOOKS

Acosta, Oscar Zeta. *The Autobiography of a Brown Buffalo*. San Francisco/New York: Straight Arrow Books/Vintage, 1972/1995.
———. *Oscar "Zeta" Acosta: The Uncollected Works*. Houston: Arte Público Press, 2006.
———. *The Revolt of the Cockroach People*. San Francisco/New York: Straight Arrow Books/Vintage, 1973/1995.
Arlt, Roberto. *The Seven Madmen*. Trans. Naomi Lindstrom. Boston: David R. Godine, 1929/1984.
Barger, "Sonny," with Keith and Kent Zimmerman, *Hell's Angel: The Life and Times of Sonny Barger*. New York: Morrow, 2000.
Berry, Jessica N. *Nietzsche and the Ancient Skeptical Tradition*. New York: Oxford, 2010.
Bingley, Will, and Anthony Hope-Smith. *Gonzo: A Graphic Biography of Hunter S. Thompson*, foreword by Alan Rinzler. London: SelfMadeHero, 2010.
Brinkley, Douglas. *The Magic Bus: An American Odyssey*. New York: Harcourt Brace, 1993.
Bruccoli, Mathew J. and Jackson R. Bryer. *F. Scott Fitzgerald: In His Own Time*. New York: Popular Library, 1971.
Bugliosi, Vincent, with Curt Gentry. *Helter Skelter—The True Story of the Manson Murders, 25th Anniversary Edition*. New York: Norton & Company, 2001.
Burroughs, William. *The Ticket That Exploded*. New York: Grove Press, 1962.
Carroll, E. Jean. *Hunter: The Strange and Savage Life of Hunter S. Thompson*. New York: Dutton, 1993.
Cleverly, Michael, and Bob Braudis. *The Kitchen Readings: Untold Stories of Hunter S. Thompson*. New York: Harper, 2008.
Cohen, Joshua. *Rousseau: A Free Community of Equals*. New York: Oxford University Press, 2010.
Cowan, Jay. *Hunter S. Thompson: An Insider's View of Deranged, Depraved, Drugged Out Brilliance*. Guilford: Lyons Press, 2009.
Day, Grove A., ed. *Mark Twain's Letters from Hawaii*. Honolulu: University of Hawaii Press, 1966.
Dickstein, Morris. *The Gates of Eden: American Culture in the Sixties*. New York: Basic Books, 1977.
Didion, Joan. *Play It as It Lays*. New York: Farrar, Straus and Giroux, 1970.
———. *Slouching Towards Bethlehem*. New York: Farrar, Straus and Giroux, 1968.
Dobyns, Jay. *No Angel: My Harrowing Undercover Journey to the Inner Circle of the Hell's Angles*. New York: Crown, 2009.
Donleavy, J. P. *The Ginger Man*. New York: Dell, 1969.
Draper, Robert. *Rolling Stone Magazine: The Uncensored History*. New York: Doubleday, 1990.
Exley, Frederick. *A Fan's Notes*. New York: Harper and Row, 1968.
Fensch, Thomas. *The Man Who Was Walter Mitty: The Life and Work of James Thurber*. Woodlands: New Century Books, 2000.
Fitzgerald, F. Scott. *The Great Gatsby*. New York: Scribner, 1925.
Gilmore, Mikal. *Stories Done: Writings on the 1960s and Its Discontents*. New York: Free Press, 2008.
Gray, Francine du Plessix. *Hawaii: The Sugar-Coated Fortress*. New York: Random House, 1972.
Hale, Dennis, and Jonathan Eisen, eds. *The California Dream*. New York: Collier, 1968.
Hemingway, Ernest. *The Sun Also Rises*. New York: Scribner's, 1926.
———. *The Old Man and the Sea*. New York: Scribner's, 1952.
Hope, William. *Curzio Malaparte: The Narrative Contract Strained*. Leicester, UK: Troubadour, 2006.
Horsfall, Nicholas. *Virgil, Aeneid 3: A Commentary*. Leiden-Boston: Brill, 2006.
Hoskyns, Barney. *Beneath the Diamond Sky: Haight-Ashbury, 1965–1970*. New York: Simon & Schuster, 1997.
Hotchner, A. E. *Papa Hemingway*. New York: Random House, 1966.

Huxley, Aldous. *The Doors of Perception*. New York: Harper, 1954/1970.

———. *Moksha: Aldous Huxley's Classic Writings on Psychedelics and the Visionary Experience*, ed. Michael Horowitz and Cynthia Palmer. Rochester: Park Street Press, 1999.

Inston, Kevin. *Rousseau and Radical Democracy*. New York: Continuum, 2010.

Kalakaua, David (King of Hawaii). *The Legends and Myths of Hawaii: The Fables and Folklore of a Strange People*. Honolulu: S. I. Publishers, 1995, reprint of 1888.

Kennedy, William. *The Ink Truck*. New York: Viking, 1969.

———. *Riding the Yellow Trolley Car*. New York: Viking, 1993.

Kerouac, Jack. *Big Sur*. New York: Penguin, 1962.

Lattin, Don, *The Harvard Psychedelic Club*. New York: HarperCollins, 2010.

Lavigne, Yves. *Hell's Angels: Into the Abyss*. New York: HarperCollins, 1996/2004.

Malaparte, Curzio. *The Skin*. Trans. David Moore with additional passages by Stephen Twilley. New York: New York Review of Books, 2013.

McEneaney, Kevin T. *Tom Wolfe's America: Heroes, Pranksters, and Fools*. Westport: Praeger, 2009.

McKeen, William. *Hunter S. Thompson*. Boston: Twayne, 1991.

———. *Mile Zero Marker*. New York: Crown, 2011.

———. *Outlaw Journalist: The Life and Times of Hunter S. Thompson*. New York: Norton, 2008.

McWilliams, Carey. *The Education of Carey McWilliams*. New York: Simon & Schuster, 1978.

Melville, Herman. *Melville: Redburn, White Jacket, Moby-Dick*. New York: Library of America, 1983.

Miller, Henry. *The Air-Conditioned Nightmare*. New York: New Directions, 1945.

———. *Big Sur and the Oranges of Hieronymus Bosch*. New York: New Directions, 1957.

———. *The Books in My Life*. New York: New Directions, 1969.

Mosely, Matthew. *Dear Dr. Thompson: Felony Murder, Hunter S. Thompson, and the Last Gonzo Campaign*. Denver: Ghost Road Press, 2010.

Murphy, Dennis. *The Sergeant*. New York: Viking, 1958.

Murphy, George, ed. *The Key West Reader: The Best of Key West's Writers, 1830–1990*. Key West: Tortugas, 1989.

Nabokov, Vladimir. *The Annotated Lolita*, ed. Alfred Appel Jr. New York: Vintage, 1991.

National Observer editors. *The Observer's World: People, Places, and Events from the Pages of the National Observer*. Princeton, NJ: Princeton University Press, 1965.

Nietzsche, Friedrich. *The Philosophy of Nietzsche*. New York: Modern Library, 1947.

Orwell, George. *Down and Out in Paris and London*. London: Secker and Warburg, 1997.

———. *Homage to Catalonia*. Boston: Harcourt, 1938/1980.

Perry, Charles. *The Haight Ashbury*. New York: Random House, 1984.

Perry, Paul. *Fear and Loathing: The Strange and Terrible Saga of Hunter S. Thompson*. New York: Thunder's Mouth Press, 1993.

Plimpton, George. *Shadow Box: An Amateur in the Ring*. Guilford: Lyons Press, 1997/2010.

Richardson, Peter. *A Bomb in Every Issue: How the Short Unruly Life of Ramparts Magazine Changed America*. New York: New Press, 2009.

Saul, John Ralston. *Voltaire's Bastards*. New York: Random House, 1992.

Rice, Grantland. *The Tumult and the Shouting: My Life in Sport*. New York: A. S. Barnes and Company, 1954.

Rodgers, Marion Elizabeth. *Mencken: The American Iconoclast*. Oxford: Oxford University Press, 2005.

Rourke, Constance. *American Humor: A Study of the National Character*. New York: New York Review of Books, 1931/2004.

Sides, Hampton. *Hellhound on His Trail: The Stalking of Martin Luther King Jr. and the International Hunt for His Assassin*. New York: Doubleday, 2010.

Spengler, Oswald. *The Decline of the West*. New York: Knopf, 1926.

Steadman, Ralph. *The Joke's Over: Bruised Memories: Gonzo, Hunter S. Thompson, and Me*. New York: Harcourt, 2006.

Stendhal. *The Charterhouse of Parma*, trans. by Richard Howard. New York: Modern Library, 1839.

Stephenson, William. *Gonzo Republic: Hunter S. Thompson's America*. New York: Continuum, 2012.

Stevens, Jay. *Storming Heaven: LSD and the American Dream*. New York: HarperCollins,1993.

Tendler, Stewart, and David May. *The Brotherhood of Eternal Love*. London: Cyan Books, 2007.

Terkel, Studs. *American Dreams: Lost & Found*. New York: Pantheon, 1980.

Thompson, Anita, ed. *Ancient Gonzo Wisdom: Interviews with Hunter S. Thompson*. New York: Da Capo, 2009.

———. *The Gonzo Way*. Golden: Fulcrum Publishing, 2007.

Thompson, Juan F. *Stories I Tell Myself: Growing Up with Hunter S. Thompson*. New York: Knopf, 2016.

Thurber, James. *Thurber: Writings and Drawings*. New York: Library of America, 1996.

Torgoff, Martin. *Can't Find My Way Home: America in the Great Stoned Age, 1945–2000*. New York: Simon & Schuster, 2004.

Torrey, Beef and Kevin Simonson, eds. *Conversations with Hunter S. Thompson*. Jackson: University of Mississippi Press, 2008.

Trudeau, Gary, B. *Action Figure! The Life and Times of Doonesbury's Uncle Duke*. Kansas City: Andrews and McMeel, 1992.

Tully, Jim. *Circus Parade*. New York: Albert & Charles Boni, 1927.

Veno, Arthur, ed. *The Mammoth Book of Bikers*. Philadelphia: Running Press, 2007.

Wagner-Martin, Linda, ed. *Hemingway: Eight Decades of Criticism*. East Lansing: Michigan State University Press, 2009.

Weingarten, Marc. *The Gang That Wouldn't Shoot Straight*. New York: Crown, 2005.

Wenner, Jann, and Corey Seymour. *Gonzo: The Life of Hunter S. Thompson*. New York: Back Bay Books, 2007.

Wethern, George, and Vincent Colnett. *A Wayward Angel: The Full Story of the Hells Angels*. Guilford: Lyons Press, 2008.

Whitmer, Peter O. *Aquarius Revisited: Seven Who Created the Sixties Counterculture That Changed America*. New York: Macmillan, 1987.

———. *When the Going Gets Weird: The Twisted Life and Times of Hunter S. Thompson*. New York: Hyperion, 1993.

Witcover, James. *The Year The Dream Died: Revisiting 1968 in America*. New York: Warner, 1997.

Wolfe, Tom. *The Kandy-Kolored Tangerine-Flake Streamline Baby*. New York: Farrar, Straus and Giroux, 1965.

———. *The New Journalism*. New York: Harper & Row, 1973.

———. *The Pump House Gang*. New York: Farrar, Straus and Giroux, 1968.

Young, Julian. *Friedrich Nietzsche: A Philosophical Biography*. Cambridge: Cambridge University Press, 2010.

SELECT ARTICLES

Barber, Benjamin. "*The Rum Diary*: An Introduction to Hunter S. Thompson's Esthetic Evolution." *Anthropoetics* 16, no. 1, 2010.

Baruth, Philip. "Beyond Realism: William Kennedy on the Surreal and the Unconscious, the Religious, the Sublime, and the Gonzo." *New England Review* 19, 1998.

Brinkley, Douglas. "Contentment Was Not Enough: The Final Days at Owl Farm." *Rolling Stone*, 24 March 2005.

Bruce-Novoa. "Fear and Loathing on the Buffalo Trail." *Melus* 6, no. 4, January 1979.

Caron, James E. "Hunter S. Thompson's 'Gonzo' Journalism and Tall Tale Tradition in America." *Studies in Popular Culture* 8, no. 1, January 1985.
Coller, Salena, "Hunter S. Thompson's Adventures in Florida" in Slate, Karen, ed., *Florida Studies: Proceedings of the 2009 Annual Meeting of the Florida College English Association*. Newcastle upon Tyne: Cambridge Scholars, 2010.
Cooper, Stephen. "John Fante's Great Gift to Los Angeles." *Los Angeles Times*, 8 April 2009.
Depp, Johnny. "A Pair of Deviant Book-ends." *Rolling Stone*, 24 March 2005.
Falconer, Delia. "From Alger to Edge-Work: Mapping the Shark Ethic in Hunter S. Thompson's *Fear and Loathing in Las Vegas*." *Antithesis* 6, no. 2, 1993.
Grassian, Daniel. "The Half-Baked Cultural Detective: *Fear and Loathing in Las Vegas* as Postmodern Noir." *Popular Culture Review* 11, no. 2, 2000.
Green, James, and others. Special issue of *Journal of Popular Culture*, summer 1975.
Hall, Brandon. "Teeth Like Baseballs." *Contemporary Literary Criticism* 229, 2003.
Hames-Garcia, Michael. "Dr. Gonzo's Carnival: The Testimonial Satires of Oscar Zeta Acosta." *American Literature* 72, 2000.
Hirst, Martin, "What Is Gonzo? The Etymology of an Urban Legend." *UQ*, January 2004.
Landreth, Elizabeth."There Shall Be No Light: Las Vegas." *Journal of Popular Culture*, 9:1, summer 1975.
Shuster, Simon. "The Curse of the Crocodile: Russia's Deadly Designer Drug." *Time*, June 2011.
Sickels, Robert. "A Countercultural Gatsby: Hunter S. Thompson's Fear and Loathing in Las Vegas and the Death of the American Dream and the Rise of Las Vegas, USA." *Popular Culture Review*, February 2000.
Stiles, Stephanie, and Randy Harris. "Keeping Curious Company: Wayne C. Booth'sFriendship Model of Criticism and the Work of Hunter S. Thompson." *College English* 71, no. 4, 2009.
Steinbrink, Jeffrey. "Mark Twain and Hunter S. Thompson: Continuity and Change in American 'Outlaw Journalism,'" *Studies in American Humor* 2, 1982.
Stull, James N. "Hunter S. Thompson: A Ritual Enactment of Deviant Behavior." *Connecticut Review* 13, no. 1, April 1991.
Tamony, Peter. "The Hell's Angels: Their Naming." *Western Folklore*, July 1970.
———. "Gonzo." *American Speech* 58, no. 1, spring 1983.
Thompson, Juan. "My Father." *Rolling Stone*, 24 March 2005.
Wenner, Jan. "My Brother in Arms." *Rolling Stone*, 24 March 2005.
Williams, Gerald. "Lolita, Who's Your Daddy?" *Massachusetts Review* 47, winter 2006.
Wright, Greg. "The Literary, Political, and Legal Strategies of Oscar Zeta Acosta and Hunter S. Thompson: Intertexuality, Ambiguity, and (naturally) Fear and Loathing." *Journal of Popular Culture* 43, no. 3, June 2010.
Wright, Luke. "The Death of the American Dream." *Virginia Quarterly Review* 85, no.4. 2009.

FILMS

Ewing, Wayne. *Breakfast with Hunter*. Wayne Ewing Films, 2003.
———. *When I Die: A Documentary on the Raising of the Gonzo Memorial*. Wayne Ewing Films, 2005.
———. *Free Lisl*. Wayne Ewing Films, 2007.
———. *Animals, Whores & Dialogue*. Wayne Ewing Films, 2010.
Finch, Nigel. *Fear and Loathing on the Road to Hollywood*. BBC, 1978.
Gibney, Alex. *Gonzo: The Life and Work of Dr. Hunter S. Thompson*. HDNet Films, 2008.
Gilliam, Terry. *Fear and Loathing in Las Vegas*. Universal Pictures, 1998.
Hicklin, William. *Hunter S. Thompson—Final 24: His Final Hours*. MVD Visual, 2006.
Linson, Art. *Where the Buffalo Roam*. Universal Pictures, 1980.

Martin, Sharon. *Biography: Hunter S. Thompson*. Biography Channel, 2004.
Thurman, Tom. *Buy the Ticket, Take the Ride*. Starz Entertainment, 2006.

INDEX

ABOUT THE AUTHOR

Kevin T. McEneaney is a freelance writer and former adjunct professor (Marist College, University of Hartford, and St. Thomas Aquinas College, among others). He is currently the cultural reporter for *The Millbrook Independent*, where he is the book page editor and music critic. He is the author of several books, including *Russell Banks: In Search of Freedom* (2010) and *Tom Wolfe's America: Heroes, Pranksters, and Fools* (2009), a *Choice* Outstanding title. As a poet, his main collections are *The Enclosed Garden* and *Longing*, which has been translated into French and Japanese.

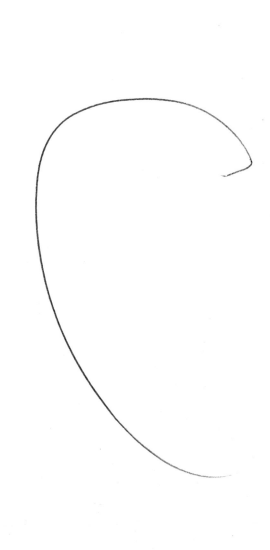